The Olympics That Never Happened

Terry and Jan Todd Series on Physical Culture and Sports

Edited by Sarah K. Fields, Thomas Hunt, Daniel A. Nathan, and Patricia Vertinsky

Also in the series

The Olympics That Never Happened

Denver '76 and the Politics of Growth

ADAM BERG

University of Texas Press   *Austin*

Requests for permission to reproduce material from this work should be sent to:
    Permissions
    University of Texas Press
    P.O. Box 7819
    Austin, TX 78713-7819
    utpress.utexas.edu/rp-form

♾ The paper used in this book meets the minimum requirements of ANSI/NISO
Z39.48-1992 (R1997) (Permanence of Paper).

Library of Congress Cataloging-in-Publication Data

Names: Berg, Adam, author.
Title: The Olympics that never happened : Denver '76 and the politics of growth / Adam Berg.
Description: First edition. | Austin : University of Texas Press, 2023. | Series: Terry and Jan Todd series
    on physical culture and sports | Includes bibliographical references and index.
Identifiers:
    LCCN 2022022511
    ISBN 978-1-4773-2645-9 (cloth)
    ISBN 978-1-4773-2646-6 (PDF)
    ISBN 978-1-4773-2647-3 (ePub)
Subjects: LCSH: Olympic Winter Games (12th : 1976 : Denver, Colo.)—Political aspects. | Olympic
    host city selection—Political aspects—Colorado—Denver. | Olympics—Planning—Political
    aspects. | City planning—Political aspects—Colorado—Denver. | Political participation—
    Colorado—Denver—History. | BISAC: HISTORY / United States / State & Local / West (AK, CA,
    CO, HI, ID, MT, NV, UT, WY) | SOCIAL SCIENCE / Sociology / Urban
Classification: LCC GV842 1976 .B43 2023 | DDC 796.4809788/83—dc23/eng/20220625
LC record available at https://lccn.loc.gov/2022022511

doi:10.7560/326459

Contents

Acronyms

ARO	Auraria Residents Organization
CCF	Citizens for Colorado's Future
CIEO	Citizens Interested in an Equitable Olympics
COC	Colorado Olympic Commission
DOC	Denver Organizing Committee (later changed to Denver Olympic Organizing Committee)
DRI	Denver Research Institute
DURA	Denver Urban Renewal Authority
FIS	International Ski Federation
HUD	Department of Housing and Urban Development
IOC	International Olympic Committee
JBC	Joint Budget Committee
MAPC	Mountain Area Protection Council
POME	Protect Our Mountain Environment
SCUSA	Colorado Ski Country USA
USOC	United States Olympic Committee
WSC	West Side Coalition

The Olympics That Never Happened

Introduction: The Game behind the Games

On 7 November 1972, Americans went to the polls. They voted for senators, governors, and the president of the United States. Yet something else awaited the judgment of citizens in the state of Colorado. Should the city of Denver host the 1976 Winter Olympics? Two and a half years prior, the International Olympic Committee (IOC) awarded the games to the Mile High City. But on this day, through a ballot initiative, it appeared Coloradans might force city and state leaders to hand back the sports spectacle.

The decision seemed momentous. According to Richard O'Reilly of the *Rocky Mountain News,* many in Colorado saw the Olympic question as "more important to the state's future than the election of any of the state's political candidates."[1] The president of Denver's Chamber of Commerce depicted the choice as one of "a dozen crucial decisions" in Colorado's "entire history."[2] Colorado state representative Richard Lamm portrayed the vote as the signal of a "quiet revolution" ready to turn the "world upside down."[3] In the words of Denver mayor William McNichols, it was "the most critical issue on the entire ballot."[4]

As these comments indicate, a deeper political contest underlay what Olympic organizers called "Denver '76." There was a game, so to speak, behind the games.[5] Several groups and individuals tried to use the event to channel Colorado's development in different and often conflicting directions.[6] While this was not strictly a matter of whether to support or oppose growth, there were significant tensions over where, how, and to what extent Colorado should expand. Indeed, for the spectrum of proponents and opponents alike, the Olympics was not the target. The Olympics was a tool for directing the trajectory of the Centennial State.[7]

A post–World War II "growth machine" initiated Denver's Olympic proposal. As the sociologist Harvey Molotch predicts, this was a collection of influential

1

businesspeople and politicians who, despite any differences, achieved mutual benefits from their shared locality's aggregate expansion. Tied together by place, the powerbrokers faced off against other location-derived cooperatives, seeking physical resources, public funds, more customers, and higher values for fixed assets.[8] Toward these ends, in line with the political scientist Clarence Stone's overlapping notion of a "governing regime," the collaborators informally enacted public policies to promote growth and simultaneously safeguard their authority.[9]

Many sport studies researchers have echoed the ideas of Molotch and Stone, examining similarly styled "growth regimes," "growth coalitions," or "growth networks."[10] As the political scientists and Olympic scholars Matthew Burbank, Gregory Andranovich, and Charles Heying contend, bids for the Olympics are "quintessential growth regime endeavors." "Without an established business-government network in place to provide a substantial level of resources over an extended period of time, an Olympic bid," they write, "would simply not occur." The authors add: "Olympic Committees are a tangible manifestation of a growth coalition."[11] In the United States, since the turn of the twentieth century, the games served consistently in this way—as a vehicle of local elites keen on fostering pro-growth cultures, building far-reaching reputations for leisure and success, attracting consumers, and legitimizing the mobilization of capital.[12]

In this process, wealthy businesspeople represented the cornerstone. As Stone suggests, while they sought to further "claims . . . on public authority and public resources," they also doled out incentives and created short-term opportunities to bring others, including politicians, into the pro-growth fold.[13] In Colorado, as the battle over the Denver Winter Games makes apparent, regime contributors hailed from local banks, utility providers, construction companies, the ski industry, and regional media outlets. It was these "place entrepreneurs" that as early as 1963 began working to bring the 1976 Winter Olympics to Colorado and Denver, hoping to gain access to public funds to promote the state's tourist industry, build advanced tourist-related infrastructure, stimulate growth generally, and thereby reap the financial rewards.[14]

While the presence of a postwar growth regime marks the starting point of the Denver '76 controversy, the broadening and malleability of the rights revolution during the 1960s and early 1970s provided the next vital component. In assorted ways, civil rights activism, a turn toward individualism by the middle class, a burgeoning environmental movement, simmering tax revolts, and anti–Vietnam War protests recalibrated people's thinking.

Rather than focusing on economic growth, many began to prioritize or be-come more outspoken about desires for social justice and/or quality of life.[15]

To articulate such points of view, various Colorado advocacy groups converged on the Denver Games and temporarily worked together toward the common end of halting the sports festival. As the Olympic researcher and political scientist Jules Boykoff would describe of this kind of situation, a "moment of movements" or an "event coalition" complicated the growth machine's agenda.[16] Mexican American and African American urbanites conveyed disquiet about their lack of inclusion in city planning as they pur-sued affordable housing for impoverished Denver residents. Citizens living west of the city in the exurbs along the Front Range foothills—who were mainly white and middle-class—embodied a brand of environmentalism characterized by class-informed lifestyle ideals and expressed contempt to-ward the aesthetic consequences of commercial growth near their homes. With these grassroots undertakings in motion, two local politicians, Richard Lamm from Denver and Robert Jackson from Pueblo, objected to the misal-location of taxpayer dollars to the Olympics and pro-growth investments broadly. They appeared to speak the mind of many a Coloradan when they asserted that the games furnished testimony that state leaders had taken the push for growth too far and at the expense of everyday people.[17] At this point, media outlets began to lend credibility to perspectives critical of the event. This book is littered with examples of how pro- and anti-Olympics forces fought over the "framing" of the games and themselves, each trying to shape public perceptions to their advantage.[18]

Colorado thus became a promising location for a small but capable crew of liberal-minded political operatives who employed the looming sports extravaganza to steer Coloradans toward their conception of a more demo-cratic and equitable society. Notably, although these activists were struck by America's inability to stop the Vietnam War and implement meaningful progressive reforms, they also realized their goals required a large umbrella. They sought an issue that could unify a diverse alliance, presented a tone and image appealing specifically to the white middle and working classes, and stressed the rights of American citizenship.

By summer 1972, these anti-Olympics coalition-builders collected enough signatures to place a measure on Colorado's upcoming ballot. It meant to bar any state funds going toward the games through an amend-ment to the state's constitution.[19] When federal legislators made their $15.5 million Olympic commitment dependent on complementary state sup-port, it became evident that Coloradans held the fate of Denver '76 in their hands.[20] If Colorado citizens voted affirmatively for the initiative, Colorado's most powerful figures would lose access to both state and federal money and have no choice but to rescind their offer to host "the youth of the world."

A growth regime that eventually turned to the rhetoric of Olympism to justify its Olympic scheme collided with an event coalition buttressed by the rights of citizenship—and citizenship appeared to win the day. Coloradans chose to block public spending and vanquished the games. Still, opposition to Denver hosting the 1976 Winter Games was inspired by a diversity of projects geared toward facilitating loftier objectives, not just stopping the event. Questions remain: How impactful was Colorado's anti-Olympics moment, for whom was it impactful, and why?

Importantly, the nature of the Denver Olympics deserves credit for exacerbating, amplifying, and providing a point of focus for the views of a range of actors. The Winter Games was a massive event born of a foreign body located a world away. It entailed significant facility construction for a temporary occurrence featuring athletic contests with minimal local followings. The deceit and unilateral decision-making that Denver bidders relied on to win over the IOC became undeniable as well. Meanwhile, public funding remained a prerequisite, as cost projections kept increasing and proved more and more untrustworthy. On top of this, the IOC mandated the direct participation of local political leaders. This led politicians and business elites to become openly aligned in the Olympic effort. As a result, the Denver Olympics provided one of the most palpable examples available of a growth machine run amok, selfishly chasing financial gains while sidelining the desires of regular people.

The Denver Games consequently served as an adaptable surrogate issue, a dispute through which assorted players could advance distinct and fundamental public policy aims.[21] For opponents, however, this foreshadowed long-term limitations. Though Olympics critics shared a common political platform, most reacted to spatially and socially confined problems. There were exceptions, but the large majority did not pursue the sustained coordination with other interest groups required to become capable of taking over governance, let alone inspire genuine sociopolitical transformation. These were, in the end, merely momentary bedfellows.[22]

Anti-Olympics forces would obtain several impressive Olympics-related gains. The narrative ahead displays the undemocratic character of the Olympics, how the event could harm community members, and how citizens could appropriate it to suit their values and visions for the future. Nonetheless, contemporaries expressed hyperbole when suggesting that the November 1972 vote operated as an irreversible tipping point. Put simply, in terms of political muscle, those who questioned the merits of hosting the games came nowhere near matching the organization and continuity of the Colorado regime in power at the time—propped up by the business community, constituted by experienced and sturdy relationships, focused on commercial growth, and in existence for the precise purpose of guiding city- and state-level policy-making.[23] The Olympics that never happened reveals the political plasticity and potential of sports mega-events, but it also showcases the difficulty of reimagining regional politics, which a few Denver Olympics opponents had hoped to do.

PART 1

THE BIDDERS

CHAPTER 1

The Origins of Olympic Dreams

Early in the bid process, Denver's team of Olympic applicants drew a list of things to "communicate" to fellow Coloradans about potentially hosting the 1976 Winter Games. "Economic benefits" and "prestige to promote tourism" stood at the top.[1] The local promoters felt comfortable conveying their reasons for seeking the sports festival, and they held firm conviction in their authority over such a pursuit.

The political history of Denver, the trajectory of the Colorado ski industry within America's post–World War II consumer culture, and dominant views of the Olympics in American society enabled that perspective.[2] Before the bid for Denver '76, for almost a hundred years, a collective of businessmen who were fixated on growth oversaw Denver's and Colorado's governance. Moreover, when World War II concluded, many western decision makers feared not only a slowdown in expansion but also a lack of diversification. If new assets sparked by the federal government stalled, the economic autonomy achieved during the war years would dissipate. Finding new ways to fan the fires of economic independence seemed essential.[3] In this figurative light, business leaders and allied elected officials turned to sports-induced tourism, and the Winter Games looked as if they fit seamlessly within such plans for the Centennial State.[4]

An elite group of business leaders founded Denver and continued to run it throughout its history. Before the Civil War, in Colorado Territory, the adjacent towns of Auraria and Denver City merged through the efforts of William Byers and General William Larimer. Byers started the *Rocky Mountain News* newspaper and, in effect, ran Auraria. Larimar invested in real estate and led Denver City. They had moved to the West anticipating

American expansion and combined Auraria and Denver City as Denver to outrun Colorado Springs and Golden in a race for regional dominance.[5]

Byers devoted the rest of his life to uniting the town's agricultural bosses, stage line and railroad magnates, financiers, real estate holders, core metal extractors, and coal barons—allies who understood their mutual interest in growth. Thus, when the Union Pacific Railroad decided to run its tracks through the less mountainous Cheyenne, Wyoming, the first-generation Denverites formed the Denver Board of Trade and, with about $2 million in capital stock, twisted arms in Congress for a land grant, made exaggerated promises of universal benefits to locals, and agreed to connect their planned railway to the Kansas Pacific line. In doing so, they were able to build a lifeline from Denver to the Union Pacific's main artery. With 600 miles of prairie separating Denver from the Missouri River, and with nearby Golden moving to build its own iron horse to Cheyenne, these moves grounded Denver's future as an economic powerhouse in the West.[6]

By the 1880s, as the historian Gunther Barth describes, Denver became an "instant city," prevailing as a center for the exchange and transportation of manufactured goods and extractive resources. Indeed, a population near 5,000 in 1870 reached almost 134,000 by 1900. At the same time, Denver elites obsessed with growth continued to guide the city's emergence. Local businessmen, newspaper owners, and politicians formed the Denver Chamber of Commerce to attract people, industry, and capital. To advertise Colorado and its central city, they sent pamphlets and salesmen back East and to Europe. And most important, outside investors from Chicago, Boston, New York, and London sent them immense sums. Discoveries of silver and gold, and additional railroad extensions, would be vital. A sound agricultural position and smelter factories filling Denver's skyline proved key. Yet without the ambition of local entrepreneurs matched to outside funding, Denver would not have grown as quickly as it did.[7]

Thus only a select group stood behind the city's development. Fewer than twenty men received the necessary loans from distant financiers to direct Denver's growth. They put most of the money toward creating monopolies in transportation, communication, manufacturing, banking, water, gas, electricity, and real estate. Amid the Gilded Age of industrial incorporation, as the population of the burgeoning outpost multiplied, the city builders accumulated enormous amounts of wealth and influence.[8] As the Denver historians Lyle Dorsett and Michael McCarthy explain: "Denver's magnates never limited themselves to one dimension of economic empire; rather, they created an interwoven and interlocked network that helped place a vise grip on virtually every significant branch of the new city's economy."[9]

*　　*　　*

As time passed, however, working with and through elected officials became critical. As Denver's population moved closer to 250,000 and Colorado's reached nearly a million, control became more difficult to maintain. The economic depression of 1893 also exacerbated unrest, bringing pangs of hunger, loss, and fear. A decade later, reformers seized on this situation to institute a new city charter. It would have placed utilities under municipal management, given local districts power over police and fire departments, abolished gambling, and imposed other measures to force many saloons out of business. Utility monopolies faced a public takeover. The business elite's control over civil servants appeared destined to weaken. Major attractions for out-of-town spenders likewise came under threat.[10]

In this moment, Robert Speer arrived as the hinge to a modified axis of power. Speer gained knowledge of Denver and loyalty within its working class while serving at different times on the police and fire boards, as police and fire commissioner, and as head of the Board of Public Works, where he oversaw half the city's budget. But he also earned the faith and financial backing of Denver businessmen by orchestrating the defeat of the new charter that would have ended their control of city utilities. In 1904, Speer thus made his way to the mayor's office, backed by those aligned with saloons, brewing, gambling, prostitution, the Denver Tramway Company, the Denver Gas and Electric Company, and the Denver Union Water Company.[11]

Speer's political acumen came through his ability to provide a greater quality of life for Denver's inhabitants while allowing the city's monopolies to endure. Following Progressive Era ideals, he pressured Denver's richest citizens and businesses to accept a level of regulation and give wealth back to the municipality. This allowed cleaner streets, parks, playgrounds, and welfare programs. As Dorsett and McCarthy describe, the time of "docile—almost puppetlike—mayors" subject to directives from "Denver's power elite" had come to an end. Nevertheless, Speer's accomplishments remained predicated on ensuring Denver's gas, electricity, telephone, and real estate moguls continued to function unobstructed. The relationship between Speer and Denver's business leaders was mutually beneficial and involved powerbrokers funneling thousands of dollars toward his election and reelection campaigns.[12]

With him and other like-minded politicians in office, pro-growth interests remained in command, continuing to market Colorado using booklets, pamphlets, and brochures aimed at tourists, new residents, and outside money. The state similarly invested in roads, as the Denver Chamber of Commerce lobbied the federal government to build dry-land irrigation facilities to attract farmers. Seeking to "Build Colorado First," the chamber hosted events such as an apple exposition, a plowing carnival, and an annual stock show, recognizing that the Mile High City would do business with agricultural communities in outlying parts of the state. The Denver Chamber and its allies focused on recruiting out-of-town travelers as well by adding hotels, restaurants, and an 11,500-seat auditorium to brand Denver a "convention city." They also worked with public officials to press Washington to establish Rocky Mountain National Park to boost tourism.[13]

Between the 1920s and the start of World War II, the drive for growth among Denver's elite would wane. A new generation inherited the set of local interconnected monopolies built by predecessors. They lived comfortably and felt pressure for frugality following the depression of 1893 and the Great Depression of the 1930s. They had witnessed some of their forbears overextend themselves. Thus, the coalition saw minimal reason to speculate in real estate, housing construction, and other new businesses or to seek investment from outsiders, which could have disrupted the localized hegemony. The "capitalists napped," the Denver historians Stephen Leonard and Thomas Noel write, "resting on their trust funds, dividends, and income property."[14]

Nonetheless, the presence of governing regime processes remained. A common selection of families still owned, operated, and held stock in the Denver Stock Yard Association, Colorado Fuel and Iron, the utility-focused Public Service Company, the expanding sugar industry, and the area's major banks. Furthermore, while elites exhibited fiscal restraint, they supported politicians and developments that could yet assist them. This included elevating Lawrence Phipps to the United States Senate. Even though Phipps spurned aid to the working class, he supported tariffs to protect the coal mine industry from foreign competition, fought for federally funded oil shale extraction studies, and voted to spend federal dollars on building highways and mountain parks in Colorado with tourism in mind. The circle of Denver decision makers also backed the election of Benjamin Stapleton for Denver mayor. Along with keeping taxes low for the business community, he oversaw the construction of an airport, gained access to water supplies from the Western Slope, and pushed through construction of Moffat Tunnel, opening a direct transcontinental rail line from Denver to the West Coast.[15]

In this setting, few Denver powerbrokers anticipated returning to a time such as the late 1800s, when growth operated as their singular passion. However, the combination of the New Deal followed by mobilization for World War II changed that mindset, setting the stage and casting many of the players for the Mile High City's successful Olympic bid. Despite resistance from politicians and upper-class businesspeople, during the Depression, President Franklin Roosevelt's New Deal flowed into the Centennial State.[16] The New Deal moved the federal government's attention westward, even though it did not, as the historian Gerald Nash contends, end the West's "colonial mentality." Western businesses still focused on production of raw materials and held limited manufacturing capabilities, remaining reliant on East Coast investors and consumers. Yet during World War II, the American government spent $70 billion in the West, creating hundreds of thousands of new jobs in aircraft, shipbuilding, aluminum, steel, and electronics-related industries.[17]

In cities like Denver, tens of thousands found work in wartime factories, while service-related trades such as banking, health care, food, and public education expanded in response.[18] In total, over 100,000 people moved to Denver during the war, increasing its population by a fifth. Colorado's overall income climbed, with earnings of about $617 million in 1940 soaring to over $1.3 billion by 1945.[19] The Centennial State and other western territories became self-sufficient, and, as Nash observes, Denver became "the 'capital' of a region 1,500 miles wide and 1,700 miles tall."[20]

After the war ended, western boosters worried that their emergent strength would abate. Therefore, they moved to compete with the East Coast, and among each other to diversify their economies, hoping to establish reliable revenue streams independent from the defense industry. Hundreds of towns formed "development commissions" and agreed to make economic growth their primary purpose.[21] In Denver, as Dorsett and Mc-Carthy assert, there was an "about face" as bankers, elected politicians, "real estate brokers, merchants, and small industrialists . . . in concert with the Chamber of Commerce[] sought growth at any price."[22] The city entered a new era of growth promotion.

In particular, the New York real estate tycoon William Zechendorf witnessed Denver's sudden promise and began building skyscrapers. In the same vein, the brothers and Dallas oilmen Clinton and John Murchison bought up city property and assembled towers of their own.[23] Descendants of the city's growth-focused pioneers also adapted. The same family had overseen the *Denver Post* since its 1895 founding. However, in 1946, the paper recruited the future Olympic bidder Palmer Hoyt to be its editor and push for growth. Likewise, since 1862, one family had run Colorado National Bank, the city's second-largest lender. A hundred years later, its president became the growth-oriented Melvin Roberts, another soon-to-be member of the Denver '76 bid team.[24] Denver's elected leaders fell in line as well. After the war, James Q. Newton was only in his midthirties but owned trusted connections to powerbrokers from the city's past. His grandfather and father worked in high-level positions for different companies owned by the powerful Boettcher family, which built a fortune selling equipment to miners in the 1870s and then investing in sugar beets, cement, and banking. Newton himself served on the boards of the Boettcher Foundation and Colorado National Bank. With support from the *Denver Post* and *Rocky Mountain News*, he became the Mile High City's first postwar mayor.[25] In addition, several other businesses enlarged or relocated to Denver and made for easy growth coalition allies. For instance, the Gates Rubber Company achieved unprecedented windfalls selling rubber "V belts" to automobile manufactures and represented another soon-to-be Olympics backer.[26] "Although the number of decision makers expanded," the urban historian Carl Abbott observes, "the dominant voices [in Denver] . . . remained the incumbent mayor, newspapers, and businessmen working through the Chamber of Commerce and downtown organizations."[27]

By this juncture, Colorado boosters had long exhibited a commitment to the tourist industry. The state possessed prime natural endowments and stunning geography. But even before considering such factors, luring vacationers was always a likely growth-machine venture. As an "export industry," tourists brought in new money, prompting spending beyond the purchasing power of regular residents. Moreover, tourists tended to be wealthier than local inhabitants, did not rely on public services to the extent of year-round citizens, and traveled expressly for consumption. They paid well and asked for comparatively little in return.[28] Thus, by the 1880s, Denver leaders described Colorado as "America's Switzerland" to tempt out-of-towners. In the late 1890s, they organized the annual Festival of Mountain and Plain, modeled after Mardi Gras in New Orleans, for the same reason. In 1915, they responded to the mass production of automobiles by opening a free auto camp within the city, enticing tourists with a place to stay before they headed farther west to the city-owned Mountain Parks system.[29]

On top of this, in reaching for tourist-associated growth, Denver's and Colorado's boosters regularly deployed sports. Sports contests throughout American history have often aided the commodification of place, enabling the construction of a "world-class city" or a "destination image."[30] Skiing competitions, especially, held unique marketing value for Colorado, as the sport came to occupy a central pace in the state's wintertime tourist economy.[31] Indeed, by 1911, the mountain settlement of Hot Sulphur Springs held its first winter sports carnival. Soon, several future resort towns, such as Steamboat Springs, followed suit. Then, in 1927, Moffat Tunnel reached completion, creating a central rail line through the Rockies and leaving recreation advocates wide-eyed. As a *Denver Post* article observed, skiing enthusiasts now "enlisted the cooperation of every service and athletic club and every civic organization in the state in . . . extensive plans for making Colorado the winter sports headquarters of the world."[32] That same year, with this goal in mind, the recently formed Colorado-based US Winter Ski Association recruited a national ski championship to the Centennial State for the first time.[33]

Multiple businesses in Denver recognized their shared interest in tourism and skiing as well. In 1936, the *Rocky Mountain News* sponsored the first "snow train," which brought spectators to Hot Sulphur Springs for its annual ski tournament and festival. After 7,000 people made the trip, Safeway groceries, the *Denver Post*, and the Montgomery Ward department store chain decided to fund similar enterprises. By 1938, snow trains ran to areas in the Colorado Rockies such as Hot Sulphur, Aspen, Steamboat Springs, Marshall Pass, and West Portal every weekend.[34] Even when Denver powerbrokers took a more cautious approach toward growth during the 1920s and 1930s, the potential for positive publicity and profits gained through skiing appealed to winter recreation impresarios, skiing boosters, and tangential businesses small and large.[35]

In light of this consensus, in the late 1930s Colorado's political and business leaders sought to advance the ski industry through the New Deal. After Moffat Tunnel made its way to West Portal, Denver authorities enlisted Colorado's congressional delegation to find funds to open what would become the Winter Park Ski Area. The director of Denver City Parks, George Cranmer, led the charge, pressing Senators Alva Adams and Edwin Johnson and Representative Lawrence Lewis to lobby Secretary of the Interior Harold Ickes. Cranmer was a reliable member of the Denver regime. After gaining wealth as a stockbroker, he had been hand-selected (and provided a "blank check") by Denver's business elite to manage Benjamin Stapleton's 1936 mayoral campaign. Later, working on behalf of Stapleton's administration, he and others convinced Ickes to come through with $9,000 in Works Progress Administration (WPA) funds. The Denver Chamber then solicited $14,000 from the Denver business community to obtain the resources needed to construct Colorado's newest skiing venture.[36] In the decade before World War II, numerous ski clubs received lesser forms of public support. The US Forest Service and New Deal programs such as the WPA, the Civilian Conservation Corps, and the Public Works Administration all helped clear trails, build lodges, and construct ski tows.[37]

As boosters welcomed federal assistance to create winter playgrounds, hosting elite ski competitions continued to prove valuable. Colorado Springs, Estes Park, Allenspark, Idaho Springs, Dillon, and Denver all hosted skiing competitions to attract consumers from out of state. In a classic example, Aspen hosted the Southern Rocky Mountain Skiing Championships in 1938, 1939, and 1940, along with the National Downhill and Slalom Championship in 1940. In the 1930s, the heir of a New York banking family, a Los Angeles real estate investor, and a local entrepreneur devised a plan to turn the mining town into a wintertime retreat. They made several miscalculations, dooming this initial attempt. Still, in later years, residents credited the skiing events for kindling Aspen's future reputation as an international leisure and recreation refuge.[38]

In truth, when World War II concluded, a slew of changes positioned the Colorado ski industry to swell. As the historian Hal Rothman describes, skiing appeared to be the epitome of the nationwide trend toward "recreational tourism." Rather than visiting and observing historical sites to imbibe a mythic past, well-off Americans began to seek physical experiences with nature to access narratives of national exceptionalism and personal authenticity.[39] Moreover, new technology such as metal skis, step-in bindings, and chairlifts made skiing easier to do. New roads likewise caused mountain slopes to become easier to reach. The nation's increased affluence and the advent of paid vacations also made the sport more affordable. Cold War culture even dictated that devoting money to recreation and leisure represented a moral good. Such spending not only nurtured the economy; it signified the presence of individual freedom and social mobility. Skiing became learnable, sellable, accessible, and symbolically validated America's capitalist system.[40]

Against this advancing backdrop, just three months after Japan's surrender in 1945, the Denver Chamber of Commerce hosted the first-ever Colorado Winter Sports Congress to figure out how to turn "winter sports into an economic and commercial asset."[41] "Winter recreation is in its infancy in Colorado," but, the Chamber urged, it "can become big business. . . . Colorado must get busy developing this big important asset."[42] The *Rocky Mountain News* correspondingly began to argue that, due to "our climate, our scenery, our place as the nation's playground," tourism was fast becoming "Colorado's most important single [economic] activity."[43] Colorado businesspeople prepared to move from an extractive mindset toward a service-oriented marketplace, with skiing representing the most noticeable prospect on their state's novel commercial landscape.[44]

By 1947, with $250,000 in Aspen Ski Company stock, investors began constructing the Centennial State's first chairlift. The following year, thanks to $100,000 in city-purchased revenue bonds, Steamboat Springs began building the world's first double-seater. Colorado's governor at the time was William Lee Knous. He attended the inaugural openings of both lifts, expressing his approval. Knous came to power in 1946, promising to spark spending in Colorado. While in office, he called Aspen's developments "Exhibit A" of his hopes for the state.[45]

A few years later, Knous's successor, Colorado governor Dan Thornton, instructed state officials and promoters to produce an abundance of literature with the intent of attracting the attention of out-of-state visitors. The strategy harkened back to some of Denver's earliest days. Through magazines, tourist brochures, guidebooks, and information packets, boosters sold Colorado as a land of clean air and sunshine, jagged peaks and fresh trout, charming ghost towns, and exciting yet safe snow-covered mountain resorts. As the historian William Philpott explains, through this integrated and coordinated effort, the "Colorado high country became more than just a region for tourists to spend money." The state itself served as "a product for consumption and an object of consumer desire."[46]

As part of this imagining of place, elite sporting events remained a constant complement. After opening its lift in 1949, Aspen gained additional recognition by hosting the 1950 World Alpine Championship. The mining town was now on its way to becoming Colorado's largest ski resort.[47] Colorado boosters also continued lobbying for federal support. In the 1950s, ski investors, western communities, local politicians, and especially Colorado governor (and former US senator) Edwin Johnson pressed President Dwight Eisenhower's administration and federal highway officials to build an extension to Interstate 70. Johnson famously gave President Eisenhower, a regular Colorado vacationer, the state's "Fishing License No. 1," along with a position paper detailing the benefits of paving the mass transit road past Denver, across the Rockies, and to the Pacific Ocean. Coloradans intended the throughway to create safe access to scenic mountain terrain for recreationists.[48] By the 1955–1956 ski season, the US government approved I-70's westward track, which in turn led future Denver Olympics allies Senator Gordon Allott and Congressman Wayne Aspinall to use their sway to obtain the Forest Service's permission for the construction of the town of Vail and its adjacent ski resort. Visible from I-70, Vail would emerge literally out of nowhere to surpass Aspen as Colorado's most sizable skiing attraction.[49] It would also occupy a central place in Denver's attempt to host the Olympics.

*   *   *

Through collective entrepreneurship and politicking, Denver's governing regime and the Colorado ski industry rose in prominence. Between 1954 and 1964, the number of visitors to the Centennial State's winter sports facilities increased from 250,000 to over a million.[50] Yet there was a promotional tool left to deploy, one that looked like a superlative avenue for continuing Denver down a road of economic and social ascendency and for turning lesser-known winter resorts such as Vail, Steamboat Springs, and Aspen into international tourist attractions.[51]

In the United States, hosting the Olympics had always been about place-based economic self-interest, and it repeatedly involved western cities or isolated eastern towns seeking to profit from the limelight generated by elite athletics and nation-versus-nation drama. In 1904, as railways lessened the importance of the Mississippi River for moving resources, St. Louis hosted the Summer Games as part of a larger struggle to remain America's western industrial hub.[52] In 1932, the local tourism promoter Dr. Godfrey Dewey and fellow residents employed the Winter Olympics to transform the secluded Adirondack village of Lake Placid, New York, into a distinguished winter resort.[53] And as the Olympic historians Mark Dyreson and Matthew Llewellyn describe, that same year, Southern California real estate developers, mortgage bankers, corporate lawyers, and filmmakers held the Summer Olympics in Los Angeles as part of "a glossy addition to the most ambitious real-estate development in American history."[54]

The games in America have also regularly functioned as a reliable mechanism for accessing public finances. The St. Louis Olympics coincided with the federally backed Louisiana Purchase Exposition, a yearlong fair commemorating the centennial of Thomas Jefferson's $15 million land acquisition from France.[55] For the Lake Placid Winter Games, then–New York governor and future president Franklin Roosevelt urged his state's legislature to support the Adirondack bid. State decision makers obliged, passing a bill to allocate $500,000 for Olympic facilities. Dewey also garnered support from the nearby town of North Elba, which agreed to issue a $200,000 bond on behalf of the Olympic project.[56] Los Angeles residents similarly committed to hosting "LA '32," voting in favor of two bond issues, one for $1 million in 1925 and another for $1.5 million in 1928.[57]

With such backing, the Lake Placid and Los Angeles Olympics, in particular, established that national and global recognition was the reward for putting on the sports extravaganza. During the Lake Placid Games, pictures of agile bodies flying over and across first-rate ski jumps, a new indoor ice rink, and a state-of-the-art bobsled run announced the presence of an area suited for sport, recreation, and consumption. The town of 3,000 had grown into a short-term city of 80,000 sports-obsessed customers.[58] Meanwhile, in Los Angeles, boosters forged indelible connections among the Olympics, mass media, and tourism.[59] Even as desperate refugees fled the Dust Bowl to the West Coast, some of them lining up at Depression-era soup kitchens operating in the shadow of the 105,000-seat Olympic Stadium, athletes socialized with Hollywood celebrities, passed recently planted nonnative palm trees throughout the city's streets, witnessed a 107-foot Olympic torch, and greeted each other at the first-ever Olympic Village. As the *Denver Post* described, thousands of pleasure-seekers made their way by plane, train, and car to the City of Angels to experience "this temporary capital of world athletes."[60]

For its part, the press in Colorado consistently framed America's 1932 Olympic forays as unquestionable successes. Although North Elba would not recoup its dept from the Lake Placid Olympics until 1973, the *Denver Post* inaccurately reported the town's "small deficit will be made up easily enough." Plus, once "all the bills are paid," the paper proclaimed, "Lake Placid will still have a beautiful arena, a magnificent ski jump, and the most thrill-provoking bobrun in the world."[61] Amid the 1932 Los Angeles Summer Games, five hundred American journalists and four hundred international reporters publicized narratives of leisure and athleticism worldwide, and at the *Denver Post*, the sports reporter C. L. Parsons proved as enamored as anyone.[62] As he put it, the famed circus magnate "Barnum was a piker if his famous shows were to be compared with the biggest athletic show in the world—the tenth Olympic games. . . . What a Spectacle!"[63] As the reporter assessed afterward, the Olympics was "a tremendous show, beautifully handled and bringing out the most spectacular performances in the history of athletics."[64]

The Los Angeles Games of 1932 especially became the embodiment of sports as an escape from life's hardships and a hope for a brighter future.[65] As the *New York Times* scribe Allison Danzig proclaimed at the start of the event, "the country may be in the midst of a depression, but there is no sign of it here."[66] One of the West Coast's most industrialized cities faced an age of misery. Yet through portraits painted by writers such as Parsons and Danzig and the efforts of local boosters, the Olympics turned Los Angeles into an apparent magnet for wealth and success.[67] As further evidence for LA '32's promotional power, officials in Nazi Germany used it to convince Adolf Hitler to remain the host of the 1936 Winter and Summer Olympics. In the most ambitious display of nationalism and propaganda in world history, the 1936 Summer Games in Berlin made the Olympics' cultural prominence and political weight irrefutable.[68]

*   *   *

Viewed through the lenses of previous Olympic organizers and sports reporters, the Olympics appeared to be an ideal vehicle for the invention of place and emphasis on recreational tourism already underway in post–World War II Colorado. Thus, not long after the fall of Nazi Germany in 1945, Centennial State tourism promoters mustered an attempt to host the 1956 Winter Games. In 1949, a luxury hotel magnate from Colorado Springs named William Thayer Tutt and the Aspen Ski Company founder Walter Paepcke orchestrated the proposal. They planned to hold the event simultaneously at Tutt's Broadmoor Hotel and Resort and Paepcke's up-and-coming ski town.[69] Tutt appears to have been the more ardent Olympics supporter. He would be at the forefront of Colorado's pursuit of the games for the next twenty years.

Like Aspen, Tutt's resort had a history of using sports as a marketing device. In 1918, the scion of a powerful Philadelphia family, Spencer Penrose, built the Broadmoor. He became wealthy in his own right as a Colorado miner and invested substantially in Colorado Springs. Penrose then constructed the upscale vacation complex outside the town and spared no expense. He hired the architect of New York City's Grand Union Station and the landscaper behind Central Park. To raise the Broadmoor's profile, he also cleared a road up nearby Pikes Peak and held automobile races to the landmark's 14,000-foot summit. Penrose persistently provided fresh sporting attractions through the years, such as a rodeo stadium, polo fields, tennis courts, an ice skating rink, and a golf course, where the Penrose could be found riding from hole to hole on an elephant from the Broadmoor's zoo. As a Colorado Springs newspaper portrayed it: "From the beginning, the Broadmoor was a sportsmen's paradise."[70]

When Penrose died in 1939, he had no surviving siblings or children, and his longtime partner in mining and real estate, Charles Tutt, took over the resort.[71] After World War II, Tutt tasked his son, William Thayer Tutt, with expanding on Penrose's earlier schemes. As Thayer Tutt recalled, the aim was to turn the Broadmoor into a "sports center" that would "attract business and develop the whole community."[72] He began by adding 2,000 seats to the Broadmoor's ice skating arena and recruiting various sports events. During the 1950s, national and international figure skating championships, the first National Collegiate Athletic Association hockey tournament, and the Soviet Union's first hockey match on American soil took place at Broadmoor World Arena. Thayer Tutt also invested millions toward enhancing the Broadmoor's golf courses, attracting high-profile events such as the 1959 US Amateur Championship.[73] As Tutt explained, referring to hosting these high-level contests: "You build your [hotel's] reputation on the free publicity you get."[74]

By comparison, Paepcke's goals for Aspen proved more quixotic. He was a Chicago industrialist, the head of the Container Corporation of America. However, he became close with a group of University of Chicago intellectuals who hoped to fuse progressive thinking with American business practices. Before World War II, Paepcke set out to create a gathering site where the nation's business leaders could study, think creatively, and share ideas toward this end. He selected Aspen for the high-minded haven.[75]

Through the 1940s, Paepcke proceeded to invest the bulk of his wealth and energy into buying up Aspen property and attempting to build what he called the "Athens of the Rockies." He worked to recruit prominent thinkers, financial elites, and celebrities to invest in and visit the town. For a time in the 1950s, the cultural sanctuary seemed to be taking form. Nonetheless, tourism quickly became part of the plan. Paepcke funded the construction of the Aspen Ski Resort and founded the Aspen Ski Company, imagining skiing as a supplement to stabilize Aspen's wanting winter economy. He meant for the town to be carried foremost by the activities of progressive collaborators during the summer months. He did not want to rely on skiing to turn a profit.[76]

But by the time of Tutt's and Paepcke's Olympic bid, it was becoming clear that out-of-town skiers, rather than thinkers, served as Aspen's economic backbone. Paepcke's cultural centerpiece, the Aspen Institute, bled cash. By contrast, skiing showed sudden and significant promise. In a "remarkably fortuitous occurrence," as Hal Rothman describes, skiing "rescued" Paepcke's legacy and fortune.[77] From Paepcke's point of view, the Olympics may have appeared to be the best of both worlds. It was an event claiming the ground of global idealism that could also publicize Aspen's true source of sustenance.

Neither were Tutt and Paepcke alone in envisioning Colorado as an Olympic host. In a setting where boosters and policy makers looked to forge growth via tourism throughout the state, backing came from politicians and other business leaders. In the spring of 1949, the governor, Colorado's two United States senators, various mayors, and numerous local chambers of commerce sent telegrams to International Olympic Committee president Avery Brundage in Rome. Brundage and the IOC met there to decide where to hold the 1956 Winter Olympics. Thus, as the *Rocky Mountain News* reported, the Coloradans made clear that the "swank" Broadmoor Hotel and the "picturesque old 'ghost' mining town" of Aspen, "launched as a winter playground three years ago," stood ready to put on the games.[78]

Unfortunately for the Coloradans, their chances to win hosting rights for 1956 were slim. Cortina d'Ampezzo, Italy, had been striving for the event since before World War II and became the IOC's consensus choice. Furthermore, the United States Olympic Committee (USOC) put its weight behind a separate bid from Lake Placid, New York. While enthusiastic about holding the games, Tutt and Paepcke failed to pass their submission through normal channels. IOC rules held that cities needed their national Olympic committee's approval before making a final pitch to the IOC, and Lake Placid represented the only American bidder of which the USOC was aware.[79]

All the same, Brundage and Paepcke knew each other. As Brundage described, his "personal friends" extended the Centennial State invitation. Brundage was also from Chicago, where he built personal wealth through construction, and would put in a good word on Colorado's behalf. "I arranged for Colorado Springs and Aspen to obtain some valuable publicity," Brundage wrote to Paepcke, "and, as a matter of fact, Colorado got twice as many votes as Lake Placid."[80] Lake Placid received one vote; Colorado earned two.[81]

With Brundage's ostensible encouragement, Tutt and Paepcke remained optimistic that Colorado Springs and Aspen might still become Olympic sites. As soon as the IOC revealed the results from its meeting in Rome, Tutt began preparing his next bid.[82] By this time, it was becoming clear that the ski industry would soon take off, and Tutt set his sights on building his own skiing facility. To do so, he hired the ski enthusiast Steve Knowlton. Knowlton would become a key Denver '76 ally. During World War II, he enlisted in the United States Army's famed 10th Mountain "Ski Troops" Division, training at Camp Hale near Aspen and facing brutal combat in the Italian Alps.[83] Afterward, along with several members of his regiment, Knowlton carried back home insight into skiing and Colorado's terrain.[84] A self-professed "ski bum," he began cutting trails for Paepcke's company, aspired to operate a ski resort of his own, and, by 1959, helped Tutt open the Ski Broadmoor facility outside Colorado Springs.[85]

In 1954, with Ski Broadmoor under construction and skiing paying Paepcke's bills, Tutt and Knowlton traveled together to Chicago to present a proposal to the USOC to host the 1960 Winter Olympics. They once more proposed to hold the event at Colorado Springs and Aspen. As the recently appointed manager of the Rocky Mountain Ski Operators Association, Knowlton spoke on behalf of a confederation of Colorado ski resorts, promising that Colorado was prepared to host the festival.[86]

Yet Tutt and Knowlton lost to another upstart ski resort from the American

West: Squaw Valley, California. More specifically, they lost to the New York attorney Alexander C. Cushing and the Southern California Olympic Organizing Committee. In 1947, Cushing raised $400,000 to purchase 574 acres in California's Sierra Nevada to start a ski complex. Like Tutt and Paepcke in Colorado, he saw the Olympics as a chance to promote his new enterprise.[87] Importantly, though, he received financial, rather than just verbal, support from California politicians. California governor Goodwin Knight endorsed the idea, and Squaw Valley's representative in the state senate introduced legislation that pledged $1 million should Cushing secure the event. The California legislature passed the proposal with ease, giving Squaw Valley an edge over its Centennial State competition.[88]

Cushing then traveled to the IOC's 1955 meeting in Paris, where the California bid narrowly defeated a rival from Innsbruck, Austria. Significantly, after receiving USOC approval, Cushing had raised $50,000 from private sources to bring an updated bid to the IOC. The bid's investors came mainly from the Cushing-led Squaw Valley Development Company. However, the event itself would be held through much larger public contributions. California, Nevada, and the federal government ultimately forked over a combined $20 million to assist Cushing in building sports facilities and infrastructure, including a stadium, a village, and a new sewage treatment plant.[89]

Historical analysis compared to initial media framing yields different interpretations of these Olympic contributions. After 1960, most of the new sports facilities built for the Squaw Valley Games went unused. California eventually acquired ownership of the venue and then sold it to another private corporation. By the 1970s, as Denver's Olympics opponents would point out, that company entered bankruptcy. Most of Squaw Valley's "white elephants" would be dismantled.[90]

Nevertheless, immediate reactions remained positive. Walt Disney and his mammoth entertainment conglomerate orchestrated extravagant opening and closing ceremonies. Hockey players and figure skaters enjoyed the first artificial ice rinks in Olympic history, tended to by a brand-new innovation, the Zamboni machine, which added a thin layer of moisture to smooth the ice. The Columbia Broadcasting System (CBS) made Squaw Valley the first Olympics televised consistently throughout the United States and one of the first sports events to reach a global audience.[91] Newspapers from California to Denver to New York also provided ecstatic local reviews.[92] The *Denver Post* expressed some skepticism, pointing to the event's price tag and the new, 8,500-seat arena that would "do little more than stand in memory" once the games concluded. Even so, the *Post* ensured its readers that "overall, the games were successful," and "there is little doubt that . . . [Squaw Valley] will become the far west's leading playground." As the paper asserted, "the name Squaw Valley now is as famous as Sun Valley or Lake Placid."[93]

Sun Valley, Idaho, represented the prototype for the posh form of recreational tourism that Aspen, Vail, and the Broadmoor tried to emulate. It was a spectacular winter sports destination located next to the small agricultural town of Ketchum. The heir to the Union Pacific Railroad, W. Averell Harriman, had designed it in the late 1930s. Inspired by an interest in skiing sparked by the 1932 Lake Placid Olympics, he sought a location reminiscent of the Austrian Alps and near his Union Pacific line. Harriman also undertook a national marketing campaign to connect skiing with status and fame, propping up the sport as an activity for Americans to idolize. From the 1940s through 1960, Sun Valley occupied a position as the first and only nationally renowned skiing attraction designed for the wealthy.[94] But now, in 1960, due to the Olympics, it seemed that Squaw Valley had joined its exclusive ranks.

With this in mind, amid a resurgence of pro-growth politics and an unprecedented emphasis on tourism in Colorado, the 1960 Squaw Valley Olympics probably left Tutt, Knowlton, Paepcke, and others with regret. However, the event also provided tactics to replicate and reasons to continue seeking the games. Colorado ski industry advocates appeared to lose out on an invaluable public relations opportunity—a priceless platform to market tourism and skiing in their state. In the same instance, they saw that establishing a relationship with elected decision makers, evidenced by a monetary commitment, carried value in the USOC's evaluation. They likewise observed that even if the bid process required bidders to use their own financial resources, they could still deploy the sports event to justify far more extensive public funding for tourism-related infrastructure and promotion. For Colorado's ski industry investors, contingent land developers, nearby property owners, local utility providers, and financiers, the games must have seemed as appealing as ever. It is little surprise that such boosters were far from ready to give up on their Olympic dreams.

CHAPTER 2

Growth Crusaders

Beginning in 1963, a collection of leading businessmen and politicians began to assemble another Colorado-based Olympic bid. This time they aimed for the 1976 Winter Games. Their effort was undergirded by over a decade of belief in growth's benevolence, a burgeoning reliance on tourism, decades of federal support for development in western states, and a century of regime politics in Denver. With sights set on creating consumption-oriented, tourist-centered growth, at the bicentennial of the United States and the centennial of Colorado, such actors confidently foresaw the Olympic flame igniting their region.

At the same time, investors in ski resorts, bankers, utility providers, construction companies, politicians at all levels, newspaper editors, and others worked in unison to bring the sports mega-event to the state. The group thereby exposed how private and public actors functioned beyond formal government structures to devise and institute city and state policy.[1] This pro-growth effort was the tangible embodiment of a governing regime.[2] Given the political economy that the bid team operated within, it did not anticipate such a formulation becoming a problem. Still, the initiative to host the 1976 Winter Olympics laid bare elements of Denver's and Colorado's political systems.

In the 1960s, local politicians proved inclined to support growth. It symbolized strong leadership, adhered to postwar expectations, and appealed to business leaders who financed campaigns and enabled policy implementation.[3] Colorado governor John Love and Denver mayors Thomas Currigan and William McNichols certainly embraced their roles as Olympics advocates; Love is probably the most prominent figure in this regard.

In fall 1962, John Love, the Republican candidate, campaigned for Colorado's governorship. He faced the Democratic incumbent governor Stephen McNichols (the older brother of the future Denver mayor William McNichols). Love was just forty-six years old, a corporate lawyer, and had never run for elected office before. According to one newspaper, his victory in the state's Republican primary represented a "major coup." But having gained the Republican nomination, Love followed in the footsteps of his political predecessors. He predicted that reducing taxes would attract more corporations to Colorado and ensure greater economic diversification. McNichols was running for a third term. Known throughout the state as "Steve," he contended that spending tax dollars wisely, at the current rates, remained the best route for Colorado's economic prosperity.[4]

Although the candidates had their differences, they agreed on the value of promoting tourism to broaden Colorado's marketplace. As part of their 1962 political platform, Colorado Republicans urged state spending on "the most effective methods of attracting out of state visitors." Also speaking of tourism, state Democrats pledged to "continue to develop facilities and programs to foster this great industry."[5] The question for Colorado citizens seemed to be: Who was the better tourist industry booster?

Love defeated McNichols, presumably convincing voters he was the best bet for attracting external capital. During his campaign, Love admitted Colorado's financial stakes had improved under his opponent, but he warned "too much of it is based on defense and federal agencies."[6] As Love rhetorically asked in a speech: "What happens to a state when its main industry is defense or defense-related . . . what happens if there's a shift in our defense posture?" The answer looked obvious. While "we all look forward to the day when we can live in true peace," Love reflected, "I don't have to tell you what will happen to the economic base in Colorado." Love, however, assured constituents that if he could just lessen the state "income and inventory taxes that choke the businessman to death, big and small . . . we can put Colorado back on the industrial map . . . [and begin to] measure our progress in industries."[7] Under his leadership, the state would witness a "decade of development," Love's campaign professed.[8]

When Love was elected, expanding the Colorado economy remained vital but challenging. He lived up to a campaign promise by cutting the state's income tax by 15 percent. Yet layoffs from the defense industry manufacturer Martin Marietta and an unforeseeable drought contributed to a downturn.[9] In response, in early 1964, Love raised the state's sales tax and increased college tuition. Political commentators reacted by mocking the novice governor's now apparently "over-enthusiastic tax cuts."[10] One cartoonist drew Love literally peeling gold plates off the dome of Colorado's capitol building to cover public expenses.[11] The recently defeated former governor McNichols went on the attack as well, outlandishly proclaiming Love's tuition hike was "going to make the greatest contribution to juvenile delinquency in the history of this state."[12] Irate college students also made their feelings known, staging sit-ins at the Capitol, picketing Love when he visited campuses, and, in one instance, hanging the governor in effigy.[13] After Love's first year on the job, many predicted the support that brought him to the governor's mansion had faded.[14]

Nevertheless, as Love recounted, he began touring the country "to find any possible economic opportunity."[15] As the sociologist Harvey Molotch suggests, in the postwar years "a key role of elected and appointed officials" was "that of 'ambassador' to industry." The task was "to communicate . . . advantages to potential investors" to "sell" an area's "business climate."[16] Accordingly, in May 1964, Love, both of Colorado's US senators, and forty local businesspeople journeyed to New York City on what they called the "Sell Colorado Mission." In Love's words, the "missionary group" aimed to inform New York executives and corporate benefactors about "one of the greatest pieces of real estate on the surface of the globe."[17]

Love and sixty-five Colorado executives traveled to San Francisco six months later, continuing to try to convince out-of-state corporations to expand into or relocate to the Centennial State. In one of the expedition's highlights, the governor spoke to Bay Area manufacturers at a luncheon hosted by his "Sell Colorado" associates. Love promised the Californians that, in Colorado, they would find a surplus of natural resources, a strong foundation for manufacturing plants, various modes of transportation, and an ideal location from which to send products throughout the United States.[18] Love pledged that new businesses would benefit from research and innovation realized at Colorado's educational facilities, a loyal and skilled labor force, and a state government friendly toward corporate and industrial enterprise. We "do hope," Love concluded in his speech, "you will consider Colorado in your expansion planning."[19] Over the next two years, Love gave similar Sell Colorado sermons in Chicago and Los Angeles. On these occasions, over a hundred Sell Colorado ambassadors from the state's business community joined the governor, lending support at their own expense.[20] Growth and development remained the barometer of success. Love and other Colorado boosters did all they could to move the needle.

Simultaneously, the same Coloradans who led the Sell Colorado program began to engineer a bid for the 1976 Winter Games. In 1963, William

Thayer Tutt reached out to Love about hosting the Olympics.[21] Love had been easy to contact. The governor grew up in Colorado Springs during the Great Depression on the opposite side of the socioeconomic tracks from Tutt's Broadmoor resort. However, in 1951, after serving as a pilot in the Pacific during World War II, attending college, and becoming a successful corporate lawyer, Love moved two blocks from the luxury retreat, joined the Broadmoor Community Church and the Broadmoor Golf Club, and then accepted a position as the resort's legal counsel. Before being elected, Love's office was located inside Tutt's hotel.[22]

Importantly, it had become clear to Tutt that a successful Olympic bid required more money than private interests would put forth. As with the 1960 Squaw Valley Olympics, hosting the games in Colorado necessitated state and federal commitments. But for Tutt and other aspiring bidders, that was probably part of the attraction. They would undoubtedly welcome public funds for marketing Colorado to tourists. Plus, enlisting the government provided an optics-related advantage. It made the promotional endeavor of business elites appear like a civic campaign connected to the "public good."[23]

Love, of course, proved amenable to Tutt's Olympic suggestion. Just six months in office, he announced his plan to bid for the sports event. In early 1964, with pressure mounting on his administration, he officially appointed individuals to the Colorado Olympic Commission (COC).[24] The original COC members were William Thayer Tutt, Peter Seibert, Merrill Hastings, Donald Fowler, Richard Olson, and Joseph Coors.[25]

Tutt had been trying to use the Olympics to promote Colorado Springs and the Broadmoor since 1949. The bid team eventually decided to hold the games in Denver, but Tutt had his own reasons to seek growth in the Mile High City and Colorado more broadly. He was a director at the First National Bank in Colorado Springs, the Mountain States Telephone Company, and the Denver & Rio Grande Western Railroad. He additionally served as the chairmen of the board for the El Pomar Investment Company and invested in, among other things, the wildly ambitious Vail Ski Resort.[26] As Tutt put it, his company had been "closely associated" with Vail "from the beginning."[27]

Peter Seibert was a central developer, operator, and owner of Vail. Moreover, although Vail would become more successful than most could have imagined, from the perspective of 1964, it still appeared to be a daring risk. In the 1950s, Seibert and others failed to get Colorado banks to support their plan to build an entire town to service a brand-new ski complex, marked by a tranquil upper-class ethos and relatively affordable second homes and con-dominiums. Seibert and his business partners ultimately sold a hundred limited partnership shares and spent their own funds to get the project off the ground. With Vail in only its second season of existence at the bid's launch, the resort's backers must have been champing at the prospect of using the Olympics to market their pathbreaking form of recreational tourism.[28]

As the publisher and owner of the nationally distributed *Skiing* magazine and the soon-to-be publisher of *Colorado Magazine,* Merrill Hastings had similarly invested in the ski industry and Colorado consumers.[29] Seibert and Hastings also had a connection to Tutt's previous Olympic partner, Steve Knowlton. All three served in the 10th Mountain Division. With their unique understanding of Colorado's mountains and skiing's improved accessibility, the army veterans positioned themselves to benefit from Colorado's emerging ski business. One source even gives Seibert and Hastings credit for instigating the bid for the 1976 games rather than Tutt.[30]

By this time, Knowlton worked as the chairperson of Colorado Ski Country USA (SCUSA), a group of ski resort leaders and related investors who promoted the sport of skiing throughout the Centennial State. By 1968, SCUSA consisted of twenty-three ski resorts and 160 allied businesses collaborating with the state-run Colorado Visitors Bureau.[31] Love was an "honorary" SCUSA member.[32] While the governor tried to sell Colorado in general, Colorado Ski Country USA labored specifically to publicize the state's up-and-coming ski towns.[33]

Predictably, the COC and SCUSA shared several contributors. Seibert and Hastings joined the Knowlton-led organization at its start, as did fellow COC member Donald Fowler.[34] Fowler, though, came to skiing from a different background. He worked as an executive director at the Denver-based United Airlines. There he devised the first joint airline and ski resort sales packages.[35] Fowler also created ski information centers at airports, skier check-in counters, and ski films for drawing in potential tourists. He never actually skied, but in 1968 he replaced Knowlton as SCUSA's top official.[36] As a private transportation provider benefiting from Rocky Mountain tourism, Fowler did not need to know how to navigate the slopes to see eye-to-eye with Colorado's ski industry champions.[37]

The last two COC members also had reasons to want to see Colorado's ski industry expand. Richard Olson occupied multiple roles. He was the president of Outdoor Industries Incorporated, a sports equipment retail outlet, a director of Vail Associates, a director at United Bank of Denver, and the vice president and general manager of Sundstrand Corporation,

Figure 2.1. December 1964. Ski Country USA chairman and industry promoter Steven Knowlton watches Governor John Love don a Ski Country USA pin. Photo by George Crouter/*Denver Post* via Getty Images.

a manufacturer of aerospace products.[38] The COC held some of its earliest meetings at Sundstrand's Mile High office.[39] Finally, Joseph Coors served as the president of Coors Porcelain and Brewing Company and acted as director of the Colorado Association of Commerce, an organization of 1,000 of the state's largest corporations.[40] He headed a group explicitly charged with promoting growth in Colorado. It is also worth adding that his son and heir, William Coors, served on SCUSA's board of trustees.[41]

At first, the ski industry looked to possess the tightest hold among the interests serving on the COC. Nonetheless, a crew of businesspeople working less directly within the world of skiing soon joined the team. Love enlisted the president of Colorado National Bank, Melvin Roberts, to run the COC's Budget and Finance Committee. The bidders would deposit their funds within Robert's institution and use its downtown location as their first formal office. Soon after that, Carl DeTemple became head of the COC's committee overseeing site selection. He was president of the Denver Brick and Tile Company, president of the Denver City Council, and an executive for the Colorado Association of Commerce.[42] Donald Magarrell and Donald McMahon also came on board in short order. Magarrell's day job was at the Colorado National Bank. In 1966, he became a vice president of the COC at Melvin Roberts's request. Roberts would step aside from his Olympic duties, leaving Magarrell as his bank's representative on the COC. After the IOC selected Denver as its host for the 1976 Winter Games, Roberts granted Magarrell a leave of absence to serve as the organizing committee's general secretary. In this role, he continued to earn a commensurate (though now publicly funded) annual salary of $37,000.[43] McMahon, meanwhile, was the director of area development for the Colorado Interstate Gas Company, a subsidiary of the powerful and long-established Public Service Company of Colorado. Public Service Company would offer several of its employees to the Olympic cause in the years come, and McMahon eventually became the COC's president and executive director.[44]

Notably, these bid-team members were directly involved with Sell Colorado. Magarrell ran Love's Sell Colorado committee, and McMahon served as Love's director of economic development.[45] In an interview with the political scientist Laura Olson, Magarrell confessed that the Sell Colorado project was McMahon's idea.[46] Indeed, when Love led his third Sell Colorado expedition, to Chicago in 1965, all the above-mentioned COC members (except for Tutt) traveled along as ambassadors.[47] For the fourth mission, to Los Angeles in 1966, each of the Olympic bidders listed took part except for Tutt and Siebert.[48]

On a 1971 television broadcast devoted to the Denver Olympics controversy sweeping across Colorado, a host asked Magarrell if the Sell Colorado campaign and the bid for the Olympics were related. After a pause, Magarrell conceded that the "Olympics would bring tourists more than anything else." Then he answered simply: "I think so."[49] Just the year before, while introducing Colorado's Comprehensive Outdoor Recreation Plan, Governor Love predicted 150,000 spectators would come to the Centennial State for the Winter Games and that, afterward, the number of annual out-of-state tourists could more than double, from 7 million to 15 million.[50] As Magarrell's hesitation appears to indicate, many Coloradans no longer embraced such growth without question. Yet his response likewise reveals that denying the obvious was futile.

With that being said, in some respects Magarrell slanted the purpose of the COC scheme. Magarrell admitted only to tourism promotion and added the qualification that he "thought," rather than "knew," that the Olympics and Sell Colorado were entwined. However, the leaders of Sell Colorado were the leaders of the COC, and the likes of DeTemple, Magarrell,

and McMahon did not fit the mold of straightforward winter sports providers. They did not represent businesses that would garner free publicity
through the Olympics. The companies they served would, nevertheless, see
increased profits from growth generally—and thus from the tourists that
Olympic advertising could bring. They were, in other words, glad to utilize
sports and sports-based tourism to advance growth writ large.[51]

While the business community provided the impetus for Denver's Olympic
bid, counterparts in the public sector remained essential. Although private
and public funds paid for Denver's forthcoming attempt to gain the games,
the bidders always expected public financing to carry the brunt of the load
when it came time to actually run the show. "We'd need a lot of money,"
the Aspen landowner and Aspen Ski Company president D. R. C. Brown
warned in 1964, "both from the state and federal government[s]."[52]

But the bidders were not perturbed. One of the purposes of forming a
growth coalition is for the beneficiaries of growth to shift the costs of their
activities elsewhere.[53] Furthermore, the bid team had good reason to think
local politicians would stand by their side. In the postwar era, state-level
representatives sought an office with a limited salary. Therefore, most came
from the upper class and were likely to share interests with, and consent to,
growth machine priorities. In her study of Colorado's 1972 anti-Olympics
ballot initiative, Laura Olson found no relationship between the positions of
Colorado General Assembly members on the games and the preferences of
their constituents. However, using a Common Cause survey from that year,
she observed a clear relationship between policy makers' individual economic interests in real estate speculation, banking, transportation, communication, and/or energy production and their likelihood of voting to enable
public funding for the sports spectacle.[54] In the same instance, such officials
sought finances to run winning campaigns. This created decent odds that
they had cozy relationships with the businesspeople behind Sell Colorado
and the COC. Through research that included interviews with 182 of the
226 members who served in the Colorado General Assembly from 1957 to
1966, the scholars Victor Hejelm and Joseph Pisciotte found that "business
interests ranked second" behind the major political parties in funding successful candidates, contributing to Democratic and Republican contenders equally.[55] In short, elected officials and business interests were likely to
benefit from working together—and often would.

Indeed, Merrill Hastings explicitly advised Governor Love on his selection of Colorado Olympic Commission members. As the COC bid got underway, the bid team also maintained easy access to the governor and other

public officeholders.[56] According to the team's legal counsel Richard Davis, a senior partner at the prominent Denver law firm Davis Graham & Stubbs, Love's door was always open to hearing Olympic-related requests.[57] Carl DeTemple also recalled that he had strong relationships and regular contacts with most state-level policy makers due to his previous position as a lobbyist for the Colorado Association of Commerce.[58]

Unsurprisingly, then, Love provided the first dose of Olympic funding through his emergency budget. Shortly thereafter, more money followed from the state's Division of Commerce and Development. Public officials used public resources to create and invest in the COC without any legislative oversight.[59] In 1967, with minimal debate, the Colorado House also passed House Joint Resolution 1032 unanimously, "extending an invitation to have the Olympic Games of 1976 in Denver" and promising Colorado Olympic organizers the "support and assistance of the citizens of this state for the successful holding" of the event. Around the same time, Colorado Senate Bill 179 backed up these words by calling to appropriate $25,000 for the COC.[60] In 1969, the City and County of Denver allocated $75,000 specifically for Denver's IOC bid, and the state followed by providing $150,000 for the same cause.[61] Even as the debate over the games heated up a few years later, as one bidder described, Olympics proponents "knew that the State Assembly would never cut off funding."[62]

As for the city of Denver, the bidders could likewise be certain of support from the mayor's office.[63] As the bid began, the mayor was the Democrat Thomas Currigan. Since the 1870s, when Currigan's grandfather moved from Ireland and became a city councilman, his family had been entrenched in Denver politics. Currigan's successor, William McNichols, was also well versed in the Mile High system. He was the son of a city auditor and brother to Colorado's former governor. He worked for Governor Steve McNichols before becoming Denver's manager of public works and then deputy mayor. He came to power when Currigan stepped down to become a vice president at Continental Airlines.[64] Currigan and McNichols wholeheartedly and expectedly backed hosting the games.[65]

At the federal level, the bidders would face ambiguity regarding the means and methods of Olympic support. How to garner dollars from Washington, DC, remained a constant topic of conversation at COC meetings.[66] Nonetheless, the Olympic planners expected to backdraft on pro-Olympics proclivities and the desires for bicentennial celebrations in the nation's capital.[67] Colorado politicians serving at the federal level assuredly conveyed fidelity to the Denver bid. Denver's Democratic US congressman, Byron Rodgers, had been tied in with Denver elites since his election in 1950.

"I wish to lend whatever assistance I can to this vital project," he wrote to Mayor Currigan in 1967; "it would spur the industrial development of the entire Rocky Mountains."[68] Republican senator Gordon Allott, a consistent advocate for tourism and growth, correspondingly penned to Currigan: "I pledge to the State and to the City of Denver every constructive effort open to me, as a United States Senator, to further this effort in support of this bid."[69] Fellow Republican senator Peter Dominick, GOP congressman Donald Brotzman, and House Democrats Wayne Aspinall and Frank Evans echoed this attitude.[70]

In 1968, to help Denver prepare its presentation to the IOC, Currigan even reached out to Democratic vice president and presidential candidate Hubert Humphrey to ask for federal funds. Humphrey replied in the affirmative.[71] A few months later, Richard Nixon defeated Humphrey to become president of the United States, but Denver's Olympic hopefuls did not need to worry. Nixon wrote to newly empowered Mayor McNichols: "You may be sure that the Denver Olympic Committee will receive full cooperation from my office."[72] Although the Nixon administration gave more attention to helping Los Angeles win its concurrent bid for the more prominent 1976 Summer Olympics, and it did not contribute money during the bid process, federal officials arranged for US ambassadors to deliver promotional material to IOC members on Denver's behalf.[73] Secretary of State Dean Rusk wrote to Governor Love as well, promising to assign a liaison to help Denver in whatever way necessary.[74] As power exchanged hands at multiple levels, the Denver bid maintained the stamp of city, state, and federal approval, not to mention, thanks to the State Department, free international postage.

With trustworthy allies functioning throughout the public realm, private interests saw the potential for positive returns and pitched in. These private players acted with knowledge of the public contributions discussed above and the assurance that more substantial public financing would follow if the bid was successful. As McMahon told the general manager of Dow Chemical in 1968, the bid team's requests for private assistance represented a "one-time effort" to win the IOC's designation. The bidders, he promised, would "have the opportunity to raise funds from sources other than the business community" and could "guarantee that the Committee will not be calling again in the future."[75]

Between 1968 and 1970, private sources provided over $212,000 to Denver's Olympic project. When collecting funds to support the all-important IOC presentation, about half the bid's $336,000 came via this pipeline.[76]

Figure 2.2. March 1968. Demonstrating support among Colorado's business community, Denver mayor Thomas Currigan, US Ski Team coach Bob Beattie, guest speaker Thomas Lowell, Broadmoor Hotel president William Thayer Tutt, Governor John Love, and Colorado Olympic Committee member Jim Stadler attend a fundraising dinner to bolster Denver's Winter Olympics bid. Photo by Melvyn E. Schieltz via Denver Public Library, Western History Collection, *Rocky Mountain News* Records.

Many of the donors had direct links to the COC. Donations included $10,000 from Thayer Tutt's El Pomar Investment firm and $15,000 from Joseph Coors's Coors Porcelain and Brewing Company. Public Service Company and Mountain States Telephone Company provided $15,000 apiece along with employees to serve on the team of bidders. Additional contributors included the Boettcher Foundation, the cement company Ideal Basic Industries, the oil and gas distributor King Resources, a collection of banks, and other businesses.[77]

Indicating the confidence of the bidders in their political position and goals, headlines such as "Central Bank Boosts Olympic Funds" ran in Denver newspapers to highlight those taking part.[78] In 1968, the press likewise celebrated as the bidders collected over $30,000 from a $100 per plate "men only" fundraising dinner. With Steve Knowlton acting as the "master of ceremonies," the gathering reportedly attracted "dignitaries," several hundred executives, Mayor Currigan, and Governor Love.[79]

The bidders also received various in-kind donations, from liquor and cars to plane trips and helicopter rides. In December 1967, along with its

$10,000 donation, Gates Rubber Company provided free travel on its private jet to Governor Love, Mayor Currigan, and Merrill Hastings when they flew to New York City to present Denver's Olympic proposal to the United States Olympic Committee.[80] In 1968, when the bidders turned their focus to the IOC, Public Service Company and the Gates Rubber flew International Ski Federation visitors by helicopter to survey potential event sites.[81] Similarly, in 1970, when the bidders made their way to Amsterdam for their final pitch to the IOC, they used a plane provided by King Resources.[82]

The ski industry also remained an eager contributor to the Olympic cause. Into the 1960s, as SCUSA meeting minutes describe, ski resorts and towns continued to use sporting events to create "widespread national and international publicity."[83] As SCUSA members declared, such occasions were "special promotions for Colorado skiing" and "gave Colorado the best press coverage."[84] Therefore, SCUSA and the COC continued to operate in tandem. As the bid got underway in 1964, Knowlton traveled Colorado to promote SCUSA's agenda and discussed the potential of hosting the games regularly.[85] "The Colorado ski business is pretty healthy right now," the booster asserted; "what better way to keep it going than with the greatest winter sports show in the world." "The winter Olympics," he exclaimed, would help the Colorado ski industry "bust right out of its britches in the next few years."[86] As SCUSA meeting minutes recount, following a late 1966 gathering in which Richard Olson, Merrill Hasting, and Carl DeTemple presented their plan to use the Olympics to "promote Colorado nationally and internationally," SCUSA officially endorsed the Colorado Olympic Commission.[87]

With the business community, politicians, and the ski industry marching in lockstep, Colorado's print media did its part as well. In the late 1960s and early 1970s, newspapers took "prime responsibility" for fostering "growth enthusiasm." For them, the nature and direction of development mattered little. As a city's population increased, local dailies became more read and more valuable. "The newspaper has no ax to grind," Molotch describes, "except the one ax which holds the community elite together: growth."[88] The bid organizers thus felt no apprehension about asking Colorado's two major presses to share Olympic-related news releases received from abroad. Neither did they sense a need to conceal the profit motive underlying such a request. As one bidder wrote to the respective editors of the *Denver Post* and *Rocky Mountain News*: "We want to be in the best possible position to know what to expect if the in-fighting for this multi-million dollar plum begins to get rough."[89]

Pro-Olympics perspectives surely extended up the chain of command at the papers. *Post* and *Rocky* editors Palmer Hoyt and Jack Foster served as informal advisers going into the 1967 proposal to the USOC; by the time the Denver bid team submitted its final plan to the IOC, they became official team members.[90] Meanwhile, reporters from both papers parroted tales of social status, exhilaration, and preparedness. *Denver Post* journalist Cal Queal characterized things this way in 1964: "Gov. John Love has launched an international mission that could bring one of the world's greatest sports attractions to Colorado." "Colorado has the raw material and the know-how to stage a first-class Olympiad . . . the finest Olympics in history," Queal exclaimed.[91] In 1966, writing from the perspective of all Coloradoans, the *Rocky Mountain News* editorialized in kind: "We boast the best snow in the nation—and the world" and "would like to be the [w]orld's winter showcase. We're keeping our skis crossed."[92]

If there were ever any doubt, it proved evident that the *Post* and the *Rocky* accepted the presumed virtues of hosting the Olympics when Governor Love, Mayor Currigan, and fellow bidders traveled to the 1968 Grenoble Winter Games. "You might expect criticism when the Mayor and the Governor set out for a junket to France in the midst of frenzied city and state business," Alan Cunningham of the *Rocky Mountain News* commented; "but Gov. Love and Mayor Currigan will have the blessings of most of their constituents when they depart on separate flights Wednesday for Grenoble," for the two leaders would be trying "to persuade members of the International Olympic Committee that the site for the 12th Winter Games eight years from now should be Colorado."[93] As Chet Nelson, the *Rocky Mountain News*'s sports section editor, affirmed during the 1968 gathering, "the benefits" of holding the event "will last long into the future."[94] After the Grenoble Games concluded, the *Denver Post* sports reporter Jim Graham shared a comparably sanguine view, musing that "on our black and white set, the spectacle of the finest winter sports athletes from 38 nations in the colorful parade sent shivers down my spine. . . . I wish every man, woman, and child in Colorado could envision through the magic of a time machine the 1976 Winter Olympics here in our own Centennial State."[95]

Perhaps most conspicuously, the editor of the *Canyon Courier* of Evergreen, Colorado, Owen Ball, also assisted the bid. Some of the earliest and most vigorous opposition to the Denver Olympics came from Evergreen, an exurban mountain town, where bidders scheduled several events. Yet upon watching the 1968 Mexico City Summer Olympics, Ball announced in the *Courier* that the "mere fact that the International Olympic Committee is considering bringing the 1976 winter games to this area gives me a good feeling all over." "I'm really not much [for] plodding around in snow on a cold winter day," he declared, "but if the Olympics come here, I'm going to be there watching those 90-meter jumps, and as many other events as possible."[96] In fact, with tensions roiling in Evergreen prior to the IOC's selection, Ball met with and pledged support to the bidders.[97] Then, weeks before the IOC made its choice, the same day that Evergreen residents met with Olympics backers and Governor Love to express their frustrations, Ball wrote to the IOC at the bid team's request to feign his community's approval. "I am sure these dedicated residents will enthusiastically support the staging of the games here," he claimed.[98]

Through the IOC selection, media outlets of various sizes continued to paint the games in a favorable light. When the bid team left for Amsterdam in May 1970, the *Denver Post* promised its readership that the "1976 Winter Games would be a definite plus for the Denver area." We wish "the Denver committee well," the paper averred, "and hope theirs is a successful trip."[99]

After Love won reelection in 1966, as he remembered, he became even "more involved in [the] 'Sell Colorado' program."[100] At the same time, the Olympics and skiing remained central to his agenda. When Love addressed the Colorado General Assembly a little over a year later, he conceded that income from Colorado ranching and farming had declined. Yet he emphasized that the state's third-largest industry, tourism, picked up the slack. Love reported that around 6.8 million tourists spent half a billion dollars in Colorado the previous year and promised that up-and-coming ski resorts and the stature brought by hosting the Olympic Games ensured that this trend would continue. "Colorado has been chosen by the United States Olympic Committee as this nation's nominee to host the 1976 Winter Olympics," Love stressed; "this . . . points to major economic and recreational advances, when we do receive the world's designation."[101] Even before the IOC selected Denver, the mere prospect of hosting the games appeared to hold positive public relations and marketing value. Thus, SCUSA invited readers of its 1968–1969 guidebook to "enjoy the ski country that beckons the world to the '76 Winter Games."[102]

The Denver-based business community, Colorado's close-knit assemblage of ski industry advocates, the city's and state's elected leaders, and the region's most widely read media outlets coordinated to host the internationally renowned festival. As Richard Olson phrased it, all worked toward "selling Colorado as a sports center."[103] Many of the individuals involved had witnessed the Great Depression, fought in World War II, and gained access to society's upper echelons amid recent postwar prosperity. Others had wielded power in the Centennial State for decades, if not generations. They were business partners, associates, and probably friends, with a shared sense of entitlement in their political authority and trust in one another, as well as common understandings of the promise of skiing, the potential of the games, and the mutual benefits of growth.[104]

CHAPTER 3

Faking an Olympic City

The Colorado bidders treated growth and the Olympics as unquestionable and interlocked goods. The games likely would have advertised Colorado ski resorts nationally and globally, brought significant utility needs, extensive construction, increased lending, greater land and property values, and a larger base of consumers in general. However, growth can be costly and come in many forms.

Note that needs for increased public services also follow growth. As a result, lower taxes or improved resources for most people are no guarantee. In addition, when businesses expand into a locality, it usually corresponds with migration. This means that an area's unemployment rate will not automatically decline. Neither are new, well-paying jobs guaranteed to go to existing (i.e., pre-growth) residents. Instead, menial laborers currently making stagnated wages and paying monthly rents could get priced out as white-collar workers move in and living expenses rise.[1] Moreover, every publicly financed pro-growth project will carry opportunity costs, taking potential resources away from other areas of public life, such as affordable housing, education, or health care. And finally, structural growth could lead to undesired cultural change. As the historian Hal Rothman details, tourism promotion in the American West frequently instigated such "side effects" for year-round inhabitants. It increased the cost of living, siphoned money from other social needs, outsourced high-end jobs, relegated neonatives to low-skilled service employment, and distorted the social and cultural atmospheres that residents valued and identified with.[2]

From this perspective, it is telling that, along with requiring the use of public money, Colorado's Olympic bid for the 1976 Winter Games had no basis in reality. It was designed purely to satisfy the IOC and represented probably the most dishonest proposal in Olympic history. As such, it indicated the extent to which the Colorado growth regime was out to advance its own interests—regardless of any wider drawbacks for the large majority of Centennial State citizens. Because the bid was utterly implausible, when the IOC awarded the games to Denver, neither the bidders nor other Coloradans could have adequately and holistically estimated the event's subsequent impacts. In truth, if anything, the bidders realized that funneling money to certain Winter Olympics sports facilities would not be smart. Notably, though, these factors did not concern the bid team. The businesses that the bidders represented did not intend to pay for the nebulous and dicey investment, even as they remained well positioned to reap its rewards.

In 1964, Colorado's Olympic planners began to form their proposal to win the right to host the Winter Games. At this juncture, their scheme included events positioned throughout Colorado. Thus, letters William Thayer Tutt carried on Governor John Love's behalf to the IOC's meeting in Innsbruck before the 1964 Winter Olympics highlighted that "Aspen, Vail, Steamboat Springs, and the Famous Broadmoor Hotel" represent "the greatest winter-sports center in America."[3] Months later, in June 1965, when the COC began informing the USOC of the details of its pending application, the group continued to locate events separated by hundreds of miles. The bidders planned for Colorado Springs and Denver to act as dual bases of operation, with far-off Aspen, Steamboat Springs, Winter Park, Vail, and Crested Butte serving as potential sites for Nordic skiing, Alpine skiing, and ski jumping.[4]

Colorado's Olympics backers agreed that this format represented their best option. "Expert observers say Colorado would have to 'farm out' the various Olympic events from Denver," Cal Queal of the *Denver Post* reported in February 1964, "rather than stage all at a single mountain location."[5] "Aspen could probably handle part of the competition," confirmed the entrepreneur and president of the Aspen Ski Company, D. R. C. Brown. "If Aspen is to take the whole thing, I'd be strictly against it."[6] The Vail owner and COC member Peter Seibert comparably told Colorado Ski Country USA's board of trustees in April 1966: "We need to sell a spread-out concept as no one ski area can feasibly accommodate all events."[7]

Yet months before Seibert made that comment, the bidders received word from the IOC president Avery Brundage that "the proximity of events" was of the utmost concern to the International Olympic Committee.[8] Indeed, IOC rules stated: "The city chosen cannot share its privilege with another" and "events must all take place in or as near as possible to the city chosen and preferably at or near the main stadium."[9] As a document from the bid team's Site Selection Committee acknowledged, Colorado's Olympic organizers became aware that the IOC wanted facilities "grouped as close together as possible."[10]

In response, in 1966, the magazine publisher Merrill Hastings suggested making Denver the singular host city and creating the Denver Organizing Committee (DOC). He then helped Denver mayor Thomas Currigan select the DOC's members, just as he had advised Governor Love when forming the Colorado Olympic Commission a few years prior.[11] Currigan officially established the new organization, which unsurprisingly looked very similar to the COC. Donald McMahon became DOC chairman, joined by Richard Olson, Donald Magarrell, Donald Fowler, Peter Seibert, Carl DeTemple, and Hastings himself.[12] Although it began to take on an "advisory" role, the COC also remained occupied by William Thayer Tutt and Joseph Coors, along with new additions such as Lieutenant Governor John Vanderhoof, the president of Loveland National Bank Paul L. Rice, King Resources president Richard King, and the Pueblo real estate mogul Samuel Jones.[13]

The creation of the DOC exemplifies the first instance of a principle that Colorado Olympic bidders followed steadfastly: fabricate appearances however necessary to appease the IOC. As the DOC legal counsel Richard Davis explained in an internal memo, Governor Love created the COC to "conduct activities on behalf of the State directed toward bringing the Winter Olympics to Colorado." The state financed the group and charged it with "promoting Colorado as host" and "conducting the games if the bid were successful." However, Davis continued, IOC rules mandated that a single city and "not a country or area" must bid for the games, host them, and maintain "a direct relationship" with the IOC. Therefore, through Mayor Currigan, the Colorado bidders formed the "organizing committee" to undertake duties that Love had already assigned to the "Olympic Commission."[14]

Several overlapping members left the COC to make the DOC appear independent.[15] Still, the two groups were a single entity. As Davis further explained, "preparation and submission of the bid to the USOC was a joint undertaking." Only "due to IOC rules" were the COC's "funds . . . made available" and "most operating functions . . . transferred to the DOC." In the summer of 1967, the COC duly sent up to $60,000 to its DOC offshoot. The DOC quickly became "paramount," even though, according to Davis, "the successful presentation of the bid, as well as staging the games, must be an all-out State effort." As Davis observed, the "DOC must represent . . . Denver as the bidder," but "the two groups must be harmonious."[16]

With this first modification complete, the DOC continued the process of adapting Colorado's bid. In the DOC's 1967 proposal submitted to the

USOC, the bidders located Nordic skiing, ski jumping, bobsled, and luge events in and around the eastern foothills town of Indian Hills. The DOC claimed that "snow cover during the game's period is usually two feet in depth" at this location.[17] The planners added that the area "consists of a natural bowl to allow for the development of a stadium concept . . . and space for parking." The DOC promised to "accommodate 20,000 people" as spectators. The conditions sounded superb.[18]

Around 1968, due to complaints levied by residents living in Indian Hills related to fears of overcrowding, the DOC moved the events a few minutes west to the town of Evergreen. The current head of the DOC's Site Selection Committee, George Robinson, stood behind the Indian Hills–Evergreen decision. Robinson was president of the Denver-based Robinson Brick and Tile Company, a director at Aspen Skiing, and a director at Colorado National Bank.[19] He reported to the bid team that Evergreen was actually more suitable than Indian Hills, and the DOC began promoting the new event site.[20] In May 1970, it officially proposed to the IOC that all Nordic events, bobsled, luge, and ski jumping take place within or adjacent to the mountain town.[21]

Nonetheless, the DOC's presentations of Indian Hills and Evergreen obscured a shared factual problem. Winter temperatures were too warm, and snow accumulation was too low to support the winter sports contests. Denver bidders were aware of this.[22] About a year before submitting their bid to the IOC, DOC officials circulated a document titled "Denver's Competition." The evaluation assessed the strengths and shortcomings of all the cities bidding for the 1976 Winter Olympics, including Denver. One of the Mile High City's "weaknesses" was "Evergreen weather for cross country events." The "confidential" DOC review noted, however, that "this negative is not known and will not be discussed."[23]

DOC researchers eventually concluded that the only plausible way for cross-country (Nordic) skiing to occur in Evergreen was if the committee used machine-made snow, covered trails with shade from trees and tarps, and ran all events before 10 a.m.[24] The DOC also considered but dispensed with the idea of hauling real snow into Evergreen from other areas.[25] Meanwhile, just months after gaining the games, the International Ski Federation (FIS) informed the DOC that it would not support such obviously inferior designs.[26] Hence, climatological specialists and winter sports facilities experts ultimately confirmed that cross-country events, in particular, could not take place in the town or, for that matter, any location within the Front Range near Denver.[27]

By March 1971, Colorado's Olympic planners aborted the idea of cross-country skiing in Evergreen.[28] At the end of the year, just before a vital presentation to the IOC at the 1972 Sapporo Winter Games, the DOC officially moved cross-country skiing and biathlon to Steamboat Springs. This is probably what the bidders planned to do all along. A month before the IOC's selection, DOC public affairs director Norm Brown, the vice president of marketing for the powerful Boettcher and Company investment firm, wrote to George Robinson. "Once the Games are obtained, the closeness of the Nordic sites is not critical," Brown observed. "Ideally, for competitors," the "cross-country and biathlon [events] would move to an area like Steamboat."[29]

To satisfy the IOC, the DOC would prepare what it called an "air bridge concept," which included using short-distance takeoff and landing aircraft to transport athletes and Olympic officials from Denver's Stapleton Airport toward its revised westward mountain sites. The Colorado organizers promised this would keep events within forty-five minutes of the Olympic Village.[30] Predictably, DOC planners knew that, with road travel included, it would take closer to two hours to get Olympians from housing in Denver to the Nordic events, and even that assumed ideal weather, zero traffic, and cars driving onto airport runways to park next to boarding ramps.[31] Of course, a straight drive by car from the Mile High City to Steamboat also took more than three hours.[32]

During the bid, the DOC had deceitfully told the IOC whatever it wanted to hear in order to win the right to host the games. As Lieutenant Governor John Vanderhoof admitted: "Picking Evergreen probably was a mistake" because it was "quite obvious there isn't a helluva lot of snow." However, he added, the "DOC had to meet all of the International Olympic Committee criteria."[33]

The story behind the DOC's plans for the Alpine competitions is a mirror image. Initially, the bidders did not commit to sites for downhill and slalom skiing. Instead, planners pointed to multiple options. Along with Vail and the Copper Mountain ski resort, the DOC put the Loveland Basin–Sniktau Complex on its radar. Vail was an 86-mile drive from Denver. Copper Mountain sat closer, at about 55 miles. The Loveland Basin ski resort and the undeveloped Mount Sniktau were closest, only about 42 miles. The DOC assured the USOC in 1967 that its Alpine Site Selection Committee had "studied all [three] potential sites in detail." Each presumably was appropriate.[34]

The bidders, though, knew such a presumption was inaccurate. Early on, the DOC asked the United States Forest Service ski expert Paul Hauk to assess the three prospective sites. Hauk had overseen ski resort feasibility studies in White River National Forest for twenty years. He studied more than fifty mountains for recreational development. DOC Site Selection Meeting minutes show Hauk refused to "recommend any Eastern Slope site [referring to the Front Range]." He cited "inadequate vertical . . . bad northwest exposure subject to wind scouring, and short snowfall" as his reasons.[35] In 1967, sensitive to the DOC's needs, Hauk eventually put his weight behind Copper Mountain. He selected Vail as a possible backup and, due to limited snow and space for parking, recommended that "Mt. Sniktau should be left untouched if this is at all possible."[36]

With the DOC's official presentation to the USOC approaching, the Colorado bidders made Vail their first choice. While many of the bid team members had connections to Vail, from a technical standpoint it looked like a reasonable option. Heeding Hauk's analysis, the Site Selection Committee also removed Sniktau and Loveland Basin from the proposal. Yet Merrill Hastings resisted the change. He believed keeping the easternmost locations as possible options allowed the bidders to claim their plan could fit within IOC guidelines.[37] It did not matter that Sniktau and Loveland Basin would never actually host the Alpine events. As DOC leader Donald McMahon told USOC member Clifford Buck, "the need for a 'close in' Alpine site was most desirable even though we all regard it as 'eye wash.'"[38]

The DOC, therefore, continued presenting Sniktau and Loveland Basin as realistic backups—even though it knew they were not. But even this would not be enough. In the fall of 1967, USOC officials visited Colorado to inspect potential Olympics sites. Upon traveling to Vail, it became apparent that the DOC's preferred Alpine venue was too distant. "Denver is where Denver is and the mountains are where the mountains are," the chairman of the USOC's Site Selection Committee publicly lamented.[39] Afterward, as a story in Hastings's *Colorado Magazine* recounted, USOC Skiing Committee chairman Malcolm McLane reached out to Hastings and told him the DOC should "switch the downhill races from Vail to some place closer to Denver." The "national committee knows," McLane explained, the IOC "won't accept such a remote competition site."[40]

In turn, for "strategy," the DOC named Sniktau and Loveland Basin its primary Alpine locations.[41] As DOC technical director Ted Farwell later acknowledged, with the USOC selection bearing down, "the effort [of the DOC] was simply to come up with something that the IOC would approve."[42] The DOC's 1967 USOC bid book thus portrayed Sniktau and Loveland Basin as it did Indian Hills. According to the book, the sites exhibited "prime qualifications" for downhill contests, including "suitable terrain and snow conditions, the free flow of traffic and the availability of large spectator

Figure 3.1. October 1968. Merrill Hastings, Alpine skiing expert Paul Hauk, and George Robinson stand on Mount Sniktau, a clearly unsuitable site, where the DOC scheduled Alpine events anyway to appease the IOC. Photo by Duane Howell/*Denver Post* via Getty Images.

areas." During the time of year in which the Olympics were to take place, the DOC claimed, the "area" had "an average snow depth over 60 inches."[43]

In the following two and a half years, with the USOC's blessing in hand, the DOC continued to embellish conditions to appease IOC voters.[44] In a 1969 report submitted to the FIS, the bidders depicted Sniktau as "having more than the required minimum vertical drop," a start "in a bowl-like location, which will assure plenty of snow," a ridge that "acts like a gigantic snow fence and contributes to the snow deposit," and "terrain features necessary for outstanding downhill competitive events for both men and women." The DOC even asserted that, "because of its excellent location, Mt. Sniktau can be developed into a major recreational skiing area by developing necessary trails for the beginner and intermediate skier."[45] The DOC's bid books to the International Olympic Committee then offered Loveland Basin for the slalom contests and Sniktau for the downhill races. As the DOC continued to allege, the sites "have always had abundant snow fall . . . matchless for alpine events."[46]

Nonetheless, months following the IOC's decision, the extent of the DOC's con became common knowledge. In early 1971, the *Rocky Mountain News* investigative journalist Richard O'Reilly visited the DOC's office, looked through its files, and found a photo of Sniktau that looked similar to the picture provided in the DOC's bid books except with much less snow on it. When O'Reilly showed the photo to a DOC representative, he was told the DOC airbrushed snow onto the image for the bid.[47] As Lieutenant Governor Vanderhoof characteristically conceded, the bidders had felt "pressed for time, so they lied a bit."[48] The same list that mentioned Evergreen's problematic weather as a "weakness" had indeed made a note of the "wind on the upper sections of Mt. Sniktau and the women's giant slalom at Loveland." These tidbits likewise were classified as "not known and not to be discussed."[49]

During February and March 1971, DOC leaders seemed to want to keep the untenable sites alive.[50] Still, a more detailed investigation commission by the DOC marked the end of Loveland Basin's and Sniktau's Olympic chances. On Sniktau, surveyors found what Hauk had years before: the "distinct possibility that wind erosion . . . could be sufficiently damaging to ski trails [so] that a competition might conceivably have to be postponed, at any given time during the winter months." The study additionally concluded that "physical features . . . seriously restrict its [Sniktau's] use for commercial development." An "overabundance of steep grades" and a "complete lack of terrain with grades that are suitable for the pure intermediate ability level [skier]" led assessors to suggest that "the development of Mt. Sniktau for skiing, either commercially or competitively, be abandoned."[51] As it turned out, there was no site "within a 90-minute *drive* of Denver" that met the "technical criteria" for downhill skiing.[52]

By November 1971, the DOC realized it needed to alter its Alpine skiing plan and further incorporate the air bridge idea.[53] After fielding multiple offers from ski resorts eager to capitalize on hosting the contests, the organizers shifted them back to Vail.[54] Hauk recalled that Richard Olson pressured the DOC in this direction. Olson was a director, shareholder, and member of the executive committee for Vail Associates and served as a director at United Bank of Denver, which provided loans to Vail Corporation.[55] Furthermore, the Vail proposal called for the construction of a brand-new skiing complex at an area called Beaver Creek, which was under consideration by the Forest Service for protection as a wilderness preserve. Vail Corporation knew that if the DOC picked Beaver Creek for the games, the Forest Service could more easily amend the boundaries of its pending wilderness classification.[56]

At the start of 1972, the organizers announced the move, again at its Sapporo presentation.[57] But as the DOC director of ski events and University of Denver ski coach Willy Schaeffler explained before the return to Vail became official, "I have always felt confident we could get the permission of the IOC and the USOC for switching to better sites than those proposed."[58] DOC members once more figured that, after they earned the right to host the games, they would be allowed to relocate events to more apt locations, even if at distances from Denver that likely would have doomed their bid if they had been disclosed in the first place.[59]

The DOC's misrepresentations did not stop there. Before deciding to list Loveland Basin and Sniktau as the sites for the Alpine races, the bidders agreed "realistically there should be 'two Olympic Villages.'" One would serve athletes competing in Denver, and another would be an "Alpine Village" with "ski base camps" to house skiers competing at sites such as Steamboat Springs and Vail.[60] With that in mind, early on the DOC shared an ambiguous plan with the USOC. It had not yet established where it would house athletes and coaches. It promised only "to provide a complete Olympic Village complex in the metropolitan Denver area that will be close to the Nordic, Bobsled, Luge, and Skating event sites."[61]

Yet weeks before the USOC's official selection, the DOC received word that this, too, would not pass muster. The USOC president Douglas Roby warned that the proposal for the Olympic Village looked overly vague and counseled the DOC to find a single and central location for Olympians to stay.[62] The DOC turned to another suspect solution. As its 1967 bid book to the USOC announced, for the Olympic Village, "the Board of Trustees of the University of Denver has granted use of university residence facilities" with "a capacity well above the 2,500 beds required."[63]

The Colorado press and DOC bulletins confirmed afterward that University of Denver dorms prepared to become Olympic dwellings. One 1968 magazine article attested that Denver organizers "received the unqualified pledge of the University of Denver to provide three student resident halls."[64] A later promotion noted that "the school's trustees are able to assure the Denver Committee that the 9,000 students enrolled at the University of Denver would be [put] on a special vacation" during the Olympic Games to make space available for athletes.[65] The DOC's May 1970 proposal to the IOC similarly read that the "University of Denver has guaranteed its modern student residence halls for the Olympic Village."[66]

However, the school had made no such assurance. In the fall of 1967, as a member of the University of Denver's board of trustees, bid-team member

Richard Olson asked Chancellor Maurice Mitchell to use the school's dorms "in principle." As DOC meeting minutes recount, this meant that the school "will cooperate in permitting reference to [the] University of Denver as [the] Olympic Village for purposes of final reports to [the] USOC."[67] Later meeting minutes clarified that "while the University of Denver is mentioned as the site of the Olympic Village in the Denver Olympic Committee presentation . . . the Board of Trustees has never given formal approval."[68] In a March 1971 letter to Donald Magarrell, Chancellor Mitchell further explained that Olson asked the university's board of trustees to "make an informal and non-binding offer" for the "possible use of the housing facilities at the University of Denver." The school agreed that its facilities "might be included in a proposal to be submitted to the International Olympic Committee." Still, Mitchell emphasized, the board of trustees "was told that it would not be held to this commitment."[69]

It is not surprising that the school's leadership proved open to working with the DOC in this way. Universities often served as "auxiliary players" in growth networks. They benefited from an increased pool of customers, many of whom could be attracted by a growth machine's urban rejuvenation and redevelopment projects. Higher education institutions may also have an eye for financial support or favors from local property owners, construction companies, money lenders, media outlets, and politicians.[70] In fact, the University of Denver quickly moved to obtain resources for itself. As Mitchell informed Magarrell, the board of trustees would still "consider the conditions under which facilities at the University of Denver might be made available."[71] These "conditions," as it turned out, equated to the funding of a new 68,500-square-foot health center and a new 111,000-square-foot student center, at a total estimated cost of $7,392,500. The school additionally asked the DOC to pay for the removal and return of student belongings, room and board for Olympic athletes, and cleaning and insurance fees.[72]

Although the DOC continued to claim Olympic housing would be at the university, the committee could not meet these demands.[73] The DOC and the school never reached an agreement.[74] It remains unclear where the organizers would have located the Olympic Village had the 1976 Denver Winter Olympic Games taken place.[75]

The impracticalities discussed above all feed into the most indicative set of DOC falsehoods: claims about how much the Olympics would cost and how much Colorado would benefit. In early 1966, the bid team hired the Denver Research Institute (DRI), associated with the University of Denver, to ascertain an "estimate of the costs and revenues of staging" the games and "to examine the associated impacts on the economy of the State."[76] The DOC would use this report to defend its agenda for years to come. Yet the DRI's findings prove to have been prearranged, incomplete, and misapplied for public consumption.

For starters, the bidders had enough confidence in the report's conclusions that they plotted to use it "to obtain legislation and funds to develop the Colorado bid" before the DRI's work even began.[77] The research group then sent a draft of its work and received feedback from Denver's Olympic planners before publishing its results.[78] On top of this, when the DRI officially shared its findings, the bidders kept it guarded. Each copy was "numbered and contained the name of the person receiving it" so that "no one would receive a copy . . . unless prior approval had been obtained."[79]

Only the bidders could view the report's admittedly tenuous conclusions. Only they would see the lead author's confession that "sites for various Olympic events are not yet selected" and that, therefore, "it will be difficult to place a price tag upon the needed facilities." Importantly, the report also added: "Until such factors as the after-use of facilities and the sources of financing are worked out, estimates pertaining to the economic impact on Colorado from staging the 1976 Winter Olympic Games are incomplete." The "estimates in the report must be considered quite rough, 'ball park,' in nature," the study stressed. "Considerable personal judgment was required."[80]

The DRI based its finding mainly on information from previous Winter Games. This enabled it to conclude that the construction of Olympic facilities would cost between $5,825,000 and $9,675,000 and that "over 80% of these facilities appear to have good to very good after-use potential." It found as well that "preparation, planning, and staging costs" would come to between $5 million and $7 million. The DRI then estimated that revenues from admissions, television, and other sources would reach between $6.4 million and $8.9 million. That left an immediate "ball park" operating margin of negative $2,272,000 to positive $2,877,000. Indeed, the DRI conceded: "Operating losses appear to be the rule rather than the expectation for past Olympics."[81]

However, the DRI still justified the DOC bid. It claimed that revenue from sales, income and gas taxes, as well as added jobs, concession dollars, and property taxes on new sports complexes, meant that the long-term "economic impact of the 1976 Winter Olympics on Colorado would appear to be sizable." The literature did not exist at the time, but this flies in the face of the consensus among sport economists today—that there are limited long-term benefits in employment and displaced (instead of added) short-term spending.[82] Beyond that, the DRI predicted "intangible benefits" that "have value even though they escape measure." Though it would not "assign a specific dollar" amount, the report asserted that such outcomes would be born from the presence of new recreation centers and "the widespread values to Colorado received from advertising." Overall, the DRI determined that the "benefits accrued, both tangible and intangible [from the Olympics], should remain for years."[83]

The DRI report confirmed at least the potential for net positive effects from hosting the Olympics. Still, the DOC made the DRI's provisional findings appear better than they were. For example, in its correspondence with the USOC, the DOC counted only immediate construction costs (ignoring preparation, planning, and staging costs) so that it could claim that the games would go for a maximum of only $10 million. The DOC then complemented this with a firm but elusive description for how these costs would "no doubt be defrayed through a combination of public and private financing." As the DOC pronounced, an "intelligent blending of aid from public sources with the private investment sector will provide a very satisfactory financing matrix."[84] The DOC did not identify what such a "matrix" entailed.

Furthermore, the DOC warped the DRI's account of federal funding. The DRI report did not provide an estimate for how much federal money the DOC should expect. It merely included data regarding previous games, such as the 1960 Squaw Valley Olympics, where the United States contributed $3.5 million. The DOC, however, lifted that number for its USOC bid, citing $3.5 million as the "anticipated" funding from federal coffers. In no way did the DRI indicate that the DOC should expect to repeat the numbers from Squaw Valley. Rather, the research group claimed the opposite, stating "Colorado would need substantial Federal financial support" such that "the level of Federal financial participation in the 1960 events would have to be expanded."[85]

Through the bid to the IOC, the Colorado team did not know the details regarding backing from Washington, DC. As DOC meeting minutes recorded, the "entire Washington picture is still clouded by uncertainty."[86] Nevertheless, as with other aspects of the bid, pinning down the logistics for this issue remained on the back burner. Winning the bid came first. At early DOC meetings, discussions about finances ran long. In response, the DOC treasurer Graydon Hubbard, of the Arthur Andersen & Company accounting firm, recommended that the topic be left for the end of the gatherings to make room for more timely matters. As he wrote to the DOC leader Robert Pringle of Mountain States Telephone Company, "I fully realize that the most important mission of the Committee is 'to get the bid,' and I share your confidence that somehow we will get the money."[87]

To make matters worse, as the IOC's selection approached, the DOC predicted financial windfalls beyond anything evidenced in the DRI's research or elsewhere. In 1968, the DOC raised its cost estimate to between $17 million and $20 million while launching potential income from the games into the stratosphere. "Estimates indicated that monetary benefits to Denver from the 1976 Games could total $150 to $200 million," a DOC press release proclaimed.[88]

It is unclear where those numbers came from, but it is evident that the DOC realized the Olympics would not, in financial terms, spark society-wide benefits. One facility the DOC needed to build to host the sports spectacle was a 400-meter speed skating oval. The bidders expected to place the track within Denver. In 1969, the bid committee hired Ahrendt Engineering Company to appraise the potential structure's costs and revenues.[89] As one DOC member described, Ahrendt Engineering concluded that to consider the arena "a self-amortizing facility will be true only if (1) a major portion of the investment does not have to be repaid and (2) the utilization by the public is excellent." This DOC contributor continued: "Either or both of these conditions are uncertain at best." Thus, "financing could prove to be a difficult problem."[90] This is a striking admission. Of all the new facilities that the DOC proposed to build, a speed skating rink near downtown Denver probably carried a better bet than most for public use.

In contrast, a ski jump, luge course, or bobsled course located in the foothills or deeper into the Rockies would have drawn much less interest. Not only would these facilities be further away from the city and more expensive to use; they required esoteric sets of skills. For instance, the only bobsled course in the United States in 1970 had been built about four decades earlier for the 1932 Lake Placid Winter Games. Bobsledding was not a popular sport for Americans.[91] If it were true the speed skating rink was a bad investment, it stands to reason that these latter event sites would have become money pits too.

Again, the bid team understood the nature of the situation. The DOC's Norm Brown speculated that it would be ideal to associate "the bob, luge, and ski jumping structures" with "alpine skiing nearby." "Without the alpine and ski tour draw," Brown wrote in a "confidential" letter, "I feel the structures may well become economically impossible to keep up."[92] The United States Ski Association president Charles T. Gibson likewise informed the DOC that, although building a ski jump near Denver would be profitable during the Olympics, the need for artificial snow would make the facility "economically infeasible" in the long term.[93] Governor Love also admitted to a group of concerned residents from Evergreen that Denver would probably dismantle the luge course scheduled for the town's outskirts after the games ended because no one would utilize it.[94] Likewise, the DOC knew that the bobsled course would become "relatively useless." For this reason, the organizers asked the IOC to let them hold the two-person bobsled event on their intended luge course and to place the four-person contest at the track in Lake Placid—or just drop it from the Olympic program altogether.[95]

When it came time to submit its IOC bid books and presentation, the DOC excluded specific expense and revenue estimates. Even so, its proposal noted, "from the standpoint of costs, eighty percent of all event and support facilities needed for the 1976 Winter Olympics already exist in Denver." The DOC thus explained, "The city does not face the almost overwhelming costs that usually accompany the Olympics."[96] Mayor Thomas Currigan had been assuring listeners that 80 percent of event facilities already existed in Colorado since his 1968 trip to the Grenoble Winter Games.[97] But this percentage was another ridiculous assertion. At least based on the DOC's proposal to the IOC, new Nordic skiing, biathlon, Alpine skiing, ski jumping, bobsled, luge, and speed skating facilities all needed to be constructed.[98]

In many respects, the disingenuousness of the DOC bid was nothing new. Throughout the history of Colorado, promoters lied about their motives and disseminated false images to spur growth. State boosters had urged authorities in the nation's capital that the country needed to extend Interstate 70 to transport resources when their real goal was creating comfortable mountain access for tourism.[99] Local tourism advocates similarly depicted small cities such as Aspen as majestic ghost towns. They sold narratives of hard-to-catch wild trout, which Coloradans bred in fisheries by the millions every year and placed upstream so anglers could easily snag them.[100] State salesmen claimed Colorado averaged 300 days of sunshine a year so often that many believed the fiction was truth.[101] It was standard practice when Denver Olympic bidders used a photo in their Olympic bid books and a model for their in-person IOC presentation that presented the Mile High City as if it sat directly at the foot of the mountains. Although Denver was miles away on the plains, Colorado advertisements had shown the city as part of the Rockies for decades.[102]

Yet the density, audacity, and fiscal implications of the DOC's dishonesty stand out. Just one week after the DOC won its Olympic bid in May 1970, the director of the DRI cautioned that, since 1967, Olympic "costs have gone up considerably." To explain this, the principal author of the DRI report publicly noted, as he had three years earlier in the report itself: "We didn't know where the sites were when we made the study."[103] Amid pronouncements

Figure 3.2. May 1970. Denver mayor William McNichols observes a display the DOC used to help win IOC approval, misrepresenting Denver's proximity to the Rocky Mountains and event sites. *Denver Post* via Getty Images.

of grand Olympic revenues, DOC members, as early as November 1968, admitted among themselves that the DRI's work was "significantly outdated, particularly sections pertaining to finance projection."[104] And, of course, the plan the DOC proposed at this time was not the one it intended to follow through with. This all makes clear that when Denver gained the 1976 Winter Games—despite what the bid team told fellow Coloradans—the DOC knew that it did not possess anything that could be construed as a sound estimate of the event's price tag or broader social effects.

The shrewd businessmen behind the bid and the companies they served put time, energy, and money into a project with unverifiable numbers. They exaggerated and misrepresented the conclusions of the DRI as well. Why would they do that? Why would they manipulate findings related to an ill-defined project that they were fronting to get underway? The answer is that the follow-up costs of running the Olympics did not matter to the DOC. Its members and supporters would see benefits, but by no means did they expect to pay for the greater part of the mega-event. If they could just get the games into their state, the broader public would foot that bill.

In summer 1972, DOC representatives explicitly spelled out the situation. With a clearer picture of where it would hold events and a funding commitment from the United States Senate, the DOC pushed the United States House of Representatives to endorse federal backing. In this effort, the planners emphasized that government funding was their only option because, as they told the House Committee on Interior and Insular Affairs, "the revenue potential of the planned facilities, when used for commercial purposes after the games, would be insufficient to attract private investment capital."[105] The DOC and its supporters desired Olympic spectators, publicity, new sports facilities, and tourists. However, they also grasped that it would not be wise to host the games if they themselves had to pay for it.

CHAPTER 4

A Mass Soft Sell

To bring the games to the Centennial State, the DOC painted a mirage of the IOC's ideal Olympics. However, it still needed to get International Olympic Committee officials to swallow the lure. Thus, after gaining USOC support at the end of 1967, the DOC devised its "Phase II Marketing Strategy." DOC members recognized that their in-person May 1970 presentation to the IOC would be "secondary to a well planned and well executed pre-selling campaign."[1] That primary "selling" effort entailed providing paid trips, parties, favors, and gifts to IOC members and influencers, as well as the use of official diplomatic channels.

By the 1960s, winning Olympic bids commonly included such methods.[2] In the same instance, the IOC realized that the corruption characteristic of its selection process could harm the organization's image. "The peculiar nature of this task," one DOC member, therefore, explained, "requires a mass selling approach in order to reach *by indirect means*."[3] In contrast to the "hard sell" observed from other recent bid cities, the DOC deployed what it dubbed a "soft sell" technique. It focused on finding ways to attract IOC support without making its overtures too obvious. As Richard Olson told fellow bidders, it "might be more effective if we more discretely told our story and not actually seek ways of asking for votes of the IOC directors." Olson realized that this was "a complex subject . . . that should be verbally discussed."[4] Nonetheless, a collection of DOC documents exposes some of the DOC's "indirect" or "soft sell" tactics, along with, as one source put it, moments of "a modest hard sell" involved.[5]

Early on, it became clear that the Denver bidders would embrace the gamesmanship involved in bidding for the Olympics, seeking creative and surreptitious ways to obtain IOC support. In 1966, Merrill Hastings and Donald

Magarrell traveled to Rome, where the IOC met to determine who would host the 1972 Winter Olympics. In Magarrell's summary of the trip, he listed their first agenda item as: "Assist, if possible, those applicants for the '72 Games who could be politically advantageous to Colorado in '76."[6] Hastings more readily admitted in an interview with the political scientist Laura Olson that the Colorado bidders went to Italy to "help Japan's bid."[7]

Sapporo, Japan, represented one of three front-runners for the 1972 Winter Games. The two others were Banff, Canada, and Salt Lake City, Utah. The Coloradans knew the IOC did not want to hold the Olympics in the same hemisphere, let alone the same country, in consecutive Olympiads.[8] Thus, Hastings and Magarrell intended to prevent the games from coming to North America too soon. Toward this end, Hastings obtained a confidential copy of Banff's bid book and shared it with Sapporo's organizing committee, hoping to give the Japanese city an edge. As Hastings told Olson, "I didn't steal it; I just got it."[9] A 1970 retelling published in Hastings's *Colorado Magazine* depicted this in detail, noting that, soon after the Sapporo contingent received the Canadian bid book, "stories began to appear in the Rome press citing Sapporo's advantages over Banff."[10] For the Coloradans, the effort appeared to pay off. Sapporo just barely took the required majority of votes on the first ballot, 32 out of 61.[11]

A few years later, in the competition for the '76 Winter Games, another Canadian bid stood in Denver's way, this time from Vancouver. Thus, when the DOC member and Public Service Company employee Neil Allen and his wife visited the Canadian city in 1969, they did reconnaissance.[12] Using the "subtle disguise" of a tourist, Allen gathered government-produced weather summaries and learned about the communication and energy infrastructure at Mount Garibaldi, where skiing events were on offer. While he sat at a coffee shop half a block away, his wife also crept into the Vancouver Organizing Committee's office. She did not learn anything of substance, but such clandestine behavior serves as another indication of the DOC's approach to procuring IOC approval.[13]

Similarly, when the DOC learned about the desire of Latin American countries to fast-track the completion of the Pan American Highway, intended to traverse the length of the Americas, the DOC president Donald McMahon and the Colorado senator Gordon Allott discussed making it happen. They suspected doing so would please the longtime Columbian IOC member Julio Gerlein-Comelia and ensure that he send his vote Denver's way.[14] While there is no evidence McMahon or Allott went through with this plan, they considered it.

To give a final and perhaps more consequential example, in early 1970 the DOC flew a group of international sports reporters to Denver to get information on competing bids, create a positive impression of itself, and seek allies with influence in IOC circles. Several Denver businesses provided donations, and Trans World Airlines supplied free travel, ensuring everything remained free for the out-of-town visitors.[15] But in particular, the DOC public relations specialist William Kostka discussed the possibility of making a deal with Vernon Morgan, the English sports editor from Reuters. Morgan "is the dean of sportswriters," Kostka wrote to Robert Pringle, the current DOC president; "I'm sure his contacts with high level IOC members are substantial." Kostka approached Morgan and then advised the DOC to give "serious consideration . . . to his [Morgan's] proposition," which involved paying his expenses for a seven-day trip to an unspecified location. In turn, Kostka explained, the DOC could "employ him in Amsterdam" during the IOC's host city election.[16]

Along with undermining its competition, lobbying the press, and trying to circuitously win the favor of IOC decision makers, the DOC's "indirectness" often became more forthright. This appeared a necessity to keep up with the bidder's foreign foes. As one DOC representative observed after attending an International Ski Federation meeting in 1969: "It seems that each candidate is currently and actively engaged in [giving] gifts to all representatives." With top adversaries Vancouver and Sion, Switzerland, acting in "contravention of acceptable rules of the game," the DOC resolved, "the concept of gifts to representatives at the Congress should be continued and perhaps expanded."[17] Thus, the Colorado bid team invited every member of the IOC and their wives to visit Denver and attend the 1969 World Ice Skating Championships held at William Thayer Tutt's Broadmoor Resort in Colorado Springs.

Twenty-six of seventy IOC members accepted first-class airfare and a week's worth of accommodations at Denver's renowned Brown Palace Hotel.[18] Along with attending the figure skating contests, the IOC members toured the nearby foothills by car and took a "sightseeing" trip by plane over the Rocky Mountains. The DOC also treated its guests to a concert by the Denver Symphony and a reception at the governor's mansion hosted by Governor Love.[19] The DOC budgeted $75,000 to cover the costs.[20]

Previously successful bidders provided similar trips to IOC voters.[21] As the DOC observed, supplying a weeklong vacation for IOC members remained a "commonly accepted practice," though it had "to be done very carefully."[22] The Olympic bidders could not let themselves be seen attempting—explicitly—to induce IOC votes. "This visitation will not be a site inspection per se," Merrill Hastings explained in a DOC memorandum; that "would not be in keeping with Olympic protocol." Instead, Hastings continued, the "intent of the visit is simply to acquaint the members of the IOC with Denver."[23] The minutes from a December 1968 DOC meeting put it more frankly: DOC members must not "give the impression to the IOC that the DOC is trying to influence the membership."[24]

Yet, of course, that was what the DOC meant to do. At the same DOC meeting just cited, organizers made clear that welcoming IOC members to Colorado represented "the most significant effort Denver could make" to enhance the city's Olympic prospects.[25] "Although this total effort must carefully avoid any hard sell appearance," McMahon reminded the DOC prior to the arrival of the IOC voters, "it will . . . be a tremendous undertaking of probably major importance to the success of our Olympic bid."[26]

Indeed, aware of IOC "rules," the DOC attempted to mask that it had scheduled the IOC visits. Rather than coming from the DOC, IOC members received their invitations from the Denver mayor's office. As DOC meeting minutes acknowledged, "The invitation will be extended by the Mayor on his stationery to avoid any charges of commercialism."[27] Denver mayor William McNichols also took the lead by disseminating a "confidential" letter on behalf of the DOC to the Colorado press, instructing local journalists to make "no mention" of Denver's Olympic bid to his ostensible IOC guests. "Do not print or broadcast comments by the IOC about Denver's bid if they should volunteer comments," the letter read; "controversial subjects would be extremely detrimental and possibly deadly to Denver's bid."[28] Here again is another salient example of businessmen, politicians, and the media working in coordination to gain the games and publicize Colorado.

The IOC president Avery Brundage, for his part, not only saw these visits for what they were; he feared they were the tip of the iceberg and worried about the appearance of IOC impropriety. Still, he made little effort to stop them. "These invitations involving very considerable expense are most embarrassing," Brundage wrote to the IOC vice president, Lord Michael Killanin. "Unfortunately, these are not the only gifts that have been accepted. Some may have even been solicited."[29] The DOC had not hidden its strategy from Brundage. It invited him to travel first-class to Denver and stay in the Brown Palace as well.[30] Donald McMahon even assured Brundage, "We have tried scrupulously to avoid any 'hard sell,'" although he conceded: "Obviously, the reason for the invitation was not missed by many of our guests." In fact, to protect the IOC's image, Brundage appears to have been the one who advised the censorship of the Colorado press. "We are grateful for the guidance you have given . . . through [Merrill] Hastings,"

McMahon told Brundage, "and will proceed with the utmost circumspection. We will brief the press beforehand and hopefully avoid any discussion of Denver's Olympic plans to the embarrassment of any member of the IOC."[31]

Since several IOC members failed to attend the World Ice Skating Championships, the DOC extended additional invitations, welcoming IOC visitors to the Centennial State whenever they pleased.[32] Many took up the DOC on the offer.[33] One such member was the Norwegian Jan Staubo, who, as a DOC report noted, had his heart set on skiing at Aspen.[34] He and his wife came to Colorado in March 1970 and experienced a schedule similar to that of earlier IOC officials.[35] The Denver bidders hoped that, through Staubo, they could obtain an entire "bloc" of IOC backing.[36] "Mr. Staubo is an influential member of the IOC," DOC meeting minutes stated; "his visit to Denver is viewed as being important to the success of our effort to secure Scandinavian support."[37]

Staubo's visit to Colorado seemed to do its job. While in the state, he offered a collection of pointers for success, and in Amsterdam the Scandinavian collective appeared to fall in line. The second round of voting went 31 votes to Sion, 29 to Denver, and 8 to Tampere, Finland. The votes for the Finnish proposal were probably symbolic support from its Nordic neighbors, the Staubo-led coalition. The USOC president Clifford Buck had informed the DOC a month before the Amsterdam meeting: "For all practical purposes, Tampere . . . may be disregarded." It was not a legitimate contender. Thus, in the third round, with Tampere out of the running and Denver and Sion left to battle for a majority of the vote, the Scandinavian OC members appeared to transfer their ballots to the Mile High City. Denver won the right to host the games, 39–30.[38]

All the while, to win the right to host the Olympics, perhaps the most important group for the DOC was the International Ski Federation. At first glance, it seems a mystery as to how skilled FIS inspectors ever approved Evergreen and Mount Sniktau as Olympic sites. The probable explanation is that FIS members and the DOC struck a deal.

At the end of October 1968, the FIS president Marc Holder led twenty FIS inspectors to Colorado. They examined Evergreen and flew by helicopter to the top of Mount Sniktau, walking down one of its proposed Alpine courses. Little snow could be found at either location. The weather during the Sniktau observation reportedly reached 62 degrees Fahrenheit.[39] Pictures published in the *Denver Post* reveal FIS members crossing a barren mountain.[40] Photos from Evergreen's local paper likewise show FIS members observing a snowless landscape.[41]

Figure 4.1. October 1968. FIS chairman Robert Faure, DOC technical director of skiing events Willy Schaeffler, FIS president Marc Holder, and FIS Alpine Courses Subcommittee chairman Hubert Spiess survey Loveland Basin, which was never a plausible location for events. Denver Public Library, Western History Collection, WH2129-2018-363.

Still, the inspectors responded to both sites with enthusiasm. Holder told the *Post*: "You have absolutely perfect courses everywhere."[42] Later, in May 1969, at the International Ski Federation Congress in Barcelona, Spain, the DOC presented studies of Evergreen and Sniktau completed by the FIS. Cross-country specialist Vladimir Pacl reported that the "proposed [cross-country] trails meet Olympic standards" and "can already be considered as excellent." Miloslav Belonozki of the FIS Ski Jumping Committee viewed Evergreen by helicopter and affirmed "the area chosen for the construction of a 70 and 90 meter ski jump is very good." FIS inspectors who visited the Alpine sites at Sniktau and Loveland Basin similarly stated that the "proposed terrains qualify."[43]

These were Nordic and Alpine experts. Given the limitations of the Nordic and Alpine sites that they purportedly studied in Colorado, the fact of their approval alone raises suspicion. It is also evident that the DOC sweetened the 1968 FIS visit with perks. The bidders paid the inspectors' travel expenses and treated them to various extracurricular activities, such as sightseeing trips, cocktail parties, and upscale dinners.[44] "Your committee certainly succeeded very well to combine a serious 'first inspection' of possible Olympic sites with the most pleasant social arrangements and very interesting and enjoyable sight-seeing," the FIS vice president Björn Kjellstrom wrote to McMahon, cryptically putting the words "first inspection" in quotation marks.[45]

Yet even if other FIS inspectors did not receive direct kickbacks or make explicit requests, there is evidence that the FIS's most powerful member did. Marc Holder's opinion was crucial to the DOC. He headed the organization that needed to approve the bidder's questionable Nordic and Alpine skiing venues. If the DOC could not get Holder to sanction its impractical plan, the chances of selling Denver to the IOC would be dashed. As DOC meeting minutes explained: "Mr. Holder can be of significant help to the DOC considering [the] technical problems involved in scheduling both the alpine and Nordic events." For this reason, the DOC invited Holder to travel from Geneva to Colorado for the 1968 Aspen Interski, making it "implicit in this invitation" that any costs for attending the world's second-largest skiing event (behind the Olympics) would be covered.[46]

Holder did not make it to the Interski, but he visited Denver in October 1968 with other FIS officials. During the trip, Merrill Hastings agreed to provide him two scholarships to the Arnold Palmer Golf Academy in Vail. DOC meeting minutes highlight this exchange.[47] Donald Magarrell also reported discussing it with Holder during the IOC's 1969 session in Warsaw, Poland. "We still have some commitment to Marc Holder to give a summer golf visitation to [the] USA," and "Marc has chosen the boy," Magarrell wrote. "This was promised by Hastings during [the] FIS visit to Denver." Magarrell then added: "I promised Holder we would contact him (Holder) regarding what can be arranged. This may present some difficulties[,] but [I] will seek assistance and suggestions."[48]

The mention of possible "difficulties" seems to signify the challenge of keeping Hastings's "promise" from public view. Nevertheless, that did not stop the transaction. The Arnold Palmer Golf Academy's tenure in Vail proved short-lived, failing after two years. Thus, from 14 July to 4 August

1970, a Swiss youth named Tony Hoerning attended the Arnold Palmer Golf Academy at Cameron Park in Shingle Springs, California. As a letter between Holder and George Robinson confirms, the DOC paid for Hoerning's airfare, attendance at the academy, and other miscellaneous expenses.[49]

It is unclear who Tony Hoerning was or what he meant to Holder. However, after his 1968 trip to Denver, Holder pledged to DOC members that the FIS "shall do whatever possible to help your case," and he appeared to live up to his word.[50] When Governor Love attended the 1969 FIS meeting in Barcelona, "promised as a vacation to Spain" by DOC members, Holder helped him access the FIS's executive council meeting, a "confidential" favor not provided to representatives from other Olympic bid cities.[51] At the same conference, the FIS actually voted for Vancouver as its preferred option for the 1976 Winter Games. Realizing this was going to happen, Holder explained to Magarrell that he would have stopped it if he could have "but was not in a position to gag the motion."[52] Holder later assured George Robinson that "the FIS vote means little" and that he would meet with the DOC "for a strategy session" on how to move forward.[53] Finally, when the DOC representative James Cotter traveled to IOC headquarters in Lausanne, Switzerland, to submit the DOC's application to host the Olympics, Holder joined him. As Cotter reported, in Lausanne the IOC member Raymond Gafner asked him "several questions about Denver's climate," but Holder, the trusted FIS leader, "promptly volunteered to answer," assuaging any concerns.[54]

Holder almost certainly lied to Gafner. He had already seen the DOC's suspect event sites. And when the DOC presented a revised proposal to the IOC in Japan in February 1972, Holder basically admitted that he knew all along that the DOC's original locations would never work. The tensest moment of the meeting came through an exchange not between the DOC and the IOC but instead among IOC members. After Holder commented that "I can confirm these [new] sites will be the best choice we can make," the IOC vice president Killanin interjected that "the only thing that worries me has nothing to do with . . . the things Denver can do. . . . We were told by the FIS, at the time of Amsterdam, that the sites selected were suitable"; now it appears they "are not suitable or there was no snow." Holder stood steadfast by replying that, "even if there is no snow in Evergreen," the DOC could have "snow brought into the area." "Was it made clear at the time of the bid," Killanin asked in turn, "that snow might have to be brought in?" Holder retorted: "We know the name of the area is Evergreen."[55]

In later years, Holder stood out as one of the few IOC members to speak candidly about bid city bribery schemes. In the 1980s, he oversaw the creation of the "Holder Rules," meant to prevent IOC members from accepting anything from bid cities that cost over $150. In the late 1990s, when reporters revealed that Salt Lake City had bribed its way to hosting the 2002 Winter Games, Holder became a whistleblower, speaking publicly about how the Salt Lake City, Nagano, and Atlanta Olympics had all been tainted by IOC members exchanging votes for favors. "To my knowledge," Holder would say, "there has always been a certain part of the vote given to corruption." When pressed, however, he proved unable to provide definitive evidence to support his assertion. He eventually admitted to sharing only speculations, fearing the Salt Lake scandal would get "swept under the carpet." Fellow IOC members wondered if the octogenarian had experienced "a stroke or some other mentally misbalancing episode." Nonetheless, Holder could have referred to his—and probably others'—dealings with the DOC.[56]

Everything considered in this chapter is based on written documentation, and Richard Olson had suggested that the details of the DOC's "soft sell" outreach to IOC voters should be kept for verbal discussion.[57] Furthermore, in the two years leading up to the IOC's selection, DOC members traveled to at least thirty-three countries and five continents, not counting North America, to "indirectly" solicit IOC votes.[58] Technical experts representing the luge, bobsled, biathlon, skating, and ice hockey federations all came to Denver to inspect potential venues as well.[59] The bidders also enlisted "outside assistance" from almost "all [United States] ambassadors at IOC countries."[60] One must wonder what conversations, offers, requests, or agreements were made during these trips, meetings, and event site surveys but never made into DOC reports, memos, meeting minutes, or letters.

In early May 1970, with an unrealistic proposal in hand and their all-out marketing strategy deployed, twenty-five Coloradans boarded a plane provided by King Resources. The group included DOC members, many of their spouses, Mayor McNichols, and Governor Love.[61] They traveled to Amsterdam to make a final appeal to host the Olympics. According to the DOC's "Final Report," it had spent $759,000 to convince the IOC that the 1976 Winter Olympics should be Denver's—with 45 percent coming from the state of Colorado, 19 percent from the city of Denver, and 36 percent from "self-generated and private sources."[62]

The DOC member and Denver marketing guru William Kostka oversaw the design of the DOC's bid books, production of a complementary film, construction of a promotional display, and the script for the DOC's oral presentation to the International Olympic Committee.[63] The former Denver mayor Thomas Currigan described the bid books to the *Rocky Mountain*

Figure 4.2. October 1968. DOC representatives George Robinson, Carl DeTemple, John Vanderhoof, and Robert McCollum, Governor John Love, and Mayor Thomas Currigan await a flight at Stapleton Airport for the Summer Games in Mexico City to lobby IOC members. Photo by Melvyn E. Schieltz via Denver Public Library, Western History Collection, WH2129-2018-362.

News editor Jack Foster as "the finest pieces of publicity material ever assembled and printed on Denver and our surrounding area."[64] Along with the books, the film showed slalom and downhill skiing at Vail, followed by inaccurate descriptions of the actual proposed sites, Loveland Basin and Mount Sniktau, the airbrushed photograph of Sniktau included. For the Nordic events in the "Evergreen area," the film pictured an unidentifiable location carpeted with snow and surrounded by jagged mountains. It was not Evergreen's golf course. Kostka also represented ski jumping, bobsledding, and luging with clips from previous Winter Games.[65] He ordered the footage from Grenoble to complete the showcase.[66]

Just as bold, Kostka's "display" for Amsterdam weighed 4,000 pounds and measured 14 by 26 feet. It included photos of various Olympic events and areas of Denver, maps of the proposed sites, a continuous slideshow, a model speed skating oval built by the Ahrendt Engineering firm, and a model of the city and surrounding areas that made Denver look closer to the mountains than it truly was. According to the DOC's "Final Report," a United Airlines employee "personally escorted the display on its Pan American flight to Europe."[67]

In addition, after receiving advice from two unnamed IOC members, the DOC tried to manage the happenings in Amsterdam. Among other things, IOC leaders suggested wearing cowboy hats, emphasizing the presence of snow at event sites, and planting questions in the audience during the bid city's presentations. "Denver should be shown under snow cover," a summary of the guidance stated; "cowboy, yes, but in snow."[68] It is unclear if the DOC brought cowboy hats to the Netherlands, but the USOC president Clifford Buck and the DOC president Robert Pringle discussed preparing "pointed questions which DOC *top leadership only* (with the utmost care) can place in the hands of an *extremely small number* of IOC members that we know beyond all doubt are for us." As Buck explained, the questions would be directed at the bid from Vancouver to expose its weaknesses.[69]

Meanwhile, the DOC presentation included familiar and unachievable promises. Donald McMahon had recently stepped down as DOC president to take a job in New York City, leaving Pringle, the new president, to make the presentation.[70] Pringle told the IOC that "80% of the cost has been met by existing facilities" and that the games would require spending only $14 million, though the number was not listed in the DOC bid book. Pringle even asserted: "Experts have advised that we could stage the Olympic Games in 12 to 18 months if need be."[71] With 1976 over five years away, this bluff was a reliable one.

When the time came for IOC members to vote, Vancouver's odds had deflated. The IOC surprisingly picked Montreal, Canada, as the host for the 1976 Summer Olympics. The committee was unlikely to send the Summer and Winter Games to the same country. Denver now stood pitted against Sion, Switzerland. On the third and final ballot, the IOC selected Denver.[72]

It must have been a gratifying moment, which was seven years in the making for many of the Colorado bidders. When Kostka passed away in 2015, the *Denver Post* remembered him as a "Denver PR legend." He had spun controversial topics such as an underground nuclear bomb detonation in Rio Blanco County, the construction of the Auraria Metro City College that displaced over 200 households, and Denver's Skyline Urban Renewal Project that required dismantling historic buildings. Yet according to his family and friends, "Kostka's proudest moment . . . was being part of the Denver team that won the bid for the 1976 Winter Olympics."[73]

The DOC and its company of promoters had put their salesmanship skills to the test, selling the most prominent international sports organization in the world a Rolls-Royce with nothing under the hood. The group spent hundreds of thousands of dollars and traveled the world to market its

Figure 4.3. May 1970. DOC president Robert Pringle and Denver mayor William McNichols return from Amsterdam after the IOC Denver officially awarded Denver the 1976 Winter Olympics. Photo by Dick Davis via Denver Public Library, Western History Collection, WH2129-2018-367.

impractical plan. It exploited guileful tactics, working within and around the conventions of Olympic bidding. And now, through these efforts, Denver's growth regime and Colorado's tourist industry stood ready for publicly funded worldwide publicity.

However, the DOC had locked its focus squarely upon the IOC. As former Mayor Currigan confessed: "We had to pay most attention to the IOC. They could vote; Denverites couldn't."[74] Little did Currigan or the rest of the DOC know that Denver and Colorado citizens would, in due time, be marking Olympic ballots of their own.

PART 2

THE OPPONENTS

CHAPTER 5

Post–Civil Rights Advocacy in the City

In May 1970, most Mexican American and African American activists and politicians in the Mile High City came from poor and rundown neighborhoods. They had limited time and resources. Moreover, during this period of federally subsidized urban renewal, they often faced the daunting task of justifying the preservation—rather than demolition—of their communities. Due to the limited purchasing power of low-income neighborhoods, allegations that their very presence depressed land values, and growth regime desires to appeal to wealthier white consumers, poorer communities, especially neighborhoods of color, were the most vulnerable to state-sanctioned transformation.[1] In Denver, as the historian Patrick Walsh contends, Mexican Americans in particular "were prisoners, not just of their own poverty and ethnicity, but also of the economic development ethos that existed everywhere around" them.[2]

Nevertheless, Brown and Black residents of Denver came to see the 1976 Winter Olympics as a vehicle for combating these challenges.[3] The question at first was not whether Denver should host the games. Instead, the city's minoritized citizens wondered how to use the event to their advantage. Whereas the Denver Organizing Committee meant to enhance the wealth of Colorado powerbrokers through tourism and commercial growth, Denverites of color ultimately looked to gain access to Olympic planning to address a systemic housing shortage that threatened low-income families.

At the same time, leaders of the Mexican American and African American communities did not always see eye-to-eye on how to accomplish that shared objective. Several grassroots activists expressed continued distrust in white authorities and demanded greater power and independence from the city's political establishment. In contrast, advocates who were more moderate began to strategically compromise and even collaborate with the

Denver machine. As the DOC's planning moved forward, both approaches hit roadblocks, leaving many in an ambiguous position regarding whether to support or oppose Denver '76—not to mention how to move forward in the struggle for equality within the post–civil rights era.

The lack of affordable housing in Denver after World War II represented a veritable crisis more than a century in the making following the Mexican–American War. Mexican Americans of the Southwest had lived in relative isolation, worked low-paying agricultural jobs, and sent their children to segregated and underfunded schools.[4] Yet a series of events brought Hispanics toward Denver in greater numbers. The Chinese Exclusion Act of 1882 and World War I increased demand for cheap labor in industries throughout the United States.[5] In Colorado, the Boettcher family's Great Sugar Company began to hire Mexican Americans from New Mexico and southern Colorado while importing migrants across the Rio Grande to its beet fields by the truckload. Company executives paid meagerly, and it became impossible for many workers to return home. Thousands thus stayed in the Centennial State and sought other employment and community in Denver during the off-seasons.[6] Despite the Ku Klux Klan taking over Colorado's political leadership in the 1920s and an upsurge of nativism and forced repatriations amid the Great Depression, Denver's Mexican American population increased to about 12,000 by 1930.[7] Then in the 1940s, additional agricultural laborers followed wartime industries into the city.[8] Discrimination prevented Mexican American and African American residents from gaining admission to industrial work during the Depression years. However, labor shortages caused by World War II opened doors to these hardscrabble jobs. By the 1950s, many Denver factories employed equal amounts of Brown and Black faces compared to white.[9]

Consequently, the city's Hispanic and African American populations doubled, sparking an affordable housing shortage, which facilitated increasingly decrepit living conditions. Property owners took advantage of high demand by converting homes for one or two families into residences that squeezed in three or four. Meanwhile, absentee landlords had little incentive to maintain or improve their holdings. As a result, limited access to water, lack of adequate heating, and the presence of vermin became commonplace.[10] Public studies continually found that Mexican Americans worked the lowest-paying jobs and faced the harshest living arrangements in the Mile High City.[11]

Other structural obstacles similar to those witnessed across the United States made matters worse. Denver authorities buttressed residential segregation through covenants, gentlemen's agreements, and redlining. It became near impossible for Brown or Black citizens to move into or simply travel through white areas. The city's schools, as the United States Supreme Court ruled in 1973, were effectively segregated.[12] Nonwhite Denverites also faced an uphill climb in obtaining home loans. As the Denver historian Richard Gould describes, local banks discriminated directly against African Americans, whereas the "darkness of skin complexion," "annotations and accents," and "degree of cultural assimilation" determined if Mexican Americans proved "Caucasian enough" for white lenders.[13] On top of this, from the 1940s into the 1970s, the Denver Police Department worked to preserve the city's racialized borders, often through directed policing and excessive force.[14]

At the same time, city boosters nationwide began to realize that the downtown's lack of desirability, rather than its accessibility, caused potential businesses and patrons to do their work, shopping, and recreating outside city limits. Middle- and upper-class whites moved from cities to suburbs, and marginalized racial and ethnic groups remained behind, making ends meet in ever more unkept, cramped, and deteriorating urban environments. Urban investors thus lobbied Congress to pass the questionably titled Housing Acts of 1949 and 1954, and in 1960 government-friendly Democrats gained control of Congress and began instituting the Great Society programs. Millions in federal funds became available and assisted urban planners in implementing locally devised development projects.[15] City boosters took advantage by exercising eminent domain and selling or leasing land to private investors at below-market value. City advocates hoped that, by building private housing, convention centers, commercial outlets, hospitals, colleges, and parks, they could protect land values, lift consumption, increase tax revenues, and preserve, if not expand, the presence of their ideal, white, middle-class clientele.[16] Although this process played out differently from city to city, it often meant displacing working-class communities of color. In many cases, Brown and Black residents moved locations, and communities became more densely populated and racially confined.[17]

For its part, in the words of the Colorado historians Carl Abbott, Stephen Leonard, and Thomas Noel, "Denver increasingly became an island of old people, poor people, and minority groups surrounded by a suburban sea of middle-class white families."[18] In response, in the 1950s, 176 firms formed the Denver Improvement Association and pushed to create the Denver Urban Renewal Authority (DURA). DURA served as a publicly funded organization led by the heart of the city's growth machine—banks, utility companies, real estate firms, and downtown merchants.[19] Most prominently, it oversaw the Skyline Project, an initiative meant to reshape the city's core by leveling twenty-six blocks consisting of the metropolis's highest concentration of poverty. The city displaced about 1,600 people, and subsidized apartments, office buildings, and retail stores eventually emerged from the rubble.[20]

Around the time DURA hatched the Skyline Project, it introduced another proposal that directly impacted the Denver Olympics debate. After World War II, higher education became more accessible for the white middle class and veterans. Yet neither the Metropolitan State College of Denver nor the University of Colorado in Denver had enough space to meet the escalating demand. Thus, in 1968, the Denver City Council selected a section of the city's West Side, known as Auraria, to become a new education complex. Auraria flanked the Skyline area and represented a stronghold for the city's Mexican American populace. Officials looked to raze thirty-eight blocks covering 169 acres and introduce a trio of colleges to service an estimated 55,000 students.[21]

As the urban geography scholars Brian Page and Eric Ross explain, Auraria was "old and deteriorating." Ninety-five percent of its residences had been built before 1910. To turn a maximum profit, landlords converted those properties to squeeze in as many families as possible. Page and Ross estimate that, in 1970, three-fourths of Auraria inhabitants rented, and over half lived below the poverty line. About nine of ten were Hispanic.[22] Auraria appeared, Page and Ross write, to be "the type of urban space that city planners across the country wanted to eradicate; its age, poor physical condition, remnant land-use jumble, minority population, entrenched poverty, and close proximity to downtown were, in the minds of many, precisely what stood in the way of successful redevelopment and the creation of an efficient, modern city."[23]

Officials would promise equivalent or improved housing and adequate compensation for displaced residents. However, Denver authorities excluded Aurarians from the decision regarding their relocation. And significantly, Auraria was a cultural foundation for Mexican Americans in the city. The West Side provided informal networks, familiar institutions, a dependable environment, security, and a forum for constructing ethnic solidarity. Urban renewal planners often avoided these types of factors in their assessments, even though, in poorer neighborhoods such as Auraria, residents relied on such elements for survival.[24] As the prominent West Sider and future Olympic negotiator Waldo Benavidez expressed, if DURA built the new colleges, many "may find a new home, but not a community."[25] A group called the West Side Action Council agreed, declaring that Denver's proposal for the higher education facilities represented "a deliberate attempt to destroy the growing potential of Mexican-American unity."[26] "Why do groups like the City Council that won't permit housing for minority people in the Anglo areas want to destroy Mexican neighborhoods," another Aurarian prodded?[27]

It also seemed probable that the campus's construction would worsen the already grim housing situation. The city meant for the colleges to become pure commuter schools, but this appeared unlikely, and as the Denver urban planner Myles Rademan pointed out, if dormitories remained absent from college grounds, then "students, with their greater affluence, diminished responsibilities, and the greater flexibility of their living arrangements[,] can usually wrest the limited supply of low and moderate-income housing from local residents." The schools "would foist the entire [housing] problem on that segment of the community least economically prepared to cope with it," Rademan warned. This proved "especially the case," he further stressed, "in an area like the West Side, where absentee ownership is a significant factor."[28]

Thus in October 1969, one month before Denver residents prepared to vote on a $5.3 million bond to gain state and federal funding to enable DURA's newest renewal effort, over 400 Aurarians packed the area's St. Cajetan's Church to convey their frustration. Led by a future Olympics challenger, the forty-one-year-old assistant pastor Peter Garcia, St. Cajetan's had stood as a communal space for Spanish-speaking worshipers for decades and became the base for a grassroots movement to stop the city's West Side proposal. The October meeting became heated, culminating when someone hurled a chair at a DURA representative.[29] Residents then spent the following weeks trying to convince fellow Denverites to vote against the bond. However, in November, the city's citizens narrowly passed it. Afterward, a lawsuit filed by 150 Auraria families failed, and follow-up efforts remained toothless. Auraria's flattening became inevitable.[30]

Months later, two days after returning home from his Olympic triumph in Amsterdam, Denver mayor William McNichols found a group of tenant rights organizations waiting outside his offices, demanding to know how Denver could spend money to host the games when a "housing crisis" continued to engulf the poor.[31] The Aurarian Peter Garcia became especially concerned. He led the attempt to stop the Auraria transformation. Now he and others stood constantly on guard against decisions made by the city without their community's involvement.

In October 1970, Garcia wrote to the DOC president Robert Pringle. Following their successful bid, Olympic organizers began to reconstitute the DOC for "Phase III: Planning and Preparation." The organizers expected to bring twenty-one to thirty Coloradans into the group's board of directors. The board would wield final authority over DOC policy, including who served on its nine-person executive council. The ex-officio executive council contributors Mayor McNichols, Governor John Love, and Colorado Olympic Commission chairman Richard Olson took charge of nominating and screening the board's membership. They would decide who ran the DOC and thereby the Denver games.[32] Garcia understood that this reorganization was underway and requested the inclusion of Mexican American and African American residents within the DOC leadership. He warned that there would be "opposition and hostility . . . toward the planned Olympics" if his demand went unmet.[33]

Garcia would display an unbending determination indicative of Chicano and Black Power protestors during the late 1960s. After World War II, the African American civil rights movement inspired various forms of nonviolent, rights-based activism marked by bus boycotts, sit-ins, freedom rides, voter registration campaigns, and marches.[34] Yet after the passage of the 1964 Civil Rights Act and the 1965 Voting Rights Act, it also became apparent to many that America still needed to enact far more profound changes. Martin Luther King Jr. faced this hard truth when he led his forces north into Chicago. There, he failed to stamp out socially and economically segregated schools, jobs, and neighborhoods.[35] "I'm convinced," King would conclude, "that many of the very people who supported us in the struggle in the South are not willing to go all the way now." As the civil rights hero professed, "It is much easier to integrate a lunch counter than it is to guarantee a livable income and a good solid job. It's much easier to guarantee the right to vote than it is to guarantee the right to live in sanitary, decent housing conditions."[36] In reaction to the limitations of federal legislation and in the absence of support from white allies, activists such as Malcolm X and later Stokely Carmichael embraced "Black Power," demanding complete freedom from white authorities, organizations, and social structures and voicing support for Black separatism, pan-Africanism, and even armed self-defense.[37]

Although these views never described the thinking of the majority of Brown or Black Americans, many younger Mexican Americans could relate. Older Hispanic leaders once sought to assimilate into white society to obtain social mobility, even presenting themselves as white.[38] But on the eve of the Denver Olympic debate, remembrances of the Mexican Revolution of 1910, the Cuban Revolution of the 1950s, the mythic figure of the

Argentinian rebel Ernesto "Che" Guevara, the 1960s youth movement in Mexico, the Vietnam War, challenges to colonialism, and the prominence of Black Power leaders combined to inspire parallel sentiments of "Brown Power" or "cultural nationalism." The Chicano movement proved ideologically heterogeneous and dynamic, shaped by specific contexts and intersecting experiences produced through class and gender.[39] The movement witnessed diverse manifestations and internal divisions. Still, it remained rooted in racial pride and desires for Mexican American autonomy.[40]

Furthermore, along with Southern California and Texas, Denver represented a point of genesis for this perspective. In March 1969, Mexican American high school students famously organized a "blowout" at Denver's West High School. The renowned Chicano leader Rodolfo "Corky" Gonzales and his organization, the Crusade for Justice, advised the students to follow the lead of over 10,000 peers from East Los Angeles. The Angelenos marched out of their schools the year prior to protest, among other problems, dilapidated and overcrowded school buildings overseen by insensitive teachers.[41] In Denver, when a teacher's repeatedly racist conduct went unpunished by school administrators, West High students did the same, marching three blocks before returning to rally outside the school, where they found police in riot gear waiting for them. As newspapers described, after the students refused to go back to class, a "fight" broke out, resulting in two hospitalizations and twenty-six people arrested, including Gonzales.[42]

The week of the West High blowout, the Crusade for Justice also hosted the first National Chicano Liberation Conference, attracting 1,500 Chicano youth to Denver and culminating with the passage of a manifesto, "El Plan Espiritual de Aztlan." In the words of the activist and political scientist Carlos Muñoz Jr., the document "merged the ideas of non-violence . . . with the more militant revolutionary Black Nationalist ideology," calling for "social and economic justice, and self-determination in the context of a Chicano cultural nationalist framework." The focus on community and ethnic pride stood in stark contrast to the individualism and assimilationism of the past.[43]

Given this backdrop, with the Olympics looming, Garcia partnered with the founder of Denver's chapter of the Black Panther Party, Lauren Watson, and his brother, Clarke Watson. Together the trio formed an organization called Citizens Interested in Equitable Olympics (CIEO). As CIEO declared, its goal was to advocate for "black and brown participation" in the planning of the games. Around this time, many Chicanos came to understand racial injustice as a national and even global economic phenomenon rooted in colonization, capitalism, and imperialism.[44] This broad and critical

Figure 5.1. December 1970. CIEO leaders Peter Garcia and Clarke Watson, with Ed Vigil, hold a press conference, expressing disappointment that they had no input in the DOC's selection of its minority membership. Photo by John Beard/*Denver Post* via Getty Images.

perspective enabled Brown and Black protesters to mingle, finding they could simultaneously participate in identity politics and coalition politics.[45] In fact, Lauren Watson joined Corky Gonzales for the West High blowout, announcing outside the school: "This is a day of black and brown unity."[46] The CIEO team thus worked together, urging the Denver City Council that, "before the City . . . approves of the Executive Council of the Denver Olympic Committee, it should have assurance that . . . all the people have meaningful input."[47]

Throughout November 1970, Garcia and the Watson brothers held weekly press conferences and attended multiple City Council meetings, insisting that they take charge of choosing individuals to represent their interests on the DOC. "The Board of Directors will not be set until I say it's set," Clarke Watson told Olympic planners.[48] At the end of the month, Garcia and the Watsons finally met with McNichols to discuss the matter. They asked him to disband and rebuild the DOC completely and remained adamant that Brown and Black Coloradans should be the ones to select who acted on their behalf.[49]

Early on, as CIEO tried to gain a hold on the DOC, it aligned with elected officials representing Mexican American and Black areas of Denver. In this way, CIEO, while ambitious, was not necessarily a radical organization. At the start of December 1970, Clarke Watson penned a proposal to Pringle. In it, he explained that CIEO and local political leaders reached an understanding over how to ensure "the most equitable, democratic and acceptable manner of selecting individuals to serve on" the DOC's board. Clarke claimed CIEO and members of the Colorado House and Senate imagined a nine-person screening committee. It would include four individuals elected by Brown and Black districts, one affiliate of CIEO, the mayor of Denver, the governor of Colorado, and two current DOC members. CIEO envisioned a group where Colorado "minorities" became a five-to-four majority.[50]

Clarke Watson even took the liberty of alerting the DOC president of the exact time and place where the committee would meet.[51] Yet the gathering he scheduled never happened. Instead, the DOC named three Mexican American and three African American members to its board of directors without consulting CIEO or other community leaders. The "screening committee" of Love, McNichols, and Olson invited Paco Sanchez (a Mexican American radio station owner, real estate developer, and politician), Joseph Torres (a Mexican American Roman Catholic priest), Donald E. Cordova (a Mexican American attorney and member of the Latin American Educational Federation), Charles R. Cousins (a Black real estate investor), William Roberts (a Black director of Metropolitan Denver Construction), and Floyd Little (a Black all-pro running back from the Denver Broncos) to become Olympic organizers.[52]

Several of the new members appeared to be standard growth-machine allies. For example, Paco Sanchez not only sold real estate. As Auraria's representative in the Colorado House and a member of the DURA board, he had supported the bond issue that made the coming Auraria relocations possible. One reason the bond to fund the Auraria campus passed was that multiple Mexican American politicians backed it.[53] Meanwhile, the attorney Donald E. Cordova admitted to buying shares in Vail Associates and the Public Service Company of Colorado after he joined the DOC.[54] The bidders could be confident these actors would go along with what they and other development-minded Olympics supporters wanted. As the DOC's legal adviser, Richard Davis, acknowledged, "the DOC did not want any obstructionists."[55]

Organizing committees often attached themselves to famous athletes and celebrities as well. During the bid, one month after Apollo 11 landed on the moon, the DOC sought out NASA astronauts to "coat-tail our cause in the limelight of their world wide popularity." The bidders thought this would help "keep Denver in the minds of the IOC" in a positive way. Accordingly, the Apollo 7 commander Willy Schirra became a committee member.[56] Similarly, the inclusion of football star Floyd Little seemed to be a means for Olympic planners to persuade Colorado's African American citizens to back the Olympic cause.

However, not every minoritized Coloradan invited to join the DOC accepted the offer. DOC decision makers probably viewed the 1952 long jump gold-medalist Jerome Biffle in the same light as Little: a positive for public relations. But by the 1960s, as everyday African Americans risked their lives at marches and sit-ins, many famous Black athletes began to feel a greater responsibility to use their fame to further the struggle for racial equality. Biffle thus progressed from an athlete of the pragmatic Cold War era into the era of athlete activism and declined a post on the organizing committee. "I want very much to do whatever I can to make these games the best in history," he wrote to mayor McNichols, "but I cannot in conscience accept an appointment made by a committee that is not broadly representative of the total Denver community."[57] The Olympian then went on television advocating on CIEO's behalf, pointing out that, even after the DOC added six "minority members," twenty-four out of the twenty-five DOC officials still represented either well-off businesspeople or politicians. "I personally can't go along with doing things this way," Biffle asserted.[58]

After the Denver City Council approved the new Brown and Black DOC members, CIEO presented a petition signed by 655 people demanding it reselect the minority delegates.[59] When that request went ignored, Clarke Watson followed with a blistering letter to McNichols. By ignoring CIEO and choosing representatives to fit its preferences, Watson alleged, the DOC selection committee acted in a manner "reminiscent of plantation masters evaluating slaves at the marketplace." Watson told the mayor that "you have turned what was a crevice into a gap between your administration and the minority community." Watson continued: "No conscientious and intelligent minority citizen in this community is willing to be duped by your dixie-cratic paternalism." "We have yet to see a true crisis rend this community," he further cautioned, "but, I would not predict that such a possibility is as remote as you seem to think."[60]

In 1966 and 1967, dozens of so-called race riots burst out in American cities, leaving scores dead, thousands injured, hundreds of buildings destroyed, and tens of millions of dollars in damage.[61] In January 1968, as the DOC entered "Phase II" of its bid, Mexican American intellectuals met in Denver to discuss "Mexican Americans in the urban area: will they riot?" Although most rejected the notion, Corky Gonzales predicted there would soon be "guerilla warfare in the southwest."[62] Likewise, Watson alluded to that possibility, threatening Denver's mayor with an extrainstitutional uprising.

Throughout this time, Clarke Watson tried to convince the six Brown and Black representatives chosen by DOC to follow Biffle's lead and refuse their appointments. He confronted Charles Cousins at his home and met Floyd Little at Stapleton Airport as the Broncos returned from an away game. He also manufactured meetings between Colorado politicians and Governor Love, where he, instead of the governor, arrived to make CIEO's case before unwitting policy makers.[63] CIEO and its supporters presented an unrelenting posture, steadfastly skeptical of the men behind the effort to make Denver an Olympic city and set on obtaining autonomous power over their fate.

It is here, though, that the Citizen Interested in an Equitable Olympics began to part ways with moderate elected Mexican American and African American leaders. One week before Clarke Watson's missive to McNichols, Elvin Caldwell, the first African American to serve on the Denver City Council, reached out to the DOC. In 1956, Caldwell beat none other than Corky Gonzales to gain his seat on the council. To do so, he carefully negotiated both Denver's white conservatism and the growing discontent of his Brown and Black constituents. By the end of the 1960s, this left Caldwell and the Watson brothers at odds. As he wrote in a public letter to Denver's chief of police in 1969: "So far as I am personally concerned, I won't be satisfied until every Black Panther is run out of Denver."[64]

Where Clarke Watson threatened to incite a violent grassroots backlash, Caldwell pressured the DOC with conventional and likely weightless political influence. According to Caldwell, the DOC assured him that "minority and disadvantaged communities would be equitably represented" in Olympic planning. By "enabling the community to have a meaningful input" and "acting in a reasonably fast manner," he called on DOC members to "demonstrate . . . they are serious about making the Olympics a total community endeavor." Caldwell added that "further delays and more promises can only serve to do further irreparable harm." Yet if the DOC failed to respond in thirty days, the councilman merely pledged to ask Denver to rescind a recent $75,000 commitment to assist Olympic organizers.[65]

Comparably, in early 1971, Betty Benavidez helped organize a meeting between Governor Love and six Brown and Black officeholders. She was Colorado's first female Mexican American state representative. At the time, Benavidez and her cohort presented themselves as sympathetic to "various matters raised" by CIEO.[66] In his letter to McNichols, Clarke Watson had similarly alluded to his partnership with the likes of Caldwell and Benavidez by couching his criticism in the notion that the screening committee presumed "our proud minority leadership, elected by our people in the finest democratic fashion, incapable of identifying individuals from their own constituencies who would best serve our interests on the Olympic Board."[67] Benavidez's husband, Waldo Benavidez, and Peter Garcia had also worked together in the recent past in opposition to the Auraria removals.[68] Nonetheless, the Benavidezes made their mark by working within Colorado's Democratic Party. Waldo Benavidez was a local kingpin, owning multiple West Side properties and regarded as the area's unofficial mayor.[69] When Betty Benavidez and her contingent, which included Caldwell, faced the governor, they therefore adopted Caldwell's more restrained tone.

They did not ask for the removal of the DOC-selected members of color. Instead, they "respectfully submitted" a set of policies for "consideration" and conveyed that they hoped to see them enacted before "additional allocations of state funds for the Olympics be permitted." The collection of proposals included specific requests, including that they "be allowed to screen and recommend" three additional "minority individuals" to join the DOC. It also called for vaguer, albeit important, actions, including that "some benefits . . . accrue . . . in the area of income to minority business enterprise and employment at *all* levels within the Olympic administration." They additionally asked that there be "some legislative assurance that facilities developed for dwelling purposes be made available to low and middle income families at the conclusion of the Games."[70]

Garcia, the Watson brothers, Caldwell, and Betty Benavidez wanted greater access to city decision-making. Still, the divide between them only widened. The team of politicians headed by Caldwell and Benavidez eventually recommended eight candidates to join the DOC board. The DOC screening committee responded by inviting none of them.[71] Afterward, Benavidez, Caldwell, and their partners in effect consented to the DOC's choices for their community's representation. As Caldwell confirmed in late December 1970, "I feel that the present minority members of the Board of Directors for the 1976 Olympics are good selections."[72]

Thus, the control of Denver's white-led business community remained squarely in place. Meanwhile, Garcia and the Watsons stood on the outside looking in, dismissed by Mayor McNichols and the DOC and seemingly at odds with Caldwell and Benavidez. The CIEO leaders did continue to seek opportunities to use the Olympic controversy to suit their own ends. In January 1971, two white state representatives began to express their worries about reckless spending and moved to halt state funding of the games.

The following week, as questions surrounding the fiscal viability of the event emerged in the Denver press, CIEO requested that the state's Joint Budget Committee begin accounting for how public dollars allotted to the DOC would impact "minority races."[73] Two months later, at a public legislative committee meeting on the Olympics, Garcia attended and stressed to city officials that "his people" needed work and housing desperately. He anticipated that hosting the Olympics would be a "disaster" unless the city built decent, affordable homes first.[74] For CIEO members, constantly fighting for ways to gain leverage in Denver, the games lingered as a viable political mechanism. At this point, though, they became less active in the Denver Olympic issue. They had taken a more militant line, moved apart from moderate counterparts, and found themselves unable to obtain the political pull for which they aimed.

From then to November 1972, other Brown and Black advocates, from Denver's West Side and East Side, not only went along with the DOC's self-chosen minority representation; they began working pragmatically with the DOC and DURA, hoping to secure affordable housing. In the earlier Skyline and Auraria schemes, Denver authorities used Great Society funds to further the city's growth network agenda. Now they again aimed to acquire federal dollars from the Department of Housing and Urban Development (HUD) to build lodging for the Olympic press. But herein lay an opportunity for minoritized Denverites.

Previous large-scale renewal projects, such as those witnessed in Denver, had sparked community resistance in several American cities. The urban historian John Mollenkopf explains that this "neighborhood activism created a new 'political space' which allowed, and sometimes forced, urban politicians and administrators to interact with new contenders for power." "These new interactions," Mollenkopf continues, "ended the days in which corporate officials and redevelopment agency administrators could quietly formulate and execute large-scale development plans on their own."[75] Indeed, in 1968, HUD responded to local unrest by issuing a directive requiring "maximum resident participation."[76] Thus, the success of urban renewal in Denver—and other cities—in the late 1960s and early 1970s would depend on an urban regime's ability to attract at least some level of community support.[77]

Before Denver won its Olympic bid, there had been discussions about using the West Side for housing the press, but locals remained under the impression that the buildings would be incorporated into the new college campus in Auraria.[78] In the summer of 1971, the city also considered a separate location that most likely would have produced motels rather than publicly funded low-income homes.[79] Yet local actors and HUD appeared to pressure Denver leaders in a different direction. As the director of DURA explained in a February 1972 memo to mayor McNichols: "Certain" Denver city councilmen, perhaps compelled by constituents, expressed "more interest in housing than the Olympics." Moreover, the DURA leader confirmed, "Our proposal is based on what HUD and [the HUD secretary George] Romney desire . . . [and] after use was a primary concern."[80] DURA therefore pledged that HUD-subsidized press housing would be repurposed into low- and middle-income homes once the games left town.

In truth, building affordable housing became advantageous for the DOC in ways beyond ensuring local consent and HUD's support. It serendipitously provided a means for Olympic organizers to try to regain the confidence of the International Olympic Committee as the nature of their fictitious proposal became known and word of opposition within Colorado spread. "In this season of discontent," McNichols informed Olympic officials, West Side residents had "taken initiative" and "proposed to sponsor and own the housing" when the games concluded. According to the mayor, this was an "encouraging and gratifying example" of Denverites taking an "active and positive interest in [Olympic] planning."[81] The affordable housing project would also bolster arguments for voting down the anti-Olympics measure scheduled for the November 1972 ballot. As Governor Love explained in a pro-Olympics advertisement, "the [current] plan for 1,400 low and middle income and senior citizen housing units built initially to house the Olympic press corps . . . will be a reality in the near future only if we stage the Olympics."[82]

Growth-regime logic had coalesced with the changing dynamics of urban renewal and the DOC's multiple Olympic needs to generate an opening for Denver's Mexican American and African American residents. Moderate community leaders thus moved to work through Colorado's growth coalition—coordinating with the DOC and DURA—to try and shape Denver's infrastructure to improve their neighborhoods. Although this meant forgoing the type of independence CIEO aspired to, it seemed a potentially auspicious route for gaining meaningful influence in the city.[83]

City planners would collect community input for the project through neighborhood meetings, public hearings, and conferences with local groups.[84] A group called the West Side Coalition (WSC), which originated during the Auraria controversy, served as the chief envoy.[85] Throughout 1971, led by Waldo Benavidez, WSC met with city and state officials and the DOC's executive board to look over architectural designs. After one meeting with the DOC late that year, as the West Side's monthly newspaper, the *West Side Recorder*, reported, "All in attendance were impressed."[86]

Figure 5.2. December 1971. Waldo Benavidez shows off a proposed housing plan for initially providing accommodations to the press, which DURA and the WSC intended to become low- and middle-income residences after Denver '76. Photo by Dave Buresh/*Denver Post* via Getty Images.

By the end of 1971, as the *Recorder* told it, the DOC appeared ready to agree to a "sensitive" design that would "provide 1,500 units of desperately needed housing for low and moderate income people." The committee promised to "aid in the economic development of the neighborhood by encouraging minority businesses and minority contractors to build and maintain units." The West Side Coalition, the DOC, and other authorities also discussed ways to create a system where working-class Mexican Americans would have a share of ownership in the new buildings, which a Mexican architect would design.[87] In the days before the Olympic vote, the *Recorder* reaffirmed that inhabitants would own the Olympics-derived units.[88] DURA's initial press housing plan certainly appeared promising. At first, it called for a combination of "garden apartments" and "townhouses" for low- and middle-income residents, along with "high rises" for the elderly, totaling 1,600 livable units. These would replace houses and single-family duplexes, most of which were over six to seven decades old and, according to the city, stood in "poor" or "very bad" condition.[89]

With this in mind and to help Denver obtain funds from HUD, Elvin Caldwell, at the request of the mayor's office, wrote to Senator Gordon Allott, asserting that "the people in my area strongly endorse the East Side Olympic Press Housing proposal."[90] Betty Benavidez and representatives of the West Side Coalition likewise sent letters to Washington.[91] Along these lines, days before the vote on the Olympic initiative, Betty Benavidez and her fellow Mexican American state representative Adolph Gomez urged Coloradans to vote for hosting the Winter Games.[92] Joseph Torres also made the new apartments and townhouses his primary focus as a DOC member.[93]

However, many Denverites of color feared that the potential for community uplift would not become a reality. The *West Side Recorder* expressed concern early on about whether the location, design, and size of the new buildings would "integrate with the surrounding neighborhood" and "accommodate . . . families." "We hope," the paper stated with caution, "HUD and [Denver] Urban Renewal will listen to us."[94] The paper's apprehension appeared validated in the summer of 1972 when, as the *Recorder* disclosed: "Those to be most affected by the ultimate plan seem to have little knowledge of it."[95] The plan DURA presented that summer was different from what even its West Side collaborators formally endorsed. Although the city received a federal grant of $15.5 million from HUD, the amount came in below its original request for $29 million. With limited time to submit a revised federal application and get the project underway, DURA proceeded to re-envision the press housing layout without seeking input from East Side or West Side residents.[96] In the words of two community organizers, the final design proved to be "a sham of resident participation."[97] Local businesses affected by the earlier proposal had also contested it, and this impacted the changes. As the chairman of DURA's board put it, some boundary alterations were driven in part by "political purposes."[98] At a community meeting led by DURA's assistant executive director, West Side residents learned that the new plans, though less expensive, called for relocating twenty fewer businesses and ninety-four more families.[99] As one West Side activist complained, it appeared DURA redrew the housing developments' boundaries "to displace residents instead of junkyards."[100]

The scale of the final scheme created unease as well. Building the press housing involved the "acquisition and clearance" of fifty-eight acres of property.[101] One report put the number of relocations at 507 families.[102] Equally concerning, had DURA undertaken the Olympic press housing project, the organization would have seized, demolished, rebuilt, and relocated Auraria, additional sections of the West Side, and parts of the East Side all at once.

It would have been a massive and emotional undertaking. Many residents expressed doubt regarding DURA's ability to relocate so many people.[103] DURA's executive director himself questioned if it was possible to pull off all three projects simultaneously.[104]

It is also important to highlight that housing was the linchpin to Olympic backing from much of the East Side and West Side. The "only tangible benefit [of the Olympics] that we can see," the *West Side Recorder* stressed, "is the possible afteruse of the housing that will be constructed."[105] When a story broke that HUD might not provide the financing to build the new residences, one Mexican American advocate responded by vowing to "melt the snow in the mountains" if the housing proposal really fell through. Another West Side representative asserted: "No housing—no Olympics."[106]

To keep Brown and Black residents on the side of the DOC, city leaders appeared to tell residents what they wanted to hear. The Benavidez-led West Side Coalition alleged as much, claiming Denver officials had "held out a carrot to gain minority support for the games."[107] Especially given the DOC's prior approach to winning IOC approval, it was not beyond the pale to suspect that the Olympic organizers and their City Hall counterparts were lying about the composition and after-use of the proposed press housing facilities. The *Recorder* began to predict there would be "a great deal of chaos and anxiety," as hasty city planning "tends to increase . . . [people's] suspicions." Many felt "city government does not consider their best interest," the paper observed.[108] Peter Garcia, for one, believed that the DOC and DURA never meant to build low- and middle-income homes. He expected to see hotels and motels in the end.[109]

Denver's minoritized citizens navigated decades of systemic impoverishment and neglect amid postwar urban renewal battles and rising Chicano and Black Power mind sets. As a collective, the situation left them unsure of how to interact with the Colorado regime based in Denver. Was working with the DOC the optimal strategy? Could the growth network be trusted? Even if the housing plan came to fruition, what would be lost by embracing an accommodationist stance? It was unclear how to respond to the Olympic issue, just as it was far from obvious how to reckon with the opportunities for and obstacles to achieving social justice in the 1970s.

Nevertheless, Chicanos, Black Panthers, moderate politicians, pragmatic community leaders, and others held two things in common. Each recognized the political capital the games created,[110] and all involved thus tried to appropriate the event to highlight and address ethnic and racial marginalization manifested through the dire state of housing options. Albeit in different and sometimes conflicting ways, Mexican Americans and African Americans in the Mile High City aimed to use the Olympics to remedy an urgent civic challenge.

In addition, urbanites of color provided fodder for and represented potential allies of other Olympics dissenters. Disregard for the best interests of Coloradans became a broader anti-Olympics complaint from different Centennial State cohorts. Other protesters would not dwell on racist urban policy to the same extent as environmental harm in the mountains or unfair taxation and reckless public spending statewide. However, they would try to contrast the needs of Denver's Brown and Black residents with the outcomes of hosting the Winter Games. Doing so bolstered the assertion that state leaders were using the Olympics to benefit themselves while running roughshod over everyone else. For certain, there were other advocates with which the DOC ran afoul—some of whom presented a stance more consolidated and as defiant as anything the DOC found inside Denver's boundary.

CHAPTER 6

Middle-Class Environmentalism in the Foothills

Like many Brown and Black citizens in Denver, white middle-class exurbanites in the Jefferson County foothills west of the city demanded input in DOC decision-making and levied location-specific demands. Generally, they did not oppose seeing the games in Colorado. However, as the DOC bid kicked into gear in the late 1960s, the mountain town residents already started to oppose new development in the vicinity of their homes. Most of these Coloradans still recognized growth as a sign of progress. But as one anti-Olympics resident living in the foothills put it, they became convinced that certain parts of the state could be "oversold."[1] Such citizens prized quiet, naturalistic settings above attracting out-of-town consumers. They did not want to see Olympic structures in their line of sight. Neither would they accept sharing open spaces, secluded neighborhoods, and spacious roadways with crowds of outsiders. As a result, with Nordic skiing, bobsled, luge, and ski jumping events slated for their area, they became ardent DOC adversaries, embracing an obstinate and unyielding environmentalist stance, which melded the language of ecology with notions of social class, aesthetic value, and expectations for self-determination.[2]

Moreover, the foothills dwellers proved well positioned to place the meanings they attached to the lands around them above and beyond conventional growth-regime imperatives.[3] Along with being well-off professionals with time and resources, they moved to the mountains for quality of life and found satisfaction in their physical surroundings. They liked things as they were and had nothing related to added infrastructure to request.[4] The mountain residents thus remained much less susceptible to the typical growth-network contention that growth or tourism were economic necessities. Indeed, within the confines of their communities, they had little reason to compromise or work with pro-Olympics forces.[5]

*   *   *

In late 1967, residents of the secluded mountain town of Indian Hills first noticed DOC surveyors assessing their properties. The community held about 350 homes and sat in Jefferson County, which started on the plains adjacent to Denver and reached into the beginning of the Rocky Mountains.[6] One of these mountainside homes belonged to a sixty-four-year-old University of Denver law professor named Vance Dittman.[7] On the verge of retirement, Dittman lived in Indian Hills with his wife, Catherine Dittman, on a fifty-acre lot. They had resided there for the previous twenty years and named the estate "Sky Meadow." The couple met at Yale University, where Vance Dittman earned his law degree.[8] With three fellow Indian Hills inhabitants—all University of Denver colleagues—Vance Dittman would galvanize a group of twenty-seven townspeople to voice objection to the DOC's Olympic proposal.[9]

Notably, this occurred amid immense transformation in Jefferson County. Between 1950 and 1970, Colorado's population rose from 1.3 million to 2.2 million.[10] In the course of this surge, middle- and upper-class citizens moved beyond Denver's borders into Jefferson County and the Front Range.[11] During the 1960s, with over 11,000 new businesses established in the area, many newcomers from across the United States relocated there as well.[12] As Denver's population increased by 100,000, outlying communities grew even faster, increasing by 560,000. From 1950 to 1970, Jefferson County alone grew from 55,686 to 235,300 residents. Even as the county's mountainous region remained relatively undeveloped, "Jeffco," as locals call it, became the fastest-growing county in the fifth-fastest growing state in the nation.[13]

With such change came important ideological shifts. In previous years, leaders of mountain locales had fought to get state and federal officials to construct new roadways and businesses near their homes to attract tourism, and Denver powerbrokers supported a semblance of land-use restrictions.[14] When a governing regime believes there is an alternative strategy that could carry greater monetary rewards, it will resist growth and development.[15] With that in mind, boosters in Colorado realized the beauty of untouched lands served to entice visitors from out of state. There was value in the simultaneous protection and commodification of nature.[16]

Yet by the late 1960s, it became apparent that tourist promoters unleashed a double-edged sword.[17] In the words of the historian William Philpott, well-off "lifestyle refugees" bought what Centennial State promoters were selling and moved in permanently, seeking a year-round mode of living centered on experiences with the outdoors.[18] Therefore, in June 1968, Dittman and other Indian Hills residents, in a letter to Denver mayor William

McNichols, Colorado governor John Love, and the DOC, detailed their fear of "an invasion" of "large crowds" that would "destroy the natural beauty of the area" in which they lived.[19] In a separate missive to the DOC, the mountain inhabitants noted that "sanitary facilities, warming houses, restaurants or lunch bars, and perhaps more undesirable businesses would be essential to the operation of" new sports complexes. "We now have nothing of the sort in our community and their presence would markedly change the whole environment of our residential area, which," Dittman and his neighbors proclaimed, "residents wish to keep residential."[20]

The references to "natural beauty" and changes in the "whole environment" allude to the construction of an environmental agenda. Broadly, around this time, middle-class suburbs played a key role in sparking America's new environmental consciousness. The movement was tied to a rising standard of living that itself caused environmental problems and placed suburbanites on the front lines of the damage, as sprawl wrought havoc on residents' health and daily life experiences. In turn, scientists and government officials, lawyers and accountants, as well as doctors and college professors began to treat clean rivers and lakes, untouched forests and mountains, fresh air, and open spaces as inherently worthy of protection.[21]

But more to the point, as the environmental historian Andrew Hurley contends, a distinct form of environmental advocacy "emerged out of the effort to protect those physical features of residential life . . . that had become central components of middle-class identity."[22] The significance of tree-covered mountains and swaths of undeveloped land lay not in health or ecological processes alone. Complemented by a private home, a collection of personal consumer goods, and a decent amount of leisure time, closeness to nature was a coveted aspect of middle-class character.[23] Many Coloradans, just like Vance Dittman and his neighbors, conveyed this environmentally inclined perspective.

The purported environmentalism stemming from Jeffco's mountains should thus be viewed, at least partly, as a rhetorical strategy born from class-inflected desires. Note that the foothills-based campaign to block Olympics-induced growth started two years before the emergence of a national environmental movement, sparked by the first Earth Day in April 1970.[24] In the late 1960s, references to financial consequences likely appeared to be a more potent resource than the keywords "environment" or "ecology" for defending one's well-off, well-designed, and well-maintained exurban hamlet. Indeed, at first, socioeconomic outcomes were an explicit component of the Indian Hills anti-Olympics argument. As Vance Dittman wrote to the Colorado Olympic Commission chair Richard Olson in 1968, "the development here . . . includes first class all season residences of substantial value. . . . I am sure that none of you wish to change the nature of an established environment or to be a means of decreasing property values of those of us who have substantial investments here."[25]

The anti-Olympics grievances of Dittman and his neighbors were also initially confined to Indian Hills. A month after the town's residents registered their objections, the DOC notified Dittman that it was considering alternative event sites. Dittman and other foothills activists had held leverage, because they voiced their frustrations before the IOC's May 1970 selection and therefore could have, at any time, moved to undermine the DOC's bid. The Denver Olympics planners thus identified two new scenarios. In one, the organizers said they would hold cross-country skiing in Indian Hills but with modifications to avoid impacting private property. For the second, they would place the skiing contests near a golf course in the town of Evergreen, a few miles northwest.[26] While Dittman was critical of the first suggestion, he expressed enthusiasm about moving events to the town next door.[27]

After all, the Indian Hills protesters supported the Olympics coming to the Centennial State. As their original letter to Colorado's political leaders and DOC officials proclaimed: "We share the wishes and hopes of the DOC that the 1976 Olympics will come to the Denver area. We realize the economic and other benefits to the state and to the city which will result from the presence of these events here, and we, as citizens of Colorado, have a stake in this too."[28] Commitment to this posture became evident in the summer of 1968, when the assistant to the DOC president wrote to Dittman to update him on the DOC's bid. The Olympic bidder promised that "many men are working at some considerable and unavoidable expense to find a better solution to the location of the Nordic events." Yet he added that, until the bid team made its changes, "it is necessary for reasons, which I am sure you can appreciate, for us to continue to list the Indian Hills area for those events." The "reasons" seem to be the community's proximity to Denver—a selling point to win over IOC voters.[29] Dittman appeared to understand and consented to the situation, writing in return, "I can assure you that none of us [in Indian Hills] are in any way opposed to the Olympics or to Denver's getting them." Rather, Dittman continued, "it is their whereabouts that concern us."[30]

In fall 1968, to mollify Dittman and other Indian Hills residents, Denver bidders changed their proposal. They left the bobsled run on Independence Mountain, about five miles from Indian Hills, and promised the event would remain on public land. However, the DOC moved the luge to nearby O'Fallon Park, adjacent to Independence Mountain, and agreed to transfer cross-country skiing, biathlon, and ski jumping away from Indian Hills, though to unspecified locations. As the DOC informed Indian Hills townspeople, it went "over this plan in some detail with Mr. Dittman" and he "seemed to be in complete agreement."[31] The first meeting of Indian Hills opponents took place at Vance Dittman's home, and Dittman worked as the front man for the group from then on.[32] Given this and his previous communications with the DOC, it appears reasonable to think that he knew—or should have suspected—that nearby Evergreen was the new location for the Nordic events.

Evergreen was a town of around 10,000 people, with one main street lined with local businesses, a small newspaper, two grocery stores, and a single stoplight.[33] It was more developed than Indian Hills but still suited to provide an equally formidable set of Olympics opponents. In response to rapid growth in the area, Evergreen residents had already created an organization called the Mountain Area Planning Council (MAPC) to promote "orderly planning and development."[34] At the outset, the MAPC's activities included preventing highways from reaching the town as well as slowing the construction of subdivisions.[35] Like those in Indian Hills, Evergreen residents were anxious about commercial growth and worried about preserving the aesthetics of their exurban retreat.

At the beginning of 1969, the MAPC learned of the DOC's revised plan and reacted with caution.[36] To the homegrown planning council, the consequences of hosting the Olympic events looked uncertain, and its stance toward the games remained undecided. Nonetheless, the organization began to draw up a list of questions for the DOC regarding how many people, cars, and parking lots would be involved. It wondered about changes to roads, sanitation facilities, and the viability of requisite water sources.[37] Finally, in March 1969, the MAPC invited DOC representatives to an "open forum" where townspeople could pose their queries. By this point, the DOC recognized that the MAPC had become the group "who now seems to be most concerned with our plans."[38]

In an apparent misstep for the bid committee, no one from the DOC attended the open forum. The March 1969 gathering represents the first time MAPC meeting minutes recorded outright dissent to the games, with an emphasis placed on the fact that the DOC had not conferred with community members in advance.[39] In addition, attendees drew up a more extensive list of questions for the bidders and further developed reasons for trepidation about hosting the sports contests. If the DOC held events in Evergreen, residents foretold, "instead of the thousands of people we now have, we will have tens of thousands—on a permanent basis." Just as Dittman and his neighbors wished to protect an "established environment," the MAPC predicted that the "Olympics will drastically and permanently alter the total community environment" of Evergreen.[40]

This turn of events drew the attention of Denver's Olympic leaders. Still, they continued to proceed in ways that exacerbated the MAPC's reservations. With the IOC selection drawing near, the DOC had less wiggle room. The bidders needed to select and stick to event sites. Thus, instead of entering a dialogue with worried Evergreen citizens, the DOC attempted to court the "top business leaders" of the mountain town.[41]

At Evergreen's Hiwan Country Club, the DOC hosted reliable growth-machine counterparts. These included the heads of Evergreen's bank and its Chamber of Commerce, the president of its Realtor association, the editor of its newspaper, and locals who worked for Public Service Company and Mountain States Telephone.[42] The Olympic hopefuls sought out Evergreen businesspeople to cultivate Olympic support, which they assumed existed complacently within the town.[43] As one Olympics official described after the country club conference, "we now have a running start on smoothing out a potentially serious public relations problem." This Olympics advocate now foresaw an upcoming face-to-face with the MAPC as an "opportunity to discuss our Olympic objectives in a straightforward and undistorted manner to the mutual benefit of everyone."[44]

But that is not what happened. In May 1969, the MAPC finally submitted its questions to the DOC; as a DOC representative in attendance described, the bidders faced "an inquisition."[45] Indian Hills opponents had spoken of the removal of trees and the loss of "natural beauty." The MAPC similarly asked the DOC to justify removing features such as mountain gulches to make room for highways and parking lots. Yet the grassroots council also went further, explaining that the DOC needed to answer its questions because "Evergreen residents were not consulted" about Olympic event locations in the first place. "Before committing the Evergreen area to the Olympics, did you call an open, public meeting of Evergreen people? If not, why not?" the MAPC badgered DOC officials. The MAPC then baited the Olympic planners, inquiring: "Since the total environment and total community will be affected, and since Evergreen residents were not consulted in any open decision making, and since residents may still feel convinced that the Olympics here means permanent devastation, . . . do you agree that we have a right to oppose the Olympics being held in our area?" Do we have, the MAPC asked, a democratic right to decide if we want to host the Winter Games near our homes?

Here MAPC members introduced a central tenet of the growing anti-Olympics sentiment emerging from Colorado's Front Range. The foothills residents considered aesthetic "devastation" generated against their wills and within their general area as a subversion of their civil liberties.[46] As the environmental scholar James Longhurst demonstrates, anxieties about the adverse environmental effects of industry and development had existed since the Progressive Era. It was an "active definition of citizenship" that made late 1960s and early 1970s environmental activism stand out. During the 1970s, Longhurst claims, the "'green revolution' on the national level . . . was built upon the 'rights revolution' that preceded and accompanied it [at the local level], equipping small, local citizen groups with knowledge of legal rights, media tactics, organization models, and rhetorical approaches."[47]

Jefferson County's foothills environmentalists fit this mold, appropriating a discourse and set of strategies recently developed and employed by far more marginalized protesters. As with Denver's Mexican American and African American citizens, they became a part of a larger, even if diffuse, movement for equal rights. In this case, though, it was a kind of bourgeoisie identity politics that became a thorn in the DOC's side.

After receiving the barrage of questions from antagonistic Evergreen residents, the DOC felt on the defensive. As one DOC official explained, "the time and effort invested in negating their [the MAPC's] influence may prove not only worthwhile but essential."[48] With the IOC selection less than a year away, "there is no question," this same DOC member concluded, that "the Evergreen community relations problem is one of the most serious challenges we have yet faced."[49]

The Denver bid team responded by hiring the trusted public relations specialist William Kostka.[50] Kostka attempted to drown out the opposition by creating a front organization dubbed "Evergreen Citizens for the 1976 Winter Olympics." The DOC dictated when this group elected its chairman, formed subcommittees, held meetings, and outlined agendas for its gatherings.[51] An Evergreen resident named Jack Rouse, who worked for Public Service Company, headed the localized pro-Olympics cause. He presented himself as a "liaison between the DOC and the Evergreen community." In this self-styled role, with the assistance of Owen Ball, the editor of the town's local paper, Rouse published a series of pro-Olympics op-eds arguing for the value of bringing the games to town.[52]

Yet the MAPC flexed its muscle in turn by threatening to "disseminate the information we have to newspapers, Governor Love, and so on, and as a last resort the IOC."[53] This included polling that showed the level of opposition to the Winter Games within Evergreen, along with facts about the area's undependable wintertime snowfall. The MAPC had followed its May 1969 meeting with the DOC by surveying the people of Evergreen and found that 61 percent of respondents did not want to play host to the games. Notably, though, by the time of the above-cited warning, the group already released this result to local and statewide media outlets. Most significant, then, the MAPC proposed sharing its polling and other damaging material with IOC members—the people who the DOC was most concerned about.[54]

Within days of receiving this threat, and with the vote in Amsterdam about five months off, the DOC reached out to the MAPC.[55] In late fall 1969, DOC president Robert Pringle and MAPC members tried to find common ground. Pringle proclaimed that Denver's bid to the IOC could not be altered. The bid books had already been sent to the printing press, and Pringle wanted to avoid "confusion . . . which would hurt the United States." Pringle did acknowledge, however, that event locations could be changed after the IOC awarded the Olympics to Colorado. He also invited one MAPC member to serve on the DOC's board of directors and, according to MAPC meeting minutes, assured Evergreen residents that he realized "holding events where they are not wanted is unwise and defeats the prime purpose of the Games."[56]

But by March 1970, after serving three months as a DOC director, the MAPC's president, Bob Behrens (a University of Denver art professor), concluded that the bidders were not taking the desires of foothills residents seriously enough. With the IOC meeting in Amsterdam within view, he made his thinking known.[57] Meanwhile, months earlier, a DOC representative had hand-delivered Denver's bid books to the IOC president Avery Brundage. In return, Brundage provided the DOC a letter he received from Evergreen citizens expressing disdain toward hosting the Olympics.[58] Afterward, the former Denver mayor and DOC advocate Thomas Currigan cautioned, "I would not be surprised if a group of Evergreen citizens wire the IOC in Amsterdam really cutting us up. . . . We could lose the battle because of Evergreen."[59] The recently appointed USOC president Clifford Buck similarly feared that a last-minute "attack" from Evergreen would "wipe out years of effort."[60]

Accordingly, Pringle and Behrens entered further negotiations. The DOC began with an offer to move ski jumping from Jefferson County. The MAPC responded by agreeing to permit cross-country skiing in Evergreen if the DOC promised to find new locations for the bobsled and luge as well.[61]

Stuck at this impasse, on Earth Day, with the IOC's selection in Amsterdam within weeks, the MAPC threatened again to send the results of its poll to the IOC unless it received "concrete evidence" that the DOC would move all its events from Jefferson County.[62] The MAPC even suggested it would send its own delegation to Amsterdam if need be.[63]

Pringle, McNichols, Love, and MAPC leaders gathered in the governor's office three days later. The Olympic bidders repeated that they could not change the format of Denver's Olympic bid. They also refused to make any written promises regarding specific changes to event locations. Love told the MAPC that it was correct to think ski jumps would be unattractive structures. He acknowledged that the bobsled course would be useless and probably removed after the games were over. Love also admitted he preferred to see cross-country events in Steamboat Springs. Even so, the governor would not provide anything other than verbal assurances that the DOC would look into relocating Olympic venues.[64]

At the end of the meeting, held at the seat of political power in Colorado and with the state's most prominent public officials in the room, the MAPC settled. The residents and the DOC agreed to a written resolution in which the DOC promised to reconsider its sites. The DOC pledged that, if Denver won the games, it would "make a complete and thorough study and review of its present plans." It promised to consider environmental well-being and citizen perspectives in the reassessment. "Based upon factual data of a scientific nature related to the environment and of complete public opinion data," the DOC assured, "the propriety and advisability [of] holding any or several Olympic events in the Evergreen area will be reevaluated." Stressing the importance of cultural and aesthetic concerns, the DOC vowed to "give particular emphasis to residential and recreational characteristics of the community."[65] Significantly, though, Pringle signed this pledge under the condition that the MAPC would wait to reveal its existence until after the IOC's decision. All the while, the DOC had not guaranteed any specific changes.[66]

Indian Hills and then Evergreen residents thought—or at least hoped—they had done enough to protect their highland harbor. As Vance Dittman later expressed to Avery Brundage, "we would have protested [to the IOC] before the award of the Games at Amsterdam, but for the fact that the DOC gave repeated assurances that the naming of these sites was only for the purpose of the bid and that good business required reevaluation—indeed that it was expected." According to Dittman, residents believed "a reevaluation would be made" and so they "needed to have no apprehension about . . . sites being final."[67] Residents of Jeffco's foothills communities knew that the DOC offered areas near their homes for the games, seemed to support Colorado hosting the Olympics, and remained optimistic that relocations away from the county were a formality.

Nonetheless, when the DOC returned from Europe, unsightly and crowd-inducing Olympic events were officially on the docket for Evergreen and areas nearby. And after more than a year of wrangling with the DOC, the people of Indian Hills and Evergreen were organized and prepared to act. On 4 June 1970, the MAPC issued an invitation through Evergreen's newspaper calling for another open forum on the Olympics with DOC members present. As part of this press release, the MAPC published a full copy of the April 1970 resolution signed by Pringle.[68] The following week, as one source described of the coming meeting, "plans were formulated for opposition."[69] Then, on 11 June, the day of the gathering, the local newspaper promoted the MAPC's event with a map displaying the DOC's Olympic plans for Evergreen on its front page. "Have your say, Olympics hearing Thursday," the headline read.[70] That evening, about 700 people crammed into the Evergreen High School gymnasium. Every seat was taken.[71]

The MAPC recorded most of the meeting with an audio reel. Three DOC members attended, including Pringle and the head of the Site Selection Committee, George Robinson. Forty-four people can be heard speaking, and about 80 percent declared disapproval of Olympic events taking place in the Evergreen region.[72] The speakers cited practical concerns, such as limited snowfall and a lack of water for artificial snowmaking. Many expressed anxieties about transporting large crowds. Some commented that the luge, bobsled, and ski jump would become "white elephants." Others noted the prospect of raised taxes due to construction and maintenance costs. Many Jefferson County inhabitants expressed concerns about a loss of plants and wildlife and the risk of soil erosion.[73]

However, another dominant theme expressed by the exurbanites was that the Olympics would ruin their community's relaxed and picturesque ethos. "We just don't want the Olympics to be in the middle of our garden," one citizen proclaimed.[74] Another reiterated, "I chose to live in Evergreen because of the fresh mountain air, meadows, the flowers, the trees," elements with which "the congestion caused by the Olympics would be completely incompatible."[75] "The Front Range west of Denver is unique," a third inhabitant asserted; "special consideration has to be given to the future development of this area so that it maintains its present aesthetic value."[76] As Doug Jones, the MAPC's president at this time, acknowledged days before, much of Evergreen's Olympic objections came "strictly from an [a]esthetic point of view."[77]

Figure 6.1. June 1970. The MAPC's president, Doug Jones, stands at the podium as DOC members Robert Pringle and George Robinson sit before a packed gymnasium at Evergreen High School, with many residents expressing displeasure at events being planned for or near to their town. Photo by Dick Davis via Denver Public Library, Western History Collection, WH2129-2018-368.

On top of this, at the meeting, the residents began to employ their aesthetics-based form of middle-class environmentalism to matters beyond the Olympic Games. Some even began to pit themselves squarely against Governor Love's most successful agenda item: selling Colorado. As George Vardaman of Indian Hills explained at the forum: "To come to the heart of the matter, Evergreen and Indian Hills are beautiful residential communities, not mountain tourist traps, and most of the residents of these communities have no desire to live in tourist traps." When another local man, Stan Deever, stood to announce he opposed the games in Evergreen, he made the connection between the event and Love's pro-growth policies even more directly. Deever carried a copy of the *Wall Street Journal*, which, he alleged, contained an advertisement paid for by "the people in our state government trying to sell Colorado to industry." The promotion depicted Colorado as an ideal area for a "growing business." "One of the drawing cards used in this ad," Deever highlighted, "is the selection of Denver as the United States' candidate for the Olympics." The "Olympics," Deever reasoned, "is only a part of the desire by a powerful group of persons for an increased exploitation and commercialization in this area."[78] This second MAPC forum thus became a platform for asserting Love's and others' most prominent political project ought to be, on certain occasions, reined in.

*   *   *

To set boundaries for when and where to sell Colorado, Jefferson County Olympics challengers began to prioritize environmentalism as well. The story of Vance Dittman exemplifies this progression. He spoke at the MAPC's June gathering, renewing his demand that Olympic events be moved. For Dittman, the bobsled and luge courses became critical. The DOC did not schedule either event at the locations that Dittman and fellow Indian Hills residents had agreed on. Instead of Independence Mountain and O'Fallon Park, the DOC planned to build structures in and around Pence Park. As one source recounts, "the DOC had in effect broken its word," and as a result the bobsled run would now travel along a portion of Dittman's property.[79]

With the bobsled threatening to cast shade on Sky Meadow, Dittman expanded his thinking about the games and development in general. At the Evergreen High School forum, he made increased taxes his major complaint.[80] Yet just a month and a half prior, millions of Americans demonstrated during the first Earth Day. In Denver, around 5,000 people joined a teach-in at Currigan Convention Center.[81] Moreover, at the June gathering, many of Dittman's neighbors articulated a salient, albeit regional, environmental consciousness. It was also around this same time that Dittman exchanged notes with a University of Denver coworker, Moras Shubert. In a letter to the DOC that he shared with Dittman, Shubert, a biologist, spelled out possible ecological consequences connected to hosting the Olympics in Evergreen. Shubert predicted that obtaining enough water to cover cross-country courses with artificial snow and to ice the luge and bobsled runs would "endanger the whole ecological nature of the area."[82]

At this point, Vance Dittman first placed the term "ecology" in his Olympics-related writing. After winning the bid, the DOC asked the Denver Research Institute to conduct a second study of its plans and make organizational recommendations. Dittman wrote to the DRI to confirm proper deliberations. He advised DRI researchers to account for "personal and financial damage," the "peace and quiet" that will be "destroyed," and the "marks on our landscape which will be unsightly." At the same instance, he added, "perhaps, most important of all," the study needed to consider "permanent injury to the ecology." "The ecology of the foothills is one of delicate balances," Dittman explained. "Once the trees, ground cover, and top soil are destroyed, or seriously disturbed, recovery is a matter of centuries, not merely a few years."[83] For Dittman, preserving his property's milieu and defending its ecological well-being became linked.

Many of Dittman's neighbors imbibed this perspective. In the summer of 1970, led by Dittman, thirteen Jefferson County residents, the majority from Indian Hills and Evergreen, established a new organization, Protect Our Mountain Environment (POME).[84] In October 1970, POME's members passed their first anti-Olympics resolution. It cited concerns related to a lack of road access and parking facilities, along with a high probability of minimal snowfall during the games. However, it also claimed the Olympics would cause deforestation and soil erosion in addition to water and air pollution. Where once diminished property values and aesthetic damage had been the fulcrum, ecological concerns now justified POME's request that Nordic events, bobsled, and luge not be staged in "Indian Hills[,] . . . Evergreen, and adjacent areas."[85]

Although POME demonstrated a willingness to use the language of ecology, it aimed more fundamentally to maintain a particular social setting. POME's executive board perhaps put it best when justifying the group's financial support of the upscale Colorado Philharmonic, which performed in Evergreen. POME fought foremost on behalf of a "cultural environment," not strictly a tangible one.[86]

As George Vardaman, an original POME member, expressed: "We in Evergreen [and] Indian Hills have deep and abiding human and social concerns."[87] Dittman similarly proclaimed to the head of the DOC's Planning Commission, Beatrice Willard, an alpine botanist herself, that POME opposed the Olympics "because of the social factors involved."[88] When POME passed a second anti-Olympics resolution in January 1971, it again warned of ecological damages. But POME also emphasized that the ruin of natural scenery especially would "degrade the whole community as a place to live." As POME's members described, holding the Olympics "in residential areas" would not just be "inconsistent with the broader concepts of the preservation of the environment"; it was also "detrimental to our preferred way of life."[89]

POME described the "way of life" or "cultural environment" to which it aspired in detail. The mountains of Jefferson County, the group explained, had "become a refuge for retired people and young families who did not want a city life for their children. . . . The areas in question, with the exception of Evergreen, have no beer or liquor outlet, nor commercial areas, but they do have schools, churches and church camps, and a beautiful setting."[90] POME thus referred to a communal sensibility, one resistant to more people, new business ventures, and large-scale facilities, though consisting of wholesome church camps and peaceful retirement homes, set in nature and apart from the drudgery of the city.[91]

By fighting to protect these social features, foothills dwellers purposely isolated themselves. According to the MAPC, single-family homes were all that the land in and around Evergreen could support. Yet as one MAPC representative acknowledged, taking this position facilitated planning and zoning policies that made it so "only the rich can live here."[92] The chairman of the Jefferson County Board of Commissioners likewise confessed that by instituting stricter zoning regulations, such as those recommended by both the MAPC and POME, "we know we're limiting the ability of the average wage earner to buy property in the mountains."[93] The MAPC's and POME's opposition to the Olympics and their broader environmentalism rested on an image that ensured their neighborhoods would remain firmly middle- and upper-class.

POME's membership list indicated as much. By the end of 1970, 476 people enlisted in the Dittman-led organization. Most lived in Indian Hills and Evergreen and identified with middle- to upper-class professions. POME's membership consisted of artists, teachers, doctors, dentists, nurses, engineers, geologists, physicists, bankers, corporation executives, accountants, lawyers, technicians, builders, and airline pilots, as well as naturalists and conservationists.[94]

Following a tactic already employed by the MAPC, these foothills inhabitants also turned to the discourse of citizen rights. As Vance Dittman vowed in December 1970, "the opposition of POME to holding the Nordic Events of the 1976 Winter Olympics in the Indian Hills–Evergreen area is based upon one fundamental approach." This "approach" had less to do with ecological awareness. Instead, Dittman declared, "citizens of the area had nothing to do with the invitation nor with the decision to hold NORDICS here. Their opinion was never asked. They never voted in any way on the question."[95] The roots of POME's opposition, Dittman claimed, resided in the fact that Olympic planners overrode its right to determine how its own town gets developed.

When it seemed helpful, POME would turn to "technical" matters, such as soil erosion, water sanitation, or the effects of downed trees. But at other times, POME abandoned these types of issues. As Longhurst observes, the "recurring emphasis on the rights and responsibilities of citizenship" often made "the new modern environmental movement" seem "not as environmental as one might expect."[96] At one point, Dittman bluntly informed Governor Love: "Any question of the physical suitability of these [Olympic] sites is entirely irrelevant." "The real issue," Dittman penned, was that "we, as citizens of Colorado . . . appeal to you as Governor." POME's secretary, Jean Gravell, shared this outlook, asserting that, because POME believed "human environmental issues come first," the group took the "stand that technical feasibility . . . is not the right measurement."[97] The gauge that mattered most to POME's members was their own preferences.[98]

Significantly, however, POME often relied on the cultural value of unobstructed naturalistic views to provide substance to the notion that its rights were being violated. POME expressed this by speaking as if it owned the picturesque features around it, referring to the "destruction" or "ruining" of "our hills and valleys and mountain peaks," "our landscape," and "our scenery."[99] The group did not adopt the name Protect *the* Mountain Environment but instead chose Protect *Our* Mountain Environment. In the minds of these residents, the aesthetic sights available from their properties and the spaciousness of their neighborhoods belonged to them.

This became evident in POME's response to a report submitted by the US Bureau of Outdoor Recreation to the United States Congress, which debated whether to subsidize the DOC. The bureau's report concluded that the Olympic Games would not, in the long run, increase the rate of growth and environmental damage in Jefferson County.[100] It even speculated that "land use decisions as they relate to the Olympics and afterwards could be environmentally beneficial in the long range." The changes POME claimed the Olympics would facilitate seemed inevitable, and if properly initiated, Olympic developments could perhaps minimize the damage.[101]

In reply, POME claimed that the Bureau of Outdoor Recreation report possessed "important inaccuracies and omissions and a general lack of depth." Nevertheless, POME did not question many of the bureau's main assertions. Rather, for POME, drawing comparisons to anticipated rates of development exposed a misunderstanding of the stakes. POME claimed that what really mattered was that, along with "water rights" and "rights from freedom from trespass," the DOC "proposes to deprive adjoining landowners of their property rights to the [a]esthetic values of their land."[102]

In late June 1972, the presence of this position surfaced again. Approximately 300 townspeople gathered once more at Evergreen High School to make their voices heard before members of the DOC. The issue at hand was the DOC's newest plans for ski jumping, bobsled, and luge facilities. Olympic organizers now hoped to see the events at Doublehead Mountain in Jefferson County, about an eight-mile drive from Indian Hills. The developer who owned the area saw an opportunity to benefit from the construction of adjoining restaurants, convenience stores, hotels, and other amenities and so offered its deed to the City and County of Denver. For its part, the DOC was still trying to keep events as close to Denver as possible.[103] At the meeting, POME's Jean Gravell railed against the DOC's newest plans, proclaiming:

Figure 6.2. August 1972. Protesters picket a DOC meeting in Denver, expressing opposition to Olympic events being held in Jefferson County. *Denver Post* via Getty Images.

"The DOC seeks to deprive us of the valuable . . . rights of quiet enjoyment of our property, freedom from encroachment by actual trespass[,] . . . and of the right to aesthetic satisfaction."[104] Gravell thus drew attention to the infringement of her presumed right to enjoy subjective experiences made possible through undeveloped lands in her home's proximity.[105]

Throughout the Olympic debate, foothills environmentalists continued to point to ecological issues and recruit other sympathetic organizations.[106] Still, the attention to ecology and coordination with other environmentalist groups carried an air of calculation. Had the well-to-do advocates from the foothills based their arguments on local aesthetic rights alone, they would have been less effective. It would have left minimal reasons for those outside the Front Range to join the cause. Furthermore, as the legal scholar Sheldon Steinbacht noted in 1970, zoning ordinances in most states "either recognized aesthetics by aligning it with an expansion of traditional notions of public welfare, or they have rejected it outright." When property owners raised the prospect of aesthetic-related injuries, the law treated such claims as valid, Steinbacht clarified, only if they "could be fitted in one of the traditional molds that encompassed public health, safety, [or] morals."[107] To protect the cultural capital accrued through undeveloped mountains, it helped to underscore complementary harms such as air pollution, water contamination, and soil erosion.

It is also worth reemphasizing that neither the MAPC nor POME opposed the Olympics coming to Colorado, at least not officially until September 1972, and both groups took this stance for the same reason they turned to ecology: it appeared to be the surest way to keep the games away from their hometowns.[108] Tellingly, the DOC would come to select an undeveloped site near Vail (Beaver Creek) under consideration to become a wilderness preserve for Alpine skiing. The purported environmentalists from Indian Hills and Evergreen did not oppose that Olympic offering. Moreover, due to poor winter conditions, the DOC eventually moved cross-country events to Steamboat Springs, and the same Bureau of Outdoor Recreation report that downplayed the long-term environmental damage caused by events in Evergreen acknowledged that the "stadium facilities and roads from Steamboat Springs to the biathlon and Nordic events would require almost complete alterations . . . [and] existing wildlife patterns would likely be disrupted."[109] Despite this finding, foothills environmentalists also did not object to events being held at Steamboat.

In late spring 1972, POME assisted in disseminating petitions to qualify the measure to bar state money being spent on the Olympics. But even then, whenever the group behind the petition drive directed discussions beyond impacts to the Front Range, the middle-class environmentalists preferred to exit the room.[110] Instead of a movement sparked by genuine concern for ecology or broader state-wide consequences, Indian Hills and Evergreen anti-Olympics environmentalists remained narrowly focused on their individual right to personal aesthetic appreciation.

The MAPC's and POME's middle-class environmentalism was far from the only reason Coloradans voted to banish the Olympics. The foothills-born grassroots undertaking could not have caused that result on its own. However, it became one of the essential pieces. Dittman, POME, and Evergreen garnered extensive media coverage, including in nationally distributed publications such as *Newsweek* and *Sports Illustrated*.[111] For many Coloradans, excessive costs and DOC dishonesty became the primary motives for wanting to nix the games. Yet concerns about environmental damage brought the issue to the forefront for many. As one leading anti-Olympics organizer recalled, "the environment is what brought it up."[112]

A large number of (presumably white) Centennial State citizens were moved by the political activism emanating from the mountains, more so—it should be emphasized—than within the city. It seemed that beautiful landscapes for white middle-class homeowners carried greater import than fair housing for the racialized poor. Thus, to an even greater extent than Brown and Black Denverites, the foothills environmentalists provided weaponry to other activists with Olympic bones to pick.

CHAPTER 7

A Liberal Tax Revolt and the Public Relations Battle

Two Democratic Colorado House representatives, Richard Lamm and Robert Jackson, became the first major figures to suggest state authorities reject the Denver Olympics outright. When the DOC's Olympic bid began to take form, they were both newly elected and thus less likely to be entangled with the state's century-old growth network. Indeed, the duo began to question the social and economic viability of investing in the Winter Games and, ultimately, tourist promotion and growth in general.

Before this, DOC leaders could barely imagine their fellow citizens working to drive out the games. Yet challengers in Denver, in the foothills, and now within the General Assembly stirred doubt. The DOC could not ignore that pressure had mounted. In response, it began an aggressive attempt to shape the image of the games in the public sphere.[1] However, when an investigation undertaken by the *Rocky Mountain News* disclosed several problematic aspects to the DOC's original proposal, it legitimized many of the fears voiced by Lamm and Jackson and further undermined the credibility of Denver's Olympic organizers. The political winds surrounding Colorado's metaphorical Olympic flames were becoming unsettled.

Richard Lamm moved to south-central Denver in 1961, where he began working as an accountant and eventually became a professor at the University of Denver's law school. By 1966, at the age of thirty-one, his district elected him to the Colorado House. Robert Jackson developed and managed car dealerships in Pueblo, about 150 miles south of Denver. In 1966, at the age of forty, his constituents sent him to the state legislature as well.[2]

During their first year in office, both freshman lawmakers supported bringing the Olympics to Colorado, voting in favor of a resolution to ask the United States Olympic Committee to advance Denver's bid. The measure passed unanimously and without discussion. Most of those working in the statehouse, including Lamm and Jackson, did not know the details of the DOC's proposal. As Lamm recalled, in that moment the prospect of holding the Olympics in Colorado seemed to him like "a great civic coupe."[3]

Yet Lamm and Jackson soon changed their views on Denver '76. With backgrounds in law, accounting, and business management, Lamm and Jackson took positions on Colorado's Audit Committee. There they began researching how much money the state should expect to spend on the games. Together they learned that no one—not even the DOC—knew how much the event would cost or how it would be paid for. The two legislators then explored the budgets of other recent Winter Olympic festivals. It was a "quite sobering experience," Lamm reflected decades later, realizing Colorado had written the DOC a "blank check" for something far more expensive than imagined.[4]

Between the DOC's successful bids to the USOC and the IOC, from January 1968 to May 1970, Lamm and Jackson placed their Olympic concerns on the back burner. Lamm, in fact, embarked on a separate and equally prickly issue: proposing and passing the nation's first state-level liberalized abortion law. Meanwhile, the DOC merely bid for the games. Paying to host the Olympics was not a problem yet. Nevertheless, when the IOC awarded the Olympics to Denver, the check Lamm and Jackson feared writing appeared headed to the DOC's coffers.

Following the DOC's May 1970 victory, the emerging politicians thus moved to thrust their worries about Olympic spending into the open. In January 1971, the DOC prepared to speak before Colorado's Joint Budget Committee (JBC). The Olympic organizers intended to offer justification for a recent $310,000 request from the state. Beforehand, Lamm reached out to JBC members and passed along information about the Olympics' probable price tag. Lamm and Jackson hoped that, upon seeing this material, they too would realize that the DOC was "lowballing" expenses.[5]

The Republican lawmaker Joe Shoemaker, in particular, ran with the baton. The DOC came to the meeting with a well-rehearsed presentation, but Shoemaker repeatedly interrupted it. How much money would the DOC need exactly? What would it spend the money on? Where precisely would requisite financial supplies come from? Shoemaker asked for specifics, and DOC members proved unable to provide them. The only solid figures the DOC put forward were the same ones it had been citing since 1967, numbers that suspiciously mirrored those of the 1960 Squaw Valley Games.[6]

At this time, as the DOC technical director Ted Farwell wrote in a letter to the DOC board, the organizers had begun to identify new sites "for illustrative purposes," but "no 'final site selection' had been made."[7] The DOC's original event sites remained unviable, and it still needed to evaluate new locations farther west, gain IOC approval, and hire engineers to study construction prospects. The organizers were far from ready to provide conclusive estimates.[8] Months after the presentation to the JBC, following a gathering between the DOC and Colorado's representatives in Washington, DC, one of Mayor William McNichols's top advisers confirmed the reality, informing his boss that several "contradictions and changing of figures" led him to conclude that "the DOC still does not have a valid handle on revenues and cost."[9] As Lamm and Jackson recognized, the DOC did not know how much the Denver Olympics would go for or how exactly the event would be funded.

In addition, the DOC wanted to keep inevitable event site changes— along with the vagueness and malleability of the situation—hidden from the International Olympic Committee. As a subsequent DOC "Weekly Staff Report" noted, at the JBC hearing the "presence of the press required restraint in revealing some of the information of our proposed planning."[10] Farwell later explained how "premature publicity" pertaining to new event locations "could seriously affect our ability to get a proper job done with the IOC."[11] The DOC had stood answerless and tongue-tied.

In response, the JBC recommended the state withhold financial support for the time being. Shoemaker explained the decision by observing, "I don't think the homework has really been done in terms of funding." Conceding that the Colorado legislature previously provided the DOC a "blank check," Shoemaker counseled that "you've reached the point in time where it's got to be done according to the same (budget request) standards we apply to everyone else."[12] As JBC chairman, the Republican representative Harry M. Locke wrote to Richard Olson three days later: "The committee wants to be completely aware now, of all commitments made by the Olympic Commission and of the total costs and funding requirements." Attached to this letter, Locke included a list of twenty-three questions that the JBC instructed the DOC to answer before it would recommend any more Olympic outlays.[13]

Significantly, this confrontation between the JBC and DOC did more than pause state funding. It gave the public cause to doubt the veracity of the DOC's cost estimates.[14] Moreover, for Lamm and Jackson, the hearing served as the first shot in a larger anti-Olympics attack. One week later, with uncertainty regarding the DOC's projections now in focus, Jackson announced that he planned to introduce a bill to bar state funds from going to the DOC for good. Jackson alleged that the $310,000 the DOC asked for was "a small part of the iceberg" and, he reasoned, "I can't see putting money

Figure 7.1. September 1972. Richard Lamm, a staunch opponent, debates DOC representative Eric Auer on the merits of hosting the Olympics. Photo by Bill Peters/*Denver Post* via Getty Images.

into a sport [such as Olympic events] . . . when there are higher priorities such as education, environmental protection, and benefits to the elderly." Jackson proclaimed that "if we're going to change our minds, this is the time to do it."[15] A few days later, Lamm stated his support of Jackson, repeating that the Denver Olympics would not be worth the cost to Colorado taxpayers.[16] "Colorado, painfully, cannot afford to host the 1976 Olympics," Lamm would later describe. "We cannot afford to do justice to our schools, to our institutions, to our many pressing needs, and as we become aware of the vast financial commitment . . . we see increasingly that we do not have the will or the tax base." Lamm warned, "we are a small state, already on the verge of a tax payer revolt."[17]

In the late 1970s, conservative activists and corporate stakeholders fought for reductions in marginal income and commercial property tax rates, as well as slashes to taxes for individual property holders. Buoyed by increased lobbying, political donations, and other methods learned from

1960s social movements, these advocates relied on discourses of freedom, participatory democracy, and patriotic dissent. Yet through the same rhetoric, some of the earliest "tax revolt" forces sought reform in the name of income redistribution, with the goal of reducing charges levied upon the average homeowner.[18] Similarly, Lamm's and Jackson's professed focus was to ensure tax dollars be properly collected and equitably spent, not irresponsibly siphoned away toward special interests. Thus, they turned against the Olympics through historically tinged claims of unfair taxation without representation.

Although Lamm and Jackson zeroed in on costs and smart spending, they also connected their anti-Olympics argument to environmental damage. In contrast, while their cause overlapped with white middle-class exurbanites, they never explicitly aligned with Brown and Black housing activists and organizers. Lamm represented one area of the city, and later he and anti-Olympics allies would reference the housing plight in Denver as evidence for the wastefulness inherent in holding the games. Still, in interviews for this book, Lamm expressed no recollection of Citizens Interested in an Equitable Olympics or the involvement of fellow officeholders Elvin Caldwell and Betty Benavidez.[19] Lamm and Jackson were less attuned to matters of affordable housing, de facto segregation, and overall neglect in the city than to pleas for quality of life echoing down from the foothills along the Front Range.

Lamm specifically was inclined to subscribe to middle-class environmentalist perspectives. As early as 1963, he had become enamored with the notion of "carrying capacity." While Governor Love began to devise his Sell Colorado program, Lamm editorialized in an essay that population growth represented America's and the world's "ultimate problem." The "belief that science can support unlimited population," Lamm cautioned, "rests on faith, not reason."[20] Furthermore, Lamm easily connected his anxieties about a world lacking essential resources to his affinity for the mountains and outdoor recreation. He had moved to Colorado after becoming captivated by the Rockies during a stint in the United States Army. A longtime member of the Colorado Open Space Council and an enthusiastic outdoorsman himself, like many Indian Hills and Evergreen residents, he became a permanent Centennial State tourist, a "lifestyle refugee."[21] He thus made sure to add in his essay about the "ultimate problem" that "recreational potential will be destroyed long before our earth's capacity to provide life is exhausted." The "matter of spiritual survival will clearly be fought long before the one for bodily survival," Lamm forecasted. "Everyone will feel the effects of crowded beaches, parks, and recreational areas." Such a view helps explain Lamm's efforts to remove billboards on state roadways and his opposition to the construction of the state's generally popular Interstate 70.[22]

Indeed, Lamm readily received anti-Olympics complaints from his law school colleague Vance Dittman. Lamm joined the school's faculty in 1969, the same year Dittman retired. Lamm took over some of Dittman's classes. According to Protect Our Mountain Environment records, during Lamm's first semester on campus, before Denver even won hosting rights, he and Dittman conferred about their "mutual concern re DOC."[23] As Lamm remembers, Dittman deserved the credit for challenging "the idea that this [the Olympics] was going to be a good thing for us growth-wise." He recalled, "Dittman definitely . . . drew a picture . . . [of] how the luge and the bobsled run would snake down those mountains and cut big scars visible from the highways."[24]

Therefore, along with objecting to costs, Lamm began to oppose the Olympics because it involved "taking good land and turning it into parking lots."[25] "There are an awful lot of us," Lamm would decry, "who don't like seeing our Garden of Eden turned into a commercial playground."[26] As the vote on the anti-Olympics ballot measure neared, repeating ideas he had held for years, Lamm further defended his anti-Olympics stance. "Colorado is under intense and growing development pressure," he proclaimed, "[and] we are becoming painfully aware that our limited water and fragile ecosystem dictate that we have a finite carrying capacity. We are paving over, plowing under and polluting Colorado at an accelerating rate; farm and open space, fishing streams and wildlife, solitude and serenity are all disappearing under the onslaught of development."[27] Jackson likewise attested: "We find these days it's in our interest to regulate growth or even stop it. We no longer think in terms of something being better just because it's bigger."[28] "Our state is attractive to us . . . because we have some uncluttered vistas and pretty streams," Jackson went on. "We should stop and think whether we want to change the open aspect of our environment here. I don't think we want to."[29]

According to Lamm, as the Olympic debate roiled in Indian Hills and Evergreen, he and Dittman remained "in very close contact."[30] It was probably no coincidence that, the same day Jackson put forth his bill to halt spending on the Winter Games, Protect Our Mountain Environment passed its own resolution asking the state legislature to cut off state funds until the DOC removed Olympic events from the Front Range.[31] Nonetheless, in a February 1972 speech, Lamm admitted that "the direct environmental abuse [of the Olympics] will be minimal. It is the financial abuse which was originally and remains now our principal question and objection." Lamm claimed his main goal was to "build fiscal sanity."[32] "We're laying off people at the state hospital and were going to spend $6,000,000 on an ice-skating rink," the representative lamented; "this is absurd."[33] Even so, middle-class environmentalism remained something Lamm and Jackson understood and appreciated, and it supplemented their main point. Committing state money to the Olympics was ill-advised.

Despite their alliance with the environmentally alarmed, it probably seemed initially that Lamm and Jackson were the underdogs. In February 1971, they proposed their bill to prevent Colorado from funding the Denver Games.[34] It never got out of the House State Affairs Committee. A few weeks later, they asked the Denver City Council to allow residents to vote on whether to host the games. This also went nowhere. The council president declared that the request made him "embarrassed for the citizens of Denver and Colorado." A fellow councilmember said that he "couldn't support such a referendum because the Olympics are the greatest thing that ever happened to Denver."[35]

Several Democrats in the Colorado House began to follow Lamm's and Jackson's lead, making Olympic spending a somewhat partisan issue and the more liberal caucus the frugal one. But most of Colorado's political leadership had no desire to let the Winter Games slip through their grasp. In April 1971, Lamm and Jackson presented what they must have known would be a series of symbolic amendments to the state's annual appropriations bill. One meant to stop state funding of the DOC for the current year. Another set a spending limit, making money allocated in the current bill the last of the state's Olympic investment. A third gave the state power to review and sanction all Olympic expenditures. None of the amendments passed.[36]

The popular press consistently condemned Lamm and Jackson as well, portraying them as baseless political agitators. After the two representatives came out against the games at the start of 1971, the *Denver Post*, taking shots at CIEO, POME, and Jackson, asserted that the "1976 Winter Olympics have been awarded to Denver and it is inconceivable that the community would allow that fact to be negated." The *Post* continued: the "award of the prestigious event . . . looms large in the history of the city and state . . . [and] it should not suffer lack of support merely because it provides a convenient lever for some to use in an effort to pry concessions for their interests." "To follow Jackson's advice," the paper professed, "would be a disastrous and stupid mistake."[37]

After Lamm and Jackson went to the Denver City Council, the *Rocky*

Mountain News especially struck back. "The almost unbelievable flap thrown up by a handful of state legislators . . . to renege on Denver's successful bid for the 1976 Olympics is the rawest kind of political pandering," the newspaper exclaimed. "We certainly hope that [the] City Council ignores that ridiculous demand." Acknowledging criticisms about costs and environmental damage, the *Rocky* retorted: "We don't buy [into] either [issue]. . . . Tourism is the state's second biggest cash crop. To hold off priming the pump of attraction would be like a beet farmer not fertilizing his field." "The environmental pitch," the paper went on, "is almost too ridiculous to take seriously."[38] The *Rocky* concluded in a separate piece, again aimed at Jackson: "We . . . trust that other legislators with less concern for political grandstanding will take a look at the facts, weigh the probabilities and possibilities, and then act without [a] closed mind, such as Jackson exhibits."[39] For the moment, the DOC could safely assume Denver's most widely read media outlets remained in its corner.

However, for Lamm and Jackson, there were incentives for standing up to the DOC and other Olympics boosters. At the start of their anti-Olympics campaign, as Lamm recalled, "we were sort of civic traitors. . . . This was like taking on motherhood."[40] They took a position that left them seemingly ostracized. Still, by taking such an apparently risky stance, the young politicians entered Colorado's political theater as main players. Just as well, they had seen the Doc's specious plans and researched Olympic costs. They knew the Olympic organizers and the growth regime that underwrote them were lying and thus vulnerable.

Therefore, the two legislators stayed on the offensive, fighting not only the games but also Colorado's political leadership. In late February 1971, the DOC returned to the Capitol to update a joint session of the Colorado House and Senate on its plans. The group went in with the intention of emphasizing that there could be no question on whether Denver should host the Olympics.[41] "We have the games for 1976," the DOC's chairman of finance and business relations avowed. "There's no moral or proper way that this fact can be reversed or refuted. . . . Our job now—yours and mine—is to stage these games the best way possible."[42]

Jackson listened and remained incredulous. "We deserve better," he told the DOC.[43] Jackson maintained, "I don't think anyone knows how much the Olympics will cost and I'm certain nobody knows exactly where the money's coming from." Similarly, Lamm argued, that when he and Jackson voted in favor of the Olympics in 1967, "we had no idea what it was going to cost." "If wisdom comes late," Lamm reflected, "that doesn't mean reject it."[44] Several other representatives also began to speak along these lines. According to Lamm's and Jackson's fellow House Democrat Wayne Knox, the DOC's presentation was nothing but "one hour of propaganda."[45]

Later in the spring, DOC members provided their most in-depth analysis of Olympic costs and revenues to date, presenting the information before a select legislative committee formed to study Olympic spending. The DOC finally provided hard numbers, projecting expenses between $18 million and $25 million. In the same instance, though, the organizers admitted that there remained many "unknowns." These included the number of people the DOC would employ, transportation requirements, expenses for housing and feeding the athletes and press, which facilities would be used, and at what rates.[46] The DOC still did not know where it would hold many events.[47]

The group of officeholders examining the approximated data decided the state should provide the $310,000 that the organizers had asked for but then set a cap of $600,000 for all future state spending. The committee specified as well that the money should be provided only for "planning and organizational tasks." It did not want state funds "used for construction of facilities or even structural planning."[48]

Yet even this left Lamm and Jackson unsatisfied. Jackson worked as a member of the group studying the DOC's budget and authored a dissenting view. He based his stance on irresponsible spending, unjust taxation, and environmental consequences. Jackson claimed it was "unreasonable to believe that, even with the best of controls, the eventual expenditure for the games has much of a chance of being under [a] $20 million net tax burden." He pointed out that although "the Denver Organizing Committee indicated an estimated range of expenditures . . . the same document has so many items specified as 'unknowns' as to make the estimates meaningless." Aware of the funding history for the 1960 Squaw Valley Olympics, Jackson predicted that in a few years Colorado would face "an 'emergency request' in order to 'save the games.'" With the event a year or two away, Jackson forewarned, policy makers would have no choice but to acquiesce. To prevent such a scenario, Jackson reiterated his demand to stop state funding straightaway. He implored that this was the right thing to do for everyday citizens. "The Olympics are a commercial enterprise," Jackson asserted. "As such they should not be a tax burden to the people of the State of Colorado."[49]

Though high costs and the misuse of taxes remained the major themes, middle-class environmentalism continued to prove a useful and revealing aspect of Lamm's and Jackson's argument. When penning his dissent, Jackson added that "environmental damage caused by an acceleration of

Figure 7.2. March 1972. Democratic Colorado House representative Robert Jackson gives a speech against Denver hosting the Olympics. Photo by John Beard / *Denver Post* via Getty Images.

uncontrolled growth throughout the state" had not been given enough attention by his fellow committee members. The committee recommended the state's Land Use Commission participate in site selections.[50] Nonetheless, Jackson avowed, if Denver holds the Olympics, "at no time in the history of this state will we have such a TV spectacular which will 'sell Colorado.'"[51] In a different context, Jackson's words could have been read as a reason for hosting the games. The purpose of the DOC and its allies was to sell Colorado. But for Jackson, selling Colorado became a point of criticism made against hosting the sports spectacle. The politics of growth appeared to be shifting—with Lamm and Jackson in the vanguard by virtue of their Olympics resistance.

The idea that Coloradans would question the DOC's pro-growth intentions shocked Olympics proponents. "Are these people against progress?" Governor Love asked in jest. "Do they want us to live in pup tents and eat organic food?"[52] However, after the emergence of Lamm and Jackson, as one DOC member put it, Denver's Olympic planners felt "constantly under attack" from "Evergreen, minorities . . . [, and] the Joint Budget Committee."[53] The organizers finally realized that they had to direct their public relations assets not only at the IOC but also toward Centennial State citizens.

The DOC did this in numerous ways. In response to Lamm and Jackson, in April 1971 it helped create House Bill 1095. At first sight, the bill ensured public oversight of Olympic spending. It tasked a committee of legislators, representatives of diverse constituencies, and technical experts with approving all DOC designs involving state funds. The bill's first draft stipulated that the Speaker of the House and president of the Senate would select six state policy makers to serve in this capacity. Nevertheless, the final version limited such representation to three members of the Colorado legislature chosen by Governor Love. After the bill passed, Love selected people he knew supported hosting the games and, as it turned out, rarely attended the group's meetings. Love also chose ski industry investors, business executives, and an environmentalist who advised the DOC as citizen delegates.[54] Unlike Lamm's and Jackson's prior attempt to mandate state oversight, this is best understood as a public relations maneuver meant to feign independent evaluation of DOC decisions. It was, in other words, another instance of powerful private actors working with elected officials to circumvent genuine citizen engagement and sanction a pro-growth project.

In attempting to appease environmentalists, the DOC followed a similar strategy, creating what it called the "Planning Commission." This group included nine members from governmental bodies and nine "experts" with specialties in architecture, civil engineering, landscape development, and ecology. The unit claimed to serve as a "community representative," providing "independent review" "to assure that the Denver Olympic Committee incorporates ecology in all planning."[55] Yet the DOC attempted to ensure that the commission's conclusions aligned with its own. As DOC meeting minutes recount, "members of the Planning Commission should be carefully screened, lest it become necessary for the [DOC] Board to override" the commission's "positions."[56] As with the oversight of state spending, the DOC intended for the Planning Commission to provide public relations protection and a rubber stamp.[57]

Interestingly, though, the DOC and the Planning Commission would sometimes take divergent views. The commission pushed DOC leadership to allow it to make its methods and findings public and to meet with Olympics objectors.[58] The commission's leader, Beatrice Willard, would also write the DOC president Robert Pringle to complain that the DOC was not permitting her team to provide sufficient input into DOC decisions. Willard warned Pringle that, if the DOC did not genuinely include the Planning Commission, members would resign.[59] Several did exactly that after the DOC selected Beaver Creek, near Vail, to host the Alpine races.[60] The commission preferred Mount Catamount near Steamboat Springs as the revised location for the Alpine events and had placed Beaver Creek fifth on a list of five options.[61]

On top of all this, while the DOC tried to appear responsive to citizen concerns, the organization ultimately kept its negotiations and decisions hidden. At the beginning of February 1971, Lamm asked for admittance to DOC board meetings. But the DOC refused him—and anyone else— entry. To justify this decision, the legal consultant Richard Davis internally warned: "From the policy standpoint . . . there have been many confidential and delicate matters discussed at meetings . . . especially including relationships with the IOC and USOC, and the financial support of private citizens and organizations."[62] George Robinson added that, "until decisions are made on sites, discussions should be carefully guarded."[63] The DOC clearly saw secrecy as in its self-interest.

Meanwhile, the organizers also began working more closely with the press to create pro-Olympics narratives for public consumption. As DOC meeting minutes note, Denver's major newspapers began appraising the organizers of "extensive research" conducted for "a series of constructive articles." By acknowledging that the *Denver Post* and the *Rocky Mountain News* undertook "research" meant from the outset to be "constructive," the DOC alluded to the papers' intent to bolster the DOC's image amid a rising public backlash.[64]

As time went on, this meant the DOC directly influencing what the media printed and broadcasted. In early March 1971, the DOC member and public relations expert Norm Brown met with the leaders of the *Post* and the *Rocky*, as well as the television stations KOA-TV, KZL, and KBTV. The "purpose of this meeting," Brown explained in a DOC memorandum, was to give "to the executive level of the major media in Denver some . . . insight into the DOC, the problems and solutions the DOC is encountering and trying to work out." As Brown clarified, this "will allow these management people to possibly head off certain elements of the press that could be destructive."[65]

This was something that at least some Denver media bosses were already doing. According to a timeline created by POME, Vance Dittman sat for an interview with the nationally distributed *Walter Cronkite Show* on 31 December 1970. When it aired on 1 March, most of the country saw a version that was twenty to thirty minutes long. In Colorado, however, the local stations cut Dittman's airtime at the DOC's request.[66] Furthermore, after the meeting with Brown, the *Denver Post*, in particular, became devoted to fostering positive views of the 1976 Winter Games.[67] When the newspaper did a series of stories on Evergreen, it consulted the DOC for "suggestions" and "accuracy."[68] By April 1971, as Brown acknowledged to fellow DOC members, the *Post* cleared all its stories on the Olympics with him.[69] The paper's executive editor, William Hornby, had attended the meeting with Brown. According to one account, he and the *Post*'s managing editor began vetting everything published on the Olympics to ensure a "coordination of effort." As Hornby told his staffers in a more colloquial moment, the *Post* meant to go "balls out" for Denver '76.[70] Once again, suffice it to say, regime politics—embodied by the pro-Olympics collaboration of DOC business-men, Colorado politicians, and the local media—persisted in the Centen-nial State.

With its array of public relations responses in play, the DOC probably felt the path to hosting the Winter Olympics remained under control, even if it had become bumpier than expected. Yet in 1971, the *Rocky Mountain News* came under the leadership of a new editorial manager, Michael Howard, an heir to the Scripps-Howard newspaper fortune. Howard also attended the gathering held by Brown with other media kingpins. He had even done reconnaissance for the DOC during its bid, visiting and reporting on Oster-sund, Sweden, a city competing to host the games.[71] Nonetheless, Howard expressed less willingness to toe the DOC line. As Brown described to Don-ald Magarrell, "Mike[,] being younger, still has some doubts and thinks we were trying to curtail the press."[72]

Howard would permit his paper to undertake the kind of coverage that the DOC wished to avoid. During the first week of April 1971, the *Rocky Mountain News* published a six-part series on the Denver Olympics written by the investigative journalist Richard O'Reilly. O'Reilly began working at the *Rocky* in January, charged by Howard to "come up with something" to explore. When O'Reilly saw the DOC's bid books submitted to the IOC, he found his first story. As he remembered, the books "had this beautiful steep mountain covered with snow, which I recognized as a place called Mount Sniktau." An avid skier, O'Reilly had driven past the mountain many times, traveling to distant resorts. He knew "that it was always bare in the winter." Sniktau "was a windblown place, and whatever snow fell just blew right off," O'Reilly recounted. "I thought, this is nonsense. That's not going to be an Alpine site."[73]

Like many Coloradans, including most Denver Olympics opponents, O'Reilly held positive views of the Winter Games in themselves.[74] He undertook his investigation aiming to clear up what the DOC needed to do to make the spectacle a success. In this respect, he fit the profile of a common growth-network editorialist. He called for "good planning" and "technical planning expertise," and time and again he became critical of particular projects. But he did not mean to stop growth broadly. O'Reilly thereby gave the *Rocky* an aura of objectivity while maintaining its traditional pro-growth mentality.[75]

Perhaps this is why the DOC granted him interviews with many of its members and contributors, one of whom admitted to the doctored picture of Sniktau. O'Reilly, though, also spoke with opponents such as Vance Dittman, Richard Lamm, and Robert Jackson. He even sought input from organizers of the 1960 Squaw Valley Olympics who expressed buyer's remorse. O'Reilly then framed the Denver Olympics as an issue with two embellished but reasonable enough sides. "Its opponents say the event will ruin our fragile mountain ecology, while its boosters say it will be the best thing ever to happen to Colorado. . . . The truth," O'Reilly posited, "undoubtedly lies somewhere in between."[76]

O'Reilly downplayed environmentalist objections, noting that although "some trees will be cut and some mountain slopes will be carved up to prepare for the games . . . the damage will be far less than that caused by normal mountain area construction and exploitation over the next five years." The crowds, he observed, would be big but no greater or more inconvenient than that of a Denver Broncos football game. O'Reilly's series also gave credence to the DOC's contentions that the games would promote tourism and become a source of local and national pride.[77]

However, O'Reilly also provided reasons to doubt not only the benefits of hosting the games but the trustworthiness of the DOC. Most noticeably, he revealed how the DOC had airbrushed snow onto a picture of Mount Sniktau to gain the IOC's approval. He cited multiple DOC members admitting that the mountain was not an ideal Alpine site.[78] He likewise established that the DOC probably could not hold cross-country events in Evergreen because of a lack of snow. The warm weather in the foothills, O'Reilly additionally observed, would make it challenging to keep frozen the 17 million gallons of water needed for the luge and bobsled courses. O'Reilly reported on the difficulties involved in using University of Denver dorm rooms for the Olympic Village as well.[79] Examining the Squaw Valley Olympics as a precedent, he also observed that those games cost thirteen times more than originally predicted and that several facilities built for the event had since proven useless, an outcome not unlikely for Denver.[80] Finally, acknowledging that the DOC's cost estimates had already risen from $14 million to as high as $25 million and that uncertainty remained over final event locations, O'Reilly concluded that "there's no way at this point to know how much . . . taxpayers will have to provide."[81]

O'Reilly's articles verified Lamm's and Jackson's criticisms, severely damaged the perceived integrity of the Olympic organizers, and offered future Olympics opponents a battery of information for the struggle ahead. As Lamm described in early 1972, until "a gentleman named Dick O'Reilly from the *Rocky Mountain News* came along, no one in the whole media . . . questioned the assumption that holding the 1976 Olympics in Colorado would be a cornucopia of benefits."[82] Another reader noted to Mayor McNichols that O'Reilly provided "quite a jolt . . . [and] for a change the public has been presented with fact, rather than fiction."[83] Indeed, one soon-to-emerge anti-Olympics organizer named Meg Lundstrom said: "I don't know that we could have done what we did without his series. His series cast such a bright light on the whole DOC operation. . . . That was the basis of all of our literature initially, and we used it heavily later on in the campaign. . . . In some ways, I don't know if anything would have happened without that series."[84] A second forthcoming Olympics objector, Sam Brown, reiterated that O'Reilly's articles proved "absolutely central to making the case" against the event.[85] Despite deemphasizing environmental concerns, O'Reilly's account even held value for middle-class environmentalists. Vance Dittman sent the entire series to the IOC, the International Ski Federation, the International Biathlon Federation, and the International Bobsled Federation. He probably hoped the articles would help convince the IOC to take it upon itself to move the games from Jefferson County, one way or another.[86]

The DOC deployed a plethora of methods to control public opinion. Yet Denver's Brown and Black activists, white middle-class environmentalists in the foothills, two fiscally judicious Colorado legislators, and a *Rocky Mountain News* reporter provided the seeds for an anti-Olympics uprising. At the end of 1971, a collection of opponents accumulated. They had not yet—individually or together—fully undercut the DOC. But the pieces were in place to forge an event coalition that could extinguish the Denver Winter Games.

Lamm continued work behind the scenes to do just that. In February 1971, he and Jackson had failed to see their bill to halt state funding receive a vote.[87] Even so, they had reason to hold out hope that state spending on the games could be stopped. They would find that there was another pivotal contingent of Olympics opponents ready to enter the fray. Thus, Lamm wrote to Dittman about nine months later, in November 1971: "Maybe there is still a chance to get a question on a ballot."[88]

CHAPTER 8

Direct Democracy for Middle America

Not long after Richard Lamm wrote his letter to Vance Dittman, a small cohort of organizers formed Citizens for Colorado's Future (CCF). From early 1972 up to the November election, it led the charge to place an initiative on Colorado ballots to stop public funding of the Olympics and in effect reject the event once and for all. CCF's principal members took up the Olympics issue because it appeared to be an effective route to challenge Colorado's political establishment. They recognized the machinations of a growth regime within the DOC. As young adults in the 1960s, CCF's main players had already committed, in varying degrees, to the peace movement, civil rights advocacy, or environmental activism. Nonetheless, by 1972 the broader counterculture had lost energy, the Vietnam War dragged on, and the conservative Richard Nixon held the presidency. In this context, Denver '76 looked like a contest the anti-Olympics organizers might yet win and that could even propel their larger goals forward.

Thus, CCF embraced the role of coalition-builder, hoping to mold those aggrieved by the DOC's action toward a common end. However, the group became convinced its agenda required the inclusion of a politically coveted sector of American society: the white middle class.[1] CCF aimed to appeal to minoritized Denverites, well-off exurbanites, tax revolters, and especially a population it described as "Middle America." CCF thus positioned itself as a moderate and mature organization while arguing that the Winter Games represented foremost a subversion of democracy undertaken by a collection of wealth-seeking elites. Through such means, the group enabled a viewpoint that allowed Coloradans to override the DOC's Olympic intentions.

The morning after the IOC selected Denver as host for the 1976 Winter Games, the *Denver Post* ran a dual front-page headline: "Denver Wins Winter

Olympics" and "Guard on Alert."[2] Governor John Love had planned to be in Amsterdam celebrating with his fellow Olympic bidders. Instead, he found himself in Colorado, preparing to order soldiers to break up a crowd of trespassers at the University of Denver. A week and a half before, National Guardsmen in Ohio shot and killed four students at Kent State University. The slain students had been protesting Nixon's decision to send ground troops into Cambodia, where America's North Vietnamese adversaries sought protection.[3] After Kent State, antiwar demonstrations broke out across the country, and Nixon ordered Love, the chair of the National Governors Association, to leave Europe for the United States to help address the unrest. In Colorado, 12,000 people marched to the Capitol Building in downtown Denver; 500 students occupied Hellems Hall at the University of Colorado in Boulder; other activists blocked the highway between Denver and Boulder for sixteen hours. Nearer to the Mile High city, at the University of Denver, 1,500 people built "a shack and tent village" christened "Woodstock West: Peace and Freedom University."[4] As the DOC pitched its proposal to the IOC, Love conferred with the chancellor of the school, Denver's chief of police, and a commander of the Colorado National Guard about the situation.[5] The night Denver won the games, just eight days after the Kent State killings, he ordered the removal of the encampment. By the time the guardsmen reached the university's ground, the protesters had left. They must have received word that regiments were on their way.[6]

This series of local events illuminates the national backdrop that inspired the political engagement of another central figure in the downfall of the Denver Olympics. At twenty-nine years old, Sam Brown was arguably the nation's most knowledgeable and successful anti–Vietnam War organizer. He hailed from a wealthy family, heirs to a successful shoe company. While in college in Southern California, he became invested in the free speech movement emanating from Berkeley, United Farm Workers of America strikes, civil rights, and various student-run antiwar protests. In 1967, he campaigned door-to-door for Vietnam Summer, a group founded to inspire antiwar actions within the middle class.[7] A year later, he became the head of the National Student Association's Alternative Candidate Task Force. In that position, Brown searched for a Democratic candidate to run against the prowar incumbent president, Lyndon Johnson. He helped recruit Senator Eugene McCarthy and guided a group called Youth for McCarthy during the senator's 1968 primary challenge. After McCarthy lost to Johnson by just 7 points in the New Hampshire primary, his campaign gained legitimacy; Robert F. Kennedy then entered the race, and Johnson withdrew.[8] Following this, in 1969, Brown organized the Vietnam Moratorium.[9] The nationwide strike included two million people. It was the largest mass demonstration in US history. Mostly made up of middle-class white Americans, it led the mainstream press to cover Vietnam protestors sympathetically for the first time, which pressured Nixon to back off plans to re-escalate the war.[10]

After the Vietnam Moratorium, Brown moved to Colorado to work on a book about the antiwar movement. He never completed that text, but after coming to the Centennial State he reached out to people he had served alongside in antiwar initiatives and made connections with members of the state's liberal base. As he remembered, his new "circle of friends" included State Representative Richard Lamm.[11] Lamm and Brown would become strategic guides for Citizens for Colorado's Future.[12]

Equally important, a foursome of lesser-known organizers took charge of the day-to-day operations for the coming anti-Olympics coalition-building project. Two of these CCF leaders followed Brown's footsteps as eager activists looking to get a leg up on Vietnam and related issues. Meg Lundstrom and John Parr were both twenty-four years old, with degrees in political science from Purdue University in Indiana. Lundstrom moved to Denver as an interlude between college and her career in journalism. Parr came to the city to work for the antiwar peace candidate Craig Barnes. Barnes was running for Denver's seat in the US House of Representatives. The war in Southeast Asia influenced both Indiana transplants. "The whole Vietnam issue opened up a lot of questions," Lundstrom recalled. "I remember . . . coming slowly to the conclusion that the government could be wrong. . . . That type of questioning attitude fueled a lot of my generation and fueled the Olympics."[13]

Parr knew Lundstrom from Purdue and brushed shoulders with Brown, who offered aid to Barnes's campaign.[14] In the summer of 1970, Barnes narrowly defeated the longtime growth-machine ally and Olympics supporter Byron Rodgers in the Democratic primary. However, many Denverites viewed Barnes as too far to the left because of his stance on racial integration. Not only did he oppose the war; he also served as one of three lawyers that argued in federal district court that Denver schools were systematically segregated. He had won that case and prepared to defend the district court's decision to impose crosstown busing at the Supreme Court. In the general election, Mike McKevitt defeated him, becoming the first Republican to represent Denver in the House in a quarter-century.[15]

After Barnes lost, he opened a Common Cause office in Denver.[16] Founded in 1970, Common Cause, among other things, advocated putting a stop to involvement in Vietnam. This venture brought Brown, Parr, and Lundstrom closer together, with each contributing to Barnes's new program.

Furthermore, during this time, Brown turned his attention to Oklahoma senator Fred Harris's run for president. Harris was a staunch supporter of Lyndon Johnson's Great Society programs, calling specifically for federal support in poor urban areas. In the same instance, he became an express critic of Johnson's and then Nixon's policies toward the Vietnam War. The self-described "new populist" represented Brown's ideal candidate.[17]

Brown recruited Parr and Lundstrom to help open Harris's western states office.[18] Yet Harris failed to raise enough money to stay in the race for more than a few weeks. It is here that Brown convened with Lamm about the Denver Olympics. As Lundstrom remembered, if Harris's campaign had garnered more support, she, Parr, and Brown would have never become involved with Denver '76. "We used to joke," Lundstrom noted, "that if the Denver Olympic Committee had known that [giving] $10,000 [to Fred Harris] would have stopped us in our tracks, it would have been easy to raise." As it turned out, not long after closing Harris's office, toward the end of 1971, Lamm, fellow State Representative Robert Jackson, Brown, Lundstrom, Parr, and about ten others formed CCF.[19]

Along with Lundstrom and Parr, two additional operatives became full-time contributors to the new anti-Olympics organization. In 1970, a New Yorker named Tom Nussbaum graduated from law school and moved to Colorado to work with the Robert Kennedy Memorial Foundation, advocating for Native American rights before the state legislature and the Bureau of Indian Affairs. When his time with the Kennedy Memorial ended, he joined the anti-Olympics project.[20] Dwight Filley grew up in Denver and, after two years of college, joined the Marine Corps. He served four years, including one as a helicopter pilot in Vietnam. Afterward, he returned to Colorado, obtained a degree in sociology, and became involved with the Sierra Club and the Colorado Open Space Council. A committed environmentalist, he learned about CCF through a meeting with like-minded environmental organizers.[21]

The CCF leaders had no hard feelings toward the games generally. They were not even that concerned with its direct consequences on Colorado. As Brown put it, the CCF team agreed with the "substantive" motives of other anti-Olympics advocates, such as socioeconomic inequality in Denver, environmental protection in the mountains, DOC dishonesty and corruption, and a need for smarter and fairer state spending. However, for them, these matters fed into larger aspirations.[22]

All the former CCF members who were still living (everyone but Parr) supplied interviews for this book. Each conveyed a desire to import genuine democratic practices into Colorado, challenge the state's political authorities, and reorient its overall trajectory. In this manner, it makes sense that the group chose the title it did instead of something such as "Citizens Against the Olympics." As Nussbaum described: "A lot of us came from opposing the Vietnam War, supporting environmental causes, working with César Chávez or with Native Americans, and seeing a certain amount of injustice in the world and wanting to change the balance of power . . . the way decisions were made, who made them. In that sense, we were all thinking in broader terms than just the Olympics."[23]

For CCF, the infusion of direct democracy served as the first step. Nussbaum recalled that he "hadn't given it [the Olympics] much thought" until he heard Governor Love pronounce that there was no need for a vote over whether to hold the international sports spectacle in Denver. This affront to democratic citizenship, Nussbaum explained, "was a major triggering event in my thinking of the games." Without much knowledge of the fiscal or environmental questions involved, Nussbaum located CCF's headquarters and spoke with Lundstrom, Parr, and Lamm about how he could help. Lundstrom expressed a similar point of view. "I didn't have a hatred of the Olympics or a burning desire to get them out," she recounted. "The important thing was the process through which people discussed the issue and came to some kind of conclusion." "All of our hearts at that point were in populist democracy," she added, "letting the people have a voice, more than anti-Olympics per se."[24] But with participatory democracy would come significant social and political change. "The Olympics were a way to ask," Lundstrom also proclaimed, "what kind of state do we want?"[25] Nussbaum affirmed that the event became "an opportunity to make a statement about the way the future of Colorado and Denver would be."[26] "The Olympics was a handle," Filley likewise stressed, "to express dissatisfaction with the way the state was going."[27]

Brown concurred and provided the most thorough account of what CCF's anti-Olympics effort meant to him. He wanted to build a coalition of citizens that could unseat the Colorado growth regime. As he spelled out: "The games were tactical. . . . What I was hoping to do was to break the stranglehold that an old elite that crossed party boundaries had over Colorado politics." "I saw it as a way," Brown emphasized, "to take on an entrenched Denver establishment and try and build a new and alternative political base." Through the Olympics, he foresaw "building a movement that would think more about what happened to the people who had been left out and left behind in the state, working people, people of color, finding a way really to speak to the interests of people whose interests were not that of the downtown business community." Brown additionally declared that "this was an opportunity to talk about who had power in Colorado and how they exercised that power and how people might actually be able to take that power away from them and take it for themselves." The veteran activist further remarked that, "strategically, my interest was in building a broader populist, if you will, democratic future."[28]

As a prominent event already fraught with dissent from various sources and forced upon Colorado by its pro-growth elites, the Winter Games became uniquely situated as a unifying stand-in for the political plight of Colorado writ large. It was an ideal means to incite criticism of and action against traditional authorities and structures. At the same time, though, the need to go through the games to enact such outcomes indicated the daunting odds Brown and CCF were up against. As they realized, they could not achieve their deeper objectives by addressing them directly. "I was interested" in the antiwar Democratic candidate George McGovern's 1972 campaign for president, Brown acknowledged, but "he was never going to carry Colorado. . . . So, it made sense to be involved in something else."[29] Filley similarly described how trying to prevent highway construction seemed unlikely, but stopping the Denver Games "was something that could be done."[30] Thus, it is apparent that part of the reason the Denver Olympics debate looked like a good place to start the long march toward a progressive populist takeover was that it, of all things, seemed winnable.

Brown and other CCF leaders also recognized that their task required a multifaceted cast of allies. When it came to the failures of the antiwar movement, the absence of democratic participation may have been part of the problem. However, it also seemed that a lack of diversity contributed. Notably, as the labor historian Jefferson Cowie observes, many liberal activists who cut their teeth on college campuses during the 1960s came to recognize that their "inability to make linkages with working people" was a "critical weakness." Prominent Democratic politicians such as Robert Kennedy and George McGovern likewise understood that, in the late 1960s and 1970s, preserving a liberal consensus necessitated a coalition of young people, people of color, women's rights activists, and white "middle America."[31]

For Brown, this rang true. Brown may have wanted "to build an alternative political establishment," but he imagined doing it without appearing to disrupt the status quo. "My interest was always at building toward the middle," Brown explained; "that is, with finding the arguments that resonated not with my peers . . . but with people for whom the flag and America were important and the idea of patriotism was very important." "What you wanted to do," Brown continued, "was create something that spoke to people's concerns where they were . . . that didn't ask them to overthrow their whole value system and accept an alternative view of the world."[32] Brown sought to create an alternative political structure without imposing anything that might be construed as a full-fledged alternative ideology.

To achieve this, Brown believed a cautious and refined attitude and appearance would be essential. When leading Youth for McCarthy, he had encouraged the group to embrace the motto "Get clean for Gene." In organizing the Vietnam Moratorium, Brown consciously sought ways to include older white middle-class Americans who might not have joined an antiwar protest before and would spurn any association with radicalism. That agenda was the reason Brown organized a strike in 1969 rather than another student-led march.[33] The book Brown moved to Colorado to work on was also meant to be an extension of an essay he wrote explaining his political calculus. As Brown argued in "The Politics of Peace," "it is not possible to build a successful peace movement simply on a student base . . . you must have a strong leadership off the campuses to set the tone and direction." He contended that within "a successful anti-war strategy . . . the appeal must be made in such a way that Middle Americans will not ignore the substance of the argument because of an offensive style." Brown pined for "a moderate peace leadership" and reiterated that "ending the war requires that people move toward Middle America."[34]

For Brown, the Olympics was another attempt to reshape "the movement"— to straighten it out and recruit older, moderate, and even conservative white Americans to political positions associated with liberalism and the counterculture. Brown imagined prideful citizens who approved of the way things were or used to be, people who would not stomach critiques of American "imperialism," who would never "condemn the country" or ask for structural makeovers but who might come to "see how their view of the world would lead them to your view on a particular incident."[35] In "The Politics of Peace," Brown admitted that he saw ending the Vietnam War itself in this way, as a "necessary first step toward meeting more difficult problems." The effort to end the war, he claimed, was "draining the nation," preventing it from addressing other social issues. But it also seemed "less intellectually intractable than the long-run problems of pollution or the distribution of wealth in America, and less emotionally deep-seated than alienation from the Protestant work ethic or the overwhelming problem of race."[36] In Brown's thinking, stopping the Olympics was akin to stopping the war. If anti-Olympics activism gained entry to middle-American living rooms, it could open new doors to success in far more significant struggles.

* * *

The collection of parties engaged with the Olympic issue must have appealed to Brown's political inclinations. For starters, Lundstrom, Parr, Nussbaum, and Filley represented his vision of young, inspired, palatable, and practical activists. As Lundstrom recalled, referencing her and Parr's upbringings in Indiana: "We knew middle-America" and "didn't have any kind of appetite for stridency."[37] Filley remembered as well how the foursome bridged the divide between the ethos that inspired their activism and the tenor of tempered white citizens. "We were clean, but we weren't exactly wearing coats and ties," he explained. "We got our spelling right, and our documents looked good . . . but we were still almost counterculture."[38] When they made public pronouncements, the CCF organizers made sure to present themselves as level-headed and conscientious, dressing well, creating polished, well-written publications, and even spending extra money on high-quality stationery.[39]

At the same time, Lamm and Jackson represented a sector of the "off-campus" leadership for which Brown also longed.[40] To borrow phrases from Nussbaum, the "young folk" of CCF tried to keep themselves out of the limelight. Instead, recognized as "authority figures," Lamm and Jackson became the group's spokespeople. Their public presence, Filley recalled, "gave a lot of credibility that would have otherwise been beyond the pale."[41] Brown agreed. Reflecting on Lamm's contribution, he noted: "He [was] older; he was in elected office; he had a reputation; so, he brought a substance . . . that was terribly important."[42] As Lamm himself described, he became the group's "titular head."[43]

Along with respected public figures and upstanding young organizers, Jefferson County's foothills residents resembled another prized sector: a moderate- to conservative-leaning, white, middle- to upper-class constituency. In Lamm's depiction, his relationship with Vance Dittman represented a novel pact between "a Democratic liberal" and "a stodgy old Republican." Dittman would both solicit and provide donations to help get CCF off the ground, and Protect Our Mountain Environment eventually worked to get CCF's anti-Olympics initiative on the ballot and then see it passed.[44] Through the common cause of rejecting the Olympics, desires for direct democracy and middle-class environmentalism converged.

CCF also reached out to people with diverse racial and ethnic backgrounds. In the first letter disseminated with CCF's letterhead, the African American state representative Paul Hamilton and the Mexican American community organizer John Zapien served as two of three signatories. Even though they were not main players in CCF, this enabled the group to appear

Figure 8.1. October 1972. Hoping to unite a diverse set of allies, CCF leaders Tom Nussbaum, John Parr, Dwight Filley, and Meg Lundstrom organized Olympic opponents, often behind the scenes, to prevent the Olympics in Colorado. *Denver Post* via Courtesy of Getty Images.

representative of a broad portion of the Colorado populace.[45] In addition, when CCF realized it needed to add a second ballot measure specific to Denver (so that Mile High officials could not attempt to fund the games by themselves), Arie Taylor helped lead another petition drive. Taylor had already broken ground as the first Black female officer in the US Air Force and, in 1972, became the first Black woman elected to serve in the Colorado House. But before joining Lamm in the Colorado Assembly, she had organized African American voters in the city on CCF's behalf.[46] In August 1972, sitting next to Tom Nussbaum at a press conference, Taylor shared what was by then a familiar CCF refrain: "Why should we spend millions of dollars in taxes for an event that lasts only ten days and which benefits only a few people?" she asked.[47]

However, John Parr conceded, CCF knew it was "walking a fine line."[48] Its umbrella could not be all-encompassing. Brown acknowledged as much, reflecting: "We tried to think at every step strategically about what our alliances needed to be and where we were going to win this thing."[49] In turn, the group highlighted how the Olympics would hurt racially marginalized citizens but in ways that remained agreeable to white middle American moderates. While this led CCF to support state and federal funding of affordable housing in the city, it never led to outright demands for or emphasis on such housing. Instead, environmental harm and unfair taxation garnered more attention. Consequently, CCF would not consolidate with Chicano and Black Power advocates or other moderate Mexican American and African American politicians.

Brown had claimed of Vietnam that "the purest anti-war position is the one that ends the war the fastest without compromising the principle that the war is wrong." This meant "priorities must be chosen and sacrifices made." The counterculture icon "Jerry Rubin may have to be excluded from a platform to keep [New York City mayor] John Lindsay," Brown soberly assessed.[50] In fact, in "The Politics of Peace," Brown admitted that even though the "position would be painful[, it] would be necessary to cultivate dovish potential among racists."[51] He was open to the possibility of making "short-run sacrifices" regarding America's more substantial social challenges because, he maintained, dealing with Vietnam had to precede them. Taking this position with regard to the games in Colorado was something Peter Garcia and the Watson brothers were unlikely to agree to do. It is also probable that Citizens Interested in an Equitable Olympics appeared too provocative and contentious to fit within the image CCF wanted to create for itself.

Moreover, it is important to note that there remained Mexican American and African American moderates who supported the games. Due to their common commitment to a pragmatic strategy, Democrats such as Elvin Caldwell, Betty Benavidez, and Waldo Benavidez could have partnered with CCF. Yet CCF embraced a measured approach to surreptitiously combat the current Colorado power structure. Conversely, Elvin Caldwell and the Benavidezes worked within that structure to obtain affordable homes. In this instance, it was CCF that pushed beyond the pale. This led CCF to oppose the Olympics, whereas a number of Brown and Black officeholders did not.

CCF did voice support for federal funds for low-income homes on the East Side and West Side. But the coalition-builders also took the position that public money should be spent on affordable housing without attaching it to the games.[52] In theory, this stance enabled CCF to oppose the Olympics while being advocates for the needs of their potential Brown and Black partners. In hazy recollections, Lamm and Brown both suggested that CCF did not take the Denver Urban Renewal Authority press housing plan seriously anyway, viewing it as another disingenuous pro-Olympics promise.[53] In this respect, Lamm and Brown agreed with Garcia.

Still, such skepticism carried a component of convenience. It allowed CCF to portray itself as unambiguously backing policies in the best interests of the racialized poor when that was not necessarily the case. Tellingly, in a 1972 essay on the Olympics, Brown noted that, despite the DOC's promises, "the land under consideration [for press housing] is thought by city planners to be too isolated for low-income housing, although suitable for hotel development."[54] He thereby indicated his distrust of DURA's proposed project. Yet Brown's account was based on information lifted from Richard O'Reilly's April 1971 series, in which O'Reilly discussed how the city looked to build press housing at the western bank of the South Platte River, not the West Side or East Side.[55] Brown opportunistically critiqued a different plan than the one the DOC and company actually put forth. Meanwhile, for their part, Caldwell, the Benavidezes, and other Mexican American and African American politicians remained convinced—and may have been correct— that supporting the games gave them the best odds to improve their communities' living conditions.

With these dynamics in play, CCF began to paint an argument that could turn a range of Coloradans against both the Olympics and perhaps even the ruling regime itself. At CCF's first meeting, the group raised money to place an ad in the *Denver Post*. Sources show Protect Our Mountain Environment representatives met with Lamm as early as November 1971 to discuss how to "frame" this imminent Olympics opposition.[56] On 2 January 1972, CCF ran its ad with the headline: "Sell Colorado? Olympics '76? AT WHAT COST TO COLORADO?"[57]

Several questions, with answers implicating the corruption and greed of Denver Olympic organizers, followed. Along with social exclusion and neglect, environmental damage, and excessive costs, the Olympics challengers asserted that the Denver Games were the product of undemocratic decisions made by wealthy, insular Colorado powerbrokers.[58] Furthermore, in line with a tactic suggested by Brown, the ad listed as its authors prominent leaders and groups from the Colorado community, including lawyers, environmentalists, Lamm, Jackson, Protect Our Mountain Environment, and the Sierra Club. The younger CCF members who did the grunt work, but carried less credibility, went unnamed.[59]

The first question the CCF advocates posed was: "Who Pays?" To which CCF answered: "YOU do." This suggested that every potential reader of the paper and thereby every person in the state would foot the Olympics bill.

CCF then highlighted that the DOC originally pegged the price tag of the Denver games at $8–10 million but now predicted a cost of about $28 million. The ad also pointed out that the 1968 Winter Olympics in Grenoble, France, cost a quarter-billion dollars, and the 1972 Summer Olympics in Munich was slated to cost West Germany more than half a billion. Given these discrepancies, CCF listed the "actual cost" of Denver '76 at "$?" The coalition-builders pointed to "HIDDEN COSTS" as well, such as highway construction, sewage expansion, military personnel and equipment, and other government services for which the DOC apparently did not account.[60] According to CCF, the DOC not only underestimated the taxpayer contribution; it purposefully concealed it.

Why would the DOC do this? "For what?" "For whom?" and "Who profits?" the CCF ad urged. The "what" was "a 10-day spectacular of winter sports in artificial snow in highly-engineered technologically contrived structures." As for the question of "who" all this was for, CCF responded the IOC and DOC. And, according to CCF, the IOC was "a self-appointed, self-perpetuating board of men who rule the Olympics," while the DOC was "a self-appointed coterie of political and business figures who privately made public decisions of broad and lasting effect on Colorado."[61] In CCF's portrayal, this "coterie" ignored and even intentionally undermined citizen input to hold a sports event for its own self-interest.

CCF additionally made it clear that these "self-appointed" powerholders neglected Coloradans of multiple backgrounds. Following the question "Who profits?" CCF provided another set of queries. "How many blacks and Chicanos will be on sports teams?" "How much low-income housing will really result?" "What quality environment will result from this kind of hard sell of Colorado's beauty?"[62] Hosting the Olympics would not be a good thing for Mexican Americans and African Americans in Denver or environmentally concerned suburban and exurban inhabitants, CCF maintained.

CCF then listed two sets of "Priorities" and their corresponding prices. One list included a bobsled course, a luge course, a speed skating rink, a ski jump, and an Alpine facility. The other noted Colorado's budget for water pollution, air pollution, handicapped children, and venereal disease. For example, CCF pointed out that, whereas a new speed skating rink would cost $6,673,000, Colorado spent only $512,874 to remedy smog-filled air.[63] As CCF contended, the games would take away vital resources from more important and neglected public needs.

CCF finally asked: "How?" How could such a misguided event be thrust upon Colorado's citizens? The answer reveals the crux of the point that the group meant to popularize. CCF claimed the people of the Centennial State were victims of a systematic usurpation of democratic practices. "NO state referendum has ever been held on either the Olympics or the Sell Colorado program of years standing," CCF professed. "ALL meetings of the Denver Organizing Committee (DOC) are held in secret with press and public barred."[64]

CCF accused the DOC and its backers of hiding costs, disregarding the preferences of citizens, and ultimately perpetuating misguided policies for its membership's self-aggrandizement. As Sam Brown claimed in a separate editorial published around the same time, titled "Snow Job in Colorado," the Winter Olympics are "sport[s] of the rich paid for by the poor in order to promote real estate and tourism."[65] This was not a new idea. The Mountain Area Protection Council in Evergreen and the African American Olympian Jerome Biffle had previously made the same point.[66] However, CCF emphasized it relentlessly, making growth-regime corruption the fundamental anti-Olympics grievance from which all others stemmed.

The day after CCF ran its ad, the organization sent a letter and its first anti-Olympics petition to 6,000 people.[67] In doing so, the group made sure to include a range of criticisms. CCF told potential signers: "We are opposed to Colorado hosting the 1976 Winter Olympics because we fear the unplanned growth and environmental damage the 'Sell Colorado' approach creates," and "we feel that Denver and Colorado taxpayers will be paying heavily for something that profits only a few."[68] With these points, the petition stated, "We, the undersigned, respectfully request that the 1976 Winter Olympics not be held in Colorado."[69]

As with the newspaper advertisement, the purported authors of the petition were not the CCF foursome running the anti-Olympics campaign but more established and diverse constituents. As Sam Brown advised in a short book that he wrote about grassroots organizing, "you must get local people deeply involved in the campaign or organization in a public and visible way." If you are new to an area, as all CCF leaders aside from Filley were, Brown instructed: "You should not be the person who opens a storefront, has a press conference, talks to the press. You should find ways to make yourself secondary to local personalities." Even if the homegrown contributor "is rarely in," Brown directed, "it's tremendously important that visibility be from a local standpoint."[70] Paul Hamilton, John Zapien, and Ruth Weiner thus took credit—an African American representative in the Colorado House, a Mexican American heading the Legal Aid Society in Denver, and a white college professor with environmentalist ties.[71] Only Zapien remained a regular CCF participant.[72]

The anti-Olympics advocates meant to use the petition to gauge how much opposition to the games existed.[73] Within three weeks, they collected over 25,000 signatures, in large part reflecting the work done by previous opponents in the city and the foothills, as well as Lamm and Jackson. After such a strong reaction, the group decided to confront the International Olympic Committee in person. CCF's members did not expect to convince the IOC to pull the games from Denver. They aimed to draw attention to their cause, gain legitimacy in the eyes of local onlookers, and continue projecting the presence of a broad coalition with a middle-American appeal.

Accordingly, CCF arranged for three of its members to travel to the 1972 Sapporo Winter Olympics with its stack of petitions in hand, along with a book of letters collected from various opponents from throughout the state, newspaper clippings detailing Olympics opposition, and a list of DOC "claims" compared to "facts." Letters came in from Lamm, Jackson, and Hamilton, the Rocky Mountain Chapter of the Sierra Club, the Rocky Mountain Farmers Union, and at least one Chicano activist.[74] Lundstrom did all the writing for CCF and put the text together, working overnight in the Denver Common Cause office until the sun came up on the day her CCF teammates left Stapleton Airport for the other side of the globe.[75]

In selecting CCF representatives to travel to Sapporo, the group stayed focused on crafting a balanced image. CCF dispatched John Parr and fellow CCF supporters Estelle Brown (no relation to Sam Brown) and Howard Gelt. Estelle Brown came to CCF through Richard Lamm. Lamm and Brown met as members of the Colorado Mountain Club and Colorado Conservation Committee. Brown also served as a founding member of the Colorado Open Space Council, had fought to prevent dams in the Grand Canyon, and advocated for environmental controls to preserve hiking, climbing, and skiing locales. She was older, white, and a well-known and respected environmentalist.[76] Although known to be "passionate" and "fierce," as Lundstrom explained, age, class, race, and gender allowed her to serve as "the proverbial little old lady in white tennis shoes."[77] Sam Brown likewise acknowledged, "we knew why she was going."[78] She appeared nonthreatening, reasonable, and presumably representative of such elements in the Colorado community.

Gelt stood as yet another young lawyer from the Midwest who also found his way to CCF through Lamm. After getting his law degree from the University of Denver, he worked as the deputy director of the Clinical Education Program at the university's law school. Richard Lamm was the director and his boss.[79] Although Sam Brown remembered the plan as laughable, in Lundstrom's words Gelt played "a gangly young lawyer who represented the voice of authority." Toward this end, Gelt himself noted that, before leaving for Japan, he "got a haircut and became the young businessman."[80]

With long hair and a beard covering his face, Parr took on the role of "the implied threat, in terms of the student protest," as Lundstrom described.[81] Gelt similarly recollected that Parr "had long hair and a beard," appearing as "the environmental hippie."[82] In multiple pictures of Parr published during the Denver Olympics controversy, he is clean-shaven. He seems to have grown facial hair with this countercultural messaging in mind.

While in Japan, perhaps due to the cover provided by her seemingly moderate positionality, Estelle Brown took the lead in propelling CCF into the spotlight. Upon arrival, the trio learned of a pre-Olympics IOC executive council meeting held at a hotel in Tokyo. The CCF members thus waited outside a conference room where IOC leaders gathered, hoping to obtain an audience. Then, as the meeting room's door opened for a lunch break, Parr and Gelt watched as Brown barged in uninvited. As Gelt described it, "Estelle, who was about five-foot-two, a little old lady with white hair, just stormed into the middle of the room." Parr and Gelt followed in time to witness Brown place CCF's petitions in front of the IOC president Avery Brundage, sitting at the head of a U-shaped table.[83]

Several journalists were present, and word of Brown's audacity and her stack of petitions spread from New York to London.[84] Richard O'Reilly had traveled to Japan to cover all things Denver Olympics and wrote about the intrusion for the *Rocky Mountain News*.[85] Moreover, after police escorted Brown, Gelt, and Parr out of the IOC meeting, the executives invited them back to have their say, signaling that they—and 25,000 signatories—had a point of view worth hearing. The CCF presentation lasted about twenty minutes and, as IOC documentation shows, included the assortment of concerns: population growth due to Olympic publicity, taxpayer burdens, damage to the mountains, and the violation of democratic ideals.[86]

"After I got through talking," Gelt recounted, "Brundage said something like, 'I'm going to piss all over your petitions.'"[87] Yet despite Brundage's "caustic remarks," this series of events allowed CCF to edge its desired picture of the Denver Games further into Colorado's public. As Parr's retelling, titled "Face to Face with the Olympic Gods," recounts, CCF used the Sapporo experience to push the idea that the people behind the Olympics were the robber barons of sports and that CCF served as the true representative of the Colorado citizenry. According to Parr, he spent his time "in the Park Hotel in Tokyo chasing down the halls after lords, counts, barons, and generals who are members of the world's most exclusive country club—the International Olympic Committee." "In that gracious world of international cocktail parties and million dollar public relations schemes," Parr continued, "we were a small voice for more fundamental realities—like breathable air, unscarred mountains, and tax money used for a more general welfare."[88] By juxtaposing the Olympic officials and CCF in this way, Parr supplemented CCF's contention that the IOC, the DOC, and other supporters of the Olympics were rulers of a sports fiefdom, living lavish lifestyles, driven by greed, and ignoring the interests of everyday people. On the other hand, CCF, from the city to the mountains, spoke for the average Coloradan's simpler—more "fundamental"—needs.

From here, CCF turned its attention to the initiative, which would bar public funding.[89] The group needed to obtain signatures from 51,000 registered Colorado voters by the end of June. It had four and a half months to reach that goal. The time was short, but the coalition-builders were well-positioned. For one, the people of Colorado already seemed inclined to take CCF's side, at least as to whether a vote on the Olympics should be held. By mid-March 1972, with CCF's electoral plans having become public knowledge, the *Rocky Mountain News* commissioned a poll that showed 68 percent of respondents wanted to cast ballots on whether to allow state funding of the Denver Games. The paper's editorial manager, Michael Howard, wrote a coinciding article and made it front-page news.[90]

CCF embraced what it knew to be proven grassroots methods as well. After observing Sam Brown at work during the run-up to the Vietnam Moratorium, through the assistance of FBI informants, Nixon aide Bob Haldeman confessed that Brown "seemed to be a genius for organization."[91] Bolstered by Brown's experience and guidance, gathering the names to get the anti-Olympics measure on the ballot became a full-time job for Lundstrom, Parr, Nussbaum, and Filley. Lundstrom took charge of writing CCF's publications and pamphlets. Parr and Nussbaum worked as field organizers, traveling throughout Colorado to create networks of support. Filley oversaw the operation at CCF's office in Denver.[92] To complement this, CCF owned an 800-person mailing list built up through the previous Sapporo petition drive.[93] After CCF asked these followers to talk to friends, an estimated 5,000 people helped solicit signatures.[94]

Within a month, CCF passed out enough petition forms to volunteers to obtain six times the names needed. The group mailed 1,000 forms to Denver residents alone.[95] Following advice found in Brown's book on organizing, CCF generated money through fundraising letters sent to known supporters and used the revenue to buy a mimeograph machine to print fliers.[96] CCF leaders and contributors spent hours standing in front of grocery

Figure 8.2. May 1972. Eventually riding 230 miles and visiting thirty-one cities, Dwight Filley (third from left) and fellow CCF supporters Bob Shaver, John Wignett, and Allan Hubbard set out from Cheesman Park with petitions to stop state spending on the Olympics via the ballot box. Photo by Bill Peters/*Denver Post* via Getty Images.

stores, shopping centers, churches, movie theaters, and sporting events to get citizens to sign. They spoke to sympathetic or potentially sympathetic groups, including the Mountain Area Protection Council and Protect Our Mountain Environment, as well as the Elks and the Rotarians. They started holding weekly press conferences, coached supporters on interacting with fellow citizens, and instructed them on how to manage additional volunteers. Though they made sure to maintain a restrained tone, they tried a few gimmicks to create buzz, such as a bicycle rally where cyclists took off from Cheesman Park carrying stacks of petitions to various parts of Colorado. In five days, led by Dwight Filley, CCF bike riders reported distributing their anti-Olympics appeal to 130 locations. A CCF press release explained, the group thereby demonstrated the lengths it would go to "make sure people in small towns have a say on whether their money should be spent on" the Winter Games.[97] In populist fashion, CCF located itself on the side that promoted and protected the voice of the people.

The technical purpose of the initiative was to make it illegal for the state to fund the event. Yet CCF understood its effort as a means to empower individuals to weigh in on whether Colorado should host the Olympics at all. "We were certain that if there wasn't any state money, there wouldn't be any Olympics," Filley remembered. "The mechanism was the tax dollars, but the purpose was to stop the Olympics."[98] Lamm similarly recollected that the "whole debate unfolded as a question [of] do we want the Olympics or not."[99] Sam Brown confirmed that, "from the base, it was a desire to stop the Olympics cold in their tracks, period."[100]

Thus, on 30 June 1972, CCF turned in petitions containing more than 77,000 names, or 26,000 more than it needed. It was the most signatures ever obtained for a Colorado ballot initiative.[101] The vote on public funding of the Winter Olympics was coming. Furthermore, if CCF's assertions resonated, an array of Colorado residents now held something in common. Whether worried about urban livability, the destruction of the environment, higher taxes, wasteful spending, DOC misconduct, or citizen exclusion from state decision-making, the state's rich and self-interested pro-growth boosters were trying to con them. With democratic citizenship now at the forefront, various people and advocacy groups, concerned with a host of issues, could tether their agendas and their ire to the games, melding a moment of movements with which a large share of middle Americans could relate.

PART 3

THE FATE AND LEGACY OF DENVER '76

CHAPTER 9

The DOC'S Credibility and the Rhetoric of Olympism

At the start of 1972, the DOC faced three existential obstacles: swaying the International Olympic Committee a second time, garnering state and federal funding, and staving off Citizens for Colorado's Future's coalition-building effort. The first two challenges were more immediate and anticipated. However, the organizers failed to navigate through them unscathed. Anti-Olympics criticism ramped up, and the DOC's credibility floundered.

Moreover, by August 1972, with CCF's initiative now approved for the November ballot, Denver '76 proponents knew that the United States Senate was probably going to make state funding a prerequisite for federal support. Thus, they understood that CCF's measure would become, in effect, a referendum on whether Colorado should host the spectacle. Carl DeTemple took over as DOC president after the Sapporo Winter Games. As DeTemple explained to Governor John Love, Mayor William McNichols, and DOC colleagues, the Senate's stipulation "rather clearly would make the November vote a 'yea or nay' proposition on the Olympics and not simply a matter of whether the state can appropriate funds." DeTemple saw a silver lining here. While citizens might want to prohibit public spending, surely, he thought, they would not outlaw the world-renowned sports event.[1]

Still, CCF had backed the DOC into a corner and forced it and its allies to recognize that the politics of growth in Colorado had changed. A large portion of the Colorado citizenry held doubts about the effects of hosting the Winter Olympics and tourism-related development. Indeed, it appeared that, if Coloradans saw the event as a pretext for commercial growth, the DOC could well be forced to return the Olympic torch to the IOC. The DOC needed to publicly deemphasize its goal of sports-inspired growth and replace it with something else.

Rather than promising economic gains, the boosters turned to the themes of youth, diversity, nationalism, state pride, and the rhetoric of Olympism. In an all-out campaign to justify keeping the Winter Games in town, the DOC and Colorado's political leaders continued to work in coordination, combining calls for national and regional exceptionalism with ideals of peace, mutual respect, and international harmony gained through sports. As the Olympics supporter and Colorado radio personality Tony Larsen artfully explained to listeners, the "bridges" that the Olympics would leave "will not span mountain streams or desecrate greenery—these bridges will span the minds of men," bringing "reason, fair play, love, dreams of a better self, and a better world."[2] If the prospect of economic growth could not convince Colorado voters to back the Olympics, then perhaps moral growth would.

About nine months after receiving IOC approval, the DOC began revising its proposal.[3] By the time the Sapporo Winter Games were held, the organizers, among other changes, moved Nordic skiing to Steamboat Springs and Alpine races to Beaver Creek, just west of Vail. The DOC readied a layout mirroring the more realistic plan it formulated years earlier, in the first half of the 1960s. Nevertheless, it was not clear whether the IOC would approve this revised setup, as the lies permeating Denver's original bid became apparent and rumors swirled that Sion, Switzerland, was prepared to take the event off Denver's hands.[4]

To make matters more complicated, the IOC president Avery Brundage appears to have enabled not only the DOC's misconduct but also tensions within the IOC itself. Before the IOC awarded the 1976 Winter Games to Denver, Brundage knew the DOC was not candid about its event sites and that unrest over them existed in foothills communities. Yet as the former Denver mayor and DOC member Thomas Currigan reported during the bid process, Brundage merely instructed the DOC to "clean up our own back yard."[5] Brundage presumably said nothing about these matters to his IOC colleagues prior to their selection of Denver. Conversely, in fall 1971, with the games in the DOC's hands, Brundage shared the addresses of IOC members with POME leader Vance Dittman at his request. Soon, letters from disaffected residents along the Front Range poured into IOC mailboxes, laying the DOC's deceit, and the brewing discontent in Colorado, bare for all to see.[6] As the IOC vice president Lord Michael Killanin wrote to another IOC leader shortly after Brundage's exchange with Dittman, IOC decision makers "may well have voted" for Denver based on "sites which were never viable."[7] Brundage was also well aware that citizens in Colorado and elsewhere would likely reject hosting the games if given a chance to do so through a popular vote. Specifically, he listed excessive costs and environmental consequences as the reasons.[8] "I am not sure you realize the strength of the forces against you," he therefore warned the USOC's then-president (and DOC member) Clifford Buck in May 1972.[9]

In truth, Brundage's behavior appears consistent with the hope that the DOC would crash, burn, and consume the entire Winter Olympics. Due to the dominance of a small group of Scandinavian and European countries and rampant professionalism and commercialism in winter sports, such as hockey and Alpine skiing, he believed it would be best for the IOC to get rid of the wintertime edition.[10] As Killanin later described, Brundage "was delighted when things began to go wrong in Denver."[11] Brundage would use his last speech as IOC president, at the 1972 Munich Summer Games, to recommend the Winter Olympics—meaning the institution as a whole—be "given a decent burial at Denver."[12]

By allowing the DOC to bungle forward into a citizen uprising, Brundage thus set up a situation where Estelle Brown could barge into the IOC executive board's Tokyo meeting. Despite Brundage's expressed displeasure toward that occurrence, it may have been exactly what he wanted to see. Afterward, board members discussed how the International Ski Federation, led by Marc Holder, had "fallen down on its responsibility," that "Denver had lied to the IOC," and that any "action which brought about 25,000 signatures against holding the Games has a derogatory effect on the IOC." In turn, the board decided to call the hotel room of the DOC's president, Robert Pringle, and demand to see him.[13]

Several DOC members were in Japan, ready to present their drastically updated proposal for the IOC to review. Pringle, DeTemple, Donald Magarrell, and George Robinson all met with the IOC Executive Board the next morning, sharing a series of half-truths to explain the DOC's new event-site layout. The IOC vice president Killanin responded by calling the altered scheme "unrecognizable." After the meeting, the whole Board concluded it would be best to move the games from Colorado but that "no action" should be taken until Brundage met again with Pringle.[14] Later that evening, Brundage once more summoned the DOC president. This time, Pringle arrived with Governor Love at his side; as Pringle recounted, they "were told ... [t]he executive committee of the IOC, by unanimous vote, had decided to resolve that the honor of hosting the 1976 Winter Olympics be withdrawn from Denver."[15] Pringle and Love thought Denver had officially lost the games. As Love likewise explained: "The way Brundage told us, it was gone."[16]

Richard O'Reilly's report in the *Rocky Mountain News* characterized what followed as the DOC's "Hectic Day in Sapporo"; the Denver '76 organizers were scrambling. They had fifteen hours before their scheduled presentation to the entire IOC.[17] Love sent word to Senator Gordon Allott, and he contacted the rest of Colorado's delegation in Washington. Senators Allott and Peter Dominick, along with Representatives Wayne Aspinall, Donald Brotzman, and Mike McKevitt, ushered an "emergency" resolution through Congress declaring support for the DOC and the 1976 Denver Olympics.[18] Secretary of the Interior Rogers Morton wired a message directly to Brundage, pledging support from President Richard Nixon and promising legislation to provide federal financial assistance.[19] On 1 February 1972, Governor Love, Mayor McNichols, and Pringle then took turns addressing the 72nd Session of the International Olympic Committee. John Parr, Howard Gelt, and Estelle Brown sat outside, wondering if they had actually convinced the IOC to take the games away from the Centennial State.[20]

Curiously, in the end Brundage urged the IOC to keep Denver afloat, perhaps expecting that the DOC would eventually implode of its own volition and drown the Winter Olympics for good. Nonetheless, after a prolonged question-and-answer session in Japan, following Brundage's guidance, the IOC allowed the DOC to stay the course.[21] Still, as Coloradans read in their local papers, for more than half a day and half a world away in Tokyo it seemed as if the DOC's chances to host the games had vaporized due to its botched planning combined with CCF's petition of signatures. As George Robinson described of CCF while in Sapporo, "they've drawn blood, there's no doubt about it."[22]

In addition, just a week later, Richard O'Reilly reported from the Sapporo games that television executives indicated to him that the DOC was overlooking the fact that it would have to pay $10–15 million on production equipment and infrastructure to broadcast events. In a front-page story for the *Rocky*, NBC's vice president of sports explained that "they [the DOC] think television is going to make everything whole for them, when really they are going to have to put up the money to make the broadcasting thing happen."[23] ABC's executive for sports production also observed that the DOC would not be able to turn a profit from television.[24] It remains unclear how the DOC's television negotiations would have panned out, but O'Reilly's revelation certainly left the organizers looking even more uninformed and unprepared. "I don't quite understand the whole thing, and I don't understand the technical factors involved," Governor Love admitted; "I don't even know if this is true."[25] DOC members further aggravated the issue by discussing openly how "there may be ways to break even." This appeared to confirm that the DOC had done some bad accounting; its previous TV broadcast–related projections were overconfident and way off.[26]

Figure 9.1. February 1972. The American flag is raised at the 1972 Sapporo Winter Olympics closing ceremony; despite resistance in Colorado, the IOC was prepared to bring the Olympics to Denver. Photo by Rolls Press/Popperfoto via Getty Images.

The happenings in Japan made the DOC look mismanaged and untrustworthy. As the Sapporo Games concluded, the American flag rose just below that of Japan's at the event's closing ceremony. In the backdrop, a large digital screen proclaimed to attendees: "We meet again in Denver '76." Yet as O'Reilly assessed it, the "DOC has created a bad credibility gap with the public, and so far, there are no signs that anything is being done to change it." The "games," he wrote, "remain a source of heated controversy."[27] About two weeks after the drama in Japan, Richard Olson indicated as much to Governor Love: "It is going to take quite an effort to get the whole community behind us," he confessed.[28]

Under intensifying scrutiny, the DOC and its backers continued to seek public money to keep their operation running.[29] In March 1972, as CCF prepared its petition drive for the ballot measure, Governor Love gave a speech to the Colorado General Assembly supporting a coming DOC request for $896,400. In defense of this appropriation, Love predicted that the overall cost of Olympic facilities and operations would reach $35 million and promised the taxpayer contribution would be no more than $5 million.[30]

Yet it soon became evident that the governor and the DOC massaged those numbers. The total of $35 million did not count an added $25 million that the DOC expected to go toward press housing and the costs of constructing the Alpine racecourses at Beaver Creek. Love's projection also did not include $10 million that the DOC anticipated obtaining from the city of Denver to improve the Denver Coliseum, the Currigan Convention Center, and Mile High Stadium. As the DOC later explained, these costs were "indirect . . . benefits derived as a result of the Games." In the DOC's portrayal, since the city needed these projects completed regardless, the Olympics should be understood as speeding them up, not causing them.[31] But the reality was that, as the DOC treasurer Graydon Hubbard described privately, "the total number [of Olympic expenses] can range anywhere from $50 million to probably well into the hundreds of millions, depending on who does the defining of 'Olympic costs' and where he strikes his total."[32] What is more, although the DOC had finally pinned down most of its event sites, it still did not yet have precise expenditure projections from engineers for facility construction.[33]

Thus, when the DOC came before the Colorado Joint Budget Committee following Love's speech, it experienced a redux of the antagonism from the year before. As a *Denver Post* reporter described, the committee chairman Donald Friedman "literally forced" larger numbers out of the DOC when, two hours into the hearing, he asserted, "I couldn't tell anyone who asked me right now how much this will cost." Friedman eventually directed Carl DeTemple to write all the DOC's needs on a blackboard, including those classified as "indirect."[34] With "direct" and "indirect" expenses combined, the price for hosting the Denver Olympics looked to be $65.3 million.[35] Then, just weeks later, the DOC publicly raised that total to between $81,169,000 and $92,813,000.[36]

As the Denver press recounted, various JBC members expressed exasperation. "If you'll pardon me my saying so," Senator Joe Shoemaker remarked to the DOC, "one of your problems is that you don't have a plan."[37] Chairman Friedman became equally disgruntled. To "restore confidence" and "have a successful Olympics," he called for the resignation of the entire DOC.[38] The JBC eventually suggested the state provide only $268,000 to the organizers, far less than requested. That was what legislators initially included in Colorado's annual budget.[39]

In response, Olympics boosters pressed back. Love reached out to fellow Republican Party leaders, while the Democratic Mayor McNichols and city council members reportedly "blitzed the State House of Representatives."[40] The staunchest resistance to funding the DOC came from House Democrats, led by Richard Lamm and Robert Jackson. Knowing this, DeTemple wrote a long explanation of the DOC's monetary needs and sent it to the House Democratic caucus, pleading for its support.[41] Enough Colorado legislators acquiesced, sending the DOC a manageable $739,000.[42] Nonetheless, Coloradans would learn through newspaper outlets that some saw reason to be disappointed by that decision. "When the DOC comes to a legislative body and says, 'have confidence in us. Give us a little more money,'" JBC chairman Friedman grumbled, "it's like the captain of the Titanic suggesting we take another voyage."[43]

Around the same time, in concert with the DOC and Denver authorities, Colorado's delegation in Washington presented identical bills in the United States Senate and House promising Denver Olympic organizers $15.5 million in federal funds.[44] Yet in the Senate, a small group led by Sam Brown confidant Fred Harris opposed the bill. Before the matter could finally come to a vote, Harris and Allott engaged in a six-and-a-half-hour debate on the Senate floor. As Harris averred, the Olympics was a "gross example of making working class people pay for rich men's games."[45] Federal authorities also pressured the DOC to provide evidence that its new sports facilities would be used after the Olympics were over, in contrast to the structures the government funded for the Squaw Valley Olympics.[46] Richard Lamm and the POME representative C. Ransom Stovall thereby took an opportunity to testify before a congressional subcommittee considering the matter and asked the federal government to withhold its sponsorship.[47]

The Senate passed the bill, S. 3531, 59–3.[48] Wester Otis of the Department of the Interior observed afterward that in Washington, "there's nobody against the Olympics. It's like apple pie and motherhood and those things."[49] Colorado lieutenant governor John Vanderhoof even told reporters: "My conversations with people high in the administration—not congress, but the [President's] administration—indicates that this (the 15.5 million) is only part of what the federal government will do for us." "There has never been a federal program that hasn't grown in size once it was established," Vanderhoof mused.[50] However, anti-Olympics pressures persisted and yielded influence. The Senate made federal support contingent on state spending, and the House decided to wait until after the November election to take up the issue of Olympic financing.[51] The DOC survived but again appeared on the defensive.

With anxieties about costs and the DOC's reliability escalating, the question was: Where would Colorado voters land? In this context, in another salient example of regime governance in Colorado, the businessmen behind the DOC asked Governor Love to take the lead in DOC's newest public relations charge. As Richard Olson instructed, Love's March 1972 speech to the Colorado legislature "should kick this effort off, and a well planned public relation program should follow immediately."[52] Two weeks after his speech, Love met with the public relations expert Sam Lusky, Olson, and other Olympic planners to strategize. Lusky was the president of a firm in Denver and joined the Olympic effort in this crucial moment at the request of several of his clients.[53] He worked with Love to form the "Committee of '76 for the Spirit of '76." Love headed the group and recruited seventy-six symbolic "core members" to assist him.[54]

Colorado business executives constituted and underwrote the Committee of '76. The Denver Chamber of Commerce solicited support on the group's behalf, and money came in from the same sources that had, in the late 1960s, paid for Denver's Olympic bid. Colorado corporations such as the Colorado National Bank, the First National Bank of Denver, the Gates Rubber Company, and the *Denver Post* provided funds.[55] Through such means, Love and Lusky raised over $36,000 in just two weeks.[56] As the DOC's longtime public relations adviser Norm Brown described, this was the beginning of the "real power play and big money."[57]

The Committee of '76 used the corporate largesse on bumper stickers, lapel badges, and advertising space in twenty-five daily newspapers. Here it endeavored to conflate Olympic support with devotion to state and nation. As Lusky described, the aim was "to make the Olympics a *piece de resistance* of the total package of [Colorado's] Centennial and [America's] Bicentennial—not a cause in and of itself."[58] As one Committee for '76 advertisement proclaimed: "We believe in Colorado. . . . We believe in the people of Colorado. . . . We believe in our Centennial. . . . We believe in our Nation's Bicentennial. . . . We believe that the Winter Olympics, held in Colorado in 1976, will give our state the worldwide prideful attention it deserves, and which may never again be possible during any of our lifetimes." The full-page promotion then asked fellow "believers" to join the pro-Olympics cause.[59]

To help the DOC further its case, it also hired William Kostka's firm, Kostka Associates. As DOC meeting minutes describe, through press releases, newsletters, and general openness with the media, Kostka's "new program will try to develop confidence in the DOC."[60] As part of this project, with no more reason to hide event relocations from the IOC, the Denver organizers permitted the public to attend its meetings.[61] They started releasing monthly financial reports and required DOC members to disclose conflicts of interest as well.[62] Then, in May 1972, the DOC prepared to "restructure" itself completely. That summer, the organization literally changed its name, becoming the Denver Olympic Organizing Committee (DOOC). As Olympic organizers announced, the DOOC board of directors would be twice the size of the old DOC's, with a membership "easily exceeding 150 people." The Olympics boosters tried to appear more diverse, seeking to include women, "minorities," environmentalists, representatives from various interest groups, and young people.[63]

However, for purposes of clarity within this book, the Denver Olympic Organizing Committee will continue to be referred to as the "DOC." This was no genuine "restructuring." As George Robinson described in a private letter, the refurbished committee "would have more generalized, but limited functions. The actual operation would be under the guidance of a chairman."[64] The Denver Olympic team hired W. R. Goodwin to take on this role. He was the chief operating officer of the land development corporation Johns Manville. Meanwhile, everyone involved with the old DOC "joined" the new DOOC, and the fourteen-member board of governors, which ran the "day-to-day operation," included many former DOC contributors. As a DOOC/DOC newsletter admitted, the "full-time staff . . . remained basically the same."[65]

In the summer of 1972, the DOC also held an essay contest titled "Seniors for '76" to promote community enthusiasm and associate the games with youthfulness.[66] The organizers challenged Colorado ninth-graders—who would be high school seniors when the Denver Olympics took place—to write about why they supported the Olympic movement. After hundreds took part, with funds loaned by the Denver Chamber of Commerce, the DOC awarded twelve winners a well-publicized trip to Europe. There, the students witnessed the 1972 Munich Olympics, visited sites from the 1968 Grenoble Winter Games, and stopped off at IOC headquarters in Lausanne.[67] Upon returning home, as the Denver press duly reported, the young scribes shared cake and ice cream with Mayor McNichols in his office.[68]

Pro-Olympics advocates comparably wanted to show that they had the allegiance of esteemed adults. Governor John Love thus oversaw the National Advisory Committee to the 1976 Winter Olympic Games. Its stated purpose was to advise Love and McNichols while mustering public and private backing from throughout the nation. Bud Wilkinson, the former University of Oklahoma football coach and President Nixon's Advisor on Physical Fitness, acted as the chairperson.[69] He began making public appearances, insisting it was "inconceivable that any American not take pride in getting to host the games."[70] Concurrently, most of the group's other eighteen contributors represented extremely wealthy businessmen and served as figureheads. When Love asked William Marriot (chairman of the board of Marriot Corporation) to join the group, the hotel executive replied that he was too busy.[71] Love convinced Marriot to take part by telling him, "I certainly understand your circumstance, but want to assure you that really all that would be required is the use of your name and very, very occasional contact."[72] Other members who provided use of their name included William Ford (vice president and director of Ford Motor Company), Archie K. Davis (chairman of the board of Wachovia Bank and Trust), David Packard (chairman of the board of Hewlett Packard), Robert Six (president of Continental Airlines), Thomas Watson (chairman of the executive committee of IBM), and Gustave L. Levy (general manager of Goldman Sachs).[73] The DOC believed association with these men would imbue the Denver Games with the respect and dependability that many now thought it lacked.[74]

But perhaps most important, Olympics proponents rested their case by espousing the IOC's professed philosophy of Olympism. They argued that, along with economic benefits, the Denver Games deserved public resources because the Olympics was an unmatched vehicle for uniting people from across the globe and celebrating human excellence.[75] As the Olympic scholars Matthew Burbank, Gregory Andranovich, and Charles Heying point out, deploying the "symbolic appeal" of the Olympics has often been vital and effective for organizers. Justifications for hosting the event based on economics are usually precarious. Organizers cannot justify their agenda on balance sheets alone. However, many find it difficult to argue against universal values such as mutual respect among the world's people and the pursuit of human potential.[76]

Denver Olympics opponents might argue that Colorado would be better off with state money going to health care, education, environmental protection, or affordable housing. Nevertheless, as former mayor Currigan asserted, while "all of these things are good . . . [i]t is ridiculous to make this kind of comparison." From Currigan's point of view, it was "impossible to measure the worth and the long-range benefits of the Olympics in dollars." "How do you measure the worth of people-to-people diplomacy? How do you measure the Olympics as an instrument of peace, as a way to foster understanding between peoples?" he asked. As Currigan contended: "Goodwill through fair competition, mutual respect, universal ideals and striving for excellence . . . simply cannot be measured in dollars and cents."[77] As a result, when Lamm, Jackson, and CCF suggested that the state focus on other more pressing local concerns, Colorado's Olympic ideologues could respond that the invaluable purposes of the Winter Games outweighed it all.

During hard times, this was how the DOC argued for public funding and approval. After its first and unexpectedly contentious meeting with the Mountain Area Protection Council, the DOC associate James Cotter reached out to the MAPC's president to explain that "the principal benefits" of hosting the Olympics would be "moral values" and that "the Olympic movement is indeed one of the few important social forces for good."[78] When the legislature's JBC first questioned Olympic spending in 1971, the DOC likewise responded in part by emphasizing that the "Olympics are described by some as the prime social force at work in the world today."[79]

The DOC's treasurer, Graydon Hubbard, brought this view to its fullest conclusion. In mid-January 1972, he drafted a memorandum to the DOC executive council and other DOC supporters in which he discussed various reasons that hosting the games appeared misguided. He admitted running an Olympics so "expenditures . . . do not exceed operating revenues . . . may not be realistic" and that staging "an Olympic games is not possible without the financial support of government." Indeed, according to Hubbard, new facilities such as a ski jump, luge course, and speed skating rink "have questionable economic after-use," require "very significant financial contribution" from the state, and thus represented a serious "financial risk."[80] Still, months later, testifying before the JBC, he justified going into the red. "Even if the cost to the government, and therefore to taxpayers, of hosting an Olympics is not recovered from added tax revenues and tourist spending in the future," the DOC treasurer told policy makers, "the price to pay seems small in comparison to the opportunity to make a contribution . . . to international goodwill and understanding." Hubbard continued: "The benefits to be derived from stimulating friendship among nations through sports and an international festival, in relation to the amount invested therein, is proportionately far greater than the benefits derived from billions in taxpayer funds spent over the years in foreign aid and similar programs." As Hubbard put it, too "many of the Olympic benefits are intangible . . . [and] simply cannot be adequately translated into dollars and cents."[81] Hubbard claimed that higher state taxes and unsustainable sports facilities were a fair price to pay to contribute to the immeasurable goals of the Olympic movement.

DeTemple took a similar line a few months later when pleading with Colorado House Democrats for funding, writing: "While we recognize the necessity for deeply probing the economic implications of the Olympic Winter Games, at this point it would be unfortunate if they were judged only in this context." The DOC leader asked the officeholders to "consider the less tangible impact" and described the "real meaning" of the Olympics as "a once-in-a-lifetime opportunity to be at the center of a truly international event of goodwill and brotherhood." "The Olympic Games," DeTemple implored, "represent the brightest hope for the future that someday peoples from all walks of life and all nationalities can discover the totality of mutual interest that will result in peaceful cooperation."[82] Given the House's eventual decision to lift state funding near the DOC's original request in the spring of 1972, at least for some members such reasoning seemed to be persuasive.

Olympism remained the keynote ringing from Olympics supporters as they entered the final stretch. In summer 1972, with the vote on CCF's initiative imminent, Love and Lusky replicated their prior strategy but to a larger extent. Love enfolded the Committee of '76 into yet another group, Coloradans for the 1976 Olympics. Businessman Charles Gates Jr. took charge of soliciting funds, and a legislative assistant to Lieutenant Governor Vanderhoof directed the operation. Meanwhile, Love, McNichols, and DOC members attended weekly briefings.[83] They anticipated a budget of $125,000. One source suggested the pro-Olympics force took in $200,000 within its first six weeks; another noted that the number reached $500,000 overall.[84] As Lusky explained to Love, the funds would make possible "a hard-hitting, dramatically publicized pro-Olympics campaign."[85]

Thus, in the month before the November election, powered by 176 ads in over fifty Colorado newspapers, 190 television commercials, and 1,274 radio announcements, Coloradans for the 1976 Olympics tried to saturate Colorado media with an Olympism-infused concoction.[86] "Colorado's Winter Olympics can bring a return to the Olympic ideal as it was meant to be," Governor Love professed in an October 1972 advertisement; it "is time for a world re-birth of the true ideals and meanings of the Olympics, and we in Colorado have it within our capability to achieve these goals: To dedicate the '76 Winter Olympics to the participants themselves, to the world of brotherhood . . . to the true spirit of competition . . . [and to] demonstrate that Colorado and Coloradans can undertake an event of such proportions." Love's plea concluded, referring to the title of the anti-Olympics measure: "Light the torch now. Vote NO on Amendment No. 8."[87]

Mayor William McNichols pushed Olympism as well, creating his own group, the Mayor's Committee for the Olympics, which included several well-known Colorado athletes.[88] As McNichols attested in a pro-Olympics pamphlet, released weeks before the initiative: "All men and women of good conscience know that when we meet people from other lands and cultures we understand them better and [we] appreciate the spirit of cooperation which must exist between all peoples of the world if we are to gain peace. . . . It is in this spirit that the competition of the Olympics was born." McNichols

Figure 9.2. October 1972. A billboard in Denver depicts DOC pro-Olympics rhetoric from Governor Love and the DOC, urging citizens to "Light the Torch Now" and vote against the anti-Olympics ballot issue. Photo by Melvyn E. Schieltz via Denver Public Library, Western History Collection, WH2129-2018-374.

promised to hold the Denver games at a reasonable cost, sparking the economy, improving the environment, and advancing the city's housing infrastructure. But moreover, the mayor professed, hosting the Olympic games and spreading Olympic ideals was simply the right thing to do. "Are we now to turn our collective back on the youth of the world?" McNichols asked. Are "we now to say that we do not wish to share understanding with our world neighbors through the cultural, philosophic, and athletic excellence of the Olympic Games?" "No!" McNichols insisted: "Join us in defeating Colorado Constitutional Amendment #8 . . . VOTE NO."[89]

As DOC president, DeTemple also made numerous television and radio appearances and sat for extensive newspaper interviews. In line with the approach taken by Love and Lusky, he tried to assuage people's worries over environmental damage and reckless spending by tethering Olympic ideals to celebrations of Colorado and America.[90] As DeTemple explained during a television spot, aside from "the practical benefits, we will be participating in the single most important example of international goodwill and peaceful competition that exists in our troubled world. In working, playing, and living with people from many nations," the DOC leader proclaimed, "we will be representing more than Denver or Colorado. We will be representing our nation and its 200 years of history, as well as our basic philosophy of freedom and individual dignity."[91]

"International sports provide one of the most permanent and unifying links between the people of the world," a separate Coloradans for the 1976 Olympics promotion began. "Recognition of this fact comes when one sees athletes from 128 nations participating in the Olympic Games." "When Coloradans go to the polls November 7 to vote on Amendment 8," the Olympics promoters urged, "all the world will watch and learn what we of this state feel about the ideals and objectives [that] the Olympics encompass."[92] Thus, Olympics backers tried to reframe the discussion. Combining Olympism, nationalism, localism, and more than a tinge of guilt, they asked Colorado citizens to stand with their state, their nation, and the Olympic movement.

It was a political move. A DOC-commissioned poll conducted in mid-September 1972 had advised Olympic advocates "against giving the impression that Colorado is going to be overrun in the future by tourists and winter sports enthusiasts." As pollsters concluded, "sports promotion is not one of the advantages [of hosting the Olympics] that will turn a lot of opponents around, although it may be an essential part of the overall thrust." Given that this poll also found that Amendment 8's chance for passing was a "toss-up," it appeared clear that to keep the Olympics in Colorado the DOC needed to convince voters that hosting the games represented something other than what it really was: a growth-oriented commercial endeavor.[93] Yet it of course remained to be seen how much weight Olympism carried with the spectrum of Centennial State voters when compared to their competing interests and ideals.

CHAPTER 10

The Event Coalition and the Rights of Citizenship

The Olympic historian Kevin Wamsley contends that, rather than the event's reason for existence, "during the twentieth century, the nebulous concept of Olympism became the structural apologetic" for the game's shortcomings. It became an "empty flask," Wamsley asserts, "to be filled by the next political, economic, educational opportunist."[1] This was how Robert Jackson read the pro-Olympics argument. The "thing about all this is that people hold the Olympics as something sacred, as something untouchable," Jackson reflected during the 1972 legislative debate over state funding. "We clothe the Olympics in a different aura, a kind of mystique," he went on. "It almost becomes what is known as the holiness of the Olympics, something removed from other sports and something that must be subsidized by state supporting monies." However, citing unknown costs, questionable benefits, and environmental damage, Jackson insisted, "I'm still for killing the Olympics."[2]

As it turned out, most Colorado voters agreed with him. They did not buy what the DOC and company were selling this time. Mexican American and African American Denverites continued to distrust the DOC and municipal authorities. Foothills environmentalists remained determined to keep events out of their middle-class refuge. Richard Lamm, Jackson, and Citizens for Colorado's Future claimed unceasingly that the Winter Olympics was fiscally misguided, environmentally dangerous, and the product of a corrupt establishment that undercut the rights of American democracy. The constant flow of grievances emanating from the city and mountains, the legitimizing voices of Lamm and Jackson, critical journalists such as Richard O'Reilly, CCF's shrewd campaigning, and persistent organizer missteps dragged the presence and politics of Colorado's growth regime out into the open. As a result, for a diversity of parties, opposing the Olympics became the preferred—even the more "American"—thing to do.

*   *   *

Within CCF's initiative to defeat the DOC, allusions to racial justice and fair housing became a relatively silent—or, perhaps more accurately, silenced—partner. The specific issues impacting Mexican Americans and African Americans took a back seat to fears of environmental damage, unjust taxation, and generalized worries about the integrity of citizenship. In CCF's effort to recruit white "middle Americans," this may have been to the coalition-builders' advantage. The white working and middle classes were probably drawn less to demands for racial inclusion and affordable homes for poor urbanites and more to the other matters involved. Nonetheless, Coloradans of color did their part to banish the games. There were multiple views among Brown and Black Denverites regarding the Olympics, but the two counties with the largest percentages of Mexican American and African American citizens produced the highest percentages of ballots cast to bar state funding of Denver '76.[3]

Local politicians such as Elvin Caldwell and Betty Benavidez supported hosting the Olympics until the finish. Others took more restrained or ambivalent stances. Some West Side and East Side residents supported the Denver Urban Renewal Authority's housing project for the press, even if they continued to express trepidation about losing control over its purported long-term outcome. As one Denverite complained, the entire thing seemed to be "rammed down our throats."[4] With the ballot measure a month away, the African American and Denver Planning Board member Beverly Biffle (the wife of Olympian Jerome Biffle) conveyed her doubts by refusing to vote on DURA's housing proposal. The board's decision was 5–0 in favor of the project. Biffle stood as a lone abstention.[5] Other West Side groups tried to leverage their exclusion from the latter stages of the planning process by refusing to endorse the city's updated housing offer until DURA agreed to additional improvements to area schools, health care facilities, recreation spaces, and shopping centers.[6]

Yet others from more militant circles turned against the games outright. In late February 1972, with the volume of Olympic objections ascending after the Sapporo Games, the Chicano pastor Peter Garcia and Lauren Watson of the Black Panthers created a new outfit, the Denver Olympic Citizen Group. Garcia and Watson no longer sought control over Olympic planning. Now, as they explained, they aimed to "unite blacks, Chicanos, Asians, Indians, women and young people in opposition to the Olympics." A little over two weeks after being released from jail on bond for conspiracy to commit a robbery, Lauren Watson proclaimed that he was ready to return to prison if it meant stopping the sports event. "We'll have mass demonstrations and anything else it takes. If we cause trouble and have to go to jail, we'll go to jail," Watson promised.[7]

Such sentiments persisted into the summer. In June 1972, with CCF's petition drive entering its final days, DURA met with West Side residents to explain its ultimate housing proposition, which it had redesigned without seeking community input. In the middle of the meeting, upon hearing the "benefits" of potential residential relocations, Peter Garcia stood up to shout in protest: "We heard the same, pardon the expression, bullshit two years ago!" Many of the estimated two hundred West Siders in attendance—aware of Garcia's reference to Auraria—applauded in response.[8] When a planning board member in attendance asked the residents if anyone still supported the housing project, he received no answer.[9] Garcia, in particular, never trusted the DOC and DURA to build low- and middle-income homes.[10]

Just as well, around this time, Lauren Watson's brother, Clarke Watson, and six other protesters parked a mule-drawn wagon in the middle of Denver's 16th Street. With traffic blocked, Clarke Watson railed against the Olympics over a loudspeaker, echoing CCF sentiments. He asserted that the mules symbolized "beasts of burned, mirroring the plight of the poor (who) are taxed for purposes that are useful only to a few members of the power elite."[11] The Chicano-inspired La Raza Unida Party also came out against the games. In its 1972 platform, the party's Colorado contingent declared that, due to "the contradictory nature of the present development of plans for the 1976 Winter Olympics, we fail to see any resulting benefits for Chicanos and the poor, and therefore oppose the diversion of badly needed financial resources from education and other crucial human issues."[12]

On top of this, Mexican American and African American actors who were less radical moved toward opposition. The Mexican American community organizer John Zapien and the African American Democratic candidate for the Colorado House Arie Taylor both worked with Citizens for Colorado's Future, recruiting petition signatures and then votes.[13] Other urbanites may have simply wished to stay in their homes or keep their communities intact. For example, after saving for years to purchase her property, the West Side's Barbara Trujillo demanded that the city let her remain there. She enjoyed her neighbors, the commute to work, and had long endeavored to shape her house to her liking. "What kind of Democratic Government is this getting to be," Trujillo lamented to Mayor McNichols, "that an individual cannot stay and live where you choose."[14] Many East Side and West Side residents expressed doubts about whether city planners would truly relocate displaced residents, a notion to which Trujillo also alluded.[15] With Denver set to contribute a portion of the overall cost for the press housing facilities, it made her "even sicker" to think her own tax dollars might pay for her and her neighbors to be "thrown out on our ear."[16]

Despite the prospect of gaining affordable housing, a large portion of Mexican American and Black stakeholders retained little faith in the impulses and assurances of Denver's growth machine. After all, Denver leaders did not take up the issue of affordable living with such verve until the games entered the balance. The Mile High City's East Side and West Side inhabitants likely speculated about the self-interest and racism that led DURA to neglect low-income housing until now and then attach it to a sports event. If it were so important, why not just build the homes regardless? Indeed, DURA circumvented citizen feedback and rushed through its final scheme to ensure the facilities would be ready for the arrival of Olympians in 1976. Olympics proponents even used housing as a point of leverage to motivate citizens to vote down the CCF initiative, claiming that without the games the project would fall through.[17] It appeared to be no secret that Denver powerbrokers cared more about tourist promotion than addressing the systemic inequities confronting marginalized Denver citizens. The Olympics, not fair housing, was the priority. When push came to shove, this state of affairs probably left many Mexican Americans and African Americans inclined to stand with CCF instead of the DOC.

White middle-class environmentalists did their share to jettison the spectacle as well. As the summer of 1972 became the fall, many foothills inhabitants concluded that, to protect their towns' naturalistic ethos, the games needed to be pushed out of Colorado altogether. At the same time, aesthetic-based environmental opposition to the Olympics began to spread to other mountain communities and attract traditional environmentalist organizations.

During most of the Olympics debate, the Mountain Area Protection Council and Protect Our Mountain Environment objected only to events taking place in certain parts of Colorado. They were not completely against the Denver Olympics. In late June, on the day CCF turned in its signature petitions to qualify the anti-Olympics measure for the November ballot, POME's Vance Dittman wrote to the DOC president Carl DeTemple and advised that "if you face the facts now and move your bobsled, luge, and ski jumps . . . you *may* salvage a degree of support otherwise lost to you."[18] The DOC, however, allowed its unrealistic plans for Jefferson County to linger for too long. As late as mid-September, the organizers still intended to see the luge, bobsled, and ski jump events in Jeffco. And although the DOC eventually moved ski jumping to Steamboat Springs in late October and made plans to combine the luge and bobsled into a single structure, at the time of the vote the organizers remained set on bringing luge and bobsled races to Jefferson County's Genesee Park.[19]

POME and the MAPC thus align themselves with CCF. As POME's Richard Kithil wrote to members in September, at "this point many of us have become convinced that we cannot reach any responsive ear if we continue to follow our past policy of having no objection to the Olympics per se, but only an objection to staging them in the Front Range of our county. We feel that we have no choice left but to strongly and effectively oppose holding the Olympics in Colorado AT ALL."[20] POME members consequently disseminated petitions, collected donations, and funded commercials to support CCF's effort to halt Olympic spending.[21] Furthermore, on the exact day of Kithal's missive to POME supporters, MAPC leaders wrote to their membership for advice. "Our representatives feel certain that the only means left to citizen groups to influence [the] relocation of [Olympic] sites is toward passage of the constitutional amendment which would deny state funding for the Games," the letter read. "Therefore, it is time to re-examine our position and determine whether we should now oppose state funding as the only way to remove the events from the area."[22] In early October, this became the MAPC's updated policy.[23]

POME and the MAPC constituted a small portion of the electorate and focused on protecting a confined cultural space; but since the moment the DOC secured the games, both groups reached far and wide to promote their common agenda. After POME formed, it started placing ads in newspapers with anti-Olympics coupons for readers to mail to county commissioners, Governor Love, and the IOC.[24] POME contributors directed over a thousand complaints to the DOC alone.[25] The MAPC also encouraged its members to keep the Olympic issue "stirred up through a letter writing campaign" aimed at Olympic planners and local officials.[26] With the 1972 Winter Olympics in Sapporo around the corner, Dittman wrote to IOC headquarters in Lausanne asking for "the names and addresses of all the members of the International Olympic Committee" so that he could "communicate with each one of them."[27] As he told Avery Brundage: "Because of the insensitivity of the DOC . . . we have resolved to take our objections" to you.[28] After Brundage acceded to the request, POME flooded the Olympic decision makers with their anti-Olympics protestations, goading them to move the games from the Front Range.[29] The foothills activists wrote to foreign Olympic committees and international sports federations. They even pleaded with Sion, Switzerland, the runner-up to Denver for the 1976 Winter Games, to try to finagle the event from the DOC.[30] Through such advocacy, POME gained local and national press coverage.[31] In fact, according to polling conducted on the DOC's behalf, while many Coloradans worried most about raised taxes and DOC corruption, respondents recognized Protect Our Mountain Environment more often than they did CCF, Richard Lamm, or Robert Jackson.[32]

Thus, the notion that the games would harm nature became ubiquitous, and other environmentalists came over to support POME and the MAPC. In April 1971, when POME penned a letter explaining its position to the International Olympic Committee and other sports federations, fifteen mostly local advocacy groups cosigned.[33] Foothills residents remained the heart of Colorado's environmentally oriented Olympics resistance. Nonetheless, by 1972, the Colorado Open Space Council, the Rocky Mountain chapter of the Sierra Club, and the Rocky Mountain Sportsmen Federation each went on record as opposing the Denver Games for environmental reasons.[34]

Amid all this, as the DOC began to reexamine event locations, other towns shared the attitude boiling up from Indian Hills and Evergreen. When the DOC considered moving cross-country skiing to Buffalo Creek in Jefferson County, 150 members of the Buffalo Park Improvement Association joined the middle-class environmentalist chorus.[35] Similarly, after officials and businesses in Aspen announced their intention to vie for the Alpine races, inhabitants of the upscale ski town rebelled. During the previous two decades, the town's old-time miners and neonatives had watched as their homes and identities became engulfed by the exploding corporate ski industry.[36] At the beginning of 1972, after the Aspen Chamber of Commerce voted to support an attempt to gain the Alpine events, over 200 townspeople seemed to have had enough, as they crammed the Pitkin County District Court House during a city council meeting to register anti-Olympics and anti-growth remonstrations.[37]

But perhaps most telling, Colorado citizens in general realized that Denver '76 provided a means through which to convey middle-class environmentalist allegiances. For instance, residents of Georgetown farther west of Evergreen never faced a direct threat from the Denver games. Yet the historic mountain rest stop, about forty-five minutes from Denver on Interstate 70, used the Olympic debate to voice its outlook on full-throttled tourist promotion. As one townsperson described, residents feared Olympic visitors would make Georgetown "disappear." The chairperson of the town's Historic Commission explained that the town, if needed, would employ architecture ordinances to preserve "esthetics" and "control what we are looking at." Georgetown's mayor put it more coarsely. If Olympic planners "come in and run all over us and use us as a 10,000-car parking lot," he warned, "we'll make Evergreen look like nothing; they'll find a bunch of s.o.b.s up here."[38]

Thanks to the ingenuity and outrage of activists in the Front Range, the Olympics became a platform for white middle-class Colorado citizens to signal their desire to slow—within the sphere of their everyday routines— the rush of postwar commercial growth and development. These opponents became so adamant that DOC pollsters determined "there is no reason to hard sell the ecologically concerned . . . [they] probably won't buy any argument."[39] Colorado boosters needed to look elsewhere to save the Denver Olympics.

According to the DOC's research, the best bet for Olympics advocates was to reassure working-class blue-collar voters that the games would not cost too much. "Business professionals, white collars, the young, and retired voters are the most reticent about supporting the Olympics," pollsters wrote, "while the working class middle-aged voter are the most supportive."[40] It was here, however, that the DOC and Olympism ran up against CCF and citizens' rights.

Several CCF members admitted that they viewed Olympics proponents as driven by a combination of motivations: pure self-interest and "pride in Colorado and Patriotism," a "badge of distinction," or "civic pride."[41] But in the months and weeks before the election, CCF focused on the former impulse. "The groups planning and promoting the Olympics," CCF alleged, "are dominated by a business and financial elite which comprise a virtual *Who's Who* of wealth, power and influence in Colorado" with "numerous instances of substantial conflicts of interest." "Just about everyone who profits from a crowd," the anti-Olympics activists argued, contributed to the Olympic cause to their own benefit. Although "certain sectors of the business community always clear big profits from games," CCF literature contended, these were "profits the taxpayer must subsidize." "No government has ever made enough money from the Olympics to cover the money put into it," the coalition-builders stressed.[42]

In addition to depicting the DOC as a group of selfish elites, in its campaign material CCF continued to construct itself as the genuine representative of mainstream citizens. The group was not shy about trying to keep up with the DOC in the contest over public perceptions. A full-page article titled "CCF, DOOC Map out Counterplans to Win Vote" exemplifies this. It noted that the pro-Olympics "Coloradans for the '76 Winter Games" would "conduct a massive media campaign," and "because the group's strength is the business community, the style . . . will resemble that of marketing a new product like toothpaste or dog food." In contrast, CCF depicted itself as "totally supported by citizen contributions," even though it had gained a substantial silent donation early on from a wealthy Coloradan named Vic Braden. Through a Lamm connection, the group benefited from a fundraising concert featuring the Grammy Award–winning folk singer and Yippie activist Judy Collins as well.[43] All the same, as CCF told it, due to its comparatively limited budget, instead of relying on money, it would use its "greatest resource—people."[44] Moreover, alongside this article, CCF featured a picture of the small house it worked out of next to a photo of the multistory building where the DOC's office could be found. CCF intentionally made it appear as if the Olympic organizers were using the entire structure, even though the opponents knew that was untrue.[45]

With the anti-Olympics measure assured in late June, CCF did effective groundwork too. After spending about $20,000 on the initiative campaign, the group would have to seek donations to cover its debts.[46] Judging by monetary assets, it was under-resourced. To raise finances during the campaign, CCF solicited donations through mailers and sold bumper stickers reading "Vote YES for NO Olympics," "The Olympics Are Taxing," "Save Our Money, Save Our Mountains—Stop the Olympics," and "Recycle the Olympics to Squaw Valley." At the same time, Lamm and Jackson went on television and radio to explain Olympic drawbacks, as CCF's younger operatives assigned volunteers to blocks, neighborhoods, precincts, and districts to distribute campaign literature door-to-door. Through an estimated 5,000 volunteers, CCF dispensed an approximated 550,000 anti-Olympics pamphlets in the month leading up to the vote.[47] CCF continued to instruct fellow Olympics opponents on how to talk with likely voters and how to organize more volunteers. It added a fifth primary coordinator named Bill Brachman, another recent law school graduate from the East Coast, who advocated for the anti-Olympics amendment on the Western Slope, the large, mostly conservative region west of Colorado's major ski resorts in Summit County and Vail. As November drew near, CCF continued to advise volunteers on ways to increase the number of foot soldiers and develop effective materials and directives to pass along. The week of the election (officially Tuesday, 7 November), the coalition-builders encouraged followers to hold anti-Olympics signs at voting sites, pass out anti-Olympics tracts, or "simply park a car with [anti-Olympics] bumper stickers on it near the polling place."[48] When the opponents learned that local television stations provided the DOC free advertising, they also successfully petitioned for equal time.[49] Through these methods, CCF made its case against the games, reached a broad audience, and embodied a genuine grassroots organization that listened to and cared about the inhabitants of the Centennial State.

And the DOC and other Olympics boosters played right into CCF's hands. The DOC could have embraced holding some form of referendum. Roger

Figure 10.1. October 1972. Dwight Filley maps out CCF's campaign strategy with three other CCF contributors, seeking to motivate voters to block state spending on the Olympics via the ballot. Photo by Melvyn E. Schieltz via Denver Public Library, Western History Collection, WH2129-2018-373.

Hansen, an environmentalist and Olympics supporter, suggested doing this. He reasoned that this strategy would serve as "a display of good faith and sincere concern over the wishes of the people" and "go far in countering the contention that the Olympics is the play thing of a 'special interest group' that cares little for the desires of the citizens of Colorado."[50] But the DOC and other prominent Olympics advocates did the opposite, opposing CCF's citizen-led initiative at every turn.

In March 1972, the *Rocky Mountain News* published a poll showing almost 70 percent of Coloradans favored a statewide vote on Olympic spending.[51] Yet Olympics supporters discouraged such citizen participation. Governor Love responded by saying a potential referendum on holding the games was "too late and destructive."[52] Mayor McNichols argued consistently that the issue had been "put to a vote of representatives of the people—the State

Legislature—in April 1967, and they voted unanimously in favor of Denver and Colorado competing for the [Olympic] designation."[53] "It would be a great hindrance to the [Olympic] effort," he claimed, to "bring this up again when the people supported it through their representatives many years ago."[54]

This shortsightedness allowed CCF to further its position as the one fighting to make democracy happen. Lamm and Jackson had already tried to implement a vote through legislative channels, and CCF literally made a vote possible through its petition and campaign. The 77,000 names CCF collected to get the constitutional amendment on the ballot thus provided an easy counterpoint to Love, McNichols, and the DOC. CCF would round down. As Lundstrom put it, although Love had his Committee of '76: "We could do our 'Committee of 76,000.'"[55]

In the final months of the controversy, CCF continued to take advantage of the DOC's blunders. In particular, the obviously well-funded pro-Olympics Coloradans for the 1976 Olympics concealed its donors, making it appear as if the money it raised came from elites acting in secret on behalf of themselves.[56] "One of our concerns has been the question of who pays and who profits from the Games," Meg Lundstrom announced at a CCF press conference. "Our observation has been that those persons instrumental in planning and promoting the Olympics have been precisely those who will profit." The "refusal to name the new committee's contributors," Lundstrom implored, "leaves us with the suspicion that the bulk of the organization's $150,000 campaign fund has been donated by those sectors of private industry which will make money from an event subsidized by the taxpayers."[57]

The DOC also did itself no favors as its cost estimates continued to rise.[58] As CCF showcased, from December 1967 to May 1970 the DOC listed costs as between $10 million and $14 million.[59] Yet in early 1971, when providing estimates to the Joint Budget Committee, it raised those numbers to between $18 million and $25 million.[60] Preceding the Sapporo Olympics in January 1972, Governor Love placed costs as high as $30 million.[61] Then, after the Sapporo Games, Love and the DOC raised that number to $35 million.[62] Still, Colorado citizens soon learned that if "indirect costs" were included, Olympic expenses would double to around $70 million.[63] Later on, the DOC's admitted estimate rose even higher.[64]

The DOC's pollsters would find that a mere 1 percent of respondents thought the games would cost near $35 million, indicating that few took the projections of political officials and the DOC seriously. By contrast, a plurality of people, 39 percent, stated that they did not know the price tag for the event.[65] Some may not have been following the issue. Still, as the spokespersons for CCF, Lamm and Jackson repeatedly claimed that "I don't know" was the correct answer; nobody knew what the final cost for the Denver Winter Olympic Games was going to be.[66] Thus, although Governor Love eventually promised Colorado would provide no more than $5 million to the DOC, CCF easily levied the charge that such a pledge should not be trusted.[67]

It "was almost like playing into our game over and over," Lundstrom recalled. "We would talk about this decision [to host the Olympics] being made by this small group, and then they announced this committee and then bought big ads. Committee of '76 for the Spirit of '76. It was like: how could you do this?"[68] Sam Brown also recollected bewilderment at the obliviousness of the Olympic organizers. "The Organizing Committee," he explained, "made a series of really stupid mistakes. They were our best friends. . . . [T]he DOC was so imprudent and thoughtless and full of itself . . . assuming, of course, it's the Olympics, and people are not going to vote against the Olympics and that they can win by just pounding the patriotic thumb." "It was a bunch of rich and powerful people," Brown reminisced, "who had really no idea what was going on."[69]

Much as Brown intended, many became convinced that Love, McNichols, the DOC, and their corporate allies were powerbrokers undermining the rights of citizenship and taking advantage of everyday people and that, therefore, opposing the Olympics represented an authentic display of Americanism. In one example, when Governor Love formed the Committee of '76 for the Spirit of '76, a lobbyist for a collection of Rocky Mountain farmers attempted to register the name as the title of his own corporation so that Love could not use it. He hoped to reserve it for 120 days. As this Coloradan saw it, Love's pro-Olympics group was "going to make use of some patriotic arguments," but a "check of history would hardly find those who were for the revolution would have voted for something like the Olympics." As the farm lobbyist claimed, permitting Love's group to use such a name did "a historical disservice" to America's true freedom fighters and its principles of democracy.[70]

With greater sarcasm, the *Denver Post*'s freewheeling editorialist Tom Gavin responded to pro-Olympics rhetoric in a parallel way. "I hadn't realized that it was in the national interest that the '76 Winter Games be held in Denver and its Vail and Steamboat Springs suburbs," Gavin wrote. "I didn't know that what we had here was a matter of national honor. . . . It simply hadn't occurred to me that to have reservations about Denver and Colorado lavishing public money on a sporting event was to be lacking in patriotism."[71] As Gavin indicated, his understanding of patriotism and the DOC's diverged.

A few months later, the journalist Ron Wolf of Boulder's *Straight Creek*

Journal, a self-avowed "alternative press," published an article titled "Who Owns the Olympics? Colorado's Financial Elite Plan 1976 Snow Job for Public." CCF could not have devised a better representation of how it meant to portray Olympics boosters. Wolf pointed out the names and professional statuses of every member of the Denver Organizing Committee, the Colorado Olympic Committee, the Committee of '76, and the National Advisory Committee. By Wolf's accounting, of these 139 Denver Olympics supporters, sixty were millionaires, sixty-nine were corporate presidents or board chairs, forty-six worked as presidents of banks or as bank directors, and four served in the Denver Chamber of Commerce. According to Wolf, the list revealed that if "you want a voice in the staging of the 1976 Winter Olympics, you had better be a millionaire and a corporate president, preferably the president of a bank."[72] The "hierarchies of committees associated with the Olympic effort . . . are dominated by a business and financial elite," Wolf proclaimed. "In fact, most of these people . . . stand to benefit either personally or for the companies they represent, by holding the games in Colorado."[73]

Yet perhaps most revealing were the letters written to Governor Love in the months leading up to the November 1972 vote. They indicated that people from across the state —including those in white, middle-class suburbs—internalized CCF's interpretation. "By hosting the forthcoming winter Olympics," Raymond Foster from Colorado Springs informed Love, "you are permitting the ecological destruction of a beautiful area. . . . Why should we, the residents of Colorado, be expected to foot a significant percentage of the bill to see our beautiful state turned into a commercial venture?" Foster then asked, "Shouldn't we be allowed to vote on whether or not we want the Olympics to be held here?"[74] Christie Drake of Denver pleaded: "I find it distressing that monies are being taken away from health areas and given to the Denver Olympic Commission. Let's once and for all ask the people of Colorado how they feel about the 1976 Winter Olympics. After all, isn't that the democratic process?!"[75] A Denverite named Mary Freed did not even take the time to list her reasons for objecting to the Winter Olympics, telling her governor he probably knew them already. "My only request," she asserted, "is that the people of Colorado be allowed to vote on the controversy."[76] Kathleen Ecceles of Littleton, a suburb of Denver, expressed a like-minded view, asking of Love, "have you forgotten you are an elected official and not a Demigod?" Ecceles concluded: "What you are doing goes against this country's very beginning; 'Taxation without Representation.'"[77]

Many of the letter writers also saw special interests as the source behind Love's apparent subversion of democratic citizenship. "We the *people* do not want the Olympics held in Colorado," wrote Fred Cocler, also from Littleton; "we the people who were not allowed to vote on this important matter; we the people who recognize that the only ones who want them are the cheap egotistic politicians, the hotel/motel owners, and the land speculators."[78] The Fahrneys, a couple from Lakewood, adjacent to Denver, echoed this claim. "The decision was never put to the people who it seems will eventually be paying for it," they wrote; "the decision was made by businessmen and politicians whose motive is selfish profit making."[79] Alicia Acord of Brighton, on the northeast outskirts of Denver, wrote along these lines as well: "The State of Colorado belongs to the people who live here, not to the Governor alone. He has been elected to serve the wishes of the majority, not a few of your friends or other politicians." As Acord told Love: "I cannot understand how you could have done this without putting [it] to the vote of the tax-payers. . . . Those games will never benefit even one percent of the people of Colorado and in your own mind you know that."[80]

Lawrence Bradley of Pueblo, Robert Jackson's hometown, made this point too. He began by comparing CCF's initial grassroots petition drive, which it presented to the IOC at the Sapporo Olympics, to the resolution that Colorado politicians rushed through the United States Congress on behalf of the DOC. Bradley then explained to Love: "Not only does the passage of the Olympic resolution reveal that you gentlemen don't represent the people of this state, but it reveals just whom you do represent. It reveals that you represent two organizations composed of people who are only minimally concerned with the welfare of the state but are maximally concerned with their own welfare: the International Olympic Committee and the Denver Organizing Committee." With this in mind, Bradley declared: "I must conclude that representative democracy is dead."[81] While many of Love's constituents listed a breadth of anti-Olympics complaints, from environmental damage to wasted public dollars, the notion that the DOC and its associates caused such havoc by subverting the rights of citizenship perhaps doomed Denver '76 more than anything else.

In Denver and throughout Colorado, for decades and decades, a coalition of business leaders aligned with politicians had collaborated to shape public policy in pursuit of their own interests. The 1976 Denver Olympics controversy enabled that reality to become more commonly accepted, confronted, and resisted.[82] Surely, Coloradans held varied perspectives on Denver hosting the games. Many businesses, community organizations, and chambers of commerce stated their support for the event prior to the election.[83] Several individuals wrote to Denver's Olympic leaders after the event was rejected, letting them know they were "sorry," "heartbroken," and "in disbelief" with the "unpardonable stupidity" of their fellow residents.[84] As one Olympics supporter lamented, "you can't always beat the idiot fringe."[85] Some pleaded with Mayor McNichols not to withdraw Denver's offer to hold the spectacle.[86]

Figure 10.2. November 1972. A lone Olympics supporter stands in the DOC's headquarters and observes vote totals at a would-be victory celebration for Colorado's pro-Olympics coalition; the ballot issue passed overwhelmingly and killed any hope to host the games. Bettmann via Getty Images.

Unbeknownst to the DOC or state leaders, a Colorado attorney named Harry Arkin flew to Lausanne, Switzerland, following the vote to convince the IOC that he could raise enough money from private investors to keep the games in the Mile High City.[87] A group led by Arkin spent the next month and a half trying to revive the Denver Olympics before finally giving up.[88]

But more Coloradans had found themselves persuaded by CCF's position. And so, on the first Tuesday in November 1972, results showed 537,400 voted "yes" while 358,906 voted "no" on constitutional "Amendment Number 8." Because Citizens for Colorado's Future wanted to make sure Olympic expenses were not absorbed solely by Denver, it had gathered enough signatures and placed a similar initiative on the citywide ballot. Denverites also voted affirmatively.[89] The Denver Olympics would not bring the people of the world together. Instead, it created a multifaceted alliance of Coloradans who successfully undercut an advertising project produced by a governing regime that included Colorado's governor, Denver's mayor, and the state's most influential businesspeople. In the context of Colorado history, the DOC had suffered a stunning defeat.

CHAPTER 11

The Momentum of the Moment

In the summer of 1972, before the Munich Olympics began, the DOC traveled to Germany to update the IOC on its planning. Beforehand, word spread that the International Olympic Committee might finally take away the Winter Games from the Mile High City. A little over half a year earlier, Richard Lamm reached out to Avery Brundage and implored the IOC do just that. As Lamm asserted: "It is both in Colorado's interest and your interest to withdraw Denver as the host."[1] Yet by the time of the meeting in Munich, Lamm had changed his mind. He and Robert Jackson wrote to the IOC and requested that the games be left in the Centennial State for the time being. "We ask," they penned, "as representatives of the people of Colorado that you not take any action on removing the Games until our November vote."[2]

This repositioning from the two legislators indicates the extent to which the Winter Olympics ricocheted back at Colorado's powerbrokers. By bringing the Olympics to the state, Olympic organizers created a venue where overt clashes over the merits of growth and the rights of citizenship could take place. In their August letter to the IOC, Lamm and Jackson claimed they wanted Coloradans to decide the future of the Denver Olympics for themselves. "We ask this," they explained, "because we believe that in a democracy the ultimate power of government resides with the people."[3] Still, for Lamm and Jackson, the Olympics fostered civic energy, attracted unlikely allies, brought topics they cared about into focus, and placed the local legislators and their grassroots counterparts on the verge of a decisive victory over their state's political establishment. The games became a commanding political resource for them. Perhaps Lamm and Jackson did not want to see Denver '76 leave Colorado too soon.[4]

However, it left eventually, and when it did, any trace of the cohesiveness required to break up or even check Colorado's traditional regime evaporated. There were significant long-term gains for some opponents. The Olympic Games had enabled activists to contend momentarily with the Colorado growth network. It did draw together diverse groups who similarly couched anti-Olympics advocacy in discourses of citizenship and democracy. But many of the central parties involved arrived at their Olympic stances due to different underlying motives. Their agendas were discrete and their unity episodic. Accordingly, their returns on investment varied, and as a whole they proved ill-suited to exert an equivalent collective influence in the future.

While the Denver Olympics exposed the workings of a growth machine, that political configuration left elected officials the most vulnerable. Citizens could vote politicians out of office and replace them; that did not hold true for the monied men. Governor Love's attachment to the DOC—the tangible embodiment of a growth regime—undoubtedly led to a decline in his political capital. Indeed, as one of Mayor McNichols's deputies noted, opposition to the Winter Olympics started to appear like an attempt "to crucify Governor Love."[5]

"Why sell Colorado? Is this vital for us to do?" Jackson had asked during the Olympics debate.[6] With more frankness, Lamm insisted that the Olympics represented "a bloated and unwise addition to Governor Love's 'sell Colorado' program."[7] "The 'Sell Colorado' approach," Lamm opined, had become "a new pollution—promotional pollution."[8] By 1972, amid a strengthening anti-Olympics uproar, Lamm called outright for Love to "repeal or substantially amend 'Sell Colorado,'" urging the governor "not to use taxpayer funds to promote" the state anymore.[9] Two weeks before the anti-Olympics vote, Lamm further professed that "over the past few years there has been tremendous change in public attitude . . . [and the Olympics] is simply the last gasp of the sell Colorado program, . . . We don't need growth."[10]

Citizen letters written to Love reveal that many understood the Olympics as a manifestation of his now apparently problematic agenda. Mary Crabbe from Littleton demanded Love "stop the Olympics from coming here." "I ask this," she declared, "as I ask you to discourage all industry and business from coming here."[11] More significant, though, the games served as a representation of Love's complicity in the denial of democracy. As Richard R. Gordon, also of Littleton, described to his governor, the "people of the State of Colorado are being denied the right, granted by the Constitution, of voicing their opinions in the way they are governed. In essence, a form of dictatorship has been imposed upon Colorado with the 1976 Winter Olympics."[12] Such views inspired citizens to consider unseating the thrice-elected state leader. "I will not support any legislator who shoves this Denver Olympics down my throat," Fred Douglas of Wheat Ridge avowed.[13] Similarly, Stanley Perkins of Denver counseled Love: "It is not too late to save your state and your re-election!"[14]

These animated writers and many others listed a collection of anti-Olympics criticisms, calling attention to raised and wasted taxes, environmental damage, and corruption. Such factors, individually or in combination, pushed even some who identified with the Republican Party over the edge. If "you waste one dime of my money on the Olympics," warned Richard Heider of Littleton, "you will have lost my vote (Republican, ordinarily) forever."[15] Likewise, the Colorado Springs resident and Olympics opponent Theo Felon informed Love he "always voted the Republican ticket" but pronounced, "I am beginning to feel that the Democratic Party is the more 'democratic' party and therefore my long support of the Republican Party is fast waning."[16]

As Sam Brown envisioned, some who turned on Love even went so far as to admit that they were beginning to see eye-to-eye with young liberals challenging social norms and institutions. Clarice Crowle of Denver identified as a "middle-aged member of the 'Establishment.'" However, as she explained to Love, "young people complain about the insensitivity of the 'Establishment,' and they certainly have a right to complain here in Colorado." Crowle had once been "enthusiastic" when she helped vote Love into office almost a decade earlier. But as she wrote in 1972, her "enthusiasm" had "long since died a slow and miserable death." The Denver Olympics seemed to be the last straw.[17]

Such sentiment also became noticeable in the Jefferson County foothills. As W. K. Brockne of Evergreen saw it, in the case of the Denver games "middle-class white Americans are a minority—the minority which pays the bill!" Alluding to anti-Vietnam marches, civil rights protests, and Black Power salutes, Brockne bemoaned: "Must we stoop to street demonstrations and raised fists before we are heard!" The exurban mountain dweller, albeit regrettably, had joined the rights revolution, demanding a voice in the face of systematic oppression. And Love appeared to be a prime target for channeling the displeasure that this structural tyranny engendered. As Brockne told Love, "I wish you to know that after 52 years I am, thanks to you, ashamed of being a Republican!"[18] In response, Love perhaps read the tea leaves. In the summer of 1973, he resigned the governorship to begin a short-lived stint as President Richard Nixon's energy czar.

On the other side of the ledger, Richard Lamm gained several assets through the Olympic controversy that proved beneficial for his pursuit to serve as

Love's replacement. The games enabled him to articulate stronger, increasingly public, and more convincing support for middle-class environmentalism, opposition to growth, fears of misused taxes, and expectations for citizen rights. The entire sporting event made him appear as the type of politician that Coloradans deserting Love could endorse.

"Democrats like you make it increasingly difficult to remain a loyal Republican," one Coloradan wrote to Lamm.[19] "Yours is the kind of thinking our government needs and I, and I am sure many other voters, will remember the next time we vote," penned another.[20] "I wish to thank you for your stand against the Olympics. We need more like you in higher office," a third Coloradan proclaimed; "if at anytime you should run for an office where the votes from the western slope [are] needed you have a lot of help here."[21] Gary O. Curtin, from Arvada, northwest of Denver, had been a "Republican for more than 15 years." Nevertheless, as he spelled out in another of Love's Olympic letters: "I really am losing faith in the Republican Party when I see you and other Republican legislators back this scheme." He therefore suggested that "perhaps men such as Dick Lamm and Bob Jackson are the *real* hope for Colorado's future!"[22]

Tellingly, when Lamm kicked off his campaign for governor in 1973, his team realized that, thanks to the Olympics, there were two distinct sectors of Colorado society to which he could turn: conventional Democrats and disaffected middle-class environmentalists. The Olympics opponent John Parr scheduled Lamm's speaking engagements in the Front Range. As a memorandum penned by Meg Lundstrom described, the purpose of these talks was to reach both "Dems and CCFers."[23] The prominent POME member and Indian Hills resident Richard Kithil would help organize a fundraising event for Lamm. Lamm "has shown special concern with our problems in Jefferson County," Kithil and others told potential donors. He "worked with us to defeat funding for the Olympics" and remained "a forceful proponent . . . of land use laws which benefit citizens rather than developers and of balanced, orderly growth patterns which deflect growth away from the front range to parts of the state which need it." "As members of POME, Plan Jeffco, the Hill and Dale Society, and the Mountain Area Planning Council," the group of exurbanites drilled home, "we feel he is *our* candidate for governor."[24]

Equally significant, to push the anti-Olympics measure over the finish line, CCF built an organization populated by skilled operatives and thousands of volunteers. The evening that Colorado defeated the games, Lamm attended a victory party for the newly elected Democratic US representative Patricia Schroeder, who also voiced objections to the Denver Olympics. At the gathering, as Lamm tells it, the Mexican American and CCF contributor John Zapien grabbed him, raised him toward the ceiling, and pronounced: "Ladies and gentlemen, the next Governor of Colorado." After that, Lamm claims, "I looked around that room and recognized we had captains in all of the major population centers. We had people with lots of enthusiasm and that same enthusiasm—I could piggyback onto it." "I became David who fought Goliath," Lamm recalled, and "all the people who had fought the Olympics were my shock troops." From "the moment of the night of the Olympic [vote]," he went on, "it was definitely in the back of my mind that the same people who defeated the Olympics could get me elected governor."[25]

Meg Lundstrom, John Parr, Sam Brown, Tom Nussbaum, Dwight Filley, and Howard Gelt all redirected their energies to Lamm's run for higher office, taking on the same roles they held during the battle over the games.[26] As Lundstrom described, we "moved pretty much as a group into that campaign."[27] Nussbaum also remembered: "We sort of just switched from one gear to another."[28] Lundstrom oversaw the campaign's publications. Filley managed Lamm's campaign office. Gelt became his deputy campaign manager. Nussbaum and Parr worked together as field organizers. CCF's pile of about 5,000 note cards with the names of the group's supporters became Lamm's initial mailing list.[29] John Parr, who earned a reputation during the Olympic debate for interpersonal skills, reached out to these contacts. As Lamm put it, Parr "knew all the people who had just taken on the establishment [to defeat the Olympics] and brought them together to help elect me."[30]

During his run, Lamm and his campaign staff continually referenced the recent Olympic debate as well. When Lamm published position papers and gave speeches on topics such as growth, environmentalism, and citizenship, his contribution to the defeat of Denver '76 verified the authenticity of his words.[31] "We look back to the Olympics," one pro-Lamm mailer proclaimed, where Lamm's "public probing" of the DOC's "financial, environmental, and managerial problems . . . led the fight against continued funding of the games."[32] As Lamm supporters further professed: "We all had hopes . . . that the resounding defeat of the games at the polls would point ou[r] state government in a new direction." Nevertheless, "the legislature has refused to pass strong land use laws . . . and so growth continues unabated. . . . [T]he best thing we can do this year for Colorado's future is to help elect as governor the one man who has shown the vision and the guts to handle these problems. That man is Dick Lamm."[33]

In contrast, issues of growth and development hindered the chances of Lamm's opponent in the general election, the former lieutenant governor (now governor) John Vanderhoof. Vanderhoof had filled the vacancy left by Love, and shortly after the Olympic vote, he could be heard conceding to the times, advocating for what he described as "regionalism." He explained that this meant "the suppression of growth in some parts of Colorado and its encouragement where it is needed." "It is high time," Lieutenant Governor Vanderhoof asserted in January 1973, "for our people and their communities to dedicate themselves to responsible land use, to conservation of resources, to self-protection from unscrupulous land developers."[34] In June of the same year, Vanderhoof went so far as to oppose building a dam to store water diverted from the Western Slope because, as critics noted, it would accelerate growth in and around the Mile High City.[35]

But given Vanderhoof's previous pro-growth attitude and his well-known Olympic advocacy, he had little chance against Lamm. Vanderhoof actually did his best to avoid growth-related topics, knowing he could not keep up with his opponent in that facet of the race. For instance, he attempted to block the United States Forest Service from deciding whether to allow the development of the Beaver Creek ski resort until after the 1974 election. Vanderhoof supported the construction of the Vail Associates project and knew this would hurt his odds against whomever the Democrats nominated. As Vanderhoof feared, the Forest Service went ahead and approved the Beaver Creek proposal, and Lamm spoke out against it at every turn.[36]

Thus, two years after the expulsion of the Denver Olympics, Lamm took the governorship, winning 53.2 percent of the vote against Vanderhoof's 45.7 percent. The Watergate scandal likely provided Lamm yet another leg up. President Nixon's crimes and resignation remained fresh as voters across the country turned on Republicans in droves. Nonetheless, as the letters to Lamm and Love cited above suggest, some who typically would have voted for Vanderhoof probably supported Lamm because of the Winter Games. Vanderhoof himself concluded that Lamm's victory hinged on low voter turnout in Republican strongholds where Olympic resentment carried the loudest reverberations, such as in Jefferson County.[37] For Lamm's part, when asked about the extent to which his resistance to the Denver Olympics impacted his gubernatorial victory, he admitted: "I think it made all the difference."[38] He was probably right.

Along with Lamm, anti-Olympics middle-class environmentalists enjoyed sustained achievements. Notably, when the initiative prohibiting Olympic spending came to the ballot, Jefferson County citizens also passed a countywide resolution to institute a local 0.05 percent open-space sales tax. The city of Boulder, just north of Jeffco, had passed the first open-space tax in the nation a few years earlier. It provided public dollars to shape the community through the purchase of lands for purposes such as agriculture and recreation. Jefferson County residents similarly raised local taxes on themselves to acquire their county's undeveloped terrain to guard against sprawl and other kinds of unsightly development.[39]

Unsurprisingly, POME's approximately 600 members aligned themselves with the organization that drafted the sales tax proposal, a Jefferson County–based group named PLAN Jeffco.[40] PLAN Jeffco, POME, and the MAPC all espoused the same middle-class environmentalist point of view. As one PLAN Jeffco brochure described: "We citizens of Jefferson County have migrated here for many and varied reasons. But we have all stayed for the *same* reason: IT'S A GREAT PLACE TO LIVE! . . . We can live in the mountains or [we] can see and smell those mountains from our homes on the plains. We like the proximity to nature that we've found here. LET'S KEEP IT THAT WAY!" The alternative, PLAN Jeffco contended, would be a community engulfed by "a sea of rooftops, even into the mountains, without the relief of bare hillside, trees or streams."[41]

POME's Vance Dittman expressed comparable thoughts when he asked the Jefferson County Planning Commission to halt the construction of new residential developments. "Will we destroy permanently the very qualities which make this environment beautiful and unique? Will we still have the unbroken open spaces, the forests, the wildlife and the serenity and quiet? Or will we be just commuters and polluters in another setting?" Dittman asked.[42] PLAN Jeffco and Dittman came to the same conclusion: the presence of "open space, the forests, [and] the wildlife" was fundamental to the essence of where they lived, and where they lived defined in large part who they were. Without these features, their beloved hamlets would dissolve—and so would their sense of self. They would become "commuters and polluters."

The MAPC's and POME's environmentalism thus extended far beyond the Olympics. Both called for a moratorium on subdivision development in Jefferson County until authorities devised a new and more acceptable comprehensive plan.[43] Amid the Olympic debate, POME especially began to concern itself with any "encroachment of industry" that it deemed "inconsistent or incompatible with the preservation of the foothills environment." POME staked out such positions on matters including sewage management, water supplies, highway construction, garbage dumps, industrial plants, snowmobile and motorcycle use, as well as horseback riding and hiking trails.[44] As the MAPC president Doug Jones observed in 1971, the Olympics spurred Jefferson County townspeople to pay closer attention to county zoning policies.[45]

Several other events pointed to an uptick in middle-class environmentalism's strength. The day Colorado citizens expelled the Olympics, they also voted out of office the three-term Republican senator Gordon Allott. Allott had been both an environmentalist foe and an Olympic backer. In contrast, his opponent, Floyd Haskell, hounded Allott about his fundraising sources and sparred with him over environmental policy.[46] The renowned pro-growth US representative Wayne Aspinall, a Democrat, had likewise lost months before in a party primary. Aspinall was a twelve-term congressman and, as with many postwar politicians, came to power by promising and fighting for economic development. Throughout his career, he expressed little patience for what he called the "non-harvesting philosophy" of the environmental movement's "over-indulgent zealots." But after the League of Conservation Voters named Aspinall its number-one congressional target, he lost his party's nomination for Colorado's 4th Congressional District to the epitome of the middle-class environmentalist: the University of Denver environmental law professor Alan Merson.[47] Merson moved to Colorado in the late 1960s and bought a second home in Indian Hills. He then became one of four University of Denver colleagues, led by Vance Dittman, who originally rallied the town's homeowners to oppose the DOC's Olympic plans. He was a founding member of POME and a contributor to CCF.[48]

Moreover, in spring 1974, state leaders reacted to the new political landscape wrought by the Olympic fight by passing two bills that gave local communities greater control over land use.[49] Then, a year later, a resident-based movement akin to that in Indian Hills and Evergreen helped block plans to expand the Marble Ski Area in Crystal Creek. As the environmental historian Michael Childers observes, the Olympics and Marble combined to signify that ski resorts "and more broadly the tourism industry" were finally "on the defensive."[50]

Yet upon closer examination, these examples evidence the limits to the kind of environmentalism reining in tourist promoters and bringing changes to Colorado. The 1974 land-use bills provided greater oversight for county governments, which suited both middle-class environmentalists and the development-minded. Local land-use restrictions on zoning and planning allowed suburban and exurban inhabitants to protect their particular environs and identities. Simultaneously, if permitting a few spots of conservation prevented broader anti-growth laws from taking hold, then real estate investors, land speculators, utility companies, and banks would welcome the provisions.[51]

Other gains of Colorado environmentalists that ensued following the

Olympics' banishment further signaled the conservatism of the state's dominant environmentalist ideology. Floyd Haskell had not outright opposed the Winter Olympics during his Senate campaign. While he signed CCF's petition and stated he would vote for the constitutional amendment banning funding, he also proposed using county ballot issues to determine whether certain counties would participate. This position opened the door for growth advocates as well as middle-class environmentalists to see promise in his election. They both could theoretically get what they wanted. Haskell referenced Jefferson Country explicitly when presenting this stance.[52] Alan Merson's appeal proved to be incomplete as well. He went on to lose in the general election to Republican James Paul Johnson. It is additionally worth noting that a localized movement, one with specifically local concerns, deserves credit for halting the development in Crystal Creek.[53]

Furthermore, the Colorado legislature repeatedly voted against statewide policies to limit growth. In the fall of 1979, a year into his second term, Lamm became so frustrated by his inability to pass broad land-use laws that he attempted to circumvent the General Assembly. He signed an executive order setting guidelines on state government actions and ensuring the review of projects receiving state and federal money. At the same time, he moved to create a "citizens crusade" to pressure elected officials to support more ambitious regional planning.[54]

But by early 1980, Lamm began to feel pushback. He had built a reputation for representing the interests of everyday people. Yet now he appeared to be the authoritarian. As one Jeffco county commissioner attested, Lamm had "usurped the power of citizens in voting to elect people to represent them." Another county-level representative averred: "I don't think we should handle people the way we do hogs. We should give the people the right to make a choice of where they live and under what conditions as long as they can afford to do so." The state legislature became emboldened by these trends and passed resolutions calling on Lamm to rescind his order, stalled his budget requests, and threatened to diminish his power over administrative decision-making.[55] Lamm's vision of a citizens-led initiative also met roadblocks. When Lamm tried to align this effort with the principles of his executive order, even the chairman of the "crusade's" coordinating committee resisted it. Lamm had no choice but to back down.[56]

In the end, Colorado's population continued to increase, and Denver and its surrounding suburbs developed apace. In the same instance, lifestyle enclaves such as Indian Hills and Evergreen, not to mention upscale "vacationlands" like Aspen and Vail, erected local barriers to growth.[57] As the historian Kenneth Jackson remarks, small-town zoning such as this often worked not as a means to environmental protection but as "a device to keep poor people and obnoxious businesses out of affluent areas"—to create, in effect, gated communities.[58] In 1990, the Denver historians Stephen Leonard and Thomas Noel described Evergreen in this way: as "a land of private driveways and NO TRESPASSING signs" that "epitomizes the suburban dream."[59]

The Colorado historian William Philpott astutely observes that many environmentalists "were hardly challenging the system." They became, instead, adherents of a dominant consumerist mindset that involved the consumption—not ecological protection—of natural settings. The "love of lifestyle," Philpott argues, "discouraged 'big picture' thinking, the sort of holistic, ecological vision needed to follow through on more comprehensive land-use reforms."[60] Thus, Lamm conceded that he did not receive the support to enact the type of environmental policies that he wanted to. When asked about his regional planning battles during his three terms as governor, he confessed: "I lost them all." "After the Olympics," Lamm reflected, "I couldn't get anything through."[61] In this regard, Lamm's career as governor confirms the political scientist Clarence Stone's insight that forming an electoral coalition and effectively directing a governing coalition are not one and the same.[62]

In Denver, the story for racially marginalized urbanites in some ways fits the theme of prolonged achievement facilitated through Olympics opposition. Brown and Black Denverites used the games to gain louder voices in Colorado's public sphere and edged city authorities toward creating affordable housing options.[63] Even if community organizers, activists, and politicians could not stop the city's overall flight toward downtown commercialization, those willing to work with "place entrepreneurs" obtained fragments of influence over urban development.[64] As the urban planning scholars Brian Page and Eric Ross conclude, in line with trends throughout the United States, by the 1970s "DURA [the city's urban renewal authority] could no longer dictate urban renewal outcomes on its own terms but instead was forced to take community interests into consideration."[65]

However, in contrast to the foothills environmentalists, Mexican Americans and African Americans of the Mile High City did not obtain the concessions from state leaders needed to fully accomplish their local goals, even if growth continued as usual everywhere else. With the games gone, such actors lost the leverage that the event created, and they needed it more than any other anti-Olympics group. As the historian Richard Gould maintains, for Denver's Hispanic community in the 1970s, in "the absence of real power at the top or at least in the absence of an administration sympathetic to the needs of the poor, the options for neighborhood organizers remained quite narrow."[66]

Perhaps it is no surprise, then, that the promised housing stemming from of Olympic planning never reached completion. Two days after the passage of Amendment 8, the regional director for the US Department of Housing and Urban Development assured that the federal agency still intended to send its money Denver's way. "If the city wants to go ahead," the HUD director claimed, "we're ready and willing."[67] But in January 1973, the Nixon administration placed a moratorium on federally funded construction, and HUD cut its commitment to Denver in half. As the historian John Mollenkopf contends, Nixon began to weaken urban development programs around 1969 but ramped up the "attack" after his landslide victory over George McGovern in November 1972. "Nixon moved forcefully to undermine the program base around which neighborhoods and Democratic City Halls had made their peace," Mollenkopf writes; "just as neighborhoods had won some influence over these programs, the Nixon administration began its onslaught against them."[68] Colorado policy makers, including Mayor McNichols, lobbied Washington to keep the full amount HUD had promised in place.[69] In March, the Denver City Council approved the entire proposal. Nevertheless, three months later, federal decision makers officially slashed a portion of what HUD had pledged.[70]

It speaks to the effectiveness of community organizers in Denver, and the platform the Olympics provided, that the press housing plan did bring some affordable housing to the city even without the games. Yet the end result did not live up to the hopes of neighborhood advocates. In the East Side, DURA spent about $3 million of city funds, plus $6 million received from HUD to clear 16.5 acres of land and add 591 housing units, consisting of mixed-income residences and homes for the elderly. The project faced criticism, however, due to a lack of transparency, a failure to come through with the mixed-income layout, and low-quality construction. The overall appearance, reliance on wood rather than brick, and dense design, along with other factors, led the moderate African American city councilman and former Olympics supporter Elvin Caldwell to report that the East Side's new quarters appeared "barrack-like" and were "totally unacceptable . . . to numerous individuals and organization[s] in the community." The housing "being built" in the East Side, Caldwell wrote to the executive director of DURA in 1976, "is not in the best interests of the community or this city."[71]

To make matters worse, the West Side initially got nothing. Waldo Benavidez and fifty fellow West Siders went straight to Mayor McNichols's office when they learned HUD's funds were going entirely to the East Side. Denver authorities made the decision without consulting the Benavidez-led West Side Coalition, which had worked with the city to design affordable homes during the Olympic debate.[72] Only after some wrangling did Denver leaders agree to spend a mere $1 million on high-rises for the elderly on the West Side as well.[73]

According to the *Rocky Mountain News*, DURA's decision to exclude the West Side had been influenced by its awareness that such projects faced "widespread criticism in the past."[74] This likely referred to the DOC's press housing plan. If this is true, internal disagreements among Mexican American advocates and distrust toward city authorities displayed during the Olympic controversy may have combined to stand in the way of obtaining at least some of the low-income housing that all agreed the West Side sorely needed. But make no mistake: equitable housing projects never became the priority in Denver throughout the post–World War II era. As the 1970s ended, through the entirety of its existence, DURA allocated a little over $11.5 million to housing rehabilitation. Over that same time span, it doled out $1.27 billion in public and private dollars toward building commercial infrastructure for Denver's central business district. Critics could easily charge the organization with subsidizing office buildings and luxury apartments for the wealthy instead of affordable homes for the working class and the poor.[75]

Despite incremental progress on several fronts, the plight of racially marginalized Denverites remained apparent. In the years following the Olympic vote, structural changes enabled moderates of Mexican descent to rise within Colorado politics. The United States Supreme Court levied a ruling requiring increased representatives from urban areas to ensure "one-person, one-vote" proportionality; the city implemented district-level elections; and the United States Congress expanded the 1965 Voting Rights Act to provide non–English speakers access to ballots and other voter information. This helped Hispanic constituents take two seats on the Denver City Council and form a solid Chicano caucus in the state House of Representatives, where politicians fought successfully for bilingual education and the institution of state-level affirmative action policies. West Siders also prevented a one-way street from splitting their neighborhood and obtained a new health care center, recreation facilities, and funding for home restorations.[76]

Still, by this time, the philosophic differences existing within the Mexican American community, exposed during the Olympic debate, had exploded, leaving Denver's grassroots Chicano movement in shambles. In 1973, pressure mounted on Corky Gonzales's Crusade for Justice. After a collection of violent confrontations between Crusaders and Denver police, and amid anxieties of infiltration by the Federal Bureau of Investigation, the "revolutionaries" began to label anyone who worked aside the system as *vendidos*, or "sell-outs."[77] The conflict between the Crusade and the Democratic Party loyalists Betty and Waldo Benavidez became so bad that locals started to call the West Side "Little Beirut" and the Benavidez home, stockpiled with weapons, "The Alamo." In this disarray, many West Siders turned on the Benavidezes, viewing them as fomenters of violence. The turmoil did not subside until 1974 when they fled to New Mexico for safety. The West Side Coalition lost its central figures, while in Denver the Crusade for Justice continued to crumble.[78]

In this context, through the 1970s into the early 1980s, gentrification in Denver displaced Mexican Americans at one of the highest rates in the nation.[79] Segregation in Denver schools and the city in general likewise remained a challenge. In 1974, the United States Supreme Court ordered the city's schools desegregated. Yet afterward, white urbanites left Denver for suburban areas, seeking locations where the decision did not apply and forced busing could be avoided. In response to the landmark decision, within months Coloradans also voted for the "Poundstone Amendment," a law that gave county residents the power to stop city annexations and limit the potential reach of the federal mandate.[80]

Alongside this, in the 1980s, as Lamm diverged from his former middle-class environmentalist allies, he similarly split with Mexican Americans on several issues. He began to advocate strict immigration policies, asserting in part that the nation's rising number of Hispanics and their refusal to "Americanize" had "splintered" the United States, giving rise to "linguistic ghettos" in the Southwest and draining the nation's economy, points he made in a book published during his third term, *The Immigration Time Bomb: The Fragmenting of America*.[81] The governor remained obsessively attentive to the risks he foresaw in relation to population growth and couched his views on ethnicity and immigration from that perspective.[82] Nonetheless, during his final years as Colorado's leader, he and the Chicano caucus in the legislature regularly found themselves at odds.[83]

In a word, as Lamm's politics suggests, the coalition of liberal organizers, prudent yet progressive politicians, middle-class environmentalists, and Brown and Black Denverites that defeated the DOC and its associates lived through and died with Denver '76. There was no equivalent unifying issue that could harness their energies into a single objective or motivate them to harmonize their actions, certainly not in any durable way. The reality was, after all, that many of the diverse actors who contributed to the DOC's downfall did not seek that style of alliance to begin with. Neither did they mean to enact fundamental changes to Colorado. Middle-class environmentalists wished to protect their own backyards and not much more. Several moderate Mexican Americans and African Americans looked to use normative channels, not upend them. CCF's call for direct democracy convinced many Coloradans when the issue was whether to host the games, but that did not equate to a readiness to use one's rights to transform the system of governance in the Centennial State.

It did not take long for this to become apparent. While much would change in the 1970s and 1980s, the presence of business interests informally shaping public policy endured. In 1973, the Organization of Petroleum Exporting Countries cut off oil supplies, causing gas prices to spike. As the United States slipped into a recession, oil and natural gas companies scoured North America for new sources of fuel. The Mile High City became the home base for these operations, which extended from the Dakota plains to the Wyoming Rockies to Colorado's Western Slope. Thus, climbing costs and long lines at the pump turned out to be a boon for Denver's residential and commercial real estate developers. From 1972 to 1982, developers constructed fifty new buildings in downtown Denver. Between 1981 and 1983 alone, the city added almost 20 million square feet of office space. The downtown, demolished in the 1960s with urban renewal funds, was finally overtaken by shops, hotels, and restaurants. Symbolically, standing above it all, the city's tallest building, just below 700 feet, took the shape of a cash register.[84]

The influx of energy extractors, other businesses, and rising skyscrapers pointed to another significant growth-related trend: economic globalization. The focus on growth remained, but the locus of power no longer rested in the cities and states. Increasingly, local powerbrokers sold their businesses to national and international corporations. In turn, politicians and businesspeople became tethered to external venture capitalists dispersed worldwide, and local people became even further removed from the levers of decision-making. For example, Gates Rubber Company was sold to a company based in Great Britain. The Public Service Company of Colorado was absorbed by a larger energy provider from Minneapolis. Colorado National Bank became part of US Bank, also headquartered in Minneapolis. Coors Brewing merged with Molson and then with Miller. A larger Chicago-based investment firm bought Boettcher and Company.[85] Resorts at Steamboat, Vail, and Aspen would all become associated with massive multinational and multiresort conglomerates. In Colorado, tourism became yet another transnational endeavor.[86] It was, tellingly, multiple Canadian developers, looking to avoid rent control, strict zoning, and higher taxes, who came to Denver and spent hundreds of millions of dollars to spearhead construction of the burgeoning skyline.[87]

In that historical backdrop, it becomes clear that the Denver Olympics represents the zenith, not the genesis, of Colorado's anti-growth resistance. As the urban studies scholar Dennis Judd observed in 1982: "Measured in terms of staying power, organization, and money, the boosters were in better position to wage a protracted campaign." "Long before the Olympics controversy and long after," Judd assessed, "they dominated the politics of growth."[88]

One could even argue that the window to create the type of populist coalition Brown hoped for passed at the same moment CCF took down the games. The shrewdly conservative Richard Nixon won reelection in 1972 decisively by focusing on cultural issues that appealed to the same subgroup that CCF had aimed to incorporate: white "middle America." In fall 1969, the president had secretly inaugurated what he called his "Middle America Committee." Its purpose was to reach "the large and politically powerful white middle-class," which, amid the counterculture of the 1960s, the committee supposed was "deeply troubled, primarily over the erosion of what they considered their values." Notably, as the historian Jefferson Cowie explains, after observing the Sam Brown–led Vietnam Moratorium—when it looked like "criticism of the war was going mainstream"—Nixon took "his strategy to the next level." In an effort that uncannily paralleled Brown's, the president deployed "workingman" and "pro-America" rhetoric to win over traditionally Democratic working-class voters and create his own "New Majority."[89] Nixon's success indicates both the uniqueness and the difficulty of maintaining the multigroup undertaking that CCF oversaw. Economic developments and fractures caused by different views on topics like immigration, religion, gender, and race would dampen prospects for the type of social movement required to challenge the socioeconomic system that, in many respects, enabled Colorado powerholders to form the DOC and bid for the Olympics in the first place.[90]

Lamm and Brown both recognized, in retrospect, that their anti-Olympics resistance yielded negligible effects. They represent probably the most prominent and successful political actors in this story, but they were also some of the boldest. They consequently expressed disillusionment at the direction of Colorado and the United States.

When pressed in an interview for this book if, as governor, he was "able to slow down growth at all," Lamm answered candidly: "No . . . this whole idea of 'selling Colorado' continued."[91] The "Colorado I was afraid was going to happen with the Olympics," Lamm similarly reflected in 1999, "happened without the Olympics." "I'm looking back on a lost opportunity," he explained. "I don't like what Denver has become. I mourn Colorado. I am truly so sorry that Colorado has become what it has become when I had a different vision."[92] In later years, Lamm would blame such "loss" on the nature of American politics. "I don't think either political party has the answer to America's problems," he decried. "I think they are both compromised by special interests and special interest money. I am appalled that this great nation does not have a more honest political system."[93]

To be sure, the type of pragmatic, diverse, and progressive populism Brown desired never reached fruition. In 1974, at the age of thirty-one, he was elected Colorado's treasurer. Brown realized that about 10 percent of deposits in Colorado banks came from the state and that the treasurer had complete authority over where that money ended up. The unrelenting strategist thus devised procedures to incentivize improved services and lending opportunities for redlined Denverites, small businesses, women, and citizens living in rural areas.[94] Yet after two years, Brown left the treasurer's office and discussions about running for Denver mayor. The president of the United States, Jimmy Carter, called him with an offer he felt, at the time, he should not refuse. Carter asked him to run ACTION, the federal government's domestic volunteer agency.[95] This drew Brown away from the Centennial State and deeper into the Democratic Party. He and his wife, Alison Valentine Teal, worked in tandem from then on to raise money, assist campaign offices, and canvass. In addition to working on behalf of many lesser-known candidates, they put the weight of their abilities behind the former anti–Vietnam War activist and then-senator John Kerry's 2004 campaign for president. Brown later served on the finance committees for Barack Obama's, Hillary Clinton's, and Joe Biden's presidential campaigns and held appointed positions in the Bill Clinton and Obama administrations.[96]

Nevertheless, in the summer of 2020, Brown expressed a point of view echoing Lamm's. "I'm fundamentally pretty discouraged about the possibility of breaking out of this . . . politics that basically is owned by elites in both parties," Brown admitted. In describing the populist alliance he hoped to forge through the Olympics and the party to which he devoted the past five decades of his life, he added with dismay: "I don't think the Democratic Party can be that vehicle because it is itself in some ways a wholly owned subsidiary of economic interests." "There is a kind of structural issue in the very nature of American politics that makes it very hard to think about how you build a coalition of the left out and the left behind to change society," Brown concluded; "It's just owned."[97]

"When we went to work for Fred Harris," Brown also remembered, "it was in the hope that he was the presidential candidate that could articulate this successfully and begin to build a coalition" to create "the kind of populist government that would have actually done things." The senator from Oklahoma failed in that effort, making way for Citizens for Colorado's Future. The Denver Olympics took the place of Harris's campaign. Nonetheless, despite the passage of Amendment 8, the battle over the games proved to be only a fleeting moment of the kind of movement that Brown sought. It was not the beginning of any kind of durable social transformation. It was not the movement itself.[98]

Through the Denver Olympics debate, in the face of decades of pro-growth boosterism, Coloradans were presented with a series of questions: Who should determine Colorado's future? Who should decide whether to host something like the Olympics—the bid designers and organizers, business elites, politicians, taxpayers, common folks, historically and structurally marginalized groups? For opponents of Denver '76, the answers sounded similar down the line: "We should decide." But that synchronous "we" did not include everyone who answered as such, even among those who felt comparably betrayed by Love, McNichols, and the DOC. For there were, of course, follow-up queries: What kind of growth do we want? What forms of development, let alone Olympic-based development, enhance or degrade social justice, quality of life, the economy, the environment, and the culture of the city and surrounding areas? What measures should be used to determine these things? Denver's Olympics opponents were not on the same page in these respects. They were not even really concerned with the same facets of these questions. They thus failed to agree on how Colorado should proceed.

There are a few things, however, that most observers should be willing to acknowledge. Growth can negatively affect local people, especially those who live in areas where business leaders manipulate public resources and infrastructure to generate wealth.[99] This may be particularly true and obvious when growth comes in the form of a huge sports enterprise.[100] As a result, the Olympics could become a siren call for regional powerbrokers. Due to its cachet, ability to move public funds, and association with tourism, the Olympics may look too alluring for investors to pass up. Yet if growth regimes try to ignite the Olympic torch, they might get burned. The chances for harms to the overall populace and the salience of growth-regime governance make attempts to host the event a ripe location for generating an anti–growth machine backlash.[101]

Mexican American and African American urbanites did use the Denver games to push city authorities to create more livable conditions for the working class and the poor. The event sparked Jefferson County's foothills residents to undertake a distinctive and, for them, efficacious environmentalist agenda. The Olympics even enabled the growth-cautious Lamm and members of CCF to oversee a variegated event coalition and become elected leaders. Within the glow of the Olympic flame, there is the political potential to advance many causes and unify multiple groups, and there is power in coordination. The games should be recognized as an opportunity for fomenting broad-based defiance to the status quo.

At the same time, though, anti-Olympics activists with far-reaching intentions should remain wary. One ought not confuse strength gained through anti-Olympics pacts with the authentic, purposeful, and long-lasting partnerships needed for deep-seated change. The legacy of Denver '76 is multifaceted, but a part of its lesson is that a common enemy does not mean a common cause.

Epilogue: The Games Go On

It seems clichéd and trite, not to mention willfully ironic, to end a book about the 1976 Denver Olympics—the games that never happened—by saying that "the games go on." But in Denver and elsewhere, through the Olympics and other sporting endeavors, they did, and they do. As several examples directly or tangentially related to Denver reveals, the game behind the games continues to be played, and the structure of cities, states, and nations, the allocation of scarce resources, and the dispersion of people remain in the balance.

In November 1977, the Los Angeles city councilman Bob Ronka flew to Denver. He traveled to meet with Colorado governor Richard Lamm and two members of his administration, John Parr and Tom Nussbaum. Los Angeles was in the process of bidding for the 1984 Summer Olympics, and Ronka was worried. Fortunately, in the Mile High City, the councilman found what he described as "invaluable" in-person advice.[1] Two days later, he returned to Southern California, sounding the alarm of cost overruns and rising taxes and threatening to gather 72,000-plus signatures to place a referendum on Los Angeles's next ballot. He meant to give Angelenos a chance to speak on whether they wanted to host the event.[2]

By this time, the Olympic movement occupied a precarious position. Following the Denver debacle, the 1976 Summer Olympics in Montreal proved to be a financial calamity. Though Montreal's mayor infamously claimed that the "Olympics could no more run a deficit than a man could have a baby," the games left the Canadian city with a $1.2 billion shortfall. It would take thirty years to repay.[3] Thus, by the 1980s, almost no one wanted to host the spectacle. Lake Placid and Los Angeles were the only cities in the world vying for the 1980 Winter Olympics and 1984 Summer Olympics, respectively.[4]

However, Los Angeles would change the path of the Olympic movement. Although the Los Angeles mayor Tom Bradley initially opposed Ronka's Olympics resistance, he and Ronka reached an agreement. Rather than a vote on whether to bid for the Summer Games, Angelenos, like Coloradans, would be given a chance to pass an ordinance restricting the use of public dollars. The difference was that Ronka and Bradley both wanted the ordinance to pass.[5] Los Angeles boosters realized they had leverage in negotiations with the International Olympic Committee because they were the only ones bidding. After the decree went through, no matter how hard the IOC pressed, the city of Los Angeles could not promise to cover excessive Olympic expenses. Meanwhile, the IOC could not send the games anywhere but the City of Angels.[6]

As Ronka wrote to Lamm, Los Angeles seized the "ability to put on spartan games on the city's terms, not according to the whims and dictates of the IOC."[7] The 1984 Los Angeles Summer Games took place without any public liability, funded for the first time through private contributions and corporate sponsorships. Moreover, since Los Angeles did not have any competition during its bid, it did not promise first-rate facilities at perfect locations. And with the University of Southern California, the University of California, Los Angeles, and facilities from the 1932 Games all contributing, the city had plenty of usable and affordable sports infrastructure. These dynamics empowered organizers to bequeath an astonishing and unmatched $222.7 million surplus.[8]

"LA '84" was not easily replicated. Yet from the late 1980s to the early 2000s, it stood out as an example of corporate investment and global image-making that many city leaders visualized for themselves, including in Denver. Denver could even be said to stand out as a troubling example of things to come nationwide.

By the mid-1980s, Denver's economy had gone from boom to bust. Businesses rejected the viability of oil shale extraction in the American West and looked to new energy sources discovered beyond American borders. Investment in the energy sector in Colorado came to a standstill. Denver lost 14,000 petroleum jobs within three years. Though many technology and communication firms remained steady, others imploded. Tens of thousands of contingent banks and service providers went insolvent. People's savings evaporated, and foreclosures became common. Over $140 million in downtown real estate faced that harsh situation, as property and land values in Denver crashed. Decentralization compounded the crisis. Due to office parks and other external commercial hubs, and to the perpetual horror of downtown interests, Denver's population decreased, and suburban shop-ping centers started to collect more sales tax than the central city. There-fore, urban officials and business leaders sought revival through tourist- and entertainment-centered development.[9]

The Mexican American mayor Federico Peña oversaw the most notable pieces of Denver's 1980s and 1990s pro-growth push. He also represents an added and complicating component of Citizens for Colorado's Future's im-pact on Centennial State politics. During their time working for the Lamm administration, Parr and Nussbaum befriended Peña, a member of the Col-orado House. The CCF duo then became part of a group of four political op-eratives that took him to lunch in 1982 and laid out a plan for how he could replace the longtime incumbent, William McNichols, and become the first minority mayor of a major majority-white American city.[10] "John [Parr] quietly and effectively showed me past voting results and demonstrated why a little-known legislator could win," Peña remembered. "Although I had my doubts, John was quite persuasive."[11] Indicating an equally significant con-tribution, Nussbaum became Peña's campaign manager for the run against McNichols and others and afterward served as his chief of staff.[12]

The Denver historians Lyle Dorsett and Michael McCarthy describe Peña's 1984 mayoral victory as "the most stunning political event in the city's mod-ern history."[13] Nevertheless, as the political scientists Susan Clarke and Mar-tin Saiz detail, Peña came to power by forming his own governing coalition following the oil bust. He ran on socially liberal pledges such as addressing environmental protection and giving low- and middle-income neighborhoods a voice in nonelectoral decisions. Yet as Clarke and Saiz write, "Peña found it necessary to be the pro-growth, fiscal conservative who could bring the busi-ness community to the table." His "rhetoric shifted," and the "new regime" was "more pro neighborhood," but, Clarke and Saiz continue, "Peña's growth strategies mirrored McNichols's unfinished policy agenda."[14]

The billionaire Marvin Davis, inheritor of Davis Oil Company and owner of Twentieth Century Fox and the Aspen Ski Company, had funded Peña's initial campaign. Peña likewise received largess from investors spe-cializing in "historic redevelopment," eyeing to revamp the warehouse dis-trict of Lower Downtown. Predictably, then, as Clarke and Saiz describe, Peña sought to build up "entertainment and tourist infrastructure" through "public-private partnerships and corporate ventures."[15] Among many other initiatives, this included building a state-of-the-art airport, a new conven-tion center, and a brand-new, publicly funded baseball stadium.

In 1990, during Peña's second term, Major League Baseball (MLB) an-nounced plans to create two expansion franchises. As with the IOC selection, the MLB had a monopoly over awarding the new teams, which allowed the league to make substantial demands of its potential "hosts." Along with a $95 million contribution up front from owners, the MLB required that new teams get scheduling priority in their home venue. This pushed "bid cities" to pay for and construct baseball-only facilities that could produce maximum revenue.[16] In familiar fashion, US senator Tim Wirth, Colorado governor Roy Romer, and Peña began to promise economic windfalls and community pride if they could get support to build the new sports complex. Businesses positioned to benefit from the stadium chipped in too, lobbying for public investment and offering donations to get approval for a cause that they would not, in the end, pay for.[17]

However, city boosters of the late 1980s and early 1990s seemed to understand that they should not approach this latest sports-infused project as directly and unilaterally as the DOC approached the Olympics. To fund the potential stadium, state legislators established the Denver Metropolitan Stadium District, which comprised six counties surrounding the proposed facility. Governor Romer appointed its board members, and Denver business leaders loaned $75,000 to get it off the ground. As the purported representative of the area's citizenry, the Stadium District introduced a ballot measure that called for a 0.1 percent sales tax increase to fund approximately 70 percent of the estimated $130 million baseball cathedral.[18] On 15 August 1990, though it would have failed if Denverites decided alone, district voters approved the tax.[19]

The "special authority" ploy appeared to garner citizen consent and insulated elected officials from a probable public backlash. The Stadium District's board—separately from Romer, Peña, and other politicians—negotiated with the new team's ownership, administered the sales tax, and borrowed money for construction. It could thereby take the brunt of the fallout from subjecting citizens to a classic "taxpayer bait and switch."[20] The estimated public contribution for the stadium rose from $97 million to $168 million after residents voted.[21] Even more concerning, before citizens submitted their ballots, authorities promised that the Stadium District's board would negotiate to acquire the maximum non–sales tax revenue generated through the new building. But due to the $95 million entry fee, Denver found it challenging to attract an ownership group willing to invest in the big leagues. To address this, the Stadium District provided the team's owners a lease that gave away 100 percent of every earnable dollar other than from ticket sales. Not one cent from concessions, parking, advertising, concerts, other nonbaseball events, and stadium naming rights would go back to taxpayers. Combined with other factors, this made the Coors Field lease the most lucrative stadium deal for ownership in all of major league baseball.[22] As the sport sociologists Kevin Delaney and Rick Eckstein describe, the Stadium District "vote was really the first of its generation," a growth-machine tactic that city boosters elsewhere, interested in sports-related growth, looked to emulate.[23]

More broadly, happenings in Denver appear to support the sport historian Sean Dinces's contention that, in the 1980s and 1990s, professional sports became part and parcel of the "exclusionary capitalism" of a "New Gilded Age."[24] When the American economy slowed in the 1970s, corporate profits contracted. In response, business leaders attacked the country's progressive taxation system, which since the New Deal supported a range of social support programs for ordinary citizens. Proponents argued that tax cuts combined with corporate subsidies would allow a "free market" to promote spending in ways that benefited everyone. Yet this marked the end of the period that saw the most egalitarian distribution of wealth in American history. It also caused federal funding for urban centers to dry up just as competition for resources went international. Cities needed to either cut off development activities or pursue extensive "public-private" partnerships aimed at worldwide competition.[25] In this context, as the history of Denver suggests, sports-inspired growth became more popular and insidious. As money moved from working- and middle-class Americans to the rich, city authorities and corporate interests often took part in the process via sports-based enterprises.[26]

At the most basic level, the nation's annual state and local outlays for sports facilities and convention centers rose from $700 million in the 1970s to $2 billion in the 1990s.[27] Yet more subtly, as with Coors Field, cities throughout the country began to give billionaire team owners tax breaks and exclusive rights to revenue from stadiums, including those built at the public's expense.[28] It was also true that, even as federal funds for social programs dwindled, the United States spent another $2 billion to assist Olympic festivals held in Los Angeles (1984), Atlanta (1996), and Salt Lake City (2002).[29] During the frugality of the era of "trickle down" economics, government proved ready and willing to invest in sports.

In fall 1991, the MLB would select Denver for its expansion prize. Coors Field opened a few years later. And as Delaney and Eckstein observed in the early 2000s, "the new stadium" was "paid for mostly with public dollars, with revenue going almost entirely into private pockets."[30] The broader economic impact of the facility also turned out to be questionable. The Lower Downtown area of Denver, where the stadium was located, witnessed impressive commercial growth and revitalization. However, many mixed-use projects anticipated in connection to the stadium's introduction remained absent as gentrification took hold and segregation persisted. From 1990 to 2013, Denver gentrified at one of the fastest rates in the nation, and by 2018 Denver County stood as the second-least affordable county in the United States.[31] On top of this, when the Supreme Court's 1974 order to desegregate the city's schools was lifted in 1995, the areas where it had been applied resegregated. In the latter half of the 1990s, Denver schools became more racially isolated, poor, and inequitable.[32] Delaney and Eckstein point out as well that a significant portion of the new development in Lower Downtown began before and at a decent distance from where the city erected its newest sporting attraction. Despite the avowals of Denver boosters, Coors Field did not necessarily deserve credit for the economic resurgence of the rebranded "LoDo" area.[33]

Still, by the 2010s, even if public funding for baseball as well as football did not instigate substantial antagonism in Denver, the same could not be said for the Olympics. Following LA '84, multiple cities started bidding again, leaving them to one-up each other and promise to cover "unplanned" expenditures. Thus, even as the 2008 Great Recession rippled across the globe, Olympic price tags reached record heights. China spent an estimated $40 billion on the 2008 Beijing Summer Olympics.[34] The 2010 Vancouver Winter Games cost $7–8 billion, with $925 million coming from public funds.[35] The cost of the 2012 London Summer Olympics rose from an estimated $5 billion to an actual $15–20 billion, and United Kingdom taxpayers bore the difference.[36] The 2014 Sochi Winter Games cost an unprecedented $51 billion.[37]

In the years between the 1984 Los Angeles Summer Games and the 2008 recession, several groups of anti-Olympics protesters from Amsterdam to Toronto to Chicago voiced their concerns in the face of Olympic bids and helped scare off IOC voters. In the United States, though urbanites of color often found themselves unable to advocate for their interests successfully, white suburbanites in the host cities of Atlanta and Salt Lake City found ways to force changes to organizing committee plans as well.[38] But after 2008, a full-fledged worldwide anti-Olympics backlash began to sprout. Cities such as Boston, Krakow, Oslo, Hamburg, Rome, Budapest, Innsbruck, and Calgary all started and then terminated Olympic bids because of local citizen dissent.[39]

Under Peña, Denver had bid in 1989 for the 1998 Winter Games.[40] In 2012, city leaders tried but failed to host the games in 2022.[41] Not long after, in August 2016, Colorado governor John Hickenlooper and Denver mayor Michael Hancock appeared ready to give the Olympics yet another go.[42]

Nonetheless, by 2017, as cities across the planet rejected the event, and with the octogenarian former governor Richard Lamm working as its front man, a Denver-based group called "NOlympics Denver" moved to halt the city's bid for the 2030 Winter Games. What is more, after the United States Olympic Committee passed over Denver to represent the United States before the IOC, the prospect of a bid for 2030 provided energy for NOlympics Denver to rebrand itself as "Let Denver Vote." The twenty-first-century Olympics opponents started to push for a broader law that would prevent public money from being used "in connection with any future Olympic Games, without the City first obtaining voter approval."[43] In spring 2019, Let Denver Vote gained the required signatures to get this proposal on the city ballot. In early June, forty-six and a half years after the banishment of Denver '76, nearly 80 percent of voters approved the measure. Denver will not be allowed to spend a dime of taxpayer money to merely explore a bid for the Olympics without gaining voter support in advance.[44] At least when it comes to hosting the games, Colorado's future rests in the same place it did in November 1972—in the hands of Coloradans.

A growing number of activists thus appear to realize the potential gain in contesting the games. For example, in 2015 in Germany, the people of Hamburg went to the polls to vote on whether to allow their city to go forward with a bid for the 2024 Summer Games. Pro-Olympics lobbyists envisioned Hamburg as a "global city" and hoped to use the games to attract investments in sports, transportation, and security. However, during public workshops, residents did not feel that their perspectives were taken seriously. Soon, grassroots anti-Olympics groups began to disseminate information about costs, the consequences of large stadiums, and a "who's who" list revealing the apparent opportunism of Olympics backers. Later that fall, when given a chance, Hamburg citizens voted against bidding for the event. By doing so, as the urban geographers Anne Vogelphole and Sybille Bauriedl claim, they attempted to take control of their city's development, expressing disapproval of "glittering" but "elitist" urban planning. The games sparked greater "public awareness for the city's future," which, Vogelphole and Bauriedl write, led inhabitants to a "critique of entrepreneurial urban policy" and to "discuss alternative futures for all citizens."[45]

As the work for this book reached completion, anti-Olympics activists in Los Angeles hoped to achieve a similar result. In 2017, the IOC selected the city to host the 2028 Summer Games. Compared to other cities, Los Angeles is probably the most suitable place on earth to hold the spectacle. It has more professional and big-time collegiate sports facilities than any other city. It is the home of Hollywood, with transportation and communications infrastructure ready to roll. All the same, that does not mean the games come without risk.[46] The city has agreed to pay for overruns, and, nine years out, organizers expected costs to reach about $7 billion.[47] If history is any indication, that number will increase.

And so, a group called "NOlympics LA" emerged to try and stop LA '28. In many respects, these latest Olympics opponents are articulating common arguments. As the group's website proclaims, the "2028 bid was hurried in profoundly undemocratic manner, informed only by the voices and interests of a few powerful figures who stand to benefit." In the same instance, the anti-Olympics activists fear the games will lead the city to neglect and worsen a crisis in homelessness and poverty caused by gentrification, unwarranted surveillance and policing, and a lack of genuine democracy. But the group realizes as well that the games are an opportunity for it. Instead "of allowing the elite to shape the future," NOlympics LA expressly intends to use "the Olympics to expose the urgent problems we face today." "We fully intend to stop the Games," the opponents claim, "but—in the process—we also want to re-imagine Los Angeles."[48]

While it remains to be seen what will come of LA '28, it suffices to say that, wherever the games go, debates about economic development, affordable housing, environmental impacts, and democratic norms and values will likely follow. Most people probably do not initially become drawn to sports or the games due to their interest in these issues. At least in part, what sparks enthusiasm for sports is the drama of competitive uncertainty, the exhilaration of physical excellence, appreciation for striving, creativity, and improvement, and the social bonds that such experiences can foster. But the things that entertain, inspire, and fulfill people can be deployed in ways that they do not expect or notice. Such things may even make individuals and communities vulnerable to exploitation, manipulation, and perhaps complicity in their own disempowerment.

Make no mistake, the Olympics does not take place inside television sets. It is more than what most Americans see every two years from their living room couch. It occurs in actual physical locations where people live, work, and survive, and it requires and will alter actual and finite physical resources—as most culturally beloved sports events do. The games and growth will therefore both always be political. Indeed, for its part, the politics of hosting the Olympics is the politics of growth.

Acknowledgments

It is a privilege to study American sport history for a living, and I certainly owe many debts to many people and institutions. At Ithaca College, between 2005 and 2009, I studied Sport Management and Sport Studies with James Gray, Ellen Staurowsky, and Stephen Mosher. They were devoted to the study of sport in society and to undergraduate education. Stephen Mosher's classes, in particular, were revelatory. From 2010 to 2016, I worked as a graduate student with Mark Dyreson, Scott Kretchmar, and Jaime Schultz within Pennsylvania State University's Kinesiology Department, specializing in Sport History and Sport Philosophy. During this time, through a graduate assistantship, Penn State provided me with waived tuition costs and a livable stipend. This setting also offered sage guidance, critical feedback, and much-needed patience. Mark Dyreson served as my dissertation chair and provided input on nearly every page of this book's earliest draft. Scott Kretchmar found a way to get me to Penn State and provided a model of mentorship during my time there. Jaime Schultz's classes constantly pushed me to read, think, and write more critically, setting bars that I continue to strive for. In addition, Penn State's History Department welcomed me with open arms. Seminars run by William Blair, Gary Cross, Alan Derickson, Lori Ginzberg, Amy Greenberg, Michael Kulikowski, and Adam Rome challenged and engaged me. A special thanks goes to Lori Ginzberg for offering critiques to my dissertation. Peter Hopsicker—who preceded me in traveling from Ithaca to State College—served on my dissertation committee as well and offered several valuable insights.

More recently, the Kinesiology Department at the University of North Carolina Greensboro embraced me, my family, and the sociohistorical study of sport. Support from UNCG KIN enabled this work to reach completion. The department also provided funding to allow me to purchase permission to use the images found in this book and to hire an indexer. I am truly grateful to the department and all my KIN colleagues.

Since 2010, the North American Society for Sport History (NASSH) has been my intellectual homebase. It is a reliable place for sharing ideas, hearing criticism, finding renewed motivation, and building community. At NASSH conferences, Malcolm McLane and Russell Field offered commentaries and questions that impacted the analysis of this book. It was also at a NASSH conference that Tommy Hunt encouraged me to submit a draft of my manuscript on the Denver Olympics to the University of Texas Press.

For the past few years, he and the UT Press editors Robert Devens and Dawn Durante answered all my questions and continued to express confidence in the project. As the copy editor, Jon Howard corrected my many mistakes and cleared up much of my writing. Mia Uribe Kozlovsky also assisted me through the multiple facets of the production phase.

As part of the publication process with UT Press, I am deeply appreciative of the thorough feedback I received from the reviewers Michael Childers and Alison Wrynn. Their two rounds of questions and comments surely improved the quality of this work. Jorge Iber and Paulina Rodriguez shared important input on Mexican American history and the Chicano movement as well. I also owe immense gratitude to Laura Lee Katz Olson for sharing her memories of sifting through the DOC's records in 1973 as she com-pleted her excellent dissertation on the Denver Olympics controversy. Her study laid the groundwork for my own. Any reading of this book's endnotes should make that obvious.

I am forever grateful to the archivists and librarians at the Colorado State Archives, the Denver Public Library, the Stephen H. Hart Research Center at the History Colorado Center, the Jefferson County Archives, and the In-ternational Olympic Committee's Olympic Studies Center. Their work made writing this book possible. For all the long days spent reading over primary sources, I cannot fathom the time and effort it took to organize it all in such an accessible manner. Moreover, Sam Brown, Dwight Filley, Richard Lamm, Meg Lundstrom, Tom Nussbaum, Howard Gelt, Richard O'Reilly, and Myles Rademan made themselves readily available for interviews. Their perspectives became a key resource. I am especially thankful to Meg Lund-strom, who— while traveling in India— served as the first interviewee and got the snowball rolling.

I am also incredibly thankful to the International Olympic Committee's Olympic Studies Center. It provided essential funding that enabled travel to archives in Denver and Lausanne, Switzerland. The support of the judges of the PhD and Early Academics Research Grant Program made much of the research for this project a reality. Furthermore, Nuria Puig's vital oversight helped me make the most of the Olympic Studies Center's resources. She remained a trusted point of contact with the IOC from the initiation of research all the way into production.

It is the hardest of all to explain my gratitude for my family. My parents, Patrice and Aaron Berg, have always been a source of vast and endless love. I am only now beginning to understand the sacrifices and investments they made for their children. My siblings, Amanda, Sara, and John, always impress me and remind me to keep pushing forward. My in-laws, Patricia Parente-Maher and Joe Maher, are a foundation of love and kindness. My best friend and partner for life, Jackie Maher, is the love of my life. She lifts my spirits and keeps me grounded every day. Our son, Hayes, and daughter, Paige, bring us immeasurable pride and joy. They are the greatest. Not sure what else to say. I love you all.

Notes

Introduction

1. Richard O'Reilly, "Growth, Funds Key Issues in Olympics Controversy," *Rocky Mountain News*, 1 November 1972, 8, 19.
2. Rex Jennings, "The Olympics Story," Transcript from Luncheon, 31 October 1972, Folder 27, Box 86, DCC DPL.
3. Richard Lamm, "Citizens Can Move Their Government," *Colorado Destiny*, 2 September 1972, 1, Folder 4, CCF DPL.
4. McNichols quoted in Charles Meyers, "Olympic Star Urges Dedication," *Denver Post*, 1 November 1972, 21. Many Coloradans engaged the issue; see Olson, "Power, Public Policy and the Environment," 248–249.
5. For previous work on the Denver Olympics, see Olson, "Power, Public Policy and the Environment"; Foster, "Denver 76"; Whiteside, *Colorado*, 145–179; Childers, *Colorado Powder Keg*, 67–95; Philpott, *Vacationland*, 267–275.
6. Throughout this book, "growth" and "development" will refer to general increases in economic activity, production, and consumption, as well as technological innovation, industrialism, materialism, and consumerism. This is how most Americans have historically understood the terms; see Collins, *More*.
7. For the inherent politics of the Olympics, see, for example, Guttmann, *The Olympics*; Boykoff, *Power Games*.
8. Molotch, "The City as a Growth Machine"; see also Logan and Molotch, *Urban Fortunes*.
9. Stone, *Regime Politics*.
10. Schimmel, "The Political Economy of Place"; Delaney and Eckstein, *Public Dollars, Private Stadiums*.
11. Burbank, Andranovich, and Heying, *Olympic Dreams*, 4–7, 11–32, 168–170 (quotations at pp. 28, 168).
12. The history of the Olympics in the United States is considered in greater depth in chapter 1. See also Riess, "Historical Perspectives on Sport and Public Policy"; Riess, *City Games*, 244.
13. Stone, *Regime Politics*, 234.

14. In *Urban Fortunes* (see pp. 30–31), Logan and Molotch define "structural speculators" as investors that seek to shape a place's relations to other places and to alter the conditions of their local market. They often use this phrase interchangeably with the term "place entrepreneurs."
15. Collins, *More*, 98–165.
16. Boykoff, *Activism and the Olympics*, 25–28; Boykoff (at p. 26) describes event coalitions as "groups coming together for a single event where there is relatively shallow, temporary cooperation between organizations that decreases after the event transpires, when demonstrators return to 'normal activism' surrounding their central issue." Boykoff is informed by Tarrow, *The New Transnational Activism*, 168–172.
17. For a similar dynamic, see Podnair, *City of Dreams*.
18. For "framing," see Entman, "Framing"; for "framing contests," see Gamson, "Bystanders, Public Opinion, and the Media," 245.
19. Colorado Winter Olympic Games Funding and Tax, Measure 8 (1972), reads as follows: "An Act to Amend Articles X and XI of the State Constitution to prohibit the State from levying taxes and appropriating or loaning funds for the purpose of aiding or furthering the 1976 Winter Olympic Games." See https://ballotpedia.org /Colorado_Winter_Olympic_Games_Funding_and_Tax,_Measure_8_(1972).
20. *Congressional Record—Senate, S 15021, 15 September 1972*, Folder 21, Box 1, DOC DPL; for likely support in the House of Representatives, see Leonard Larsen, "Initial U.S. Olympics Aid Sought," *Denver Post*, 25 September 1972, 3; Robert Threlkeld, "House Unit Gives Denver Strong Boost for Olympics," *Rocky Mountain News*, 26 September 1972, 1, 6. For contemporary dollar values, readers may consult www.usinflationcalculator.com.
21. For the theoretical underpinnings of this contention, see Price, "On Seizing the Olympic Platform"; Hartmann, "Rethinking the Relationship Between Sport and Race in American Culture." In the case of the Denver Olympics, it was a *debate over sports*—not the occurrence of a sports event itself—that created the "platform" and provided a "contested terrain." In particular, the discourse over whether to host the Winter Olympics served as the political vehicle where people could struggle over the course of growth and what the rights of citizenship should entail.
22. This analysis aligns with Stone's "social production model" and Burbank and colleagues' conclusions pertaining to the American-held games of Los Angeles (1984), Atlanta (1996), and Salt Lake City (2002). See Stone, *Regime Politics*, 219–233; Burbank, Heying, and Andranovich, "Anti-Growth Politics or Piecemeal Resistance?"
23. Stone, *Regime Politics*, 131–134, 193, 227–231.

Chapter 1: The Origins of Olympic Dreams

1. "What Do We Want to Communicate," n.d., Folder Board of Directors, Box S4130, ARDOC CSA.
2. This chapter provides a synthesis of secondary research and represents an interpretation geared toward showing why Denver bidders had such great confidence in their ability to bid for and host the Olympics. The chapter should not be

considered a comprehensive account of Denver's or Colorado's history. It should also not be assumed that the "successes" of Denver elites and ski industry boosters were universally fair or just. Indeed, a fuller telling would emphasize events such as the Sand Creek Massacre and the Ludlow Massacre, along with the overall invasion of the unceded lands of the Cheyenne, Arapaho, and Ute peoples, as well as racism, gender discrimination, and corporate exploitation within various industries. See Limerick, *The Legacy of Conquest*; Hoig, *The Sand Creek Massacre*; Kelman, *A Misplaced Massacre*; Andrews, *Killing for Coal*; Scott Martelle, *Blood Passion*; Goldberg, *Hooded Empire*; Leonard and Noel, *Denver*, 13–22, 91–97, 174–177, 186–190; Dorsett and McCarthy, *The Queen City*, 87–117.

3. Nash, *The American West Transformed*, 201–216.
4. For an excellent examination of tourism promotion in general in Colorado, see Philpott, *Vacationland*.
5. Dorsett and McCarthy, *The Queen City*, 1–25.
6. Dorsett and McCarthy, *The Queen City*, 1–25; Leonard and Noel, *Denver*, 32–42.
7. Barth, *Instant Cities*; Dorsett and McCarthy, *The Queen City*, 57–86; Leonard and Noel, *Denver*, 39–44, 116–127. The men behind this effort included William N. Byers, Jerome B. Chaffee, Charles Kountze, David H. Moffat, John Evans, James Duff, Walter S. Cheeseman, Henry R. Wolcott, James Archer, J. B. Grant, Rodger Woodbury, William Gray Evans, Fred D. Solomon, and Charles Boettcher.
8. Trachtenberg, *The Incorporation of America*; Dorsett and McCarthy, *The Queen City*, 1–25, 57–86.
9. Dorsett and McCarthy, *The Queen City*, 57–86 (quotation at p. 68).
10. Dorsett and McCarthy, *The Queen City*, 129–131, 134; Leonard and Noel, *Denver*, 65–71, 128–139.
11. Dorsett and McCarthy, *The Queen City*, 121–148; Leonard and Noel, *Denver*, 132–134.
12. Dorsett and McCarthy, *The Queen City*, 134–148 (authors' quotation at p. 134); Leonard and Noel, *Denver*, 140–149.
13. Dorsett and McCarthy, *The Queen City*, 124–129.
14. Leonard and Noel, *Denver*, 238; Dorsett and McCarthy, *The Queen City*, 187–200, 228; members of this new generation included Gerald Hughes, John Porter, Chester and John Morey, John C. Mitchell, Charles Boettcher, George Trimble, John Campion, Dennis Sullivan, A. V. Hunter, and H. L. Doherty.
15. Dorsett and McCarthy, *The Queen City*, 197–208; Leonard and Noel, *Denver*, 240–242.
16. Dorsett and McCarthy, *The Queen City*, 231–233; Leonard and Noel, *Denver*, 203–218; see also White, *"It's Your Misfortune and None of My Own,"* 463–494.
17. Nash, *The American West Transformed*.
18. Major wartime employers in Denver included the Rocky Mountain Arsenal (which produced ammunition and poisonous gases), the Remington Arms Company (which made small-caliber bullets), and a US Maritime Commission prefabrication plant (which specialized in constructing parts for submarine chasers).
19. Dorsett and McCarthy, *The Queen City*, 237–238; Leonard and Noel, *Denver*, 219–232; Nash, *The American West Transformed*, 82–84.
20. Nash, *The American West Transformed*, 56.

21. Nash, *The American West Transformed*, 200–216.

22. Dorsett and McCarthy, *The Queen City*, 251, 253; see also Abbott, Leonard, and Noel, *Colorado*, 315–325.

23. Dorsett and McCarthy, *The Queen City*, 263–265; Leonard and Noel, *Denver*, 247–248.

24. Leonard and Noel, *Denver*, 240, 243; Goodstein, *Denver in Our Time*, 11–13.

25. Leonard and Noel, *Denver*, 243–250.

26. Dorsett and McCarthy, *The Queen City* (for businesses moving to Denver, see pp. 260–262; for the Gates Rubber Company, see 227–228, 240); see also Leonard and Noel, *Denver*, 235–250. Piggybacking on President Harry Truman's call for decentralization, boosters recruited the United States Air Force Academy in Colorado Springs and tens of thousands of federal employees. Corporations such as IBM, Honeywell, Johns Manville, Sundstrand, Ball Brothers Research, and Beech Aircraft also became prominent Denver employers.

27. Abbott, *The New Urban America*, 124–126 (quotation at p. 126).

28. Fainstien and Stokes, "Spaces of Play"; Rosentraub and Joo, "Tourism and Economic Development"; Rothman, *Devil's Bargains* (one of the central claims of Rothman's work is that growth coalitions are behind tourism promotion in general despite drawbacks to local residents).

29. Dorsett and McCarthy, *The Queen City*, 82–83; Leonard and Noel, *Denver*, 120, 123, 263.

30. Whitson and Macintosh, "Global Circus."

31. Whitson and Horne, "Underestimated Costs and Overestimated Benefits," 74.

32. Coleman, *Ski Style* (quotation at p. 79).

33. Rothman, *Devil's Bargains* (for general ski promotions, see pp. 168–179; for the national ski championship, see 179).

34. Coleman, *Ski Style*, 87–88; Rothman, *Devil's Bargains*, 180–181.

35. Dorsett and McCarthy, *The Queen City*, 217–218; Leonard and Noel, *Denver*, 120.

36. Childers, *Colorado Powder Keg*, 32–35, 173n57. Dorsett and McCarthy (*The Queen City*, 219) state the WPA granted $38,000, but the source for this number is unclear; for an overview of Cranmer, see 208–219.

37. Coleman, *Ski Style*, 89–97.

38. Coleman, *Ski Style*, 77–81; Rothman, *Devil's Bargains*, 183–184.

39. Rothman, *Devil's Bargains*, 24, 149–153, 166–170.

40. Coleman, *Ski Style*, 120–126; Cohen, *A Consumer's Republic*.

41. Quotation Philpott, *Vacationland*, 139.

42. L. R. Kendrick (Chairman of the Winter Sports Committee, Denver Chamber of Commerce) to Winter Sports Enthusiasts throughout Colorado, Announcement, 26 November 1945, Folder 5, Box 1, George Cranmer Collection, Denver Public Library, Denver, Colorado.

43. "Colorado Looks Ahead," *Rocky Mountain News*, 21 April 1946, 14; Philpott, *Vacationland*, 44–48.

44. On the emergence of a service economy in the West generally, see White, *"It's Your Misfortune and None of My Own,"* 517–519.

45. Knous quoted in Philpott, *Vacationland*, 43; Coleman, *Ski Style*, 120–122.

46. Philpott, *Vacationland*, 42.

47. Rothman, *Devil's Bargains*, 204–226; Philpott, *Vacationland*, 25–46.
48. Childers, *Colorado Powder Keg*, 39–67; Philpott, *Vacationland*, 99–109; Leonard and Noel, *Denver*, 273.
49. Philpott, *Vacationland*, 138; Childers, *Colorado Powder Keg*, 53.
50. Olson, "Power, Public Policy and the Environment," 31. By the 1955–1956 ski season, about 20 percent of Colorado skiers traveled from beyond the state's borders, contributing around $3 million in ski industry revenue alone; see Allen, "Colorado Ski and Winter Recreation Statistics," 35.
51. For examples of cities that used the Olympics to define themselves around this same time, see Witherspoon, *Before the Eyes of the World*; Schiller and Young, *The 1972 Munich Olympics and the Making of Modern Germany*.
52. Barnett, "St. Louis 1904"; Dyreson, *Making the American Team*, 73–77.
53. Fea, "Lake Placid 1932"; Anzalone, *Battles of the North Country*, 11–35.
54. Dyreson and Llewellyn, "Los Angeles Is the Olympic City," 1993; see also White, "The Los Angeles Way of Doing Things"; Dinces, "Padres on Mount Olympus"; Dyreson, "The Endless Olympic Bid"; Siegel, *Dreamers and Schemers*. The real estate mogul William May Garland led the charge for the bid with the backing of film studio executives such as MGM's Louis B. Mayer as well as the city's three major newspapers.
55. Barnett, "St. Louis 1904"; Dyreson, *Making the American Team*, 73–77.
56. Fea, "Lake Placid 1932."
57. Dyreson and Llewellyn, "Los Angeles is the Olympic City"; Keys, "Spreading Peace, Democracy, and Coca-Cola." Los Angeles boosters also found ways to access public resources for building Memorial Coliseum, which served as the Olympic Stadium; see Riess, "Power Without Authority," 52–53.
58. Anzalone, *Battles of the North Country*, 11–35.
59. Keys, "Spreading Peace, Democracy, and Coca-Cola."
60. Pieroth, "Los Angeles 1932"; Keys, "Spreading Peace, Democracy, and Coca-Cola," esp. 171; "Tourists Descend on Games," *Denver Post*, 29 July 1932, 27.
61. Quentin Reynolds, "American Victory in Bobsled Final Climaxes Great Meet," *Denver Post*, 15 February 1932, 26.
62. Keys, "Spreading Peace, Democracy, and Coca-Cola," esp. 171.
63. C. L. Parsons, "Impressive Ceremony Opens Meet at Los Angeles Olympics," *Denver Post*, 30 July 1932, 11.
64. C. L. Parsons, "Colorful Ceremony Marks Completion of Record Event," *Denver Post*, 15 August 1932, 16.
65. Senn, *Power Politics and the Olympic Games*, 3.
66. Allison Danzig, "Thousands Crowding into Los Angeles for Opening of Olympic Games," *New York Times*, 29 July 1932, 1, 19.
67. Pieroth, "Los Angeles 1932"; Keys, "Spreading Peace, Democracy, and Coca-Cola," 165.
68. Mandell, *The Nazi Olympics*.
69. William Thayer Tutt to Avery Brundage, Telegraph, circa April 1949, File 0004, Film 108, ABC IOCA; Walter Paepcke to Avery Brundage, Telegraph, circa April 1949, File 0004, Film 108, ABC IOCA.
70. "The Broadmoor Colorado Springs"; Sharon Miller, "It Was the Largest Event in the Town's History," *Gazette Telegraph* (Colorado Springs), 29 June 1968, 4C–6C.

71. Penrose and Tutt built their initial fortunes though the sale of a Cripple Creek gold mine, followed by a smelter business, and then mining copper; see "Colorado Experience: Spencer & Julie Penrose," PBS Colorado, www.pbs.org/video /colorado-experience-spencer-julie-penrose.

72. William Thayer Tutt, Colorado Springs, Colorado, 12 June 1975, interviewed by David McComb, 20, OHR SHHRC.

73. "Thayer Tutt Catapults Area into World-Wide Sports Role by Using Broadmoor Facilities," *Gazette Telegraph* (Colorado Springs), 29 June 1968, 42C; "William Thayer Tutt," www.coloradosports.org/index.php/who-s-in-the-hall/inductees /item/216-william-thayer-tutt. Penrose planned the Broadmoor's first invitational golf tournament in 1921 and achieved national attention when playing host to the Trans-Mississippi Tournament of 1927; William Thayer Tutt, McComb interview, SHHRC26.

74. William Thayer Tutt, McComb interview, 20, 25, SHHRC.

75. Rothman, *Devil's Bargains*, 205–226.

76. Rothman, *Devil's Bargains*, 205–226.

77. Rothman, *Devil's Bargains*, 205–226 (quotation at p. 214).

78. William Lee Knous to Avery Brundage, Telegraph, circa April 1949, File 0004, Film 108, ABC IOCA; Eugene D. Millikin to Avery Brundage, Telegraph, circa April 1949, File 0004, Film 108, ABC IOCA; Ed C. Johnson to Avery Brundage, Telegraph, circa April 1949, File 0004, Film 108, ABC IOCA; Avery Brundage to Walter Paepcke, Letter, 20 June 1949, Folder VII, Winter Olympic Games 1956 Bid Colorado Spring, Colo., File 0004, Film 108, ABC IOCA.

79. Session of the International Olympic Committee, 21–27 April 1949, Sessions IOCA.

80. Avery Brundage to Walter Paepcke, Letter, 20 June 1949, Reel 108, Folder VII, Winter Olympic Games 1956 Bid Colorado Spring, Colo., ABC IOCA.

81. Session of the International Olympic Committee, 21–27 April 1949, Sessions IOCA.

82. William Thayer Tutt to Avery Brundage, Letter, 22 June 1949, Folder VII, Winter Olympic Games 1956 Bid Colorado Spring, Colo., File 0004, Film 108, ABC IOCA; Avery Brundage to William Thayer Tutt, Letter, 27 June 1949, Folder VII, Winter Olympic Games 1956 Bid Colorado Spring, Colo., File 0004, Film 108, ABC IOCA; William Thayer Tutt to Avery Brundage, Letter, 25 September 1954, Folder VII, Box 187, Winter Olympic Games 1956 Bid Colorado Spring, Colo., File 0004, Film 108, ABC IOCA.

83. For the Tenth Mountain Division, see Coleman, *Ski Style*, 97–107; Sheldon, *Conquer to Climb*.

84. Coleman, *Ski Style*, 97–107.

85. "Steven Knowlton," www.skihall.com/index.php?_a=document&doc_id=11&id =173; "Ski Country Seen from Broadmoor," *Gazette Telegraph* (Colorado Springs), 29 June 1968, 26C.

86. Colorado Springs–Aspen Invitation Winter Olympic Games, 28 November 1954, Crawford Family United States Olympic Archive, Colorado Springs, Colorado; Denver Olympic Organizing Committee, Final Report, 29 December 1972, "History" section, Folder 3, Box 1, DOOC SHHRC.

87. Ashwell, "Squaw Valley."

88. Ashwell, "Squaw Valley."

89. Ashwell, "Squaw Valley."
90. Ashwell, "Squaw Valley."
91. Barney, Wenn, and Martin, *Selling the Five Rings*, 75.
92. Ashwell, "Squaw Valley," 337–343; "Squaw Valley Hailed: Top Ski Officials Call 1960 Winter Olympics Best Ever," *New York Times*, 27 February 1960, 14; "Pageantry Writes Finish to Olympics," *Denver Post*, 29 February 1960, 37.
93. "Pageantry Writes Finish to Olympics."
94. Rothman, *Devil's Bargains*, 186–201.

Chapter 2: Growth Crusaders

1. Stone, *Regime Politics*, 3; Burbank, Andranovich, and Heying, *Olympic Dreams*, 158.
2. Burbank, Heying, and Andranovich, "Anti-Growth Politics or Piecemeal Resistance?," 336.
3. Logan and Molotch, *Urban Fortunes*, 57–85; Stone, "Paradigms, Power, and Urban Leadership."
4. "Young Republicans Strengthened by Political Novice Love's Win," newspaper clipping, circa September 1962, Folder 8, Box 1, John Love Papers JLP DPL.
5. "GOP Plank Favors Reducing Taxes So State Is on 'Pay-As-You-Go' Basis," *Denver Post*, 7 October 1962, 6D; "Dems Take Pride in State Regime," *Denver Post*, 7 October 1962, 6D.
6. Morton L. Margolin, "Opponent Hits Steve on Spending Policies," *Rocky Mountain News*, 15 August 1962, 8.
7. John Love, Speech, circa 1962, Folder 16, Box 1, JLP DPL.
8. News Release, "Let's Elect John Love," 25 October 1962, Folder 12, Box 1, JLP DPL.
9. Walker, "John A. Love," 30; "Martin Co. Drops 250 Employees," *Denver Post*, 9 January 1964, 1.
10. Leonard Larsen, "GOP Move to Hike Tuitions Likely Campaign Issue," *Denver Post*, 25 January 1964, 22A.
11. "Get the Rest of that Gold Off!," clipping, circa 1963–1964, Folder 2, Box 5, JLP DPL.
12. McNichols quoted in Tom Gavin, "2nd Dist. Dems Hear Steve Rip Love's Tuition," *Denver Post*, 26 January 1964, 26A.
13. "Sit-in Protests Tuition Boost," *Denver Post*, 23 January 1964, 59; Joanne Ditmer, "Love Picketed at CU Campus," *Denver Post*, 21 January 1964, 15; "CU Students Hang Governor in Effigy," *Denver Post*, 17 January 1964, 18.
14. "State Poll Predicts Love Popularity Loss," *Rocky Mountain News*, 2 January 1964, 66; Walker, "John A. Love," 30–31.
15. Walker, "John A. Love," 31.
16. Molotch, "The City as a Growth Machine," 313; Logan and Molotch, *Urban Fortunes*, 57–62.
17. "Love Troup Guests of New York Bank," *Denver Post*, 14 May 1964, 16; "Love Paints Glowing Picture of Colorado," *Rocky Mountain News*, 15 May 1964, 8.
18. Vincent Dwyer, "Love Sings Praises of Colo. In Bay Area," *Rocky Mountain News*, 18 November 1964, 5; Vincent Dwyer, "Gov. Love Tells Bay Area of Colorado's Advantages," *Rocky Mountain News*, 19 November 1964, 5.

19. John A. Love, Speech, "'Sell Colorado—San Francisco,'" 18 November 1964, Box 66948, JLF CSA.

20. Dick Johnson, "Colo. Trade Leaders Court Chicagoans," *Denver Post*, 1 November 1965, 29; Dick Johnson, "LA Labor Costs Spur Bid," *Denver Post*, 25 May 1966, 19.

21. Olson, "Power, Public Policy and the Environment," 90.

22. Walker, "John A. Love," 4, 20.

23. Logan and Molotch, *Urban Fortunes*, 36.

24. "Love Will Seek Winter Games," *Denver Post*, 27 June 1963, 34; Denver Olympic Organizing Committee, Final Report, 29 December 1972, "History" section, Folder 3, Box 1, DOOC SHHRC.

25. Denver Olympic Organizing Committee, Final Report, "History" section.

26. "William Thayer Tutt," www.coloradosports.org/hall-of-fame/athletes/1972-inductees/william-thayer-tutt.

27. William Thayer Tutt, McComb interview, 23, SHHRC.

28. "Peter Seibert, Soldier Skier Who Built Vail Is Dead at 77," www.nytimes.com/2002/07/28/us/pete-seibert-soldier-skier-who-built-vail-is-dead-at-77.html; Rothman, *Devil's Bargains*, 229–237; Philpott, *Vacationland*, 170–186.

29. Olson, "Power, Public Policy and the Environment," 90–91; "Merrill George Hastings Jr.," www.postindependent.com/article/20080501/OBITUARIES/377242619>.

30. John Henry to Jim Cotter, Letter, 6 April 1970, Folder 11, Box 100, WMP DPL.

31. "Ski Country USA Widely Hailed," *Denver Post*, 16 April 1968, 6.

32. Colorado Ski Country USA, Pamphlet, 1968–1969, Folder 7, Box 1, SCUSA DPL.

33. Coleman, *Ski Style*, 147–181.

34. Board of Trustees 1968–69, Folder 7, Box 1, SCUSA DPL

35. After Chicago, Denver became United's second largest hub; see Leonard and Noel, *Denver*, 432.

36. Board of Trustees 1968–69, Folder 7, Box 1, SCUSA DPL; "Donald S. Fowler—Sport Builder—1983," www.skimuseum.net/halloffame/hall_of_fame_details.php?HallOfFameID=48; Colorado Ski Country USA, Annual Meeting Minutes, 8 June 1968, Folder 7, Box 1, SCUSA DPL.

37. Logan and Molotch, *Urban Fortunes*, 74.

38. "Richard Hugo Olson," www.legacy.com/obituaries/denverpost/obituary.aspx?n=richard-hugo-olson&pid=16562181.

39. Richard Olson, Colorado Olympic Commission Meeting Minutes, 12 November 1965, Folder 2, Box 48, DCC DPL.

40. Olson, *Public Policy and the Environment*, 92.

41. Board of Trustees 1968–69, Folder 7, Box 1, SCUSA DPL.

42. Colorado Olympic Commission to the Office of the Mayor, Letter, 30 September 1966, Folder 22, Box 99, WMP DPL; for deposits in Colorado Bank, see paperwork designating signatory powers in Box 4149, ARDOC CSA.

43. For Magarrell's leave of absence, see Olson, "Power, Public Policy and the Environment," 137; G. D. Hubbard, Memorandum, 1 April 1971, Box 4128, ARDOC CSA.

44. Dwyer, "Gov. Love Tells Bay Area of Colorado's Advantages"; "McMahon to Head Olympic Bid Drive," *Rocky Mountain News*, 17 March 1967, 112; Denver Olympic Organizing Committee, Final Report, "History" section.

45. Dwyer, "Gov. Love Tells Bay Area of Colorado's Advantages"; "McMahon to Head Olympic Bid Drive," *Rocky Mountain News*, 17 March 1967, 112.
46. Olson, "Power, Public Policy and the Environment," 97–98.
47. Governor John A. Love's Itinerary for Chicago "Sell Colorado Mission," 1–4 November 1965, Folder Sell Colorado Trip Los Angeles, Box 66998, JLF CSA.
48. "Governor John A. Love's Itinerary for Los Angeles "Sell Colorado Mission," 23–25 May 1966, Folder Sell Colorado Trip Los Angeles, Box 66998, JLF CSA.
49. KTMA-TV (Denver television station), Environmental Hotline, 1971, aired 15 March 1971, Denver Public Library, Denver Colorado.
50. John Love in *1970 Colorado Comprehensive Outdoor Recreation Plan*, 1, 32, Folder Federal Bureau of Outdoor Recreation, Box S4130, ARDOC CSA.
51. Logan and Molotch, *Urban Fortunes*, 62–75; Richard Davis, F. George Robinson, and William Kostka Jr. were likewise positioned as key Olympic contributors and Sell Colorado Ambassadors and will be discussed in following the pages.
52. Brown quoted in Cal Queal, "Winter Olympics 1976," *Denver Post*, 6 February 1964, 62.
53. Logan and Molotch, *Urban Fortunes*, 34–37.
54. See Olson, "Power, Public Policy and the Environment" (for an analysis of constituent preferences, see pp. 247–249; for economic interests, see pp. 251–254).
55. Hjelm and Pisciotte, "Profiles and Careers of Colorado State Legislators," 715 (campaign contributions).
56. Donald Magarrell, Memorandum Re: Meeting with Governor Love and Mayor Currigan, 20 June 1966, circa 20 June 1966, Box S-4147, ARDOC CSA.
57. Olson, "Power, Public Policy and the Environment," 256.
58. Olson, "Power, Public Policy and the Environment," 255.
59. Olson, "Power, Public Policy and the Environment," 207–208.
60. Colorado General Assembly, H.J. Res. 1032. *46th General Assembly, 1st Session*, 1967. Though this resolution has been misplaced at the Colorado State Archives and Records, a copy can be found at Folder 26, Box 99, WMP DPL; Colorado General Assembly, S.B. 179. *46th General Assembly, 1st Session*, 1967, CSA.
61. Agreement, 15 January 1969, Folder 8, Box 100, WMP DPL; Richard M. Davis, Denver Organizing Committee Meeting Minutes, 15 August 1969, Folder 8, Box 100, WMP DPL.
62. Pringle quoted Olson, "Power, Public Policy and the Environment," 255.
63. Tom Currigan to John A. Love, Letter, 7 June 1965, Folder 23, Box 99, WMP DPL.
64. Dorsett and McCarthy, *The Queen City*, 308; Noel and Leonard, *Denver*, 401.
65. Currigan's and McNichols's roles will be explored in more depth in following chapters.
66. Thomas Currigan to Donald McMahon, Letter, 22 August 1968, Folder 1, Box 100, WMP DPL; Richard M. Davis, Denver Olympic Committee Meeting Minutes, 29 March 1968, Folder 3, Box 100, WMP DPL; Richard M. Davis, Denver Olympic Committee Meeting Minutes, 9 May 1968, Folder 3, Box 100, WMP DPL; Richard M. Davis, Denver Olympic Committee Meeting Minutes, 11 July 1969, Folder 3, Box 100, WMP DPL.
67. G. D. Hubbard to Robert J. Pringle, Letter, 17 March 1970, Book 3, Box S4150, ARDOC CSA.

68. Byron Rodgers to Thomas G. Currigan, Letter, 10 April 1967, Folder 1, Box 1, DOC DPL. For Roger's background, see Leonard and Noel, *Denver*, 249.

69. Gordon Allott to Thomas G. Currigan, Letter, 11 April 1967, Folder 1, Box 1, DOC DPL.

70. Peter H. Dominick to Thomas G. Currigan, Letter, 24 April 1967, Folder 1, Box 1, DOC DPL; Wayne N. Aspinall to Thomas G. Currigan, Letter, 11 April 1967, Folder 1, Box 1, DOC DPL; Donald G. Brotzman to Thomas G. Currigan, Letter, 9 May 1967, Folder 1, Box 1, DOC DPL; Frank E. Evans to Thomas G. Currigan, Letter, 19 April 1967, Folder 22, Box 99, WMP DPL.

71. Tom Currigan to Hubert H. Humphrey, Letter, 6 September 1968, Folder 1, Box 100, WMP DPL; Hubert H. Humphrey to Thomas Currigan, Letter, 16 September 1968, Folder 1, Box 100, WMP DPL.

72. Richard Nixon to W. H. McNichols, Letter, 4 August 1969, Folder 1, Box 101, WMP DPL.

73. Sarantakes, "Moscow versus Los Angeles," 137–157, esp. 143.

74. Denver Olympic Organizing Committee, Final Report, "History" section.

75. Donald McMahon to Loyd Joshel, Letter, 13 December 1968, Box S4152, ARDOC CSA.

76. Olson, "Power, Public Policy and the Environment," 210–213.

77. Olson, "Power, Public Policy and the Environment," 213; see also Box S4150 ARDOC CSA. For correspondences between the donators and the bid team, see Folders 8 and 11, Box 100, WMP DPL.

78. "Central Bank Boosts Olympic Fund," *Rocky Mountain News*, 25 May 1968, 90.

79. W. J. Stadler Jr. to Thomas Currigan, Letter, 28 March 1968, Folder 1, Box 100, WMP DPL; Chet Nelson, "Olympic Bid Gets Big Shot in Arm," *Rocky Mountain News*, 19 March 1969, 48; "Lowell Thomas to Speak at Denver Olympic Dinner," *Rocky Mountain News*, 10 March 1968, clipping, Folder 25, Box 99, WMP DPL; Barley Key, "Cherry Hills Fete Keys Olympic Bid," *Rocky Mountain News*, 3 March 1968, 56; Denver Olympic Organizing Committee, Final Report, "History" section.

80. Donald F. McMahon to USOC Presentation Team, Letter Re: Flight Schedule, 8 December 1967, Folder 22, Box 99, WMP DPL.

81. "Olympics in Colorado?," *Denver Post*, 30 October 1968, 92. Jeep Corporation donated a Jeep; see Richard M. Davis, Denver Olympic Committee Meeting Minutes, 1 March 1968, Folder 3, Box 100, WMP DPL. Hertz and Kumpf Lincoln-Mercury Company each provided two vehicles, and Davis Brothers Incorporated donated liquor for an International Sports Federation reception; see F. George Robinson to John C. Davis, Letter, 1 November 1968, Folder 4, Box 100, WMP DPL; F. George Robinson to Florian Barth, Letter, 1 November 1968, Folder 4, Box 100, WMP DPL; F. George Robinson to Jim Schorsch, Letter, 1 November 1968, Folder 4, Box 100, WMP DPL. IBM provided the DOC goods and services; see Donald F. McMahon to R. J. Whalen, Letter, 5 February 1969, Folder 8, Box 100, WMP DPL.

82. Denver Olympic Organizing Committee, Final Report, "History" section.

83. Colorado Ski Country USA, Board of Trustees Annual Meeting Minutes, 3 June 1966, Folder 19, Box 1, SCUSA DPL; Colorado Ski Country USA, Annual Meeting Minutes, 8 June 1968, Folder 7, Box 1, SCUSA DPL; Richard M. Davis, Denver

Organizing Committee Meeting Minutes, 13 June 1968, Folder 3, Box 100, WMP DLP; "Interski May Aid Denver Olympic Bid," *Denver Post*, 9 April 1968, 31.

84. Bob Parker to Board of Trustees, Your Letters Regarding the Future of the Ski Country USA Program, 14 December 1966, Folder 19, Box 1, SCUSA DPL; Steve Knowlton, Colorado Ski Country USA Newsletter, 1 April 1964, Folder 2, Box 1, SCUSA DPL.

85. Steve Knowlton, Colorado Ski Country USA Newsletter, 1 November 1964, Folder 2, Box 1, SCUSA DPL.

86. Steve Knowlton quoted in Queal, "Winter Olympics 1976."

87. Board of Trustees—RMSAOA Combined Luncheon Meeting, 11 November 1966, Folder 17 or 18, Box 1, SCUSA DPL.

88. Molotch, "The City as a Growth Machine"; Logan and Molotch, *Urban Fortunes*, 70–73.

89. Olson, "Power, Public Policy and the Environment," 117; see also box S4151 ARDOC CSA.

90. Denver Organizing Committee, Denver Organizing Committee's Response to Questionnaire for Bid Cites, April–May 1967, Folder 1, Box 1, DOC DPL; Denver Olympic Committee Roster, Folder 23, Box 99, WMP DPL; William H. Mc-Nichols Jr. to Palmer Hoyt, 22 July 1969, Folder 8, Box 100, WMP DPL; Richard M. Davis, Denver Organizing Committee Meeting Minutes, 11 September 1969, Folder 9, Box 100, WMP DPL. "Mayor Expands Olympic Panel," *Denver Post*, 17 September 1969, 3.

91. Queal, "Winter Olympics 1976."

92. "Winter Olympics for Colorado," *Rocky Mountain News*, 16 December 1966, clipping, Folder 25, Box 99, WMP DPL.

93. Alan Cunningham, "Love, Currigan, Flying to Olympic Site," *Rocky Mountain News*, 31 January 1968, 5; John Morehead, "Olympic Pitch Set by Denver," *Denver Post*, 11 January 1968, 28; "Coloradans Carry Bid for Olympics to Grenoble," clipping, 31 January 1968, Folder 25, Box 99, WMP DPL.

94. Chet Nelson, "The Winter Olympics," *Rocky Mountain News*, clipping, circa February 1968, Folder 25, Box 99, WMP DPL.

95. Jim Graham, "Olympic Pomp 'Seen in Colo.,'" *Denver Post*, 7 February 1968, 74.

96. Owen K. Ball, "Ball Points," *Canyon Courier* (Evergreen), 31 October 1968, clipping, Folder 6, Box 6, MAPC JCA.

97. Richard M. Davis, Denver Organizing Committee Meeting Minutes, 11 September 1969, Folder 9, Box 100, WMP DPL.

98. Owen K. Ball to International Olympic Committee, Letter, 23 April 1970, File 0010, Film 110, ABC IOCA.

99. Bick Lucas, "Good Luck, Denver, On Winter Olympics," *Denver Post*, 3 May 1970, clipping, Folder 2, Box 6, MAPC JCA.

100. Walker, "John A. Love," 40. As Love's campaign trumpeted, he had brought "129 new industries in[to] Colorado during the last four years and 119 major expansions of existing businesses." Brokering a land acquisition deal to attract Kodak and reporting an unemployment rate as low as 3.3 percent were major victories; see "Love For Colorado: Election Fact Sheet," circa 1966, Folder 23, Box 1, JLP DPL.

101. "Text of Love Address to General Assembly," *Denver Post*, 9 January 1968, 44.

102. Colorado Visitors Bureau, "1968–69 Colorado Skiing: Resorts, Lodges, Services, Transportation," circa 1968, Folder 1, Box 1, SCUSA DPL.
103. Richard Olson, Colorado Olympic Commission Meeting Minutes, 12 November 1965, Binder COC Minutes, 12 November 1965–30 June 1970, Box S-4147, ARDOC CSA.
104. For an example of the close relations of many of the bidders, see Merrill G. Hastings to Executive Committee, Letter, 20 March 1969, Box 4149 ARDOC CSA.

Chapter 3: Faking an Olympic City

1. Logan and Molotch, *Urban Fortunes*; for the effects on taxes, see pp. 85–88, and for the effects on jobs, see 89–91.
2. Rothman, *Devil's Bargains*. For a similar analysis, see Anzalone, *Battles of the North Country*.
3. John Love, Letter, circa 1964, 1964.01.01–1973.12.31, Candidatures in general and of the cities of Denver, Grenade, Grenoble, and Innsbruck for the Olympic Winter Games in 1976: invitation, correspondence, speeches, lists, presentation, questionnaires, and report, CC IOCA.
4. "Ski Colorado: Bid for the Winter Olympics," circa 1965, Folder 23, Box 99, WMP DPL.
5. Queal, "Winter Olympics 1976."
6. Brown quoted in Queal, "Winter Olympics 1976."
7. Colorado Ski Country USA, Board of Trustees Annual Meeting Minutes, 27 April 1966, Folder 19, Box 1, SCUSA DPL.
8. Merrill Hastings, Colorado Olympic Commission Board of Directors Meeting Minutes, 9 February 1966, Box S-4147, ARDOC CSA.
9. "From the Olympic Rules: Useful Information for the Press," Extract, Folder 23, Box 99, WMP DPL; see also International Olympic Committee, Olympic Rules and Regulations, Lausanne, Switzerland, 1971, 11, 35.
10. Site Selection Committee, Memo, circa 1966, Folder 22, Box 99, WMP DPL.
11. Donald Magarrell, Memorandum Re: Meeting with Governor Love and Mayor Currigan, 20 June 1966, Box S-4147, ARDOC CSA; Sidney Cornwall, Special Meeting of the Colorado Olympic Commission, 30 January 1967, Box S-4147, ARDOC CSA.
12. Thomas Currigan to United States Olympic Committee, Letter, 1 December 1966, Folder 22, Box 99, WMP DPL; Office of the Mayor, Press Release, 31 March 1967, Folder 22, Box 99, WMP DPL; "Denver Group Set to Push For '76 Olympics," *Rocky Mountain News*, 1 April 1967, 74. An undated note suggests Hastings alone selected the DOC members, which Currigan officially appointed; see Folder 22, Box 99, WMP DPL; see also Thomas Currigan to Donald McMahon, Letter, 24 March 1967, Folder 22, Box 99 WMP DPL. Other original DOC members included Robert O'Donnell (president of Harmon, O'Donnell, & Henninger Associates Inc.), F. George Robinson (president of Robinson Brick & Tile), Charles Smuckler (president of Alameda National Bank), Walter Hellmich (chairman of the Colorado Council of Arts & Humanities), Russ Writer (manager of Writer's Manor), Robert Pringle (vice president of Mountain States Telephone Company), and James H. Smith (former assistant secretary of the US Navy);

John H. Boyd (director of public relations for Martin Marietta Company) joined a month later; Richard Davis (a senior partner at Davis, Graham, and Stubbs) took on the role as the DOC's legal adviser and eventually became a member. See Denver Olympic Organizing Committee, Final Report, 29 December 1972, "History" section, Folder 3, Box 1, DOOC SHHRC.

13. Denver Olympic Organizing Committee, Final Report, "History" section.
14. "COLORADO OLYMPIC COMMISSION / DENVER OLYMPIC COMMIT-TEE: Definition and Allocation of Responsibilities and Duties," circa May–June 1968, Folder 1, Box 100, WMP DPL; Davis is referenced as the author in Richard M. Davis, Denver Organizing Committee Meeting Minutes, 17 April 1968, Folder 3, Box 100, WMP DPL; see also Thomas Currigan to Richard Olson, Letter, 6 June 1968, Folder 1, Box 100, WMP DPL; John A. Love to Richard Davis, Letter, 10 June 1968, Folder 1, Box 100, WMP DPL.
15. Donald Magarrell to John A. Love, Letter, 13 March 1968, Folder 3, Box 100, WMP DPL; F. George Robinson to John A. Love, Letter, 13 March 1968, Folder 3, Box 100, WMP DPL; Donald Fowler to Richard H. Olson, Letter, 13 March 1968, Folder 3, Box 100, WMP DPL; Merrill Hastings to John A. Love, Letter, 13 March 1968, Folder 3, Box 100, WMP DPL. George Robinson, who served in both organizations, also resigned from the COC.
16. "COLORADO OLYMPIC COMMISSION / DENVER OLYMPIC COMMIT-TEE"; see also Donald Magarrell, Denver Organizing Committee Meeting Minutes, 8 August 1967, Folder Board of Directors, Box S4130, ARDOC CSA.
17. Denver, Colorado, USA, 1967, XII Olympic Winter Games (1967), Denver Public Library, Denver, Colorado.
18. Denver Organizing Committee, Denver Organizing Committee's Response to Questionnaire for Bid Cites, circa 1967, 5–8, Folder 1, Box 1, DOC DPL; see also Denver, Colorado, USA, 1976, XII Olympic Winter Games (1967), 11–13.
19. Robinson replaced Peter Seibert. Seibert stepped down from his DOC post to focus on managing Vail; see Peter Seibert to Thomas Currigan, Letter, 2 May 1967, Folder 22, Box 88, WMP DPL.
20. Richard Davis, Denver Organizing Committee Meeting Minutes, 8 August 1968, Folder 3, Box 100, WMP DPL; Committee of Candidature for the XII Winter Olympic Games, International Bulletin, 1 November 1968, Folder 2, Box 1, DOC DPL; Denver US Candidate for the XII Winter Olympic Games 1976, International Bulletin, May 1969, Folder 29, Box 3, POME SHHRC.
21. Denver Organizing Committee, Book One, Denver: The City, Denver: United States Candidate for the XII Winter Olympic Games, 1976 (1970), 47–49, Bid Books IOCA.
22. J. B. Cotter to F. G. Robinson, D. F. Magarrell, G. F. Groswold, J. W. Rouse, N. C. Brown, L. Grant, and W. Kostka, "Re: Weather Information," 28 October 1969, Folder Sites Environmental General, Box S4143, ARDOC CSA; Lewis O. Grant to James B. Cotter, Letter, 21 April 1970, Folder 27, Box 2, DOC DPL. Grant found odds were there would be five or more inches of snow on the ground in Evergreen during just four days in the month of February.
23. J. B. Cotter to R. M. Davis, T. Hildt Jr., R. J. Pringle, G. D. Hubbard, D. V. Dunklee, R. S. McCollum, R. D. Barnard, C. H. Buck, N. H. Allen, T. G. Currigan, R. H. Olson, Letter Re: Competitive Comparisons, 13 May 1969, Folder 8, Box 100, WMP DPL.

24. Ted Farwell to Lewis Grant, Letter, 3 December 1970, Folder Sites Environmental General Folder Number I, Box S4143, ARDOC CSA; Ted Farwell to Warren Hartmann, Marvin Elkins, Sven Wiik, Don Barrett, Marvin Crawford, Dean Williams, and John R. Fetcher, Letter, 30 March 1972, Folder 9, Box 102, WMP DPL; Technical Division to General Secretary and Manager Public Affairs, Report No. 2, 8 March 1971, Folder 2, Box 2, DOC DPL.

25. Technical Division to the DOC Executive Committee, Report No. 1, 14 January 1971, Folder 2, Box 2, DOC DPL.

26. Ted Farwell to C. Allison Merrill, Letter, 3 December 1970, Folder 18, Box 1, DOC DPL; C. Allison Merrill to Ted Farwell, Letter, 9 December 1970, Folder 18, Box 1, DOC DPL.

27. Robert Burns, "Olympic Officials Hint Nordic Events Shift to Steamboat," *Rocky Mountain News*, 25 February 1971, 5; Technical Division to General Secretary and Manager Public Affairs, Report No. 2, 8 March 1971, Folder 2, Box 2, DOC DPL; Cross Country Advisory Committee Meeting Minutes, 22 March 1971, Folder 19, Box 2, DOC DPL.

28. Technical Division to General Secretary and Manager Public Affairs, Report No. 2, 8 March 1971, Folder 2, Box 2, DOC DPL.

29. Norm Brown to Bob Pringle, Don Magarrell, F. G. Robinson, Letter, 6 April 1970, Book 4, Box S4150, ARDOC CSA.

30. Technical Division to General Secretary, Memorandum Re: Report of attendance at the 28th FIS Congress, Opatija, Yugoslavia, 20–31 May 1971, 22 June 1971, Folder 37, Box 2, DOC DPL; Technical Director to DOC Board and COC Board, Inter-Office Memorandum, 14 December 1971, Folder 15, Box 2, DOC DPL.

31. Mayor William McNichols to DOC Executive Council, Memorandum, 8 December 1971, Folder 5, Box 101, WMP DPL.

32. Denver Olympic Committee Executive Council Meeting Minutes—Revised, 21 December 1971, Folder 28, Box 1, DOC DPL; Denver Organizing Committee Board of Directors Meeting Minutes, 22 December 1971, Folder 19, Box 1, DOC DPL.

33. Vanderhoof quoted in "Vanderhoof: Evergreen Out," *Denver Post*, 9 March 1971, 40; see also Robert Pringle to Robert Behrens, Letter, 10 April 1972, Folder Competition Sites Nordic Events, Box S4149, ARDOC CSA.

34. Denver Organizing Committee, Denver Organizing Committee's Response to Questionnaire for Bid Cites, circa 1967, 1–5, Folder 1, Box 1 DPL DOC; Colorado Olympic Committee Meeting Minutes, 14 March 1967, Binder COC Minutes, 12 November 1965–30 June 1970, Box S4147, ARDOC CSA.

35. Site Selection Meeting Minutes, 20 February 1967, Binder 2, Box 1, PHP DPL; Site Selection Committee Meeting, 14 March 1967, Binder 2, Box 1, PHP DPL; Paul Hauk to George Robinson, Letter, 29 September 1967, Binder 2, Box 1, PHP DPL. All PHP DPL sources used are also included in Hauk, *Beaver Creek Ski Area Chronology*.

36. Paul Hauk to George Robinson, Letter, 13 September 1967, Binder 2, Box 1, PHP DPL; Site Selection Committee Meeting Minutes, 6 April 1967, Binder 2, Box 1, PHP DPL; Paul Hauk to George Robinson, Letter, 29 September 1967, Binder 2, Box 1, PHP DPL; Paul Hauk to George Robinson, Letter, 16 October 1970, Binder 2, Box 1, PHP DPL.

37. Site Selection Committee Meeting Minutes, 6 April 1967, Binder 2, Box 1, PHP DPL.

38. Donald McMahon to Clifford Buck, Letter, 26 September 1967, Folder Competition Sites Alpine Events, Box S4149, ARDOC CSA.

39. Newbold Black quoted in William Marvel, "Colo. Snow Trips Olympic Site Unit," *Rocky Mountain News*, 4 November 1967, 83.

40. McLane quoted in "Long Road '76," *Colorado Magazine*, November–December 1970, 11–16, 102–107.

41. Site Selection Committee Meeting Minutes, 6 April 1967, Binder 2, Box 1, PHP DPL. This source suggests the Sniktau and Loveland Basin were always included for strategic purposes, not a literal proposal.

42. Farwell quotation from David Sumber and Ted Farwell, "The Olympic Bubble," *Colorado: Rocky Mountain West*, January/February 1973, 28; see also Technical Division to the DOC Executive Committee, Report No. 1, 14 January 1971, Folder 2, Box 2, DOC DPL; Olson, "Power, Public Policy and the Environment," 104.

43. Denver, Colorado, USA, 1976, XII Olympic Winter Games (1967), 6–7, DPL.

44. Richard M. Davis, Denver Olympic Committee Meeting Minutes, 17 April 1968, Folder 3, Box 100, WMP DPL.

45. Denver US Candidate for the XII Winter Olympic Games, Proposed Nordic and Alpine Sites: Prepared for International Ski Federation Congress 1969, presented 18–25 May 1969, Folder 33, Box 3, POME SHHRC.

46. Denver Organizing Committee, Book One, Denver: The City, Denver: United States Candidate for the XII Winter Olympic Games, 1976 (1970), 17, Bid Books IOCA.

47. Richard O'Reilly, interview with author, Pasadena, California, 1 June 2016, recording in the author's possession; see also O'Reilly, "The Olympics and Colorado, 1st of a Series: Olympics Good or Bad in Colorado?"

48. Vanderhoof quoted in Richard O'Reilly, "DOC Disclosure of Alpine Site Selection Delayed," *Rocky Mountain News*, 30 January 1972, 3, 6.

49. J. B. Cotter to R. M. Davis, T. Hildt Jr., R. J. Pringle, G. D. Hubbard, D. V. Dunklee, R. S. McCollum, R. D. Barnard, C. H. Buck, N. H. Allen, T. G. Currigan, R. H. Olson, Letter Re: Competitive Comparisons, 13 May 1969, Folder 8, Box 100, WMP DPL.

50. Donald F. Magarrell, Executive Council, 25 February 1971, Folder 26, Box 1, DOC DPL; Technical Division to General Secretary and Manager of Public Affairs, Report No. 2, 8 March 1971, Folder 2, Box 2, DOC DPL.

51. Joseph Cushing Jr. to Theodore Farwell, letter, 11 June 1971, Folder 37, Box 2, DOC DPL; Sno-Engineering Inc., "Preliminary Site Evaluation: Mount Sniktau," Spring 1971, Folder 37, Box 2, DOC DPL.

52. Technical Director to DOC Executive Council, Inter-Office Memo, Subject: Sport Site Reevaluation—General Alpine Site, 1 November 1971, Folder 37, Box 2, DOC DPL.

53. Technical Director to DOC Executive Council, Inter-Office Memorandum, Subject: Sport Site Reevaluation—General Alpine Site, 1 November 1971, Folder 37, Box 2, DOC DPL; Technical Director to DOC Board and COC Board, Inter-Office Memorandum, 14 December 1971, Folder 15, Box 2, DOC DPL; Denver Organizing Committee Board of Directors Meeting Minutes, 22 December 1971, Folder 19, Box 1, DOC DPL.

54. Richard M. Davis, Denver Organizing Board of Directors Meeting Minutes, 16 December 1971, Folder 19, Box 1, DOC DPL; "Copper Mountain: A Summary," December 1971, Folder 16, Box 101, WMP DPL; "Keystone Olympic Prospectus," December 1971, Folder 32, Box 2, DOC DPL; "Proposal for Consideration of Steamboat Springs–Mount Badly as Official Site for the 1976 Winter Olympic Games," January 1972, Folder 34, Box 2, DOC DPL; Vail Associates, "Beaver Creek," circa December 1971, Folder 35, Box 2, DOC DPL; Peter W. Seibert to Executive Council of the Denver Organizing Committee, Letter, 19 December 1971, Folder 35, Box 2, DOC DPL; Jerry D. Jones (General Manager of Snowmass) to Robert Pringle, Letter, 5 January 1972, Folder 22, Box 2, DOC DPL; W. V. N. Jones (President of Aspen Highlands Skiing Corporation) to Denver Olympic Committee, Letter, 5 January 1972, Folder 22, Box 2, DOC DPL; Sumber and Farwell, "The Olympic Bubble," 35.

55. Hauk, *Beaver Creek Ski Area Chronology*, 4. See also Olson, "Power, Public Policy and the Environment," 150–156.

56. Olson, "Power, Public Policy and the Environment," 154.

57. This will be discussed in greater detail in chapter 9.

58. Schaeffler quoted in Richard O'Reilly, "The Olympics and Colorado: Olympic Alpine Conflict Brewing, 4th of a Series"; for Schaeffler's influence in the Sniktau selection, see F. George Robinson to Willy Schaeffler, letter, 1 November 1968, Folder 4, Box 100, WMP DPL.

59. Technical Director to DOC Executive Council, Inter-Office Memo, Subject: Sport Site Reevaluation—General Alpine Site, 1 November 1971, Folder 37, Box 2, DOC DPL.

60. Richard Olson, Colorado Olympic Commission Meeting Minutes, 12 November 1965, DCC DPL. Site Selection Meeting Minutes, 20 February 1967, Binder 2, Box 1, PHP DPL; Site Selection Committee Meeting, 14 March 1967, Binder 2, Box 1, PHP DPL.

61. Denver Organizing Committee, "Denver Organizing Committee's Response to Questionnaire for Bid Cites," circa 1967, 59, Folder 1, Box 1, DOC DPL; the DOC listed Colorado School of Mines, Metropolitan State College, Arapahoe Junior College, and the Lowry Field and Fitzsimons Hospital military installations as possibilities.

62. William Marvel, "Colo. Snow Trips Olympic Site Unit," *Rocky Mountain News*, 4 November 1967, 83.

63. Denver, Colorado, USA, 1976, XII Olympic Winter Games (1967), 17, DPL.

64. "Olympics: Denver Organizing Committee for the XII Olympics," *Colorado: Rocky Mountain West*, Mid-Winter 1968, 27. This article was written by a DOC member or someone in close contact with the group. Many of the pictures used in the DOC's 1967 USOC bid book also accompanied the piece; see also Committee of Candidature for the XII Winter Olympic Games, International Bulletin, 1 November 1968, Folder 2, Box 1, DOC DPL.

65. Denver US Candidate for the XII Winter Olympic Games 1976, International Bulletin, circa 1969, Folder 26, Box 99, WMP DPL.

66. Book Two, Denver: Technical Information, Denver: United States Candidate for the XII Winter Olympic Games, 1976 (1970), 8, Bid Books, IOCA.

67. Donald Magarrell, Denver Organizing Committee Meeting Minutes, 25

September 1967, Folder Board of Directors, Box S4130, ARDOC CSA; Donald Magarrell, Denver Organizing Committee Meeting Minutes, 6 December 1967, Book 1, Box S4150, ARDOC CSA.

68. Richard M. Davis, Denver Olympic Committee Meeting Minutes, 17 April 1968, Folder 3, Box 100, WMP DPL.

69. Maurice Mitchell to Don Magarrell, Letter, 12 March 1971, Folder 13, Box 2, DOC DPL.

70. Logan and Molotch, *Urban Fortunes*, 75–76.

71. Maurice Mitchell to Don Magarrell, Letter, 12 March 1971, Folder 13, Box 2, DOC DPL.

72. Maurice B. Mitchell to Robert J. Pringle, Letter, 3 August 1971, Box 67053, JLF CSA; see also Agreement Between the University of Denver (Colorado Seminary) and the Denver Organizing Committee XII Winter Olympic Games 1976, Box 67503, JLF CSA.

73. For the DOC continuing to list the university as the site of the Olympic Village, see Denver Olympic Committee, Report: The Denver XII Olympic Winter Games Prepared for the International Olympic Committee Executive Board, May 1972, IV7, Folder 23, Box 1, DOC DPL.

74. John Morehead, "Housing Knotty Problem in Olympics," *Denver Post (Bonus)*, 25 September 1972, 6.

75. Denver Olympic Organizing Committee, Final Report; see "Olympic Village" and "Alternative Site For Olympic Village."

76. Theodore D. Browne, Preliminary Estimate of Costs, Revenues, and Economic Impact Associated with Staging the 1976 Winter Olympic Games in Colorado, 4 January 1967, iii, Folder 2, Box 1, DOC DPL. Browne was a professional business consultant.

77. Donald Magarrell, Colorado Olympic Commission Meeting Minutes, 19 September 1966, Box S4147, ARDOC CSA.

78. Donald Magarrell, Colorado Olympic Commission Meeting Minutes, 29 November 1966, Box S4147, ARDOC CSA; Special Meeting of the Colorado Olympic Commission, 15 December 1966, Box S4147, ARDOC CSA.

79. Donald Magarrell, Colorado Olympic Commission Meeting Minutes, 5 January 1967, Box S4147, ARDOC CSA.

80. Browne, Preliminary Estimate of Costs, iii–iv.

81. Browne, Preliminary Estimate of Costs (quotation at p. vi). Browne provides these number on v–vi but goes into much more detail regarding how the DRI reached them throughout the report.

82. Zimbalist, *Circus Maximus*.

83. Browne, Preliminary Estimate of Costs, 36 (for "tangible" and "intangible" benefits, see pp. 29–36).

84. Denver Organizing Committee, "Denver Organizing Committee's Response to Questionnaire for Bid Cites," circa 1967, 76, Folder 1, Box 1, DOC DPL. This line about a financing matrix was repeated in Denver, Colorado, USA, 1976, XII Olympic Winter Games (1967), 45, DPL.

85. Browne, Preliminary Estimate of Costs, 27.

86. Richard M. Davis, Denver Organizing Committee Meeting Minutes, 17 April 1969, Folder 8, Box 100, WMP DPL.

87. G. D. Hubbard to Robert J. Pringle, Letter, 17 March 1970, Book 3, Box S4150, ARDOC CSA.

88. "Information for Immediate Release," 18 September 1968, Folder 36, Box 1, DOC DPL; see also Charles Meyers, "Denver's Olympic Bid Paying Off, DOC says," *Denver Post*, 13 December 1969, 10.

89. Richard M. Torrisi to Denver Olympic Committee, Letter Re: Speed Skating Rink, 19 June 1968, Folder 3, Box 100, WMP DPL.

90. J. B. Cotter to T. Hildt Jr., D. F. Magarrell, F. G. Robinson, R. J. Pringle, G. F. Groswold, A. Zirkel, P. J. Gallavan, K. Dybevik, W. Kostka Jr., Letter Re: Speed Skating/Hockey Complex Proposal, Ahrendt Engineering Co., 8 May 1969, Folder 12, Box 2, DOC DPL; Ahrendt Engineering's analysis is located with the Cotter letter in Folder 12, Box 2, DOC DPL. However, its cover page is labeled "Denver Olympic Village for the Denver Organizing Committee for the 1976 Winter Olympics, Inc."

91. "Sledding Dropped from 1976 Games," *New York Times*, 25 August 1972, 23.

92. Norm Brown to Bob Pringle, Don Magarrell, F. G. Robinson, Letter, 6 April 1970, Book 4, Box S4150, ARDOC CSA.

93. Charles T. Gibson to Marvin Crawford, Letter, 3 January 1972, Folder 16, Box 2, DOC DPL.

94. Tommy Patterson, Mountain Area Planning Council Conversation w/Gov. Love, 23 April 1970, Folder 24, Box 1, MAPC JCA.

95. Technical Director and Public Information Director to Executive Council, Inter-Office Memo, 19 April 1972, Subject: What do we do about the bobsled?, Folder 25, Box 102, WMP DPL. Mayor William McNichols also expresses concern about the economic viability of the bobsled run and ski jump; see Denver Olympic Committee Board of Directors Meeting Minutes, 22 December 1971, Folder 19, Box 1, DOC DPL.

96. Denver Organizing Committee, Book One, Denver: The City, Denver: United States Candidate for the XII Winter Olympic Games, 1976 (1970), 98, Bid Books IOCA.

97. Bob Lochener, "Press Polite on Denver's Bid," *Denver Post*, 13 February 1968, 23.

98. Denver Organizing Committee, Book Two, Denver: Technical Information: United States Candidate for the XII Winter Olympic Games, 1976 (1970), Bid Books IOCA. For Alpine events, see pp. 18–43; for ski jumping, 50–55; for cross-country skiing, 56–63; for the biathlon, 63–68; for speed skating, 86–89; for bobsled and luge, 90–103.

99. Philpott, *Vacationland* (see p. 103 for highways as essential for moving resources).

100. Philpott, *Vacationland*, 135; see also Brown, *Trout Culture*, 77–91.

101. Philpott, *Vacationland*, 64–75, 83.

102. Philpott, *Vacationland*; for representing Denver as part of the Rockies, see p. 157; for the DOC picture with a telephoto lens, see p. 269.

103. John Morehead, "Olympian Job Ahead for Denver," *Denver Post*, 17 May 1970, 1, 3.

104. Richard M. Torrisi to DOC-IOC Members, Letter Re: Informational/Promotional Materials Inventory, 14 November 1968, Book 1, Box S4150, ARDOC CSA.

105. The Controller General, Report to the Committee on Interior and Insular Affairs, House of Representatives, Plan for Staging the 1976 Winter Olympic Games in Colorado, August 1972, Folder 16, Box 102, WMP DPL.

Chapter 4: A Mass Soft Sell

1. PHASE II MARKETING STRATEGY, Revised July 1969, Book 2, Box S4150, ARDOC CSA.
2. Dichter, "Corruption in the 1960s?"
3. Richard M. Torrisi, Olympic Designation—Phase II, 31 March 1968, Folder 1, Box 100, WMP DPL.
4. R. H. Olson to Don McMahon, John Love, Thomas Currigan, Cliff Buck, Merrill Hastings, Tom Hildt, Don Magarrell, Robt. Pringle, F. George Robinson, Charles Smukler, Report on the Xth Winter Olympic Games: Grenoble, 28 February 1968, Book 1, Box S4150, ARDOC CSA.
5. PHASE II MARKETING STRATEGY, Revised July 1969, Book 2, Box S4150, ARDOC CSA.
6. Donald F. Magarrell to Richard Olson, Letter, 2 May 1966, Folder 23, Box 99, WMP DPL.
7. Hastings quoted in Olson, "Power, Public Policy and the Environment," 97.
8. Denver Olympic Organizing Committee, Final Report, 29 December 1972, "History" section, Folder 3, Box 1, DOOC SHHRC.
9. Olson, "Power, Public Policy and the Environment," 97.
10. "Long Road '76," 11–16, 102–107 (quotation at p. 14); see also Donald F. Magarrell to Richard Olson, Letter, 2 May 1966, Folder 23, Box 99, WMP DPL.
11. 64th Session of the International Olympic Committee, 24–30 April 1966, Sessions IOCA.
12. Denver Olympic Organizing Committee, Final Report, "History" section.
13. Neil Allen, trip to Vancouver, BC, 3, 4, 5 August 1969, 11 August 1969, Book 2, Box S4150, ARDOC CSA.
14. Olson, "Power, Public Policy and the Environment," 117. See also Box S4152, ARDOC CSA.
15. Norm Brown to William Kostka Jr., Letter, 2 February 1970, Book 3, Box S4150, ARDOC CSA; Richard M. Davis, Meeting Minutes, 12 March 1970, Book 3, Box S4150, ARDOC CSA; Olson, "Power, Public Policy and the Environment," 115.
16. William Kostka Jr. to Robert Pringle, Memorandum, 16 March 1970, Book 3, Box S4150, ARDOC CSA.
17. Gerry Groswold, Report on Attendance at FIS Congress—Barcelona, Spain, 18–25 May, 5 June 1969, Folder 13, Box 102, WMP DPL.
18. International Olympic Committee Guests, Folder 8, Box 100, WMP DPL; Thomas G. Currigan and William H. McNichols Jr. to Reginald S. Alexander, Letter, 23 December 1968, Folder 4, Box 100, WMP DPL.
19. Schedule of Planned Activities for International Olympic Committee Visit, 25 February–4 March 1969, Folder 8, Box 100, WMP DPL.
20. Richard M. Davis, Denver Olympic Committee Meeting Minutes, 17 April 1969, Folder 8, Box 100, WMP DPL.
21. Ditcher, "Corruption in the 1960s?"
22. Richard M. Davis, Denver Olympic Committee Meeting Minutes, 14 November 1968, Folder 4, Box 100, WMP DPL.
23. Merrill G. Hastings Jr. to All DOC Directors, Memorandum, 26 December 1968, Folder 4, Box 100, WMP DPL.

24. Richard M. Davis, Denver Olympic Committee Meeting Minutes, 12 December 1968, Folder 4, Box 100, WMP DPL.

25. Davis, Denver Olympic Committee Meeting Minutes, 12 December 1968.

26. D. F. McMahon to COC/DOC Members, Re: IOC Visit, February 25–March 4, 1969, 27 January 1969, Book 2, Box S4150, ARDOC CSA.

27. Richard M. Davis, Denver Olympic Committee Meeting Minutes, 12 December 1968, Folder 4, Box 100, WMP DPL.

28. John G. Griffin to William H. McNichols, Letter, 20 February 1969, Folder 8, Box 100, WMP DPL; John G. Griffin to William H. McNichols, Letter, 24 February 1969, Folder 8, Box 100, WMP DPL. For McNichols confirming that the DOC drew up the letter, see William H. McNichols to John G. Griffin, Letter, 21 February 1969, Folder 8, Box 100, WMP DPL.

29. Avery Brundage to Michael Lord Killanin, letter, 15 September 1969, 1969.07. 01–1969.12.31, Correspondence of Avery Brundage, PB IOCA.

30. Thomas Currigan and William McNichols to Avery Brundage, 23 December 1968, Folder XII Winter Games–1976–Denver, Colorado Bid, File 0006, Film 110, ABC IOCA.

31. D. F. McMahon to Avery Brundage, Letter, 3 February 1969, Folder XII Winter Games–1976–Denver, Colo.–Organizing Committee (1970–1971), File 0010, Film 110, ABC IOCA.

32. William H. McNichols to Dr. Adbel Mohamed Halim, Letter, 6 August 1969, Folder 8, Box 100, WMP DPL; see also Book 2, Box S4150 ARDOC CSA.

33. Tentative IOC Denver Visitation Program—January, 21–27, 1970, circa January 1970, Folder 11, Box 100, WMP DPL; William H. McNichols to George von Opel, Letter, 29 October 1969, Folder 9, Box 100, WMP DPL; William H. McNichols to Rudolf Nemetschke, Letter, 2 December 1969, Folder 9, Box 100, WMP DPL.

34. Tom Hildt, Report from Europe, 17 November 1969, Book 3, Box S4150, ARDOC CSA.

35. William McNichols Jr. to Jan Staubo, Letter, 23 January 1970, Folder 11, Box 100, WMP DPL.

36. For discussion of voting blocs, see Richard M. Davis, Denver Organizing Committee Meeting Minutes, 13 June 1968, Folder 3, Box 100, WMP DPL; Donald Magarrell to DOC Office, Report from Don Magarrell on IOC Visit to Warsaw, Poland, 10 June 1969, Folder 9, Box 100, WMP DPL; William Kostka Jr. to Robert J. Pringle, Re: Press Visit, 16 March 1970, Book 3, Box S4150, ARDOC CSA.

37. Richard M. Davis, Denver Olympic Committee Meeting Minutes, 12 March 1970, Folder 11, Box 100, WMP DPL.

38. D. F. Magarrell to DOC Executive Council, Letter, 19 March 1970, Book 3, Box S4150, ARDOC CSA; DOOC, Final Report, "History" section; Clifford Buck to R. J. Pringle, Letter, 3 April 1970, Book 4, Box S4150, ARDOC CSA.

39. Charlie Meyers, "Proposed Olympics Please FIS Inspecting Unit," *Denver Post*, 30 October 1968, 87.

40. "Olympics in Colorado?," *Denver Post*, 30 October 1968, 92.

41. "Olympic Committee Looks Over Site," *Canyon Courier* (Evergreen), 31 October 1968, clipping, Folder 6, Box 6, MAPC JCA.

42. Holder quoted in Meyers, "Proposed Olympics Please FIS Inspecting Unit," 87.

43. Denver US Candidate for the XII Winter Olympic Games, Proposed Nordic and

Alpine Sites: Prepared for International Ski Federation Congress 1969, presented 18–25 May 1969, Folder 33, Box 3, POME SHHRC.

44. Bjorn Kjellstrom to Richard Torissi, Letter, 8 November 1968, Folder 4, Box 100, WMP DPL; Graham S. Anderson to Merrill G. Hastings Jr., Letter, 1 November 1968, Folder 4, Box 100, WMP DPL; Al Merrill to Richard Torissi, Letter, 5 November 1968, Folder 4, Box 100, WMP DPL; Bjorn Kjellstrom to Donald McMahon, Letter, 12 November 1968, Folder 4, Box 100, WMP DPL; Ski Industry Advisor to Ski Writers, Letter, Subject: Press Conference for F.I.S. Officials, 13 November 1968, Folder 4, Box 100, WMP DPL.

45. Bjorn Kjellstrom to Donald McMahon, Letter, 12 November 1968, Folder 4, Box 100, WMP DPL.

46. Richard M. Davis, Denver Olympic Committee Minutes, 1 March 1968, Folder 3, Box 100, WMP DPL.

47. Richard M. Davis, Denver Organizing Committee Meeting Minutes, 8 May 1969, Book 2, Box S4150, ARDOC CSA.

48. Donald Magarrell to DOC Office, Report from Don Magarrell on IOC Visit to Warsaw, Poland, 10 June 1969, Folder 9, Box 100, WMP DPL. Cotter later reported, using his own curious quotation marks, that Holder "does expect to be able to come to Denver in March to 'look things over again' "; see James B. Cotter to William H. McNichols Jr., DOC Executive Board, Norman C. Brown, and William Kostka Jr., Letter Re: Official Denver Application Presentation, Lausanne, Switzerland, 7 January 1970, Folder 11, Box 100, WMP DPL.

49. George Robinson to Marc Holder, Letter, 6 July 1970, Folder Visitations to Denver, Box S4129, ARDOC CSA; George Robinson to Arnold Palmer Golf Academy, Letter, 6 July 1970, Folder Visitations to Denver, Box S4129, ARDOC CSA.

50. Marc Holder to Richard M. Torrisi, Letter, 6 November 1968, Box 66195, JLF CSA.

51. Hastings notes the promised vacation in Olson, "Power, Public Policy and the Environment," 115; for Holder's help, see George F. Robinson, Report from Barcelona—FIS Conference, 18–25 May 1969, Folder 9, Box 100, WMP DPL.

52. Donald Magarrell to DOC Office, Report from Don Magarrell on IOC Visit to Warsaw, Poland, 10 June 1969, Folder 9, Box 100, WMP DPL; for additional FIS members working with the DOC at this meeting, see Gerry Groswold, Report on Attendance at FIS Congress—Barcelona, Spain, 18–25 May, 5 June 1969, Folder 13, Box 102, WMP DPL.

53. F. George Robinson, IOC Congress—4–10 June 1969—Warsaw, Poland, circa June 1969, Book 2, Box S4150, ARDOC CSA.

54. James B. Cotter to William H. McNichols Jr., DOC Executive Board, Norman C. Brown, and William Kostka Jr., Letter Re: Official Denver Application Presentation, Lausanne, Switzerland, 7 January 1970, Folder 11, Box 100, WMP DPL.

55. Denver Organizing Committee for the Denver Organizing Committee of the XII Olympic Winter Games, Report to the 72nd Session of the International Olympic Committee, 1 February 1972, Games of Denver IOCA; 72nd Session of the International Olympic Committee Minutes, Sapporo 1972, Sessions IOCA.

56. Wenn, Barney, and Martyn, *Tarnished Rings*, 18–20.

57. R. H. Olson to Don McMahon, John Love, Thomas Currigan, Cliff Buck, Merrill Hastings, Tom Hildt, Don Magarrell, Robt. Pringle, F. George Robinson, Charles

Smukler, Report on the Xth Winter Olympic Games: Grenoble, 28 February 1968, Book 1, Box S4150, ARDOC CSA.

58. William H. McNichols to William J. Porter, 9 September 1969, Folder 9, Box 110, WMP DPL; Richard M. Davis, DOC Meeting Minutes, 13 November 1969, Folder 9, Box 100, WMP DPL; Richard M. Davis, Denver Organizing Committee Meeting Minutes, 12 February 1970, Folder 11, Box 100, WMP DPL; Donald Magarrell to William H. McNichols Jr., Letter, 25 January 1970, Folder 11, Box 100, WMP DOC; Richard M. Davis, Denver Organizing Committee Meeting Minutes, 11 December 1969, Folder 11, Box 100, WMP DPL; Richard M. Davis, Denver Organizing Committee Meeting Minutes, 15 January 1970, Folder 11, Box 100, WMP DPL; DOOC, Final Report, 29 December 1972, "History" section.

59. Denver Olympic Organizing Committee, Final Report, "History" section.

60. J. H. Smith to D. F. McMahon, Memorandum Re: IOC Contact, 26 December 1968, Book 1, Box S4150, ARDOC CSA.

61. "Denver Delegation," booklet, 69, Session International Olympic Committee Amsterdam, May 1970, Folder 7, Box 1, DOC DPL.

62. Denver Olympic Organizing Committee, Final Report; see "Financial Summary" section.

63. William Kostka Jr. to DOC Board of Directors, Letter Re: Marketing Activities, 15 January 1970, Folder 11, Box 100, WMP DPL; William Kostka Jr. to William H. McNichols Jr., John Love, Robert J. Pringle, Walter M. Schirra Jr., Letter Re: Amsterdam Presentations, 21 April 1971, Folder 11, Box 100, WMP DPL; "Denver's Winter Olympic Hopes—The Hour of Decision," *Empire Magazine* (*Denver Post*), 10 May 1970, 14–19.

64. William H. McNichols to Jack Foster, Letter, 3 April 1970, Folder 11, Box 100, WMP DPL.

65. Unimark & Summit Productions, *The Denver Olympic Story*, AV Box 21, DCC DPL; see also www.youtube.com/watch?v=dRybd-l2too.

66. William Kostka Jr. to DOC Board of Directors, Letter Re: Marketing Activities, 15 January 1970, Folder 11, Box 100, WMP DPL.

67. Denver Olympic Organizing Committee, Final Report, "History" section; Shipper's Export Declaration, US Department of Commerce, 30 April 1970, Folder Visitation from Denver Amsterdam, Box S4130, ARDOC CSA; Packing List US Candidate for the XII Winter Olympic Games 1976, Folder Visitation from Denver Amsterdam, Box S4130, ARDOC CSA.

68. Comments Made By Two IOC Members During a Breakfast Meeting on January 27, 1970, Book 3, Box S4150, ARDOC CSA.

69. Clifford Buck to R. J. Pringle, Letter, 3 April 1970, Book 4, Box S4150, ARDOC CSA.

70. Donald McMahon to William McNichols, Letter, 1 August 1969, Folder 8, Box 100, WMP DPL.

71. Denver Committee of Candidature, Amsterdam, Netherlands, Script, Presented on 10 May 1970, Folder 11, Box 100, WMP DPL.

72. 69th International Olympic Committee Session, 12–16 May 1970, Sessions IOCA.

73. Tamara Chuang, "Obituary: Denver PR Legend Bill Kostka Remembered for Drive, Grace: Former Rocky Mountain News Man Turned Public Relations

Legend Handling Controversial Topics," *Denver Post*, 30 December 2015, www
.denverpost.com/business/ci_29326256/obituary-denver-pr-legend-bill-kostka
-remembered-drive.
74. Currigan quoted in Denver Olympic Organizing Committee, Final Report, "History" section.

Chapter 5: Post–Civil Rights Advocacy in the City

1. Logan and Molotch, *Urban Fortunes*, 112–116.
2. Walsh, "Young and Latino in a Cold War Barrio," 6.
3. To avoid redundancy, the term "Hispanic" will be used interchangeably with
"Mexican American." The former term came into popularity in the 1970s and
includes people of Latin American and Spanish descent. The large majority of
Hispanic people in Denver were Mexican American. "Hispanic" is a fraught
term because of its inclusion in the United States Census starting in 1980. Not
everyone who fell under its umbrella preferred the label. However, the term was
used in the late 1960s and early 1970s, often in the masculine form of "Hispano."
The label of "Chicano" will also be used to denote Mexican Americans harboring
commitments to ethnic pride and cultural independence. This term also carries
a contested history, as in the early twentieth century it referred to an uneducated
and lower-class status. Yet Mexican American activists repositioned the label
by 1960s as a badge of pride and commitment to cultural autonomy. The term
"Brown" will be used to describe Mexican Americans in the context of Mexican
American and African American relations (i.e., Brown and Black relations). This
is a term that Mexican Americans in this history applied to themselves.
4. Deutsch, *No Separate Refuge.*
5. Kanellos, *Chronology of Hispanic-American History*, xix.
6. Deutsch, *No Separate Refuge*, 153–154, 168–172; Dorsett and McCarthy, *The Queen City*, 226; Leonard and Noel, *Denver*, 388–389.
7. Goldberg, *Hooded Empire*; Dorsett and McCarthy, *The Queen City*, 124, 226; Kanellos, *Chronology of Hispanic-American History*, 198–199; Leonard and Noel, *Denver*, 388–390; S. J. Holmes, "Perils of the Mexican Invasion," *North American Review*, 227, 5 (1929): 615–623.
8. Deutsch, *No Separate Refuge*, 153–154, 168–172; Dorsett and McCarthy, *The Queen City*, 226; Leonard and Noel, *Denver*, 388–389.
9. Gould, *The Life and Times of Richard Castro.*
10. Dorsett and McCarthy, *The Queen City*, 240–242; Leonard and Noel, *Denver*, 368, 391–392.
11. Leonard and Noel, *Denver*, 391–392; Page and Ross, "Legacies of a Contested Campus," 1299. Page and Ross cite University of Denver, Bureau of Business Research, *Housing Trends in Denver, 1939–1949* (Denver: Housing Authority of Denver), Denver Public Library.
12. *Keyes v. Denver School District No. I*, 413 U.S. 189 (1973); Leonard and Noel, *Denver*, 374–380.
13. Walsh, "Young and Latino in a Cold War Barrio," 48; Noel and Leonard, *Denver*, 368, 388; Gould, *The Life and Times of Richard Castro*, 84–85. Rothstein, *The*

Color of Law. "Mapping Inequality: Redlining in New Deal America," https://dsl
.richmond.edu/panorama/redlining/#loc=14/39.7275/-105.0020&opacity=0.8
&city=denver-co&sort=23&area=D7.

14. Walsh, "Young and Latino in a Cold War Barrio," 102–127; Gould, *The Life and Times of Richard Castro*, 49–53; Vigil, *The Crusade for Justice*, 18–20, 33–38, 100, 127–130; Abbott, Leonard, and Noel, *Colorado*, 4th ed., 355–360; Frank Plaut, "Minority Group—Governmental Agency Relations: Investigation and Recommendations," The State of Colorado, 1967, Folder 20, Box 4, JLP DPL. For a similar dynamics in other cities, see Diamond, *Mean Streets*, esp. chapters 5 and 6; Pagán, *Murder at the Sleepy Lagoon*, 2–3, 49, 55, 58–59, 72–74, 134–135, 162, 227; US Civil Rights Commission, *Mexican Americans and the Administration of Justice.*

15. To obtain urban renewal funds, a locality had to provide one-third of a project's cost. However, after the Housing Act of 1954, local funds could be subsidized by private funds and developments were no longer required to be residential. The 1954 act also reduced red tape, decentralizing government decision-making and empowering local businesspeople; see Mollenkopf, *The Contested City*, 117.

16. Fogelson, *Downtown*, 317–380; Jackson, *Crabgrass Frontier.*

17. Fogelson, *Downtown*, 317–380; Mollenkopf, *The Contested City*, 17, 79–81, 114–119, 162–212; Hirsch, *Making the Second Ghetto*; O'Connor, *Building a New Boston*; Schwartz, *The New York Approach*, 108–143; Sugrue, *The Origins of the Urban Crisis*, 48–51. For another example focused on displacement of Hispanic resident from urban renewal, see Fernández, *Brown in the Windy City.* Through long-term tax revenue, cities contended it was in their interest to subsidize construction for middle- and upper-class homes and private services. For a focus on attracting white consumers, see Avila, *Popular Culture in the Age of White Flight.*

18. Abbott, Leonard, and Noel, *Colorado,* 4th ed. (quotation at p. 325; see also 323–325, 367–391).

19. Judd, "From Cowtown to Sunbelt City," 178–182.

20. Page and Ross, "Legacies of a Contested Campus," 1316.

21. James Crawford, "2 Hispano Student Units Rap Auraria School Site," *Rocky Mountain News*, 20 October 1969, 38; Auraria Renewal Authority, Status Report, January 1969, Folder 21, Box 94, WMP DPL; Page and Ross, "Legacies of a Contested Campus." The complex included Metropolitan State College, the University of Colorado's Denver campus, and a new community college.

22. Page and Ross, "Legacies of a Contested Campus," 1302.

23. Page and Ross, "Legacies of a Contested Campus" (quotation at pp. 1330, 1302–1303); see also Denver Urban Renewal Authority, *Auraria Environmental Impact Assessment* (Denver, CO: Denver Urban Renewal Authority, 1969), Denver Public Library, Denver Colorado; Denver Urban Renewal Authority, *Relocation Survey of Residents in the Proposed Auraria Urban Renewal Project Area: Summary*, 4 September 1969, Denver: Denver Urban Renewal Authority, Denver Public Library, Denver, Colorado. http://digital.denverlibrary.org/cdm/ref/collection/p15330coll6/id/657.

24. Logan and Molotch, *Urban Fortunes*, 103–110; Mollenkopf, *The Contested City*, 174.

25. Benavidez quoted in Pat McGraw, "Auraria Gains, Losses Listed," *Denver Post*,

31 October 1969, 3, 16; see also Richard Castro quoted in Crawford, "2 Hispano Student Units Rap Auraria."

26. "West Side Action Council Opposes Issue," *Denver Post*, 2 November 1969, 37.

27. Mrs. Ernest Virgil, "Home in Auraria," *Denver Post*, 30 October 1969, 23.

28. Myles C. Rademan to Community Renewal Program Staff, Memorandum Re: Olympic Press Housing and its Relation to the West Side Neighborhood, 13 September 1971, Folder 18, Box 102, WMP DPL.

29. "Auraria Meet Generates More Heat Than Light," *Rocky Mountain News*, 30 October 1969, 68.

30. Gallegos, "The Forgotten Community," esp. 20.

31. George Lane, "Housing Dissenters Turn Ire on HUD, Olympics," *Denver Post*, 30 May 1970, 28; see also Richard Tucker, "Housing Unit Opposes Olympic Bid," *Rocky Mountain News*, 6 November 1970, 8.

32. As part of this process, members of the bid team, including Pringle, George Robinson, and Donald Magarrell, took seats on the Executive Council.

33. "Chronology," Report, circa 1971, Folder 13, Box 100, WMP DPL.

34. Tarrow, *Power in Movement*, 140–156; Muñoz Jr., *Youth, Identity, Power: The Chicano Movement*, 66; Isserman and Kazin, *America Divided*, 21–42, 81–87, 126–133; Terry H. Anderson, *The Movement and the Sixties* (New York: Oxford University Press, 1996), 43–82; Chafe, *Civilities and Civil Rights*; Dittmer, *Local People*; Carson, *In Struggle*; Garrow, *Protest at Selma*.

35. Ralph, *Northern Protest*. For de facto segregation in Chicago, see Hirsch, *Making the Second Ghetto*.

36. Martin Luther King Jr., "The Other America," 14 April 1967, www.youtube.com /watch?v=dOWDtDUKz-U.

37. Joseph, *Waiting 'til the Midnight Hour*.

38. Muñoz Jr., *Youth, Identity, Power*, 31–60.

39. Gutiérrez, *Walls and Mirrors*; Fernández, *Brown in the Windy City*.

40. Muñoz Jr., *Youth, Identity, Power*; Mariscal, *Brown-Eyed Children of the Sun*.

41. Garcia and Castro, *Blowout!* The protest in Los Angeles proved key in the emergent Chicano identity; see Haney-Lopez, *Racism on Trial*. For a similar dynamic in Houston, see Miguel, *Brown, Not White*; Muñoz Jr., *Youth, Identity, Power*, 79–81.

42. Muñoz Jr., *Youth, Identity, Power*, 86; Bill Marvel, "West High School Students and Police Fight," *Rocky Mountain News*, 21 March 1969, 1; "Gonzales Trial: Police Blamed for Violence at West," clipping, Folder 52, Box 6, RGC DPL; "Corky, Five Enter Pleas of Innocent," clipping, Folder 52, Box 6, RGC DPL; "Police, Students and Others Clash at West High," clipping, Folder 52, Box 6, RGC DPL; see also Vigil, *The Crusade for Justice*, 81–87.

43. Muñoz Jr., *Youth, Identity, Power*, 3, 91–95; Mariscal, *Brown-Eyed Children of the Sun*, 140–170.

44. Oropeza, *¡Raza Si! ¡Guerra No!*

45. Mantler, *Power to the Poor*; Mariscal, *Brown-Eyed Children of the Sun*, 171–209, 190–200; Vigil, *The Crusade for Justice*, 29–30, 34. At times, Native American rights activists also joined this multiracial coalition. However, research for this book found no evidence of Indigenous participation in the Olympics debate.

46. "Militants Join Move for Boycott at West," clipping, Folder 10, Box 5, RGC DPL.

47. Ottawa W. Harris to John Kelly, Letter, 4 November 1970, Folder 13, Box 100,

WMP DPL; George Lane, "Minority Olympic Role Request Will Be Aired," *Denver Post*, 11 November 1970, Clipping, Olympic Clippings DPL; Goodstein, *How the West Side Won*, 89.

48. "Chronology," Report, circa 1971, Folder 13, Box 100, WMP DPL.
49. Lane, "Minority Olympic Role Request Will Be Aired." Marcella Trujillo joined them; she was director of Mexican American Studies at the University of Colorado in Denver and a La Raza Unida Party member.
50. Clarke Watson to Robert Pringle, Letter, 1 December 1970, Folder Board of Directors, Box S4130, DOC CSA.
51. Watson to Robert Pringle, Letter, 1 December 1970.
52. George Lane, "McNichols Adds 16 to Olympic Board," *Denver Post*, 6 December 1970, 3.
53. "21 Denver Legislators Favor Auraria," *Denver Post*, 2 November 1969, 33; Goodstein, *How the West Side Won*, 89.
54. Donald E. Cordova to Carl DeTemple, Letter, 17 April 1972, Box S4129, ARDOC CSA.
55. Davis quoted in Olson, "Power, Public Policy and the Environment," 141; see also 137–142.
56. J. B. Cotter to Executive Board, R. S. McCollum, N. C. Brown, and W. Kostka Jr., Letter, 21 August 1969, Book 2, Box S4150, ARDOC CSA.
57. Biffle quoted in Jonathan Shikes, "A Place in History," www.westword.com/news /a-place-in-history-5069009. For changes in how Black athletes dealt with politics through sports from the 1950s into the 1970s, see Moore, *We Will Win the Day*.
58. "Chronology," circa 1971, Folder 13, Box 100, WMP DPL; "Mayor Plans No Meet with Minorities of DOC," *Denver Post*, 15 December 1970, 3; Technically, twenty-three out of twenty-five DOC board members were businessmen or politicians. Floyd Little and Joseph Torres were the exceptions. Also, one woman served on the DOC board, Nancy Harrington.
59. Olson, "Power, Public Policy and the Environment," 140.
60. Clarke R. Watson to William H. McNichols, Letter, 4 December 1970, Folder 13, Box 100, WMP DPL.
61. Isserman and Kazin, *America Divided*, 166–170; Horne, *Fire This Time*; Banfield, *The Unheavenly City*, 185–209.
62. Gonzales quoted in Vigil, *The Crusade for Justice*, 50; "Will Mexican Minority Riot?," *Rocky Mountain News*, 29 January 1968, 8; Bob Saile, "Gonzales Predicts 'Guerilla Warfare,'" *Denver Post*, 29 January 1968, copy in the author's possession.
63. "Chronology," circa 1971, Folder 13, Box 100, WMP DPL.
64. Caldwell quoted in Leonard and Noel, *Denver*, 382.
65. Elvin R. Caldwell to Denver Organizing Committee, Letter, 27 November 1970, Folder 19, Box 1, DOC DPL.
66. Betty Benavidez to William McNichols, Letter, 6 January 1971, Folder 23, Box 102, WMP DPL; as members of the DOC nominating committee, Mayor McNichols and Richard Olson were also invited; it is unclear if they attended.
67. Clarke R. Watson to William H. McNichols, Letter, 4 December 1970, Folder 13, Box 100, WMP DPL.
68. See *Denver Post*, 24 October 1968 and 29 October 1969.

69. Goodstein, *How the West Side Won*, 241–244.

70. Representative Betty Benavidez, Representative Leo Lucero, Senator George Brown, Representative Paul Hamilton, Representative Jerome Rose, Senator Roger Cisneros, Representative Ruben A. Valdez to John Love, Letter, 15 January 1971, Folder Olympics, Box 2, RLC SHHRC.

71. Representative Betty Benavidez, Representative Leo Lucero, Senator George Brown, Representative Paul Hamilton, Representative Jerome Rose, Senator Roger Cisneros, Representative Ruben A. Valdez to William McNichols, Letter, 26 February 1971, Folder 4, Box 101, WMP DPL.

72. "Chronology," Report, circa 1971, Folder 13, Box 100, WMP DPL.

73. "Minority Group Protests: Olympic Funding Delay Urged," *Denver Post*, 11 January 1971, 27.

74. Norm Brown to Don Magarrell, Letter Re: Legislative Committee meeting March 5, 1971 (Open Meeting) at the Capital, 2:00–4:30 p.m., Folder 12, Box 1, DOC DPL; Fred Brown, "Ski Officials to Inspect Alternate Colo. Olympic Sites," *Denver Post*, 6 March 1971, 1, 3.

75. Mollenkopf, *The Contested City*, 190–191.

76. Mollenkopf, *The Contested City*, 192.

77. Logan and Molotch, *Urban Fortunes*, 37–39; this is a major theme in Stone, *Regime Politics*.

78. Pat McGraw, "Auraria Gains, Losses Listed," *Denver Post*, 31 October 1969, 3, 16.

79. David Lucy, Development Feasibility Study—Press Housing Site, Left Bank, Platte Valley, 8 July 1971, Folder 18, Box 102, WMP DPL. Lucy writes, the "motel-apartment complex" would be "used as designed" after the Olympics and that the "operation will not produce a great amount of low income housing"; see 3, 2.

80. Louis R. LaPerriere to William McNichols, Memorandum, 17 February 1972, Folder 6, Box 102, WMP DP; Cf. "Housing Plan OK Sought," *Denver Post*, 25 June 1972, 25. This article contends housing the press was the "secondary" concern.

81. William McNichols, Transcript, Progress Report, Denver Organizing Committee XII Olympic Winter Games 1976, 1 February 1972, Folder 19, Box 102, WMP DPL.

82. Advertisement, "Colorado's 1976 Olympics: A Statement from John Love," *Rocky Mountain News*, 5 October 1972, 51.

83. Logan and Molotch, *Urban Fortunes*, 51, 39; Mollenkopf, *The Congested City* 191, 197.

84. Joe Simmons to Louis R. LaPerriere, Memorandum, 7 February 1972, Folder 18, Box 102, WMP DPL.

85. Jerry Garcia to Bob Wielder, Letter, 16 June 1972, Folder 18, Box 102, WMP DPL; Goodstein, *How the West Side Won*, 238.

86. "Olympic Press Village Plans Reviewed," *West Side Recorder*, January–February 1971, 1.

87. "Residents View Press Village Plans," *West Side Recorder*, December 1971.

88. "City Council Support Olympic Press Housing," *West Side Recorder*, November 1972, 1.

89. Denver Community Renewal Program, Denver Olympic Press Housing: Plans for Development and After-Use, 20 March 1972, 3, Appendix II, and Appendix III, Folder 15, Box 102, WMP DPL; Denver Community Renewal Program,

Proposed Olympic Press Housing: Preliminary Draft, circa 1971–1972, Folder 1, Box 104, WMP DPL.

90. Elvin Caldwell to Gordon Allott, Telegram, 13 April 1972, Folder 18, Box 102, WMP DPL; John Henry to Mayor [William McNichols], Letter Re: Olympic Housing, 13 April 1972, Folder 18, Box 102, WMP DPL.

91. "Denverites Lash Anti-Olympic Drive," *Rocky Mountain News*, 15 April 1972, 5.

92. "Two Councilmen Boost Olympics," *Denver Post*, 5 November 1972, 82.

93. Richard M. Davis, Denver Olympic Committee Board of Directors Meeting Minutes, 16 December 1971, Folder 19, Box 1, DOC DPL; Richard M. Davis, Denver Olympic Committee Board of Directors Meeting Minutes, 16 March 1972, Folder 21, Box 1, DOC DPL; "Olympic Housing Plan Praised," *Rocky Mountain News*, 14 April 1972, 3.

94. "Olympic Press Village Plan in Progress," *West Side Recorder*, October 1971, 1, 8.

95. "Citizen Participation Education—For—Olympic Housing," *West Side Recorder*, August 1972.

96. Jeff Rosen, "Olympic Press Housing Plan Criticized," *Rocky Mountain News*, 22 June 1972, 25.

97. Sister Anna Koop and Fred Kahane to Gordon Allott, Letter, 20 June 1972, Folder 18, Box 102, WMP DPL.

98. Holland quoted in "Housing Plan OK Sought," *Denver Post*, 25 June 1972, 25.

99. Rosen, "Olympic Press Housing Plan Criticized"; "West Side Residents Rap New Olympic Housing Plan," *Denver Post*, 22 June 1972, 23. Cf. McEncroe, *Denver Renewed*, 626.

100. Jerry Garcia to John J. Wilder, Letter, 27 June 1972, Folder 18, Box 102, WMP DPL.

101. William McNichols to DURA Board of Commissioners, Letter, 7 April 1972, Folder 6, Box 102, WMP DPL; for the final proposal, see Robert J. Cameron to Denver City Council, Letter, Subject: Urban Renewal Plans for East Side Housing and West Side Housing—NDP Urban Renewal Areas, 6 October 1972, Folder 18, Box 102, WMP DPL.

102. Denver Community Renewal Program, Proposed Olympic Press Housing: Preliminary Draft, circa 1971–1972, Folder 1, Box 104, WMP DPL.

103. John Morehead, "Housing Plan OK Sought," *Denver Post*, 25 June 1972, 18.

104. J. Robert Cameron to William McNichols, Memorandum, Subject: Olympic Press Housing, 16 February 1972, Folder 17, Box 102, WMP DPL.

105. "Olympic Press Village Plan in Progress," *West Side Recorder*, October 1971, 1, 8; this point was made on several occasions; see also "Denverites Lash Anti-Olympics Drive," *Rocky Mountains News*, 15 April 1972, 5.

106. Cecil Jones, "Olympic Press Housing Project Hits Roadblock," *Rocky Mountain News*, 2 June 1972, 5, 6; John Morehead, "Minorities Spokesmen Want Olympic Housing," *Denver Post*, 9 June 1972, 3.

107. Westside Coalition quotation from McEncroe, *Denver Renewed*, 665; John Morehead, *Denver Post*, 6 June 1972, 3.

108. "Citizen Participation Education—For—Olympic Housing," *West Side Recorder*, August 1972.

109. Olson, "Power, Public Policy and the Environment," 184.

110. For yet another example, see Colorado Senator George Brown in Richard Tucker, "Senate Hikes State Outlays to $2 Million," *Rocky Mountain News*, 15 April 1972, 5.

Chapter 6: Middle-Class Environmentalism in the Foothills

1. Stoepplewreth quoted in Douglas Bradley, "Olympic Foes Voice Concerns," 29 June 1972, clipping, Folder 4, Box 6, MAPC JCA.
2. The complexity of this environmentalism aligns with analysis in Anzalone, *Battles of the North Country*, esp. 138.
3. Logan and Molotch, *Urban Fortunes*, 213–215.
4. Logan and Molotch, *Urban Fortunes*, 134–139.
5. A similar dynamic appears in Rothman, *Devil's Bargains*.
6. Goodstein, *Denver in Our Time*, 152.
7. Olson, "Power, Public Policy and the Environment," 106–107.
8. Vance R. Dittman, Statement Made At Meeting of MAPC and DOC, 11 June 1970, Folder 50, Box 5, POME SHHRC; Marsh, "Vance R. Dittman Jr.—Lawyer's Law Professor."
9. The Denver professors were law instructors Vance R. Dittman and Alan Merson, the business management scholar George Vardaman, and the philosophy professor Francis Brush; see note cards in Folder 64, Box 6, POME SHHRC.
10. See www.census.gov/dmd/www/resapport/states/colorado.pdf.
11. Abbott, Leonard, and Noel, *Colorado*, 4th ed., 323–325, 367–391.
12. Olson, "Power, Public Policy and the Environment," 26–31.
13. Denver SMSA [standard metropolitan statistical area], "Populations by County, Denver SMSA 1900 to 2000," cited in Maynard B. Barrows and Gairald H. Garrett, "Mountain Area Planning Council: Report of Land Use and Zoning," 13 March 1969, Folder 23, Box 1, MAPC JCA; see also Olson, "Power, Public Policy and the Environment," 28.
14. Philpott, *Vacationland*, 85, 110–125.
15. Logan and Molotch, *Urban Fortunes*, 209–215.
16. Philpott, *Vacationland*, 224–237. This mirrors recreational planning in New York's Adirondack State Park Forest Preserves decades earlier; see Anzalone, *Battles of the North Country*; for examples of consumer environmentalists, see John Love, Speech, "Re: Air Pollution," 8 March 1963, Box 66948, JLF SCAR; Roger Hansen, "A Blue Print for Action—Now or Never," speech at the CMC Breckenridge Conference, 26–27 September 1964, Folder 19, Box 8, CECR DPL.
17. Rothman, *Devil's Bargains*.
18. Philpott, *Vacationland*, see esp. chapter 5.
19. Vance R. Dittman to John A. Love, Thomas G. Currigan, Richard Torrisi, George Robinson, Don McMahon, Merrill G. Hastings Jr., Gerald Groswold, Letter, 1 June 1968, Folder 23, Box 2, POME SHHRC. As early as February 1968, the DOC knew about the anti-Olympics views in Indian Hills; see Gerald Groswold to George Robinson, Letter, 14 February 1968, Folder 60, Box 6, POME SHHRC.
20. Vance R. Dittman, George Vardaman, Emil G. Gadeken, and Lyman C. Sourwin to Richard Torrisi, Letter, 8 August 1968, Folder 3, Box 100, WMP DPL.
21. Historians debate the origins of this environmentalism and the extent to which it was driven by specialists and government officials versus suburbanites themselves. However, there is agreement that the development of white middle-class suburbs proved key to the movement's origins and popularization; Hays, *Beauty,*

Health, and Permanence; Adam Rome, *The Bulldozer in the Countryside*; Sellers, *Crabgrass Crucible.*

22. Hurley, *Environmental Inequalities*, 46–76 (quotation at p. 47).

23. Bartiz, *The Good Life*; Philpott, *Vacationland*, 127–188; Rome, *The Bulldozer in the Countryside*, 1–15.

24. Rome, *The Genius of Earth Day.*

25. Vance R. Dittman to Richard Olson, Letter, 15 August 1968, Folder 60, Box 6, POME SHHRC.

26. Gerald F. Groswold to Mr. and Mrs. Vance R. Dittman, Letter, 5 July 1968, Folder 60, Box 6, POME SHHRC.

27. Vance R. Dittman to Gerald F. Groswold, Letter, 11 July 1968, Folder 60, Box 6, POME SHHRC.

28. Vance R. Dittman to John A. Love, Thomas G. Currigan, Richard Torrisi, George Robinson, Don McMahon, Merrill G. Hastings Jr., Gerald Groswold, Letter, 1 June 1968, Folder 23, Box 2, POME SHHRC.

29. Richard M. Torrisi to Vance R. Dittman, Letter, 21 August 1968, Folder 60, Box 6, POME SHHRC.

30. Vance R. Dittman to Richard M. Torrisi, Letter, 24 August 1968, Folder 60, Box 6, POME SHHRC. Dittman even suggested using Bergan Park, a twelve-mile drive from Indian Hills.

31. Richard M. Torrisi to Vance Dittman, Letter, 27 September 1968, Folder 60, Box 6, POME SHHRC; Richard M. Davis, Denver Organizing Committee Meeting Minutes, 12 September 1968, Folder 4, Box 100, WMP DPL.

32. Richard Davis, Denver Organizing Committee Meeting Minutes, 8 August 1968, Folder 3, Box 100, WMP DPL. The Evergreen-based Mountain Area Planning Council appointed Dittman the "chairman" of the "Olympic situation"; see Pat M. O'Hara (President of MAPC) to Vance R. Dittman, Letter, 14 October 1968, Folder 60, Box 6, POME SHHRC.

33. "'Nevergreen,'" *Newsweek*, 14 December 1970, 94.

34. Mountain Area Planning Council, By-Laws, 14 March 1968, Folder 4, Box 1, MAPC JCA.

35. Mountain Area Planning Council, By-Laws, 14 March 1968; "Evergreen Protests Plan to Build Bypass Highway," *Rocky Mountain News*, 20 June 1968, 61; Tommy Patterson, Mountain Area Planning Council Meeting Minutes, 23 September 1968, Folder 22, Box 1, MAPC JCA; John Dunning, "Evergreen Road Issue Heats Up," *Denver Post*, 20 June 1968, 37.

36. Tommy Patterson, Mountain Area Planning Council Meeting Minutes, 13 January 1969, Folder 23, Box 1, MAPC JCA.

37. Tommy Patterson, Mountain Area Planning Council Meeting Minutes, 17 February 1969, Folder 23, Box 1, MAPC JCA.

38. Richard M. Davis, Denver Organizing Committee Meeting Minutes, 20 March 1969, Folder 8, Box 100, WMP DPL.

39. Tommy Patterson, Mountain Area Planning Council Meeting Minutes, 13 March 1969, Folder 23, Box 1, MAPC JCA.

40. Mountain Area Planning Council, Introduction to the May 8, 1969 Questions to DOC, Folder 23, Box 1, MAPC JCA; Mountain Area Protection Council, Summary of Questions, 8 May 1969, Folder 23, Box 1, MAPC JCA.

41. Denver Organizing Committee Meeting Minutes, 17 April 1969, Book 2, Box S4150, ARDOC CSA.

42. Jack Rouse to Jim Cotter, Letter, 17 April 1969, Book 2, Box S4150, ARDOC CSA; Gerald Groswold to George Torrison, Letter, 24 April 1969, Book 2, Box S4150, ARDOC CSA; James B. Cotter to Jack Rouse, Letter, 2 May 1969, Book 2, Box S4150, ARDOC CSA.

43. Denver Organizing Committee Meeting Minutes, 17 April 1969, Book 2, Box S4150, ARDOC CSA.

44. James B. Cotter to Jack Rouse, Letter, 2 May 1969, Book 2, Box S4150, ARDOC CSA.

45. James Cotter to N. C. Brown, W. S. Law, R. S. McCollum, G. F. Groswold, S. Wiik, P. J. Gallavan, N. H. Allen, W. Kostka Jr., Re: Evergreen Community Relations Mountain Area Planning Council Meeting—5/8/69, 12 May 1969, Book 2, Box S4150, ARDOC CSA.

46. Mountain Area Protection Council, Summary of Questions, 8 May 1969, Folder 23, Box 1, MAPC JCA; Cf. Michael W. Childers, *Colorado Powder Keg*, 68–95.

47. Longhurst, *Citizen Environmentalists* (quotations at pp. xi–xvi); see also Sellers, *Crabgrass Crucible*.

48. J. B. Cotter to Executive Board, N. C. Brown, W. S. Law, R. S. McCollum, G. F. Groswold, S. Wiik, P. J. Gallavan, N. H. Allen, W. Kostka Jr., Letter, 12 May 1969, Book 2, Box S4150, ARDOC CSA.

49. J. B. Cotter to Executive Board, K. Dybevik, G. F. Groswold, R. H. Olson, P. J. Gallavan, J. W. Rouse, N. C. Brown, W. S. Law, W. Kostka Jr., Re: Evergreen Community Relations, 22 May 1969, Book 2, Box S4150, ARDOC CSA.

50. J. B. Cotter to DOC Executive Board, W. Kostka Jr., N. C. Brown, J. W. Rouse, G. F. Groswold, W. S. Law, R. H. Olson, R. S. McCollum, P. J. Gallavan, K. Dybevik, Letter, 4 June 1969, Folder 9, Box 100, WMP DPL; Richard M. Davis, Denver Organizing Committee Meeting Minutes, 19 June 1969, Folder 8, Box 100, WMP DPL.

51. Evergreen Community Relations, 29 July 1969, Box S4147, ARDOC CSA.

52. "Evergreen Olympics Group Being Formed," 17 July 1969, clipping, Folder 6, Box 6, MAPC JCA; William Kostka Jr. to Donald Magarrell, Re: Evergreen Meeting, 4 September 1969, Book 3, Box S4150, ARDOC CSA.

53. Tommy Patterson, Mountain Area Planning Council Meeting Minutes, 2 September 1969, Folder 23, Box 1, MAPC JCA.

54. The MAPC polled 3,065 houses; 1,032 returned the ballot; 392 or 38% favored the Olympics; 630 or 61% opposed the Olympics; four households were divided and six or 1% were undecided. "MAPC Reports Result of Survey on Olympics," *Canyon Courier* (Evergreen), 11 September 1969, clipping, Folder 6, Box 6, MAPC JCA; "Olympic Plan Response Chilly," *Denver Post (Zone 3)*, 17 September 1969, 3.

55. Tommy Patterson, Mountain Area Planning Council Meeting Minutes, 10 November 1969, Folder 23, Box 1, MAPC JCA.

56. Tommy Patterson, Mountain Area Planning Council Executive Board Meeting Minutes, 25 November 1969, Folder 23, Box 1, MAPC JCA.

57. Tommy Patterson, Mountain Area Planning Council Meeting Minutes, 9 March 1970, Folder 24, Box 1, MAPC JCA; Richard M. Davis, Denver Organizing Committee Meeting Minutes, 12 March 1970, Folder 11, Box 100, WMP DPL.

58. Ben Eastman Jr. and Martha Eastman to International Olympic Committee, Letter, 30 December 1969, Book 3, Box S4150, ARDOC CSA.

59. Thomas G. Currigan to Robert Pringle, Letter, 24 March 1970, Book 3, Box S4150, ARDOC CSA.

60. Clifford Buck to R. J. Pringle, Re: Munich Meeting of GAIF, 3 April 1970, Book 3, Box S4150, ARDOC CSA.

61. Tommy Patterson, Mountain Area Planning Council Meeting Minutes, 13 April 1970, Folder 24, Box 1, MAPC JCA; Robert Pringle, "Resolution of Denver Organizing Committee Board of Directors," circa April 1970, Folder Site General II, Box S4130, ARDOC CSA; Tommy Patterson, Mountain Area Planning Council Meeting Minutes, 13 April 1970, Folder 24, Box 1, MAPC JCA; Tommy Patterson, Mountain Area Planning Council Meeting Minutes, 15 April 1970, Folder 24, Box 1, MAPC JCA.

62. Tommy Patterson, Mountain Area Planning Council Meeting Minutes, 20 April 1970, Folder 24, Box 1, MAPC JCA.

63. Olson, "Power, Public Policy and the Environment," 132.

64. Tommy Patterson, Mountain Area Planning Council Conversation w/Gov. Love, 23 April 1970, Folder 24, Box 1, MAPC JCA; Robert Pringle to Bob Behrens, Letter, 24 April 1970, Folder Site General II, Box S4130, ARDOC CSA.

65. Denver Organizing Committee, Resolution, 10 April 1970, Folder Competition Sites Nordic Events, Box S4149, ARDOC CSA; Folder 24, Box 1, MAPC JCA.

66. Tommy Patterson, Mountain Area Planning Council Meeting Minutes, 11 May 1970, Folder 24, Box 1, MAPC JCA.

67. Vance R. Dittman to Avery Brundage, Letter, 6 November 1971, Folder 16, Box 1, POME SHHRC.

68. "Agenda Set for Meeting on Olympics June 11," *Canyon Courier* (Evergreen), 4 June 1970, clipping, Folder 6, Box 6, MAPC JCA.

69. Timeline, Folder 60, Box 6, POME SHHRC.

70. "Have-Your-Say Olympics Hearing Thursday," *Canyon Courier* (Evergreen), 11 June 1970, 1, 4.

71. Chuck Green, "Evergreen Expresses Olympiphobia," *Denver Post*, 12 June 1970, 76; Gary Gerhardt, "Olympic Objections Cited in Evergreen," *Rocky Mountain News*, 12 June 1970, 8; Mountain Area Planning Council, Public Meeting Re: Olympic Games, 11 June 1970, Folder 24, Box 1, MAPC JCA.

72. "Letter to Courier," *Canyon Courier* (Evergreen), 18 June 1970, clipping, Folder 6, Box 6, MAPC JCA; Tape of June 11, 1970 MAPC Meeting—Side 1 and Side 2, MAPC JCA; Green, "Evergreen Expresses Olympiphobia"; Gerhardt, "Olympic Objections Cited in Evergreen," 8. Newspapers reported about fifty residents spoke at this meeting.

73. Tape of June 11, 1970 MAPC Meeting—Side 1 and Side 2, MAPC JCA.

74. Tape of June 11, 1970 MAPC Meeting—Side 1, MAPC JCA.

75. Tape of June 11, 1970 MAPC Meeting—Side 2, MAPC JCA.

76. Tape of June 11, 1970 MAPC Meeting—Side 1, MAPC JCA.

77. Jones quoted in Todd Phipers, "Evergreen Icy to Ski Jump Plan," *Denver Post*, 7 June 1970, 23.

78. Tape of June 11, 1970 MAPC Meeting—Side 2, MAPC JCA.

79. Timeline, Folder 60, Box 6, POME SHHRC; Vance R. Dittman to Robert Pringle, letter, 22 June 1970, Folder 60, Box 6, POME SHHRC.

80. Vance R. Dittman, Statement Made at Meeting of MAPC and DOC, 11 June 1970, Folder 50, Box 5, POME SHHRC.

81. John A. Love, Speech, "Earth Day," 22 April 1970, Speeches of Gov. John A. Love, Box 66950, JLF SCAR; Steve Wynkoop, "Teach-in for Earth Day Draws 5,000," *Denver Post*, 23 April 1970, 1, 3.

82. Dr. Moras L. Shubert to the Denver Olympic Committee, Letter, 9 June 1970, Folder 44, Box 4, POME SHHRC.

83. Vance R. Dittman to John Wells (Denver Research Institute), Letter, 30 June 1970, Folder 60, Box 6, POME SHHRC; Dittman specifically references Shubert's letter to the DOC here.

84. Protect Our Mountain Environment, Inc. Articles of Incorporation, 26 August 1970, Folder 40, Box 4, POME SHHRC; see also John Toohey, "Olympic Plans Draw Fire," *Denver Post*, 25 October 1970, 24.

85. Protect Our Mountain Environment, Resolution, 29 October 1970, Folder 40, Box 4, POME SHHRC.

86. Board of POME to Owen K. Ball, Letter, 17 August 1970, Folder 60, Box 6, POME SHHRC.

87. George T. Vardaman to John G. Well, Letter, 10 July 1970, Folder 60, Box 6, POME SHHRC.

88. Vance Dittman to Dr. Beatrice Willard and DOC Planning Commission, Letter, 30 November 1971, Folder 53, Box 5, POME SHHRC.

89. Resolution, 8 January 1971, Folder 30 or 40, Box 4, POME SHHRC; for similar reasoning, see Vance R. Dittman to Avery Brundage, Letter, 6 November 1971, Folder 16, Box 1, POME SHHRC; Doug Jones quote in Pat McGraw, "Evergreen Nordic Site Re-Evaluation Pledged," *Denver Post*, 11 November 1970, 76.

90. Letter to the International Olympic Committee, 26 April 1971, Folder 48, Box 4, POME SHHRC; fifteen other, mostly local, advocacy groups consigned this letter with POME: North Turkey Creek Associations (Pine Hills, Marschner, Chinook Chapters), Wild Rose Grange, Marshdale Homeowners Association, Evergreen Naturalists, Hill and Dale Society, Indian Hills Improvement Association, El Pinal Association, Genesee Grange, Kittredge Home-owners Association, Buffalo Park Association, V.F.W. Post 3471, Inter-Canyon Environmental Improvement Association, Crescent Park Land and Home-owners Association, Upper Bear Creek Homeowners Association. Almost identical letters were also sent to the international skiing, luge, bobsled, and biathlon federations; see letter to International Ski Federation, n.d., Folder 16, Box 2, POME SHHRC.

91. For a further example, see Vance R. Dittman to Avery Brundage, Letter, 6 November 1971, Folder 16, Box 1, POME SHHRC.

92. Cheryl Hayes, *Dear Earth* (Denver Colorado), April 1971, 9, 10.

93. Jack Tresize quoted in John Toohey, "Mountain Developing Slowed," *Denver Post*, clipping, circa December 1971, Folder 6, Box 6, MAPC JCA.

94. Membership information, 21 December 1970, Folder 47, Box 3, POME SHHRC; Vance R. Dittman to John A. Love, Letter, 18 November 1970, Folder 17, Box 2, POME SHHRC; Vance R. Dittman to Joe Ciancio Jr. (Manager of Parks and Recreation), Letter, 11 December 1970, Folder 17, Box 2, POME SHHRC; Vance R. Dittman Jr. to Clifford H. Buck, Letter, 8 December 1970, Folder 4, Box 4, POME SHHRC.

95. Vance R. Dittman, Introductory Statement, 18 December 1970, Folder 47, Box 4, POME SHHRC.

96. Longhurst, *Citizen Environmentalists*, x.

97. Jean Gravell, "Open letter to the Evergreen Chamber of Commerce, Att'n Mr. Jack Moore; From Protect Our Mountain Environment, Inc. Jean Gravell, Secretary and Treasurer," *The Canyon Courier* (Evergreen), 27 November 1970, clipping, Folder 17, Box 2, POME SHHRC.

98. Vance R. Dittman to Rodolphe J. Leising, Letter, 23 November 1970, Folder 17, Box 2, POME SHHRC; Vance R. Dittman Jr. to Clifford H. Buck, Letter, 8 December 1970, Folder 40, Box 4, POME SHHRC.

99. Protect Our Mountain Environment, General Membership Meeting, 29 October 1970, Folder 40, Box 4, POME SHHRC; Vance Dittman to Jack Wolf (Chairman of County Planning Commission, Jefferson County), Letter, 31 May 1972, Folder 51, Box 5, POME SHHRC; Vance R. Dittman to Roger P. Hansen, Letter, 21 April 1972, Folder 53, Box 5, POME SHHRC; Michael Holland to Comite International Olympique, Letter, 10 November 1971, Folder XII Olympic Winter Games 1976 Denver, Colo. Protests (1969–1971), File 0012, Film 110, ABC IOCA; John S. Irwin to Governor Love, telegraph, 31 January 1972, Administrative Correspondence Box 67068, JLP SCAR.

100. Bureau of Outdoor Recreation, Department of the Interior, Environmental Statement DES 72 65: Proposed 1976 Denver Olympic Games, 8 June 1972, esp. 22 and 27. The Bureau of Outdoor Recreation was part of the Department of the Interior; a copy of the source is available in Folder 6, Box 1, POME SHHRC.

101. Bureau of Outdoor Recreation, Department of the Interior, Environmental Statement DES 72 65: Proposed 1976 Denver Olympic Games, 8 June 1972; for quotation, see introductory section, "Summary of environmental impact and adverse environmental effects"; for more on benefits of sound planning, see pp. 36–37. For the effects on water, air, and wildlife in Jefferson County, 28–32.

102. Officers of Protect Our Mountain Environment, Comments of 'Protect Our Mountain Environment' Regarding Draft Environmental Statement DES 72, 11 June 1972, Folder 6, Box 1, POME SHHRC.

103. The offer was contingent on the City and County of Denver agreeing to allow construction surrounding the event sites, which would have been denser than what people in Jefferson County would wish for. John Henry to Mayor [William McNichols], Letter Re: Doublehead Ski Jump Proposal, 8 May 1972, Folder 9, Box 102, WMP DPL. An additional offer was for Denver to buy the land for $500,000, rather than receive it for free. In that case, no promise for rezoning would be required. See Paul D. Ambrose and Ronald Lewis to William McNichols, Letter, 12 May 1972, Folder 9, Box 102, WMP DPL; Ronald Lewis to William McNichols, Letter, 9 June 1972, Folder 9, Box 102, WMP DPL; John Henry to Earl Thraser, Letter, 16 June 1972, Folder 8, Box 102, WMP DPL; Peter Blake, "Olympic Site near Tiny Town Identified," *Rocky Mountain News*, 3 February 1972, 5, 6; Thomas E. Kristopelt to John Henry, Letter, 4 April 1972, Folder 9, Box 102, WMP DPL; Ted Farwell to Ron Lewis, Letter, 27 April 1972, Folder 7, Box 103, WMP DPL.

104. Gravel quoted in "We Don't Want Olympics, DOC Is Told," *Canyon Courier* (Evergreen), 29 June 1972, 1, 5.

105. For an additional example of this view, see Michael S. Holland to Senator George McGovern, Letter, 6 May 1972, Folder 42, Box 4, POME SHHRC; Michael S.

Holland to Senator Edward Kennedy, Letter, 6 May 1972, Folder 42, Box 4, POME SHHRC; Michael S. Holland to Senator Robert Dole, Letter, 8 May 1972, Folder 42, Box 4, POME SHHRC.

106. Coordination with other environmentalist groups will be discussed in chapter 9.

107. Sheldon Elliot Steincacht, "Aesthetic Zoning: Property Values and the Judicial Decision Process," *Missouri Law Review* 1, no. 2 (Spring 1970): 1–11 (quotation at pp. 1–2).

108. This will discussed in more detail in chapter 10.

109. Bureau of Outdoor Recreation, Department of the Interior, Environmental State DES 72 65: Proposed 1976 Denver Olympic Games, 8 June 1972 (quotations at p. 38), POME SHHRC. In contrast, the report noted that "long-term Olympic impacts on the vicinity of [Jefferson County's] Doublehead Mountain" were "not judged to be significant because of the present growth patterns in the area"; see 42.

110. Olson, "Power, Public Policy and the Environment," 187.

111. "Nevergreen," *Newsweek*, 14 December 1970, 94; Edith D. Decker, Vance R. Dittman Jr., "Letters: A 'Tasteful Rape,'" *Newsweek*, 4 January 1971, 5; Roger Rapoport, "Olympian Snafu at Sniktau," *Sports Illustrated*, 15 February 1971, 60–61; "What's Up DOC," *Sports Illustrated*, 20 December 1971, 11–12.

112. Gelt Interview.

Chapter 7: A Liberal Tax Revolt and the Public Relations Battle

1. The DOC and Olympics opponents engaged in a "framing contest"; see Boykoff, *Activism and the Olympics*, 29–30.

2. Lamm Interview (2016); Leonard Larsen, "Colorado Legislature—1967," *Denver Post Bonus*, 1 January 1967, 1.

3. Olson, "Power, Public Policy and the Environment," 209; Lamm Interview (2016).

4. Lamm Interview (2016).

5. Lamm Interview (2016).

6. Lamm Interview (2016); Fred Brown, "Colorado Olympic Plan Termed Too General," *Denver Post*, 4 January 1971, 14.

7. Ted Farwell to DOC Board, Letter, 9 December 1971, Folder Board of Directors, Box S4130, ARDOC CSA.

8. G. D. Hubbard Jr. to DOC Executive Council, Letter, 6 January 1971, Folder 28, Box 1, DOC DPL; Technical Division to the DOC Executive Committee, Report No. 1, 14 January 1971, Folder 2, Box 2, DOC DPL.

9. John Henry to Mayor [William McNichols], Letter, 19 August 1971, Folder 7, Box 104, WMP DPL.

10. Weekly Staff Report—Weeks of December 28, 1970 & January 4, 1971, 8 January 1971, Folder 19, Box 1, DOC DPL.

11. Richard M. Davis, Denver Organizing Committee Board of Directors Meeting Minutes, 18 November 1971, Folder 19, Box 1, DOC DPL; Richard O'Reilly, "DOC Directors Vote to Conduct Open Meetings," *Rocky Mountain News*, 25 February 1972, 5.

12. Shoemaker quoted in Fred Brown, "Colorado Olympic Plan Termed Too General," *Denver Post*, 4 January 1971, 14.

13. Harry M. Locke to R. H. Olson, Letter, 7 January 1971, Folder 10, Box 1, DOC DPL.

14. Brown, "Colorado Olympic Plan Termed Too General."

15. "Bill Planned to Bar Funds for Olympics," *Denver Post*, 10 January 1971, clipping, Folder 65, Box 6, POME SHHRC.

16. "Many Pay, Few Gain: Legislators Challenge Olympics for Colorado," *Denver Post*, 15 January 1971, 24.

17. Richard Lamm to Avery Brundage, Letter, 22 November 1971, Folder Olympics—Correspondence, Box 2, RLC SHHRC.

18. Hall, *American Patriotism, American Protest*, 95–116; Martin, *The Permanent Tax Revolt*, 74–79, 98–99; Lo, *Small Property versus Big Government*, 4–5.

19. Lamm Interview (2016); Lamm (2020).

20. Lamm, "The Ultimate Problem."

21. Philpott, *Vacationland*, 270.

22. Lamm, "The Ultimate Problem."

23. Timeline, Folder 60, Box 6, POME SHHRC.

24. Lamm Interview (2016).

25. Lamm quoted in Cal Queal, "Yes, They Want No Olympics," *Denver Post*, 7 February 1971, 7.

26. Lamm quoted in "How Many Care? The U.S. May Lose Out on the Winter Olympics," *Current Events*, 31 January 1973, 1–2.

27. Richard Lamm, "Citizens Can Move Their Government," *Colorado Destiny*, 2 September 1972, 1, Folder 4, CCF DPL.

28. Jackson quoted in Queal, "Yes, They Want No Olympics."

29. Jackson quoted in Richard O'Reilly, "Benefits of the Olympics Are Disputed," *Rocky Mountain News*, 9 April 1971, 8.

30. Lamm Interview (2016).

31. Pat McGraw, "Citizens Unit Asks DOC Funds Cutoff," *Denver Post*, 10 January 1971, 29.

32. Richard Lamm, "Promotional Pollution: The Case for Not Holding the 1976 Winter Olympics in Colorado," speech transcript, 12 February 1972, Folder 2, CCF DPL.

33. Richard Lamm quoted in Douglas S. Looney, "Blah . . . Say a Lot of Colorado Folks When Talk Turns to the Olympics," *The National Observer*, clipping, Folder 3, Box 103, WMP DPL.

34. Colorado, H.B. 1156, 48th General Assembly, 1st Session 1971, CSA.

35. Quotations from "Olympic Vote in Denver Goal of 9 Legislators," *Rocky Mountain News*, 26 January 1971, 21. Lamm and Jackson were joined by Representatives John S. Carroll, Charles J. DeMoulin, Hubert M. Safran, Eldon W. Cooper, Wayne N. Knox, Betty L. Benavidez, Ruben A. Valdez, and Gerald H. Kopel.

36. Olson, "Power, Public Policy and the Environment," 223–224, 242–246.

37. "Sniping Clouds the Olympics without Solving Any Problems," *Denver Post*, 12 January 1971, 18.

38. "Sabotaging the Olympics," *Rocky Mountain News*, 27 January 1971, 38.

39. "Looking on the Blind Side," *Rocky Mountain News*, 27 February 1971, clipping, Folder 68, Box 6, POME SHHRC.

40. Lamm Interview (2016).

41. Richard M. Davis, Denver Organizing Committee Board of Director's Meeting Minutes, 18 February 1971, Folder 19, Box 1, DOC DPL.
42. Leonard Larsen, "Games Must Go On, Solons Told," *Denver Post*, 26 February 1971, 3. For the DOC's preparation for the joint session, see Richard M. Davis, Denver Organizing Committee Board of Director's Meeting Minutes, 18 February 1971, Folder 19, Box 1, DOC DPL; Robert Olson, Outline of Presentation to Joint Session of the Legislature, Thursday, February 25, 1971—11 a.m.—State House Chambers, 18 February 1971, Folder 13, Box 1, DOC DLP.
43. Jackson quoted in Larsen, "Games Must Go On, Solons Told."
44. Lamm and Jackson quoted in Cal Queal, "Yes, They Want No Olympics."
45. Knox quoted in Larsen, "Games Must Go On, Solons Told."
46. Legislative Committee to Study Plans for the 1976 Winter Olympic Games, Minutes of Meeting, 4 March 1971, Folder 10, Box 1, DOC DPL; Richard Olson to Senator Harry M. Locke, Letter, 20 January 1971, Folder 10, Box 1, DOC DPL.
47. Donald F. Magarrell to Board of Directors, Status Report, 10 June 1971, Folder 4, Box 48, POME SHHRC.
48. The 1971 Legislative Committee on the Olympics, "State Participation in the 1976 Winter Olympic Games," 25 March 1971, Folder 45, Box 4, POME SHHRC; for the formation of the committee, see Forty-eighth General Assembly, Senate Joint Resolution No. 9, 27 January 1971, CSA.
49. Robert Jackson, "Minority Findings of the 1971 Legislative Committee on the Olympics," 25 March 1971, Folder 42, Box 4, POME SHHRC.
50. When the DOC reselected Nordic and Alpine sites, they were supposed to run the plans through the State's Land Use Commission, but never did; see "DOC hit for site selections," *Golden Daily Transcript*, 11 February 1972, 1; G. D. Hubbard Jr. to DOC Executive Council, Memo, Subject: DOC's Obligations to the State Land Use Commission, 14 February 1972, Folder 29, Box 1, DOC DPL.
51. Jackson, "Minority Findings of the 1971 Legislative Committee on the Olympics."
52. Love quoted in Douglas S. Looney, "Blah . . . Say a Lot of Colorado Folks When Talk Turns to the Olympics," *The National Observer*, clipping, Folder 3, Box 103, WMP DPL.
53. Technical Division to the DOC Executive Committee, Report No. 1, 14 January 1971, Folder 2, Box 2, DOC DPL.
54. Olson, "Power, Public Policy and the Environment," 220–223.
55. Paul I. Bortz (with Theodore D. Browne), Prepared for the Denver Organizing Committee for the 1976 Olympic Winter Games, Inc., Organization of the XII Olympic Winter Games: Objectives, Tasks, and Organizational Structure, October 1970, Folder 6, Box 1, DPL DOC; D. F. Magarrell, Denver Olympic Committee: Planning Commission Concept (adopted 21 January 1971), 25 January 1971, Folder 19, Box 1, DOC DPL; "Denver Olympic Committee Planning Board Policy Guidelines," n.d., Folder Planning Board General, Box S4132, ARDOC CSA; Robert J. Pringle, Minutes of the Nominating Committee for the Planning Commission of the Denver Olympic Committee, 4 March, 1971, Folder 33, Box 1, DOC DPL; Magarrell, Planning Board Meeting Minutes, 31 August 1971, Folder 33, Box 1, DOC DPL.
56. Richard M. Davis, Denver Organizing Committee Board of Directors Meeting Minutes, 18 March 1971, Folder 19, Box 1, DOC DPL.

57. Phil E. Flores, Planning Board Meeting Minutes, 28 September 1971, Folder 33, Box 1, DOC DPL; Phil E. Flores to Carl DeTemple, Ted Farwell, Norm Brown, and Jack Watson, Inter-Office Memo, 7 January 1972, Folder Planning Board Meeting, Box S4132, ARDOC CSA.

58. Beatrice Willard to Carl DeTemple, Letter, 20 January 1971, Folder Planning Board General, Box S4132, ARDOC SCAR; Norm Brown to Carl DeTemple, Ted Farwell, Jack Watson, Phil Flores, Ellen Jenson, Inter-Office Memo, 18 January 1972, Folder Planning Board Meeting, Box S4132, ARDOC CSA.

59. Beatrice E. Willard to Robert Pringle, Letter, 18 February 1972, Folder Planning Board General, Box S4132, ARDOC CSA; Childers, *Colorado Powder Keg*, 90; Hauk, *Beaver Creek Ski Area Chronology*, 4; Olson, "Power, Public Policy and the Environment," 149–156.

60. Richard M. Davis, Minutes of the Denver Olympic Committee Board of Directors, 20 January 1972, Folder 21, Box 1, DOC DPL; Carl DeTemple to Dr. Beatrice Willard, Letter, 25 January 1972, Folder 29, Box 1, DOC DPL.

61. Planning Board Meeting Minutes, 18 January 1972, Folder 18, Box 101, WMP DPL; Sumber and Farwell, "The Olympic Bubble," 28.

62. Richard M. Davis to the Executive Council, Memorandum, Subject: Public Attendance at Meetings, 9 February 1971, Folder 28, Box 1, DOC DLP.

63. Robinson quoted in Richard M. Davis, Denver Organizing Committee Board of Director's Meeting Minutes, 18 February 1971, Folder 19, Box 1, DOC DPL; see also Brigitte Bastian, Site Selection Committee Meeting Minutes, 29 September 1970, Folder Site General II, Box S4130, ARDOC CSA; Richard M. Davis, Denver Organizing Committee Executive Council Meeting Minutes, 28 October 1971, Folder 28, Box 1, DOC DPL; Denver Olympic Committee Board of Directors Meeting Minutes, 22 December 1971, Folder 19, Box 1, DOC DPL; Richard O'Reilly, "DOC directors vote to conduct open meetings."

64. Richard M. Davis, Denver Organizing Committee Board of Director's Meeting Minutes, 18 February 1971, Folder 19, Box 1, DOC DPL.

65. Norm Brown to Don Magarrell, Memorandum Re: Media Executive Advisory Committee Meeting on March 8, 1971 at the DOC offices between members of the DOC staff and Mr. Charles Buxton, Bill Hornby, and John Rogers of Denver Post; Mike Howard of the Rocky Mountain News; Don Faust, General Manager, KOA-TV; Hugh Terry and Sheldon Peterson, KLZ; and Al Flanagan, president of Mullins Broadcasting (KBTV), 11 March 1971, Folder 39, Box 1, DOC DPL.

66. Timeline, Folder 60, Box 6, POME SHHRC.

67. "Right Steps Taken to Brighten Outlook for 1976 Winter Games," *Denver Post*, 2 April 1972, 25.

68. Richard M. Davis, Denver Organizing Committee Board of Directors Meeting Minutes, 18 March 1971, Folder 19, Box 1, DOC DPL.

69. Staff Meeting Minutes, 2 April 1971, Folder 44, Box 2, DOC DPL.

70. "The Word from Olympus: The Post Hierarchy Dictates How News of 1976 Winter Olympics will be Managed. Brace Yourself of a Snow Job," *The Unsatisfied Man*, April 1971, 3.

71. Denver Organizing Committee Meeting Minutes, 17 April 1969, Book 2, Box S4150, ARDOC CSA.

72. Norm Brown to Don Magarrell, Memo Re: Media Executive Advisory Committee Meeting on March 8, 1971 at the DOC offices between members of the DOC staff and Mr. Charles Buxton, Bill Hornby, and John Rogers of Denver Post; Mike Howard of the Rocky Mountain News; Don Faust, General Manager, KOA-TV; Hugh Terry and Sheldon Peterson, KLZ; and Al Flanagan, president of Mullins Broadcasting (KBTV), 11 March 1971, Folder 39, Box 1, DOC DPL.

73. O'Reilly Interview.

74. O'Reilly Interview.

75. Logan and Molotch, *Urban Fortunes*, 72–73.

76. Richard O'Reilly, "The Olympics and Colorado, First of a series: Olympics— Good or Bad in Colorado?," *Rocky Mountain News*, 4 April 1971, 1, 5, 8. Much of what O'Reilly reported (including problems with Evergreen and Sniktau) was reported two months earlier in *Sports Illustrated*; see Roger Rapoport, "Olympian Snafu at Sniktau," *Sports Illustrated*, 15 February 1971, 60–61. Rapoport's article did not seem to reach Coloradans as effectively as O'Reilly's series.

77. Richard O'Reilly, "The Olympics and Colorado: Benefits of Olympics Are Disputed, 6th of a series," *Rocky Mountain News*, 9 April 1971, 8.

78. Richard O'Reilly, "The Olympics and Colorado: Olympic Alpine Conflict Brewing, 4th of a series," *Rocky Mountain News*, 7 April 1971, 6, 8, 18.

79. O'Reilly, "The Olympics and Colorado: Olympic Alpine Conflict Brewing, 4th of a series"; Richard O'Reilly, "The Olympics and Colorado: Snags Arise in Olympic Site Selection, 3rd of a series," *Rocky Mountain News*, 6 April 1971, 8, 22.

80. Richard O'Reilly, "The Olympics and Colorado: 60 Winter Olympics Cost Skyrocketed, 2nd of a series," *Rocky Mountain News*, 5 April 1971, 8, 16.

81. Richard O'Reilly, "The Olympics and Colorado: Olympic Cost Estimates Vary Widely, 5th of a series," *Rocky Mountain News*, 8 April 1971, 8, 18.

82. Richard Lamm, "Promotional Pollution: The Case for Not Holding the 1976 Winter Olympics in Colorado," speech transcript, 12 February 1972, Folder 2, CCF DPL.

83. R. A. Smith to William McNichols, Letter, 9 April 1971, Folder 4, Box 101, WMP DPL.

84. Lundstrom Interview.

85. Brown Interview (2016).

86. Vance R. Dittman Jr. to Avery Brundage, Letter, 4 May 1971, File 0012, Film 110, ABC IOCA; Vance Dittman and Jean Gravell to All POME Members, Bulletin, May 1971, File 0012, Film 110, ABC IOCA.

87. Olson, "Power, Public Policy and the Environment," 224–225; Colorado, H.B. 1156, 48th General Assembly, 1st Session 1971, CSA.

88. Richard Lamm to Vance Dittman, Letter, 18 November [1971], Folder 18, Box 2, POME SHHRC.

Chapter 8: Direct Democracy for Middle America

1. Cowie, *Stayin' Alive*, esp. chapters 2 and 3.

2. *Denver Post*, 13 May 1970, Front Page; the headlines at the *Rocky Mountain News* also read: "Jubilant Denver is Winner in 1976 Bid for Winter Olympics" and

"Gov. Love Pleads for Peace on Campus," see *Rocky Mountain News*, 13 May 1970, Front Page.

3. Isserman and Kazin, *America Divided*, 250–252, 254–256.
4. Abbott, Leonard, and Noel, *Colorado*, 4th ed., 349.
5. Bill Logan, "Love and Key Officials Confer on DU Crisis," *Rocky Mountain News*, 12 May 1970, 8.
6. James Crawford, "Negotiation Fails to End DU Impasse," *Rocky Mountain News*, 13 May 1970, 5. Walker Jr., "John A. Love," 42; Abbott, Leonard, and Noel, *Colorado*, 349–350.
7. Wells, *The War Within*, 168–170.
8. Wells, *The War Within*, 223–226; with Brown heading Youth for McCarthy, McCarthy won Democratic presidential primaries in Wisconsin, Pennsylvania, New Jersey, Illinois, and Oregon; see also "Vietnam: A Television History; Interview with Sam Brown, 1982."
9. Brown Interview (2016); Brown also worked for Harold Hughes's successful 1969 campaign for US Senate.
10. Wells, *The War Within*, 328–331, 370–379; as Wells also points out, there is reason to believe American military capabilities played as large a role (and maybe the decisive role) in Nixon's decision to back off the "Duck Hook" plan.
11. Brown Interview (2016).
12. Filley Interview; Lundstrom Interview.
13. Lundstrom Interview.
14. Lundstrom Interview; "Barnes-McKevitt Race Closest," *Denver Post*, 1 November 1970, 5; Parr also knew Lamm fairly well as a lobbyist in the Colorado legislature for Common Cause; see Norman Udevitz, "Small but Artful Activist Wielding Rare Power," *Denver Post*, 11 October 1972, 32–33.
15. Leonard and Noel, *Denver*, 78, 380.
16. "Love Elected to 3rd Term, McKevitt Wins; Colo. GOP in Control," *Denver Post*, 4 November 1970, 1, 3.
17. Harris, *Now Is the Time*; Lowitt, *Fred Harris*.
18. Lundstrom Interview; see also Udevitz, "Small but Artful Activist Wielding Rare Power."
19. Lundstrom Interview; see also Udevitz, "Small but Artful Activist Wielding Rare Power."
20. Nussbaum Interview (2016).
21. Filley Interview.
22. Brown Interview (2016); Lundstrom Interview; Nussbaum Interview (2016); and Filley Interview; Lamm Interview (2016); all express positive or indifferent views of the Olympics.
23. Nussbaum Interview (2016).
24. Lundstrom Interview.
25. Lundstrom Interview.
26. Nussbaum Interview (2016).
27. Filley Interview. Filley made essentially the same point in 1972, stating the "Olympics will reorder our state priorities"; see Filley quoted in "Where Voters Battle Over the Olympics," *Business Weekly*, 28 October 1972, 78.
28. Brown Interview (2016).

29. Brown Interview (2016).
30. Filley Interview.
31. Cowie, *Stayin' Alive* (for the need to reach beyond campuses, see pp. 68–70; for trying to create a coalition that included middle America, see chapter 2).
32. Brown Interview (2016).
33. Wells, *The War Within*, 371.
34. Sam W. Brown Jr., "The Politics of Peace," *Washington Monthly*, August 1970, 24–46 (quotation at pp. 42, 43, 31).
35. Brown Interview (2016).
36. Brown, "The Politics of Peace," 34.
37. Lundstrom Interview.
38. Filley Interview.
39. Lundstrom Interview; Nussbaum Interview (2016).
40. Brown, "The Politics of Peace," see esp. 42–43.
41. Filley Interview.
42. Brown Interview (2016).
43. Lamm Interview (2016); Lundstrom Interview; Brown Interview (2016); for an example of Lamm in this role, see Norman Udevitz, "Cost of Olympic Games Debated," *Denver Post*, 29 September 1972, 42.
44. Lamm Interview (2016).
45. Paul L. Hamilton, Ruth Weiner, and John Zapien to Friend, Letter, 1 January 1972, Folder XII Winter Games 1976, Denver, Col. Organizing Committee (1972), File 0011, Film 110, ABC IOCA; Brown Interview (2020).
46. Nussbaum Interview (2016).
47. Richard O'Reilly, "Drive to Bar City Olympic Funding is Formally Launched," *Rocky Mountain News*, 18 August 1972, 6.
48. Parr quoted in Ron Wolf, "Yes, We Have No Olympics," *Straight Creek Journal*, 21 November 1972, 3.
49. Brown Interview (2020).
50. Brown, "The Politics of Peace," 33.
51. Brown, "The Politics of Peace," 33.
52. "CCF Asks Denver Housing Aid," clipping, circa 1972, Folder 4, Box 48, POME SHHRC; CCF ally Oklahoma Senator Fred Harris took the same position; see Leonard Larson, "Harris Backs $29.1 Million for Low-Income Housing," *Denver Post*, 11 May 1972, 34.
53. Lamm Interview (2020); Brown Interview (2020).
54. Sam W. Brown, "Snow Job in Colorado," *New Republic*, 29 January 1972, 18.
55. Richard O'Reilly, "The Olympics and Colorado: Olympic Alpine Conflict Brewing, 4th of a series," *Rocky Mountain News*, 7 April 1971, 6, 8, 18; notably, the after-use plan for the bank of the Platte River included motel and hotels; see David Lucy, Development Feasibility Study—Press Housing Site, Left Bank, Platte Valley, 8 July 1971, Folder 18, Box 102, WMP DPL.
56. Timeline, Folder 60, Box 6, POME SHHRC.
57. Advertisement, "Sell Colorado? Olympics '76? AT WHAT COST TO COLORADO?," *Denver Post*, 2 January 1972, 41.
58. This perspective echoed that of the influential social theorist C. Wright Mills; see Mills, *The Power Elite*; Miller, "*Democracy Is in the Streets*," 78–91.

59. Brown, *Storefront Organizing*, 62.
60. Advertisement, "AT WHAT COST TO COLORADO?"
61. Advertisement, "AT WHAT COST TO COLORADO?"
62. Advertisement, "AT WHAT COST TO COLORADO?"
63. Advertisement, "AT WHAT COST TO COLORADO?"
64. Advertisement, "AT WHAT COST TO COLORADO?"
65. Brown, "Snow Job in Colorado," 18.
66. Mountain Area Protection Council, "Summary of Questions," 8 March 1969, Folder 23, Box 1, MAPC JCA; Biffle quoted in "Mayor Plans No Meet with Minorities of DOC," *Denver Post*, 15 December 1970, 3.
67. Citizens for Colorado's Future, "A Presentation to the International Olympic Committee from the Citizens for Colorado's Future," SD: Brochure de presentation des protestation 1972, 1972.01.01–1972.12.31, 1976 Olympic Winter Games of Denver (not celebrated), Games of Denver IOCA; see section titled "Citizens for Colorado's Future: A Brief History."
68. Paul L. Hamilton, Ruth Weiner, and John Zapien to Friend, Letter, 1 January 1972, Folder XII Winter Games 1976, Denver, Col. Organizing Committee (1972), File 0011, Film 110, ABC IOCA.
69. Concerned Citizens of Colorado to International Olympic Committee, Petition, circa January 1972, Box 2, JPP DPL.
70. Brown, *Storefront Organizing*, 29.
71. Paul L. Hamilton, Ruth Weiner, and John Zapien to Friend, Letter, 1 January 1972, Folder XII Winter Games 1976, Denver, Col. Organizing Committee (1972), File 0011, Film 110, ABC IOCA.
72. Brown Interview (2020); Lamm Interview (2020).
73. Lundstrom Interview.
74. Citizens for Colorado's Future, "A Presentation to the International Olympic Committee from the Citizens for Colorado's Future," 1972.01.01–1972.12.31, 1976 Olympic Winter Games of Denver (not celebrated), Games of Denver IOCA.
75. Lundstrom Interview.
76. Lamm Interview (2016); Philpott, *Vacationland*, 222–223.
77. Lundstrom Interview.
78. Brown Interview (2020).
79. Lamm Interview (2016); Gelt Interview.
80. Gelt Interview.
81. Lundstrom Interview.
82. Gelt Interview.
83. Gelt Interview; John Parr, "Face to Face with the Olympic Gods," *Capital Ledger*, March 1972, 1, 3: 4–11, esp. 5–7.
84. Olson, "Power, Public Policy and the Environment," 176; John Hennessey, "Mrs. Brown Invades Meeting of the IOC's Elder Statesmen," *The Times of London*, 29 January 1972, clipping, 1971.01.01–1972.12.31, Press Cuttings from the 1976 Olympic Games of Denver, Games of Denver IOCA. "Denver Group, Against Having Games, Crashes IOC Meeting," *New York Herald*, 30 January 1972, clipping, 1971.01.01–1972.12.31, Press Cuttings from the 1976 Olympic, Games of Denver IOCA.

85. Richard O'Reilly, "Olympic Protester Crashes IOC Meeting," *Rocky Mountain News*, 29 January 1972, clipping, Folder 4, Box 6, MAPC JCA.

86. International Olympic Committee Executive Board Meeting Minutes, 28–30 January 1972, EB IOCA.

87. Gelt Interview.

88. Parr, "Face to Face with the Olympic Gods," 5–6.

89. Lundstrom Interview.

90. Michael Balfe Howard, "News Survey Indicates Heavy Support for Olympic Referendum," *Rocky Mountain News*, 13 March 1972, 1; John Ashton, "Drive Launched for Referendum," *Denver Post*, 16 March 1972, 25.

91. Haldeman quoted in Wells, *The War Within*, 376.

92. Lundstrom Interview.

93. Dwight Filley, Meg Lundstrom, and John Parr to Friend, Letter, 30 March 1972, CCF DPL.

94. Nussbaum estimated CCF garnered 4,000–6,000 volunteers; Lundstrom estimated 5,000; Richard O'Reilly, "Volunteer Unit to Petition for Olympic Site Change," *Rocky Mountain News*, 6 January 1972, 8.

95. "Olympic Spending Petitions Sent Out," *Denver Post*, 2 April 1972, 2.

96. Brown, *Storefront Organizing*, 38.

97. For soliciting signatures, see Filley Interview and Brown Interview (2016); for speaking with various groups, see Nussbaum Interview and Gelt Interview. For the bicycle rally, see Lundstrom Interview and "Taking Olympic-Funder Petition on Tour," *Denver Post*, 28 May 1972, 45; Olson, "Power, Public Policy and the Environment," 188; see also Dwight Filley, Meg Lundstrom, and John Parr to Friend, Letter, 10 May 1972, Folder 28, Box 2, MAPC JCA.

98. Filley Interview.

99. Lamm Interview (2016).

100. Brown Interview (2016).

101. Dwight Filley, Meg Lundstrom, and John Parr, Citizens for Colorado Newsletter, 25 June 1972, Folder 50, Box 5, POME SHHRC.

Chapter 9: The DOC'S Credibility and the Rhetoric of Olympism

1. Carl DeTemple to Governor Love, Mayor McNichols, W. R. Goodwin, and Eric Auer, Memo, 31 July 1972, Folder 17, Box 102, WMP DPL.

2. Tony Larson, Script, "A Bridge to Span the Minds of Men," 14 January 1971 (6:10m), Folder 4, Box 101, WMP DPL. KOSI broadcasted Larson's comments.

3. Technical Division to General Secretary and Public Affairs Manager, Report No. 2, 8 March 1971, Folder 2, Box 2, DOC DPL.

4. John Henry to Mayor [William McNichols], Letter, 14 October 1971, Folder 19, Box 102, WMP DPL.

5. Thomas Currigan, Report by Phone, 11 February 1970, Folder 11, Box 100, WMP DPL; see also Avery Brundage to William H. McNichols, Letter, 20 April 1970, Folder XII Winter Games–1976–Denver, File 0011, Film 110, ABC IOCA.

6. Avery Brundage to Vance R. Dittman, Letter, 1 November 1971, Folder 16, Box 2, POME SHHRC. For protest letters (mostly from Evergreen and Indian Hills),

see Folder XII Olympic Winter Games 1976 Denver, Colo. Protests (1969–1971), File 0012, Film 110, ABC IOCA; see also 1971.10.01–1971.10.30, Letters of Protest against holding the 1976 Olympic Winter Games in Denver (not celebrated), Games of Denver IOCA; 1971.11.01–1971.12.31, Letters of Protest against holding the 1976 Olympic Winter Games in Denver (not celebrated), Games of Denver IOCA.

7. Lord Killanin to Monique Berlioux, Letter, circa November 1971, 1970.01.01–1972.12.31, Correspondences of the Organizing Committee of the 1976 Olympic Winter Games in Denver (not celebrated), Games of Denver IOCA.

8. Avery Brundage to Monique Berlioux, Letter, 18 April 1970, 1970.01.01–1970.06.30, Correspondence of Avery Brundage, PB IOCA; Avery Brundage, "Olympic Games in Danger," Speech, 10 May 1970, 1940.01.01–1972.12.31, Speeches given by Avery Brundage, PB IOCA; Avery Brundage to Monique Berlioux, Letter, 18 April 1970, 1970.01.01–1970.06.30, Correspondence of Avery Brundage, PB IOCA.

9. Avery Brundage to Clifford Buck, Letter, 17 May 1972, Folder 66, Box 2, DOC DPL.

10. Avery Brundage to Jan Staubo, Letter, 6 July 1968, 07.01.1968–09.31.1969, Correspondence of Avery Brundage, PB IOCA; Avery Brundage to Bjorn Kjellstrom, Letter, 6 July 1968, 07.01.1968–09.31.1969, Correspondence of Avery Brundage, PB IOC; Brundage, "Olympic Games in Danger," Speech, 10 May 1970, 1940.01.01–1972.12.31, Speeches Given By Avery Brundage, PB, IOCA; Guttmann, *The Games Must Go On*, chapters 8, 11, 13; Llewellyn and Gleaves, *The Rise and Fall of Olympic Amateurism*, chapter 7.

11. Killanin, *My Olympic Years*, 57.

12. Brundage quoted in Richard O'Reilly, "Denver Officials Mixed in Reaction to Brundage," *Rocky Mountain News*, 21 August 1972, 5.

13. International Olympic Committee Executive Board Meeting Minutes, 28–30 January 1972, Executive Board, 20, 11–12, EB IOCA; see also Richard O'Reilly, "Decision Climaxes Hectic Day in Sapporo: Denver Will Keep the Games, Olympic Committee Rules," *Rocky Mountain News*, 1 February 1972, 1, 6.

14. International Olympic Committee Executive Board Meeting Minutes, 28–30 January 1972, 27–29 and 35, EB IOCA; Killanin and Constantin Andrianov wanted to end Denver '76 themselves, while Brundage wanted to see the DOC withdraw on its own.

15. Pringle quoted in Richard O'Reilly, "Decision Climaxes Hectic Day in Sapporo."

16. Love quoted in John M. Lee, "Denver Suffers Sapporo Ordeal"; Charlie Meyers, "IOC Reaffirms Denver as '76 Winter Games Host," *Denver Post*, 1 February 1972, 1, 2.

17. Richard O'Reilly, "Decision Climaxes Hectic Day in Sapporo"; John M. Lee, "Denver Suffers Sapporo Ordeal."

18. Leonard Larsen, "Congress Acted in 'Emergency,'" *Denver Post*, 1 February 1972, 9. Every member of Colorado's congressional delegation sponsored the bill except for Representative Frank Evans, who could not be reached because he was sick with the flu; see Richard O'Reilly, "Denver's Chance for U.S. Funds for Games Sites Seen as Good," *Rocky Mountain News*, 6 February 1972, clipping, Folder 68, Box 6, POME SHHRC.

19. Rogers C. B. Morton to Avery Brundage, Wire, 31 January 1972, Folder XII Winter Games–1976–Denver, Colo.–Organizing Comm. (1970–1971), File 0010, Film 110, ABC IOCA.

20. Lundstrom Interview.

21. Denver Organizing Committee for the Denver Organizing Committee of the XII Olympic Winter Games, Report to the 72nd Session of the International Olympic Committee, 1 February 1972, Games of Denver IOCA; 72nd Session of the International Olympic Committee Minutes, Sapporo 1972, Sessions IOCA. The audio recording and transcript are in the author's possession.

22. Robinson quoted in "Olympics Opposition Will Continue Battle," *Denver Post*, 2 February 1972, 2.

23. Lindemann quoted in Richard O'Reilly, "DOC Face $10 million Broadcasting Cost," *Rocky Mountain News*, 8 February 1972, 1, 6.

24. Richard O'Reilly, "DOC Mulls Ways to Cut TV Cost," *Rocky Mountain News*, 10 February 1972, 5.

25. Love quoted in "Governor, Mayor Puzzled by Report of Games TV Cost," *Rocky Mountain News*, 9 February 1972, 5.

26. Norm Brown quoted in O'Reilly, "DOC Mulls Ways to Cut TV Cost."

27. Richard O'Reilly, "Olympic Committee Difficulties Evaluated, Criticized," *Rocky Mountain News*, 20 February 1972, 19.

28. Richard Olson to John Love, Letter, 23 February 1972, Box 67089, JLF CSA.

29. G. D. Hubbard Jr. to Members of the DOC Executive Council and Tom Currigan and Members of the Colorado Olympic Commission, 17 January 1972, Folder 29, Box 1, DOC DPL; "Colo. Olympic Fund Short, Says Love," *Denver Post*, 6 February 1972, 2.

30. John A. Love, Speech, Address to the Legislature Re: Olympics, 3 March 1972, Box 66951, Speeches of Governor John A. Love, JLF CSA.

31. Richard O'Reilly, "$70 million Total Help Possible: $35 Million Olympic Cost Fails to Cover City Extras," *Rocky Mountain News*, 19 March 1972, 8.

32. G. D. Hubbard to DOC Board and COC Board, Letter, Subject: Financial Summaries of Prospective Olympic Activity, 30 March 1972, Folder 21, Box 1, DOC DPL; Charlie Meyers, "DOC Meets to Tie Together Aid Bids," *Denver Post*, 3 April 1972, 2.

33. Carl DeTemple to Governor John A. Love, DOC Inter-Office Memo, Subject: Proposed Statement, 27 March 1972, DOC DLP; Sport Facilities—Capital Modification Budget, March 1972, Folder 9, Box 2, DOC DPL; see this source for exact cost and modification details.

34. Friedman quoted in Charlie Roos, "Budget Committee Grills Olympic Leaders," *Denver Post*, 22 March 1972, p. 3.

35. Richard O'Reilly, "Joint Budget Committee Exacts $65.3 Million from DOC," *Rocky Mountain News*, 22 March 1972, 5.

36. Richard O'Reilly, "DOC Pegs Costs at Low of $81 Million," *Rocky Mountain News*, 4 April 1972, 16, 17.

37. Shoemaker quoted in O'Reilly, "Joint Budget Committee Exacts $65.3 Million from DOC."

38. Friedman quoted in Olson, "Power, Public Policy and the Environment," 234.

39. Richard Tucker, "1.2 Billion Budget Okayed by JBC; Olympic Funds Cut," *Rocky*

Mountain News, 4 April 1972, 5; "Long Bill Cuts Games Budget," *Denver Post*, 3 April 1972, 2.

40. Richard O'Reilly and Robert Burns, "DOC Expects Legislature to Restore Olympics Funds," *Rocky Mountain News*, 5 April 1972, 5, 7; "Mayor at Capitol: City Pleads Olympics Case," *Denver Post*, 7 April 1972, 10.

41. Carl N. DeTemple to Representative Thomas T. Farley, Letter, 6 April 1972, Folder 46, Box 1, DOC DPL; "DOC Replies to Dems Questions," *Rocky Mountain News*, 8 April 1972, 134.

42. The Colorado Senate would raise the number to $783,500 with a $5,000,000 overall ceiling for future funding; see Olson, "Power, Public Policy and the Environment," 235–236.

43. Freidman quoted in "House Votes $739,000 for Olympics," *Denver Post*, 7 April 1972, 3.

44. S. 3531, 92nd Congress 2nd Session, 25 April 1972, Folder 17, Box 102, WMP DPL; Leonard Larsen, "Olympic Fund Bills Offered," *Denver Post*, 25 April 1972, 3. The DOC initially requested $19.9 million. The United States Congress reduced the number to $15.5 million based on the assumption that bobsled races would be held in Lake Placid, New York. For coordination with Mayor McNichols's office, see Folder 17, Box 102, WMP DLP.

45. Harris quotation from Robert Threlkeld, "Senate OKs $15.5 Million Olympics Funding," *Rocky Mountain News*, 16 September 1972, 5, 6. Along with Harris, there was resistance to funding the Denver Olympics from South Dakota Democratic senator George McGovern, Iowa Democratic representative H. R. Cross, and Maryland Democratic representative William F. Ryan; see Robert Threlkeld, "DOC Faces Uphill Fight for U.S. Funds," *Rocky Mountain News*, 20 February 1972, 5; "Harris to Hold Talks on Winter Olympics," *Rocky Mountain News*, 24 March 1972, 18; Leonard Larsen, "Harris Urges Ban of U.S. Funds for Denver Olympics," *The Denver Post*, 13 April 1972, 32; Leonard Larsen, "Twin Bills for Federal Olympics Aid Gather 4 Opponents," *Denver Post*, 26 April 1972, 49.

46. Webster Otis to Robert J. Pringle, Letter, 9 December 1971, Folder 37, Box 2, DOC DPL; Statement by Senator Gordon Allott to Denver Olympic Committee, 16 December 1971, Folder 8, Box 1, DOC DPL; Robert Threlkeld, "DOC's Request for Funds Expected To Be Cut," *Rocky Mountain News*, 6 April 1972, 5; Leonard Larson, "No Fund Amount Set: Olympics Aid Bill 'Open Ended,'" *Denver Post*, 20 April 1972, 25.

47. 1976 Denver Winter Olympics, Hearing before the Subcommittee on Parks and Recreation of the Committee on Interior and Insular Affairs, United States Senate, Ninety-Second Congress Second Session, S. 3551, 9 June 1972; for Lamm's statement, see 48–61; for Stovall's statement, see 168–179.

48. Congressional Record—Senate, S. 15021, 15 September 1972, Folder 21, Box 1, DOC DPL. The nay votes came from Oklahoma senator Fred Harris, Connecticut senator Abraham A. Ribicoff, and Arkansas senator J. W. Fulbright.

49. Otis quoted in Richard O'Reilly, "Denver's Chance for U.S. Funds for Games Sites Seen as Good," *Rocky Mountain News*, 6 February 1972, clipping, Folder 4, Box 6, MAPC JCA; see also Webster Otis to Robert J. Pringle, Letter, 14 February 1972, Folder 6, Box 103, WMP DPL.

50. John Vanderhoof quoted in Robert Barnes, "Vanderhoof Says IOC Won't

Cancel," *Rocky Mountain News*, 17 August 1972, 8. The bill left open the possibility that more than $15.5 million could be appropriated, reading: "There is authorized to be appropriated by the Secretary of the Interior a sum not exceeded $15.5 million (December 1971 prices), *plus or minus such amounts, if any, as may be justified by reason of ordinary fluctuation in construction costs*" (author's italics); see Congressional Record—Senate, S. 15021, 15 September 1972, Folder 21, Box 1, DOC DPL.

51. For likely support in the House of Representatives, see Leonard Larsen, "Initial U.S. Olympics Aid Sought," *Denver Post*, 25 September 1972, 3; Robert Threlkeld, "House Unit gives Denver strong boost for Olympics," *Rocky Mountain News*, 26 September 1972, 1, 6.

52. Richard Olson to John Love, Letter, 23 February 1972, Box 67089, JLF CSA; Carl DeTemple also confirmed Love's actions were in response to DOC request; see Olson, "Power, Public Policy and the Environment," 180.

53. Sam Lusky to John A. Love, Letter, Subject: Operation Impact Re: The Colorado Citizens of 76, 17 March 1972, Box 67089, JLF CSA. For the presence of other DOC backers at the meeting, see Olson, "Power, Public Policy and the Environment," 180.

54. "'Committee of 76' to back Olympics," *Rocky Mountain News*, 25 March 1972, 5.

55. Sam Lusky to John Love, Letter, Subject: Update Report Re Status of Fund Collections For Committee of 76, 9 May 1972, Folder 32, Box 87, DCC DPL; "Governor Lists Committee of 76," *Denver Post*, 26 March 1972, 3.

56. John A. Love to Sam Lusky, Letter, Subject: A Review of the activities and expenditures of the Committee of 76/For the Spirit of 76, 25 July 1972, Box 67089, JLF CSA.

57. Brown quoted in Olson, "Power, Public Policy and the Environment," 181.

58. Lusky quoted in Richard O'Reilly, "Olympic Column Wipeout," *The Unsatisfied Man*, April 1972, 1.

59. Advertisement, "This We Believe," clipping, circa 20 March 1972, Folder 49, Box 5, POME SHHRC; see also Advertisement, "Thanks! And It's Only the Beginning!," *Denver Post*, 2 April 1972, clipping, Folder 4, Box 6, MAPC JCA; Advertisement, "You Support the 1976 Olympics and the Colorado Centennial!," *Canyon Courier* (Evergreen), 13 April 1972, clipping, Folder 67, Box 5, MACP JCA.

60. Richard M. Davis, Denver Olympic Committee Board of Directors Meeting Minutes, 16 March 1972, Folder 21, Box 1, DOC DPL; "Kostka Will Handle PR," *Denver Post*, 5 March 1972, 3.

61. Denver Olympic Committee Board of Directors Meeting Minutes, 24 February 1972, Folder 21, Box 1, DOC DPL; Richard O'Reilly, "DOC Directors Vote to Conduct Open Meetings," *Rocky Mountain News*, 25 February 1972, 5.

62. Denver Olympic Committee, Press Release, 16 March 1972, Folder 44, Box 1, DOC DPL. Denver Olympic Committee, Press Release, Subject: Expenditures since 1965, 24 March 1972, Folder 44, Box 1, DOC DPL; Carl DeTemple to Board of Directors and DOC Planning Board, Inter-office Memorandum, Conflict of Interest Board Resolution, 12 April 1972, Folder 21, Box 1, DOC DPL.

63. Richard M. Davis, Preliminary Draft of Proposal—5/5/72: Reorganization of the DOC, 5 May 1972, Folder 32, Box 1, DOC DPL; "Proposal of Special Committee

Composition of DOOC," Folder 3, Box 102, WMP DPL; Denver Olympic Committee, *Olympic News*, July 1972, Folder 49, Box 1, DOC DPL. For the suggestion of 150 members, see Denver Olympic Organizing Committee, Press Release, 19 October 1972, Folder 21, Box 1, DOC DPL.

64. George Robinson to Gerald F. Groswold, Letter, 14 July 1972, Folder 21, Box 1, DOC DPL.

65. Denver Organizing Committee Board of Directors Meeting Minutes, 18 July 1972, Folder 21, Box 1, DOC DPL; Denver Olympic Committee, *Olympic News*, July 1972, Folder 49, Box 1, DOC DPL.

66. Molotch, "The City as a Growth Machine," 315.

67. Itinerary for Seniors for '76, Folder 38, Box 87, DCC DPL; Seniors for '76: Total Contributions Received and Total Expenses, Folder 38, Box 87, DCC DPL. The Denver Chamber of Commerce loaned just under $12,000; see also Denver Olympic Committee, *Olympic News*, August 1972, Folder 49, Box 1, DOC DPL; Essay Contest for Children for the 1976 Olympic Winter Games in Denver (not celebrated), 1972.01.01–1972.12.31, Games of Denver IOCA.

68. "Mayor Hosts 12 Essayists," *Denver Post*, 24 September 1972, 3.

69. Wilkinson was a candidate for US senate in 1964 and, coincidentally, lost to Fred Harris.

70. Wilkinson quoted in John Ashton, "Wilkinson Heads Games Unit," *Denver Post*, 1 August 1972, 3.

71. William Marriott Jr. to John A. Love, Letter, 18 July 1972, Box 67089, JLF CSA.

72. John A. Love to William Marriott Jr., Letter, 26 July 1972, Box 67089, JLF CSA.

73. National Advisory Committee [Members], Folder 23, Box 102, WMP DPL; National Advisory Committee [Mission], Folder 23, Box 102, WMP DPL.

74. Charles Gates Jr. stressed this point; see Olson, "Power, Public Policy and the Environment," 181.

75. International Olympic Committee, Olympic Rules and Regulations, Lausanne, Switzerland, 1971, 11; pollsters found that those who wanted—or could be convinced to support—the games were also most convinced the event would be an economic benefit. Moreover, there appeared a clear correlation between supporting the Olympics and believing in the tenets of Olympism and vice versa (i.e., opposing the Olympics and disbelieving Olympism); see William R. Harrison, "A Study of Voters' Opinions toward Colorado's Hosting the 1976 Winter Olympics (Prepared For: Coloradans for the '76 Winter Games)," September 1972, 24, Folder 2, Box 103, WMP DPL.

76. Burbank, Andranovich, and Heying, *Olympic Dreams*, 160, 165.

77. Thomas Currigan, Speech, March 1972, Folder 12, Box 102, WMP DPL.

78. James B. Cotter to Robert K. Behrens, Letter, 13 May 1969, Book 2, Folder S4150, ARDOC CSA.

79. Richard Olson to Senator Harry M. Locke, Letter, 20 January 1971, Folder 10, Box 1, DOC DPL.

80. G. D. Hubbard Jr. to Members of the DOC Executive Council and Tom Currigan and Members of the Colorado Olympic Commission, 17 January 1972, Folder 29, Box 1, DOC DPL.

81. G. D. Hubbard, "Presentation to Joint Budget Committee," circa April 1972, Folder 12, Box 104, WMP DPL. In this presentation, Hubbard also did not

abandon the notion that the Olympics could "stimulate . . . Colorado's tourist economy."

82. Carl N. DeTemple to Representative Thomas T. Farley, Letter, 6 April 1972, Folder 46, Box 1, DOC DPL.

83. Olson, "Power, Public Policy and the Environment," 194–195.

84. Olson, "Power, Public Policy and the Environment," 194; Ron Wolf, "Yes, We Have No Olympics," *Straight Creek Journal*, 21 November 1972, 3.

85. Sam Lusky to John A. Love, Letter, Subject: A Pro-Olympics Campaign to Defeat the Referendum, 25 July 1972, Box 67089, JLF CSA.

86. "Colorado for the '76 Olympics Newspaper Recap," Report, 12 October 1972, Folder 7, Box 104, WMP DPL; Frye-Still Inc. Media Department, "Coloradans for the '76 Winter Games Broadcast Schedule," 13 October 1972, Folder 7, Box 104, WMP DPL.

87. Advertisement, "Governor Love: Colorado's Winter Olympics Can Bring a Return of the Olympic Ideal," *Rocky Mountain News*, 19 October 1972, 42.

88. "Mayor's Committee for the Olympics," Folder 3, Box 102, WMP DPL.

89. "Let's Team Up on Nov. 7 and Keep the Olympics in Colorado," Pamphlet, circa October–November 1972, Folder 3, Box 102, WMP DPL. See also William McNichols to Stephen King, Letter, 18 September 1972, Folder 3, Box 103, WMP DPL; William McNichols to J. T. McAdams, Letter, 18 September 1972, Folder 3, Box 103, WMP DPL; William McNichols to Grace Merz, Letter, 6 October 1972, Folder 3, Box 103, WMP DPL.

90. Carl DeTemple, Transcript, Statement Presented 9:00m. Newscast, Channel 2, 8 March 1972, Folder 21, Box 1, DOC DPL; Carl DeTemple, Transcript, KOSI Candid Comment, "Major Olympic Questions," 16 March 1972, Folder 44, Box 1, DOC DPL; Carl DeTemple, Transcript, Statement of Carl DeTemple— KWNG, 9:00m. News, 11 April 1972, Folder 44, Box 1, DOC DPL; Mark Wolf, "An Interview with DOC Head De Temple," *The Sentinel* (Lakewood, Colorado), 13 April 1972, 13; Mark Wolf, "DeTemple Responds to Olympics Critics," *The Sentinel* (Lakewood, Colorado), 20 April 1972, 17.

91. Carl DeTemple, Statement of Carl DeTemple—KWNG, 9:00m. News, 13 April 1972, Folder 44, Box 1, DOC DPL.

92. H. C. Kimbrough, "Coloradans for the 1976 Olympics," Folder 3, Box 102, WMP DPL.

93. William R. Harrison, "A Study of Voters' Opinions toward Colorado's Hosting the 1976 Winter Olympics (Prepared For: Coloradans for the '76 Winter Games)," September 1972 (quotations at pp. 4, 12–13), Folder 2, Box 103, WMP DPL.

Chapter 10: The Event Coalition and the Rights of Citizenship

1. Wamsley, "Laying Olympism to Rest" (quotations at pp. 231, 232); See also Lenskyj, *Inside the Olympic Industry*, 99–102, 131, and 148.

2. Jackson quoted in Ray Broussard, "Solon Raps Subsidizing of Olympics by State," *Gazette Telegraph* (Colorado Springs), 11 April 1971, clipping, Board of Directors Folder, Box S4130, ARDOC CSA.

3. Olson, "Power, Public Policy and the Environment," 272–274.

4. Cecil Jones and Jeff Rosen, "An Olympic Housing Gap," *Rocky Mountain News*, 20 August 1972, 4.

5. "Planners Approve Olympic Housing," *Rocky Mountain News*, 5 October 1972, 31.

6. Neighborhood Improvement Board, Westside to District 8—Geographical Area Committee of Model Cities, Memorandum, 21 July 1972, Folder 18, Box 102, WMP DPL.

7. "Minorities Launch Anti-Olympics Drive," *Denver Post*, 28 February 1972, clipping, Folder Olympics, Box 4, Rocky Mountain Center on the Environment, Denver Public Library, Denver, Colorado.

8. Garcia quoted in "West Side Residents Rap New Olympic Housing Plan," *Denver Post*, 22 June 1972, 23.

9. Jeff Rosen, "Olympic Press Housing Plan Criticized," *Rocky Mountain News*, 22 June 1972, 25.

10. Olson, "Power, Public Policy and the Environment," 184.

11. Al Knight, "Rush Hour Protest of Olympics Held," *Rocky Mountain News*, 15 March 1972, 5; "Olympic Foes Tie Up 16th Street," clipping, circa March 1972, SD1: Wish for Referendum—Citizens Opposition 1972, Press Cuttings Arranged by Subject from the 1976 Winter Games in Denver (not celebrated), Games of Denver IOCA.

12. Colorado Platform: La Raza Unida Party, Greeley, Colorado, 5 August 1972, cited in Marin, *A Spokesman of the Mexican American Movement*, 41–46 (quotation at p. 43).

13. See chapter 8.

14. Barbara Trujillo to William McNichols, Letter, 26 June 1972, Folder 18, Box 102, WMP DPL.

15. "Housing Plan OK Sought," *Denver Post*, 25 June 1972, 25.

16. Barbara Trujillo to William McNichols, Letter, 26 June 1972, Folder 18, Box 102, WMP DPL.

17. Advertisement, "Colorado's 1976 Olympics: A Statement from John Love," *Rocky Mountain News*, 5 October 1972, 51.

18. Vance Dittman to Carl DeTemple, Letter, 30 June 1972, Folder 3, Box 103, WMP DPL.

19. Charlie Myers, "Steamboat Springs OKd for Jump Site," *Denver Post*, 20 October 1972, clipping, Folder 8, Box 103, WMP DPL; Denver Olympic Committee, "Denver XII Olympic Winter Games 1976: Report [to] International Olympic Committee, Munich Germany August 1972," Report on the organization of the 1976 Olympic Winter Games in Denver (not celebrated), 1970.01.01–1972.12.31, Games of Denver IOCA; Denver Olympic Organizing Committee, Final Report, 29 December 1972; see "Luge" section, Folder 3, Box 1, DOOC SHHRC.

20. Richard Kithil to Members of Protect Our Mountain Environment, Letter, 15 September 1972, Folder 47, Box 4, POME SHHRC.

21. Vance R. Dittman, President's Annual Address, 28 August 1972, Folder 40, Box 4, POME SHHRC; Tommy Patterson, Mountain Area Planning Council Meeting Minutes, 11 September 1972, Folder 26, Box 1, MAPC JCA.

22. Tommy Patterson to MAPC Members, Letter, 15 September 1972, Folder 16, Box 1, MAPC JCA.

23. Tommy Patterson, Mountain Area Planning Council Meeting Minutes, 9 October 1972, Folder 26, Box 1, MAPC JCA.

24. Timeline, Folder 60, Box 6, POME SHHRC.

25. Vance R. Dittman Jr. to Clifford H. Buck, Letter, 8 December 1970, Folder 4, Box 4, POME SHHRC.

26. MAPC, Newsletter, circa 1970, Folder 14, Box 1, MAPC JCA; Tommy Patterson, Mountain Area Planning Council Meeting Minutes, 22 June 1970, Folder 24, Box 1, MAPC JCA; Tommy Patterson, Mountain Area Planning Council Meeting Minutes, 13 July 1970, Folder 24, Box 1, MAPC JCA; Tommy Patterson, Mountain Area Planning Council Meeting Minutes, 14 September 1970, Folder 24, Box 1, MAPC JCA; Tommy Patterson, Mountain Area Planning Council Meeting Minutes, 13 September 1971, Folder 25, Box 1, MAPC JCA.

27. Vance R. Dittman to Monique Berlioux, Letter, 24 October 1971, Folder 16, Box 2, POME SHHRC; Vance R. Dittman to Avery Brundage, Letter, 26 October 1971, Folder 16, Box 2, POME SHHRC.

28. Vance R. Dittman to Avery Brundage, Letter, 6 November 1971, Folder 16, Box 1, POME SHHRC.

29. Vance R. Dittman to Mark Brewer, Letter, 24 November 1971, Folder 17, Box 2, POME SHHRC.

30. Catherine P. Ditmann et al. ("representative citizens of Colorado") to Sion Olympic Committee, Letter, 19 October 1971, Folder 3, Box 1, POME SHHRC; Vance R. Dittman to Serge Lang, Letter, 21 October 1971, Folder 16, Box 2, POME SHHRC.

31. "Nevergreen," *Newsweek*, 14 December 1970, 94; Edith D. Decker, Vance R. Dittman Jr., "Letters: A 'Tasteful Rape,'" *Newsweek*, 4 January 1971, 5; Roger Rapoport, "Olympian Snafu at Sniktau," *Sports Illustrated*, 15 February 1971, 60–61; "What's Up DOC," *Sports Illustrated*, 20 December 1971, 11–12; "CBS to Air Olympic Opposition," clipping, n.d., Folder 65, Box 6, POME SHHRC.

32. William R. Harrison, "A Study of Voters' Opinions toward Colorado's Hosting the 1976 Winter Olympics (Prepared For: Coloradans for the '76 Winter Games)," September 1972, Folder 2, Box 103, WMP DPL.

33. Letter to the International Olympic Committee, 26 April 1971, Folder 48, Box 4, POME SHHRC; the other groups cosigning included: North Turkey Creek Associations (Pine Hills, Marschner, Chinook Chapters), Wild Rose Grange, Marshdale Homeowners Association, Evergreen Naturalists, Hill and Dale Society, Indian Hills Improvement Association, El Pinal Association, Genesee Grange, Kittredge Home-owners Association, Buffalo Park Association, V.F.W. Post 3471, Inter-Canyon Environmental Improvement Association, Crescent Park Land and Home-owners Association, Upper Bear Creek Homeowners Association. Almost identical letters were also sent to the International Skiing, Luge, Bobsled, and Biathlon Federations; see letter to International Ski Federation, n.d., Folder 16, Box 2, POME SHHRC.

34. Olson, "Power, Public Policy and the Environment," 128, 182–183. Olson notes the Colorado Open Space Council did not contribute substantially to the effort to block state funding; see 188.

35. Olson, "Power, Public Policy and the Environment," 144–145.

36. Rothman, *Devil's Bargains*, 243–251, 269–279; see 275 for consideration of the Denver Olympics.

37. Tom Carter, "Olympics Provide New Gist for Aspen's Argumentative Mill," *Aspen Today*, 5 January 1972, 3; Guido Meyer, "Don't Give Olympics Away because of a Few Nuts," *Aspen Today*, 5 January 1972, 3; "Aspen Olympics Meet: Chamber, Citizens at Odds," *Denver Post*, 19 January 1972, 24.

38. All quoted in Joan White, "Georgetown Rumblings Portend Growth," *Denver Post*, 18 July 1972, 31, 44.

39. William R. Harrison, "A Study of Voters' Opinions toward Colorado's Hosting the 1976 Winter Olympics (Prepared For: Coloradans for the '76 Winter Games)," September 1972, iii, 9, Folder 2, Box 103, WMP DPL.

40. Harrison, "A Study of Voters' Opinions."

41. Lundstrom Interview; Nussbaum Interview; Lamm Interview (2016); see also Lamm quote from in Norman Udevitz, "Small but Artful Activist Wielding Rare Power," *Denver Post*, 11 October 1972, 32–33.

42. "Who Will Be Profiting?," *The Colorado Destiny*, 2 September 1972, CCF DPL.

43. For Braden's donation, see Lamm Interviews (2016 and 2020); Brown Interview (2020); for Judy Collins, see "Where Voters Battle Over the Olympics," *Business Weekly*, 28 October 1972, 78, and Lamm Interview (2020).

44. "CCF, DOOC Map Out Counterplans to Win Vote," *The Colorado Destiny*, 2 September 1972, CCF DPL.

45. Lundstrom Interview.

46. Norman Udevitz, "Small but Artful Activist Group Wielding Rare Power," *Denver Post*, 11 October 1972, 32–33; Lamm Interview (2016 and 2020); Dwight Filley, Meg Lundstrom, and John Parr to Friend, Letter, 13 November 1972, Folder 15, Box 101, WMP DPL.

47. Ron Wolf, "Yes, We Have No Olympics," *Straight Creek Journal*, 21 November 1972, 3.

48. Dwight Filley, Meg Lundstrom, and John Parr to Friend, Letter, 2 November 1972, Folder Citizens For Colorado's Future, Box 2, RLC SHHRC; Dwight Filley, Meg Lundstrom, and John Parr, Citizens for Colorado Newsletter, 25 June 1972, Folder 50, Box 5, CCF DPL; on Brachman, see Lundstrom Interview.

49. Lundstrom Interview; Nussbaum Interview (2016).

50. Rodger P. Hansen to Colorado Olympic Commission, Memorandum Re: Referendum on Colorado Olympics Spending, 11 May 1972, Folder Colo. Olympic Commission, Box S4132, ARDOC CSA.

51. Michael Balfe Howard, "*News* Survey Indicates Heavy Support for Olympic Referendum," *Rocky Mountain News*, 13 March 1972, 1.

52. Love quoted in John Ashton, "Drive Launched For Referendum," *Denver Post*, 16 March 1972, 25; Robert Burns, "Love Calls House Olympic Referendum Date Too Late," *Rocky Mountain News*, 14 March 1972, 5, 6.

53. William McNichols to John McIntosh, Letter, 1 March 1972, Folder 6, Box 102, WMP DPL; see also William McNichols to Mrs. Alfred Crowls, Letter, 8 March 1972, Folder 6, Box 102, WMP DPL.

54. McNichols quoted in Cecile Jones, "McNichols Doubts Referendum Value," *Rocky Mountain News*, 15 March 1972, 8, 10.

55. Lundstrom Interview.

56. Olson, "Power, Public Policy and the Environment," 194.

57. Lundstrom quoted in "Group Refuses Donor Names," *Denver Post*, 21 September 1972, 3.

58. "How Much Will the 1976 Winter Olympics Cost," *The Colorado Destiny*, 2 September 1972, CCF DPL.

59. Gordon S. White Jr., "Denver Picked to Bid for '76 Winter Olympics," *New York Times*, 18 December 1967, 76; Charles Meyers, "Denver's Olympic Bid Pay Off, DOC Says," *Denver Post*, 13 December 1969, 10; "Denver Triumph a 7-Year Effort," *New York Times*, 13 May 1970, 53.

60. "Budget Panel Gets Olympic Cost View," *Denver Post*, 4 February 1971, 3.

61. "Love Confident Colo. to Hold '76 Olympics," 31 January 1972, clipping, Folder 4, Box 6, MACP JCA.

62. "1976 Olympics Will Cost $35-Million, Denver Says," *New York Times*, 12 March 1972, S5.

63. Richard O'Reilly, "$70 Million Total Help Possible: $35 million Olympic Cost Fails to Cover City Extras," *Rocky Mountain News*, 19 March 1972, 8.

64. Leonard Larson, "Total Cost of Olympics Estimated at $76.5 Million," *Denver Post*, 24 March 1972, 3; Robert Threlkeld, "Total Public Olympic Cost is $77 Million," *Rocky Mountain News*, 24 March 1972, 5; Richard Starnes, "'76 Winter Olympics—Victim of Political Alliance?," *Rocky Mountain News*, 2 April 1972, 5; Richard O'Reilly, "DOC Pegs Costs at Low of $81 Million," *Rocky Mountain News*, 4 April 1972, 16, 17.

65. William R. Harrison, "A Study of Voters' Opinions toward Colorado's Hosting the 1976 Winter Olympics (Prepared For: Coloradans for the '76 Winter Games)," September 1972, 16, Folder 2, Box 103, WMP DPL.

66. "How Much Will the 1976 Winter Olympics Cost?," *The Colorado Destiny*, 2 September 1972, CCF DPL.

67. For Love's promise, see John A. Love, Speech, Address to the Legislature Re: Olympics, 3 March 1972, Box 66951, Speeches of Governor John A. Love, JLF CSA.

68. Lundstrom Interview.

69. Brown Interview.

70. "Lobbyist Moves to Halt Name Use," *Rocky Mountain News*, 2 April 1972, 24.

71. Tom Gavin, "Someone Upstairs Likes the Olympics," *Denver Post*, 15 May 1972, 19.

72. Ron Wolf, "Who Owns the Olympics? Colorado's Financial Elite Plan 1976 Snow Job for Public," *Straight Creek Journal* (Boulder, Colorado), 24 August 1972, 3, 5–6.

73. Wolf, "Who Owns the Olympics?"

74. Raymond W. Foster to Governor John Love, Letter, 10 April 1972, Folder Olympics, Box 67608, Administrative Correspondence, JLF CSA.

75. Christine Drake to Governor John Love, Letter, circa 5 May 1972, Folder Olympics, Box 67608, Administrative Correspondence, JLF CSA.

76. Mary Freed to Governor John Love, Letter, 1 February 1972, Folder Olympics, Box 67608, Administrative Correspondence, JLF CSA.

77. Kathleen Eccles to Governor John Love, Letter, 7 February 1972, Folder Olympics, Box 67608, Administrative Correspondence, JLF CSA.

78. Fred Colcer to Governor John Love, Letter, 6 January 1972, Folder Olympics, Box 67608, Administrative Correspondence, JLF CSA.

79. Mr. and Mrs. Dan Fahrney to Governor John Love, Letter, 15 January 1972, Folder Olympics, Box 67608, Administrative Correspondence, JLF CSA.

80. Alicia M. Acord to Governor John Love, Letter, 10 April 1972, Folder Olympics, Box 67608, Administrative Correspondence, JLF CSA.

81. Lawrence Bradley, Open Letter to Governor John Love and the members of the Colorado Congressional delegation, 2 February 1972, Folder Olympics, Box 67608, Administrative Correspondence, JLF CSA.

82. For additional letters similar to those cited above, see Box 67068, JLF CSA.

83. Folder XII Winter Games–1976–Denver, Colo.–Organizing Comm. (1970–1971), File 0010, Film 110, ABC IOCA; Folder 1, Box 101, WMP DPL; Folder 24, Box 97, DCC DPL.

84. James H. Harris to William McNichols, Letter, 9 November 1972, Folder 9, Box 104, WMP DPL; John G. McFee to William McNichols, Letter, 9 November 1972, Folder 9, Box 104, WMP DPL; Laraine Thompson to William McNichols, Letter, circa November 1972, Folder 9, Box 104, WMP DPL.

85. Eldon Hayes to William McNichols, Letter, 19 December 1972, Folder 9, Box 104, WMP DPL.

86. Larry Dreiling to William McNichols, Letter, 10 November 1972, Folder 104, Box 9, WMP DPL.

87. Harry L. Arkin to United States Olympic Committee, Letter, 13 November 1972, Folder 5, Box 102, WMP DPL.

88. Richard Tucker, "Pro-Olympics Group Seeks Response," *Rocky Mountain News*, 15 December 1972, 65.

89. Norm Udevitz, "Voters Reject Funding for '76 Olympics," *Denver Post*, 8 November 1976, 1, 3.

Chapter 11: The Momentum of the Moment

1. Richard Lamm to Avery Brundage, Letter, 22 November 1971, Folder Olympics—Correspondence, Box 2, RLC SHHRC.

2. Robert Jackson and Richard Lamm to [the International Olympic Committee], Letter, 15 August 1972, Folder Olympics, Box 2, RLC SHHRC; see also Alan Cunningham, "Games Foes Send 'Surprise' Letter to IOC Members," *Rocky Mountain News*, 16 August 1972, 5, 6.

3. Jackson and Lamm to [the International Olympic Committee], Letter, 15 August 1972.

4. Olson, "Power, Public Policy and the Environment," 270–271.

5. M. R. Licht to Ben Bezoff, Memorandum, Subject State House Meeting—February 9, 1972, 10 February 1972, Folder 7, Box 102, WMP DPL.

6. Jackson quoted in Richard O'Reilly, "The Olympics and Colorado: Benefits of Olympics are Disputed, 6th of a series," *Rocky Mountain News*, 9 April 1971, 8.

7. Richard Lamm, "Open Forum: Games' Removal from State," *Denver Post*, 1 March 1972, 27.

8. Richard Lamm, "Promotional Pollution: The Case for Not Holding the 1976 Winter Olympics in Colorado," speech transcript, 12 February 1972, Folder 2, CCF DPL.

9. "Colorado Sold Enough; Lamm Asks for Repeal," *The Colorado Democrat*, 8 January 1972, 1.

10. Lamm quoted in "Winter of '76 Colorado Olympic Picture," *Denver Post*, 25 September 1972, 1, 3, 7.

11. Mary Crabbe to Governor John Love, Letter, 15 May 1972, Folder Olympics, Box 67068, Administrative Correspondence, JLF CSA.

12. Richard R. Gordon to Governor John Love, Letter, 15 March 1972, Folder Olympics, Box 67068, Administrative Correspondence, JLF CSA.

13. Mr. & Mrs. Fred Douglas to Governor John Love, Letter, 8 February 1972, Folder Olympics, Box 67068, Administrative Correspondence, JLF CSA.

14. Stanley F. Perkins to Governor John A. Love, Letter, circa January 1972, Folder Olympics, Box 67068, Administrative Correspondence, JLF CSA.

15. Richard J. Heidler to Governor John Love, Letter, 2 March 1972, Folder Olympics, Box 67068, Administrative Correspondence, JLF CSA.

16. Theo M. Fenlon to Governor John Love, Letter, 19 June 1972, Folder Olympics, Box 67068, Administrative Correspondence, JLF CSA.

17. Clarice M. Crowle to Governor John Love, Letter, 25 February 1972, Folder 6, Box 102, WMP DPL.

18. W. W. Brockne to Governor John Love, Letter, 27 March 1972, Folder Olympics, Box 67068, Administrative Correspondence, JLF CSA.

19. Mrs. Robert Owen to Richard Lamm, Letter, n.d., Folder Correspondence to Committee, Box 2, RLC SHHRC.

20. Mrs. H. R. Haskett to Richard Lamm, Letter, 15 January 1971, Folder Correspondence to Committee, Box 2, RLC SHHRC.

21. Robert Whittaker to Richard Lamm, Letter, 12 February 1972, Folder Correspondence to Committee, Box 2, RLC SHHRC.

22. Gary O. Curtin to Governor John Love, Letter, 18 February 1972, Folder Olympics, Box 67068, Administrative Correspondence, JLF CSA.

23. Meg to Dick, John, Bob, Harris, Margie, Maria, Sam, and Jim, Memorandum, Subject: Decisions of May 25th Meeting, circa 1973, 1st Race for Gov., Folder Internal, Box 1210, RLC SHHRC.

24. John and Jeanne Canny, Richard and Jinner Kithil, and Richard and Margot to Friend, Letter, 11 February 1974, Folder Funding Memos, Box 26, RLC SHHRC; see also Catherine P. Dittman to Robert Jackson, Letter, 18 January 1971, Folder Correspondence to Committee, Box 3, RLC SHHRC; Catherine P. Dittman to John A. Love, Letter, 13 January 1970, Folder Olympics, Box 2, RLC SHHRC.

25. Lamm Interview (2016); Robert Jackson also considered a run for governor; see Tom Gavin, "Bob Jackson Looking Higher," *Denver Post*, clipping, Folder 49, Box 5, POME SHHRC.

26. Lamm Interview (2016); Jim Monaghan, the architect of Alan Merson's primary upset of Wayne Aspinall, joined them too; see Aldo Svaldi and Karen Crummy, "Jim Monaghan, Political Guru, Anschutz Confidant, Dead at 66," *Denver Post*, 15 May 2013, www.denverpost.com/2013/05/15/jim-monaghan-political-guru-anschutz-confidant-dead-at-66. For Merson's upset of Aspinall, see below.

27. Lundstrom Interview.

28. Nussbaum Interview (2016).

29. Nussbaum Interview (2020).

30. Lamm quoted in "Wyoming Crash Kills Three," *Denver Post*, 23 December 2007, www.denverpost.com/2007/12/23/wyoming-crash-kills-three.

31. Richard Lamm, "Announcement Speech," 1 October 1973, Folder First Campaign for Governor, Box 19, RLC SHHRC; Richard Lamm, "Speech to the Colorado Labor Council," 8 September 1973, Folder Colorado Labor Council, Box 3, RLC SHH; Richard Lamm, "Colorado Should Seek Balance, Not Growth," circa 1973, Folder Colo. Growth, Box 3, RLC SHHRC; Richard Lamm, "A Need for A Land Use Bill," *Rocky Mountain News*, 19 August 1973, clipping, Folder July–August 1974, Box 24, RLC SHHRC; see also Folder July–August 1974, Box 24, RLC SHHRC.

32. Richard D. Lamm, "Summary of Legislative Record," circa 1973, Folder Miscellaneous, Box 19, RLC SHHRC.

33. Campaign letter, 25 April 1974, Binder July–August 1974, Box 2, RLC SHHRC.

34. Vanderhoof quoted in "Games Vote Shows Priorities: Vanderhoof," *Rocky Mountain News*, 6 January 1973, 11; John G. White, "Land Use Warning Issued," *Denver Post*, 7 January 1973.

35. Olson, "Power, Public Policy and the Environment," 285.

36. Childers, *Colorado Powder Keg*, 108, 111.

37. John Vanderhoof, Interviewed by David McComb, OHR SHHRC. See also differences between vote percentages by county at https://uselectionatlas.org/RESULTS.

38. Lamm Interview (2020); in 1974, Democrat Gary Hart also defeated Republican senator and Olympic Supporter Peter Dominick.

39. "1972 Open Space Resolution," www.planjeffco.org/about-us_our-history.html.

40. Protect Our Mountain Environment, Motion by Hugh Dewigh, 20 April 1972, Folder 40, Box 4, POME SHHRC.

41. Plan Jeffco Citizens Organization, "Vote for the Open Space Land Proposals," Pamphlet, Folder 10, Box 1, POME SHHRC.

42. Vance R. Dittman Jr. to Jefferson County Planning Commission, Letter, 26 July 1971, Folder 40, Box 4, POME SHHRC.

43. "Resolution Before the Board of County Commissioners of the County of Jefferson State of Colorado: Moratorium and P.O.M.E," 15 December 1971, Folder 11, Box 1, POME SHHRC; William S. Willson to Jefferson County Board of Commissioners, Letter, 4 October 1971, Folder 25, Box 1, MAPC JCA; clipping, Folder 7, Box 8, MAPC SHHRC; John Toohey, "Year Long Moratorium Urged," *Denver Post (Zone 3)*, 7 April 1971, 3.

44. Quotations from POME Bulletin No. 5, "Protect Our Mountain Environment," published in the *Canyon Courier* (Evergreen), 17 September 1970, Folder 53, Box 5, POME SHHRC; see also POME's Local Activities, Folder 6, Box 4, POME SHHRC. For a more comprehensive listing of POME's environmentalist engagements, see POME, First Annual Membership Meeting, 10 August 1971, Folder 4, Box 4, POME SHHRC.

45. "Anti-Olympic Action 'Pluses' Listed," *Denver Post*, 22 January 1971, 4.

46. Fred Brown, "Senate Veteran Allott Upset by Haskell," *Denver Post*, 8 November 1972, 77; Leonard Larson, "Haskell Gets Campaign Tip," *Denver Post*, 29 September 1972, 9; Robert Threlkeld, "Haskell in Washington to Seek Funds," *Rocky Mountains News*, 30 September 1972, 5.

47. Schulte, *Wayne Aspinall and the Shaping of the American West* (Aspinall quotations at pp. 2–3); see also 268–278.

48. Ernest B. Furgurson, "Congress Wary of Aspinall Defeat," *Rocky Mountain News*, 19 September 1972, 33.

49. Childers, *Colorado Powder Keg* (see p. 105 for the land-use bills). House Bill 1034, or "The Local Government Land Use Control Enabling Act," regulated land use to ensure adequate environmental protection. House Bill 1041, or "the Areas and Activities of State Interest Act," sought to broaden local and state oversight over land-use development, considered a "matter of public interest," including mineral resource areas, historical, natural, or archaeological resources, and key facilities where development may have material effect. Together the bills placed greater control of growth and development in county governments. Notably, the bills often backfired, as rural county governments still tended to support development.

50. Childers, *Colorado Powder Keg*, 101.

51. Logan and Molotch, *Urban Fortunes*, 191–192.

52. "Haskell: Olympic Decision Should be County Wide," *Lamar Tri State Daily*, 5 September 1972, clipping, Binder Clippings other than DP [*Denver Post*] and RMN [*Rocky Mountain News*], Box 24, RLC SHHRC.

53. Childers, *Colorado Powder Keg*, 101.

54. Judd, "From Cowtown to Sunbelt City," 190–194.

55. Judd, "From Cowtown to Sunbelt City," 190–194.

56. Judd, "From Cowtown to Sunbelt City," 190–194.

57. Philpott, *Vacationland*, 286–287.

58. Jackson, *Crabgrass Frontier*, 242; see also Philpott, *Vacationland*, 286–287.

59. Leonard and Noel, *Denver*, 312–319 (quotation at p. 312).

60. Philpott, *Vacationland*, 275–297 (quotation at pp. 281 and 280). Other factors that weakened the environmental movement included the oil crisis and recession of 1973–1975 and a backlash from the New Right, which viewed environmentalists as enemies of free enterprise, private property, and thus American ideals.

61. Lamm Interview (2016).

62. Stone, *Regime Politics*, 63. Peter Garcia held this view; see Olson, "Power, Public Policy and the Environment," 269.

64. Mollenkopf, *The Contested City*, 197.

65. Page and Ross, "Legacies of a Contested Campus," 1293–1328 (quotation at pp. 1311–1312).

66. Gould, *The Life and Times of Richard Castro*, 44.

67. John Morehead, "Housing Project Still On," *Denver Post*, 9 November 1972, 3.

68. Mollenkopf, *The Contest City*, 209.

69. "McNichols Hopes to Keep HUD Funds," *Rocky Mountain News*, 18 January 1973, 6.

70. McEncroe, *Denver Renewed*, 630–631.

71. Caldwell quoted in McEncroe, *Denver Renewed*, 646–647 (for a broader set of controversies surrounding this development, see pp. 633–660); see also Tom Morris, "The Destruction of a Place Called the Neighborhood," *Rocky Mountain News*, 9 July 1978, 2, 4; T. R. Witcher, "This Old Housing Project," *Westword*, 31 August 2000, www.westword.com/news/this-old-housing-project-5064130.

72. Olson, "Power, Public Policy and the Environment," 294.

73. McEncroe, *Denver Renewed*, 661–668.

74. Jeff Rosen, "Denver Cut from Urban Renewal Plan," *Rocky Mountain News*, 6 June 1973, 10, 11.

75. Judd, "From Cowtown to Sunbelt City," 181–182.

76. Richard Gould, *The Life and Times of Richard Castro*, 147–171; Leonard and Noel, 403–404.

77. Navarro, *La Raza Unida Party*, 99–100; Gould, *The Life and Times of Richard Castro*, 105–145; Leonard and Noel, *Denver*, 386–387.

78. Gould, *The Life and Times of Richard Castro*, 105–145.

79. Judd, "From Cowtown to Sunbelt City," 198.

80. Judd, "From Cowtown to Sunbelt City," 195–197.

81. Lamm and Imhoff, *The Immigration Time Bomb*.

82. Infamously, Lamm also proposed that terminally ill and suffering Americans had a "duty to die" to limit health care costs and ensure a well-functioning economy; see "Gov. Lamm Asserts Elderly, If Very Ill, Have 'Duty to Die,'" *New York Times*, 29 March 1984, 16; his focus on immigration and Americanization also lasted into recent years; see "Gov. Richard Lamm: My Plan to Destroy America," *Washington Examiner*, 20 April 2006, www.washingtonexaminer.com /gov-richard-lamm-my-plan-to-destroy-america-35408; https://khow.iheart.com /content/2019-03-22-former-co-gov-dick-lamm-on-politics-now-and-then -and-on-multiculturalism; "Richard Lamm on Immigration," www.youtube .com/watch?v=Yd8N-sjwMx4; "Keynote Speaker: Richard Lamm," www.youtube .com/watch?v=gg0J1DvM8Es.

83. Gould, *The Life and Times of Richard Castro*, 154–190.

84. Judd, "From Cowtown to Sunbelt City," 167–201; Leonard and Noel, *Denver*, 407–423; Abbott, Leonard, and Noel, *Colorado*, 397–420; Murray, "Denver."

85. Abbot, Leonard, and Noel, *Colorado*, 402–405.

86. Rothman, *Devil's Bargains* (for the incorporation of the ski industry, see pp. 252–286; for the incorporation of tourism and the rise of "entertainment tourism," see 287–312).

87. Dorsett and McCarthy, *The Queen City*, 327–238.

88. Judd, "From Cowtown to Sunbelt City," 177; see also Leonard and Noel, *Denver*, 274.

89. Cowie, *Stayin' Alive*, chapter 3 (see pp. 128–129 for Nixon's committee and response to the Moratorium; see p. 144 for Nixon's focus on appearances rather than policy).

90. Cowie, *The Great Exception*.

91. Lamm Interview (2016).

92. Lamm quoted in John Sanko, "Colorado Only State Ever to Turn Down Olympics," *Rocky Mountain News Capital Bureau*, http://co-mmc.civicplus.com /Files/AgendaCenter/Items/30/Colorado%20only%20state%20ever%20to%20 turn%20down%20Olympics_201205071617158193.pdf; see also "Colorado the Only State to Turn Down Winter Olympics After Winning Bid," *Games Monitor*, 20 January 2008, www.gamesmonitor.org.uk/node/546.

93. Lamm quoted in https://khow.iheart.com/content/2019-03-22-former-co-gov -dick-lamm-on-politics-now-and-then-and-on-multiculturalism.

94. Grace Lichtenstein, "Colorado Bankers Shaken by Ex-Antiwar Organizer," *New York Times*, 4 May 1975, 72; Brown Interview (2016).
95. Brown Interview (2020).
96. Brown Interview (2020). Under Clinton, Brown acted as the United States ambassador to the Organization of Security and Cooperation in Europe, which addressed issues of arms control, human rights, and freedom of the press. Later, under President Barack Obama, he worked as the director of the Fulbright Scholarship Board, overseeing grants for research and teaching.
97. Brown Interview (2020).
98. Brown Interview (2020).
99. Thomas Piketty concludes that "growth can harm some while benefiting others," in Piketty, *Capital in the Twenty-First Century*, 16; see also Logan and Molotch, *Urban Fortunes*, 34, 290; Stone, *Regime Politics*, 201.
100. Dinces, *Bulls Markets*; Lipsitz, "Sports Stadia and Urban Development"; Zimbalist, ed., *Sports, Jobs, and Taxes*; Rosentraub, *Major League Losers*; Coats and Humphreys, "The Growth Effects of Sport Franchises, Stadia, and Arenas"; Coats and Humphreys, "Do Economists Reach a Conclusion on Subsidies for Sports Franchises, Stadiums, and Mega-events"; for evidence of tourism's contribution to such outcomes, see Rothman, *Devil's Bargains*; Anzalone, *Battles of the North Country*; Eisinger, "The Politics of Bread and Circuses"; Judd, "Constructing the Tourist Bubble."
101. This aligns with Eisinger's work on subsidized projects geared toward entertainment and tourism in general; see Eisinger, "The Politics of Bread and Circuses," 328.

Epilogue

1. Richard Lamm to Bob Ronka, Letter, 11 November 1977, Folder Olympics LA 1977, Box 2, RLC SHHC; Bob Ronka to Richard Lamm, Letter, 16 November 1977, Folder Olympics LA 1977, Box 2, RLC SHHRC.
2. "Ronka Seeks Olympic Vote by Angelenos," *Los Angeles Herald Examiner*, 14 November 1977, 2; Joyce Peterson, "Ronka Tells Olympics Concern," *Valley News and Green Sheet*, 15 November 1977, 6.
3. Jean Drapeau quoted in "The 40-Year Hangover: How the 1976 Olympics Nearly Broke Montreal," *The Guardian*, 6 July 2016, www.theguardian.com.
4. 75th International Olympic Committee Session, 21–24 October 1974, International Olympic Committee Sessions, Sessions IOCA.
5. Kenneth Reich, "Drive to Place Olympics Issue on Ballot Gains," *Los Angeles Times*, 15 November 1977, 1, 30, 31; Kenneth Reich, "Olympics Cost Measure Due for Ballot," *Los Angeles Times*, 22 February 1978, 1, 5; Wilson, "Los Angeles"; Dyreson and Llewellyn, "Los Angeles Is the Olympic City"; Llewellyn, Gleaves, and Wilson, "The Historical Legacy of the 1984 Los Angeles Games."
6. Reich, *Making It Happen* (see p. 24 for Bradley refusing to take on financial liability).
7. Bob Ronka to Richard Lamm, Letter, 19 October 1978, Folder Olympics LA 1977, Box 2, RLC SHHRC.

8. Kenneth Reich and Bill Boyarsky, "IOC Approves L.A. Bid of '84 Olympics," *Los Angeles Times*, 10 October 1978, 1, 22. For a more critical appraisal of the 1984 Los Angeles Olympics, see Boykoff, *NOlympians*, 56–66.

9. Leonard and Thomas, *Denver*, 411–416, 423–425; Murray, "Denver: City Profile."

10. "Tribute to John Parr," *National Civic Review* (Summer 2008), 10; Federico Peña Interview, 5 October 2018, www.historycolorado.org/story/collections-library/2018/10/05/federico-pena-his-own-words.

11. Peña quoted in "Tribute to John Parr," *National Civic Review* (Summer 2008), 10; see also Federico Peña, Interview, 5 October 2018, www.historycolorado.org/story/collections-library/2018/10/05/federico-pena-his-own-words.

12. Nussbaum Interview (2016).

13. Dorsett and McCarthy, *The Queen City*, 305–322 (quotation at p. 305).

14. Clarke and Saiz, "From Waterhole to World City" (quotations at pp. 170, 168, and 194); see also Muñoz Jr. and Henry, "Rainbow Coalitions in Four Big Cities," 607.

15. Clarke and Saiz, "From Waterhole to World City" (quotations at pp. 168 and 194); see also Muñoz Jr. and Henry, "Rainbow Coalitions in Four Big Cities," 607.

16. Long, *Public/Private Partnerships for Major League Sports Facilities*, 35; Rosentraub, *Major League Losers*, 47.

17. Sage, "Stealing Home."

18. Sage, "Stealing Home." Initially, citizens were told they would pay only 50 percent at cost of $100 million; see Clarke and Saiz, "From Waterhole to World City," 183.

19. Rosentraub, *Major League Losers*, 46. Rosentraub claims the creation of the Stadium District weakened the position of groups likely to oppose the stadium deal. The sales tax would hinder poorer residents, given their need to spend a more significant portion of their income to get by. At the same time, well-off Coloradans were more likely to save their money than spend it. In turn, wealthier voters living outside the city were more likely to favor public funding through the sale tax mechanism.

20. Eisinger, "The Politics of Bread and Circuses," 324–325.

21. Sage, "Stealing Home"; Rosentraub, *Major League Losers*, 46–49; Eisinger, "The Politics of Bread and Circuses," 326.

22. Sage, "Stealing Home"; Rosentraub, *Major League Losers*, 46–49; the deal was later adjusted to allow the Rockies to build a larger stadium. In the renegotiation, the Stadium District gained concessions, including 20 percent of game-day parking revenue; see Delaney and Eckstein, *Public Dollars, Private Stadiums*, 112. Meanwhile, the overall cost with interest reached $231 million. The public contributed $215 million by 1997; see Clarke and Saiz, "From Waterhole to World City," 199 (note 53) and 187.

23. Delaney and Eckstein, *Public Dollars, Private Stadiums*, 109.

24. Dinces, *Bulls Markets*; for the "New Gilded Age," see Cowie, *Stayin' Alive*, esp. 71.

25. Burbank, Andranovich, and Heying, *Olympic Dreams*, esp. 14–20.

26. Harvey, *A Brief History of Neoliberalism*, 164–165; Piketty, *Capital in the Twenty-First Century*, 294–296.

27. Eisinger, "The Politics of Bread and Circuses," 319.

28. Dinces, *Bulls Markets*; see also Long, *Public/Private Partnerships for Major League Sports Facilities*, 88.

29. US General Accounting Office, *Olympic Games.*

30. Delaney and Eckstein, *Public Dollars, Private Stadiums,* 114.

31. *Denver Comprehensive Plan 2000: A Vision for Denver and Its People,* 7, www
.denvergov.org/content/dam/denvergov/Portals/646/documents/planning
/comprehensiveplan2000/CompPlan2000.pdf; Aldo Svaldi, "Not So Full Employment," *Denver Post,* 25 October 2015, 1A, 18A; Michael Roberts, "Denver's
Home Affordability Is Second Worst in USA," *Westword,* 3 July 2018, www.west
word.com/news/denvers-home-affordability-is-second-worst-in-usa-10449670.
See also Aldo Svaldi, "Housing in Denver is 'Seriously Unaffordable,' Among
Worst in Nation Study Finds," *Denver Post,* 12 December 2017, www.denverpost
.com/2017/12/12/denver-housing-affordability-among-worst-in-nation
-point2homes; Joe Rubino, " 'Gentrification Moves Fast': A Hard Look at Economic Displacement in Denver's Most Historic Black Neighborhood," *Denver
Post,* 15 December 2017, www.denverpost.com/2017/12/15/denver-five-points
-gentrification. For another example where growth seems to have backfired in
Denver, see Shaw, *Generation Priced Out,* 125–126; Bardaka, Delgado, and Florax, "Causal Identification of Transit-Induced Gentrification and Spatial Spillover Effects," 15–31.

32. Chungmie Lee, *Denver Public Schools.*

33. Delaney and Eckstein, *Public Dollars, Private Stadiums,* 115–117.

34. Geoffrey A. Fowler and Stacy Meichtry, "China Counts the Cost of Hosting the Olympics," *Wall Street Journal,* 16 July 2008, www.wsj.com/articles
/SB121614671139755287; "Olympic Challenge: How Do Host Cities Fair After
the Games?," *CBS News,* 24 February 2014, www.cbsnews.com/news/olympic
-challenge-how-do-host-cities-fare-after-the-games.

35. Betti Fong, "B.C. Taxpayers Olympic Cost: $925 million," *Toronto Star,* 9 July
2010, www.thestar.com/sports/olympics/2010/07/09/bc_taxpayers_olympic_cost
_925_million.html.

36. Zimbalist, *Circus Maximus,* 47, 114–125.

37. James Gaines, "Putin's $51 Billion Sochi Plan Blew Up in His Face," *Business In-
sider,* 5 February 2015, www.businessinsider.com/putin-51-billion-dollar-sochi
-olympics-2015-2.

38. Burbank, Andranovich, and Heying, *Olympic Dreams* (for Los Angeles '84, see
pp. 66–73; for Atlanta '96, 101–116; for Salt Lake City '02, 140–147; for a com-
parative analysis, 165). One exception came from Utah, where pressure from
affordable housing advocates forced the city's mayor to withdraw a plan to locate
a new speed skating oval downtown.

39. Dempsey and Zimbalist, *No Boston Olympics*; "Voters Deliver Resounding No to
Munich 2022 Winter Olympics Bid," www.dw.com/en/voters-deliver-resounding
-no-to-munich-2022-winter-olympics-bid/a-17217461; "Stockholm Drops Its Bid
to Host the 2022 Winter Games," www.bbc.com/sport/winter-olympics/25783574;
"Krakow Withdraws 2022 Olympic Bid after Residents Vote 'No,' " www
.washingtonpost.com/news/early-lead/wp/2014/05/27/krakow-withdraws-2022
-olympic-bid-after-residents-vote-no; "Oslo's 2022 Olympic Winter Games and
Delusions of Grandeur," www.norwegianamerican.com/featured/oslos-2022
-olympic-winter-games-and-delusions-of-grandeur; "2024 Olympics: Hamburg
says 'No' to Hosting Games," www.bbc.com/news/world-europe-34960208;

"Italy Withdraws Role [in] 2024 Olympic Games Bid," www.bbc.com/news/world-europe-37624948; Marton Dunau, "Budapest Withdraws Bid to Host 2024 Olympic Games," www.reuters.com/article/us-olympics-2024-budapest-idUSKBN16842G; "Innsbruck Won't Bid for 2026 Winter Games After Referendum," www.usatoday.com/story/sports/olympics/2017/10/15/tyrol-residents-reject-innsbrucks-2026-olympics-bid/106689616; Jamie Strashin, "Why Calgary Passed on the 2026 Olympics—And What's Next for the Games Nobody Seems to Want," CBC Sports, 14 November 2018, www.cbc.ca/sports/olympics/calgary-2026-plebiscite-jamie-strashin-1.4904585.

40. Peña actually considered bids on multiple occasions; see Charlie Myers, "Peña Backing Sought for '92 Olympic Bid," 7 April 1985, *Denver Post*, A1, A16; Joni H. Blackman, "City Will Consider Bid for '96," *Denver Post*, 10 April 1985, clipping, Olympic Clippings, DPL; William Schmidt, "Colorado Spurns Olympics No More," *New York Times*, 23 April 1989, 18.

41. Andrew Blevins, "U.S. Olympic Committee Passes on 2022 Bid, Stalling Colorado Effort," *Denver Post*, 3 July 2012, www.denverpost.com/2012/07/03/u-s-olympic-committee-passes-on-2022-bid-stalling-colorado-effort.

42. John Murray, "Colorado Group Seeks Lessons from Rio for Potential Olympics Bid," *Denver Post*, 22 June 2016, www.denverpost.com/2016/06/22/colorado-group-seeks-lessons-from-rio-for-potential-olympics-bid.

43. Patricia Calhoun, "Let Denver Vote Makes the Denver Ballot . . . Just Not in May," *Westword*, 5 February 2019, ww.westword.com/news/denver-voters-will-have-say-in-future-olympics-bid-11216628.

44. Patricia Calhoun, "Game Over: Initiative Passes," *Westword*, 4 June 2019, www.westword.com/news/denver-approves-measure-requiring-vote-for-any-olympic-subsidy-11366950; John Aguilar, "Denver Prop 302: Measure Requiring Voter Approval Before City Spends on Olympic Bids," *Denver Post*, 4 June 2019, www.denverpost.com/2019/06/04/denver-olympics-funding-election.

45. Anne Vogelphole and Sybille Bauriedl, "Hamburg's Bid for the 2024 Games: Political Misconceptions of Citizens' Concerns," *Play the Game*, 24 October 2018, www.playthegame.org/news/comments/2018/074_hamburgs-bid-for-the-2024-games-political-misconceptions-of-citizens-concerns.

46. Dempsey and Zimbalist, *No Boston Olympics*, 163–165.

47. David Wharton, "Estimated Cost of 2028 Los Angeles Olympics Jumps to $6.9 billion," *Los Angeles Times*, 30 April 2019, www.latimes.com/sports/la-sp-la-2028-olympics-budget-20190429-story.html.

48. "NOlympics LA and the Road to 2028: A Platform for Changing the Conversation and Winning," https://nolympicsla.com/platform. For more on the Los Angeles protesters, especially their *differences* to previous anti-Olympics activists, see Boykoff, *NOlympians*.

Bibliography

Primary Sources

Archival Collections

Colorado State Archives (CSA), Denver, Colorado

Administrative Records of the Denver Organizing Committee (ARDOC CSA)
John Love Files (JLF CSA)

Denver Public Library (DPL), Western History Collection, Denver, Colorado

Citizens for Colorado's Future, C MSS – M881 (CCF DPL)
Colorado Environmental Coalition Records, CONS137 (CECR DPL)
Denver Chamber of Commerce, WH1216 (DCC DPL)
Denver Organizing Committee for the 1976 Winter Olympics Records, WH1143 (DOC
    DPL)
Denver Urban Renewal Authority, WH914 (DURA DPL)
George Cranmer Collection, WH479 (GCC DPL)
John Love Papers, WH1084 (JLP DPL)
John Parr Papers, WH2033 (JPP DPL)
Olympic Clippings (Olympic Clippings DPL)
Paul Hauk Papers, C MSS WH1304 (PHP DPL)
Rodolfo Gonzales Collection, WH1971 (RGC DPL)
Ski Country USA Records, WH1045 (SCUSA DPL)
William McNichols Papers, WH1015 (WMP DPL)

Jefferson County Archives (JCA), Golden, Colorado

Mountain Area Protection Council Records (MAPC JCA)

*International Olympic Committee Archives (IOCA), Olympic Studies Center,
Lausanne, Switzerland*

1976 Olympic Winter Games of Denver (not celebrated) (Games of Denver IOCA)
Avery Brundage Collection (ABC IOCA)

Candidatures of Cities (CC IOCA)
International Olympic Committee Executive Board (EB IOCA)
International Olympic Committee Sessions (Sessions IOCA)
President Brundage (PB IOCA)
President Killanin (PK IOCA)

Stephen H. Hart Research Center (SHHRC), History Colorado Center, Denver, Colorado

Denver Olympic Organizing Committee Collection (DOOC SHHRC)
Protect Our Mountain Environment (POME SHHRC)
Richard Lamm Collection (RLC SHHRC)

Bid Books

Colorado Springs–Aspen Invitation Winter Olympic Games, 28 November 1954
Denver, Colorado, USA, 1976, XII Olympic Winter Games (1967)
Denver Organizing Committee, Book One, Denver: The City, Denver: United States
 Candidate for the XII Winter Olympic Games, 1976 (1970)
Denver Organizing Committee, Book Two, Denver: Technical Information, Denver:
 United States Candidate for the XII Winter Olympic Games, 1976 (May 1970)

Legal Documents

Colorado General Assembly, *H.J. Res. 1032, 46th General Assembly, 1st Session, 1967*
Colorado General Assembly, *S.B. 179, 46th General Assembly, 1st Session, 1967*
Colorado General Assembly, *H.B. 1156, 48th General Assembly 1st Session, 1971*
Colorado General Assembly, *Senate Joint Resolution No. 9, 27, 48 General Assembly 1st
 Session, January 1971*
Keyes v. Denver School District No. I, 413 U.S. 189 (1973)

Oral Histories and Interviews

Brown, Sam W. "Vietnam: A Television History; Interview with Sam Brown, 1982."
 08/11/1982 [August 11]. Video recording at WGBH Media Library & Archives.
 http://openvault.wgbh.org/catalog/V_A55BE9295E024182AD926622157A9791.
Brown, Sam W. Telephone interview with author. 11 April 2016. Recording in author's
 possession.
Brown, Sam W. Telephone interviews with author. 24 and 25 June 2020. Recordings in
 author's possession.
Filley, Dwight. Telephone interview with author. 21 May 2016. Recording in author's
 possession.
Gelt, Howard. Telephone interview with author. 21 May 2016. Recording in author's
 possession.
Lamm, Richard. Telephone interview with author. 9 May 2016. Recording in author's
 possession.
Lamm, Richard. Telephone interview with author. 22 June 2020. Recording in author's
 possession.
Love, John A. Interview with David McComb. Ideal Basic Industries, Denver,

Colorado. 20 March 1974. Transcript at Oral History Reports, Stephen H. Hart Center, Denver, Colorado

Lundstrom, Meg. Telephone interview with author. 30 March 2016 and 19 May 2016. Recording in author's possession.

Nussbaum, Tom. Telephone interview with author. 6 April 2016. Recording in author's possession.

Nussbaum, Tom. Telephone interview with author. 18 June 2020. Recording in author's possession.

O'Reilly, Richard. Interview with author. Author's home, Pasadena, California. 1 June 2016. Recording in author's possession.

Tutt, William Thayer. Interviewed with David McComb. Broadmoor Hotel, Colorado Springs, Colorado. 12 June 1975. Transcript at Oral History Reports, Stephen H. Hart Center, Denver, Colorado.

Vanderhoof, John. Interview with David McComb. Denver Chamber of Commerce Building, Denver, Colorado. 19 June 1975. Transcript at Oral History Reports, Stephen H. Hart Center, Denver, Colorado.

Newspapers and Magazines

Aspen Times
Aspen Today
Capital Ledger (Denver, CO)
Chicago Tribune
Colorado Democrat
Colorado Magazine
Colorado: Rocky Mountain West
Dear Earth (Denver, CO)
Denver Post
Gazette Telegraph (Colorado Springs, CO)
Los Angeles Herald Examiner
Los Angeles Times
National Civic Review
New Republic
New York Times
Reuters
Rocky Mountain News
The Sentinel (Lakewood, CO)
Skiing
Sports Illustrated
Straight Creek Journal (Boulder, CO)
Valley News and Green Sheet
Washington Monthly
West Side Recorder

Websites

ballotpedia.org

bbc.com
businessinsider.com
cbc.ca
cbsnews.com
census.gov
coloradosports.org
deadspin.com
denverpost.com
gamesmonitor.org.uk
historycolorado.org
latimes.com
legacy.com
money.cnn.com
nolympicsla.com
nytimes.com
pbs.org
planjeffco.org
playthegame.org
postindependent.com
qz.com
reuters.com
skihall.com
skimuseum.net
theguardian.com
thestare.com
uselectionatlas.org
usinflationcalculator.com
westword.com
wjs.com
youtube.com

Secondary Sources

Abbot, Carl. *New Urban America: Growth and the Politics of the Sunbelt.* Chapel Hill: University of North Carolina Press, 1981.

Abbott, Carl, Stephen J. Leonard, and Thomas J. Noel. *Colorado: A History of the Centennial State.* 4th ed. Boulder: University Press of Colorado, 2005.

Allen, Gerald L. "Colorado Ski and Winter Recreation Statistics." Manuscript, Business Research Division, Graduate School Administration, University of Colorado at Boulder, 1969.

Anderson, Terry H. *The Movement and the Sixties.* New York: Oxford University Press, 1996.

Andrews, Thomas G. *Killing for Coal: America's Deadliest Labor War.* Cambridge, MA: Harvard University Press, 2008.

Anzalone, Johnathan D. *Battles of the North Country: Wilderness Politics and Recreational Development in the Adirondack State Park, 1920–1980.* Amherst: University of Massachusetts Press, 2018.

Ashwell, Tim. "Squaw Valley." In *Encyclopedia of the Modern Olympic Movement*, edited by John E. Findling and Kimberly D. Pelle, 337–344. Westport, CT: Greenwood, 2004.

Avila, Eric. *Popular Culture in the Age of White Flight: Fear and Fantasy in Suburban Los Angeles*. Berkeley: University of California Press, 2004.

Banfield, Edward C. *The Unheavenly City: The Nature and Future of Our Urban Crisis*. Boston: Little, Brown, 1970.

Bardaka, Eleni, Michael S. Delgado, and Raymond J. G. M. Florax. "Causal Identification of Transit-Induced Gentrification and Spatial Spillover Effects: The Case of the Denver Light Rail." *Journal of Transport Geography* 71 (2018): 15–31.

Barnett, C. Robert. "St. Louis 1904." In *Encyclopedia of the Modern Olympic Movement*, edited by John E. Findling and Kimberly D. Pelle, 33–40. Westport, CT: Greenwood, 2004.

Barney, Robert, Stephen Wenn, and Scott G. Martin. *Selling the Five Rings: The International Olympic Committee and the Rise of Olympic Commercialism*. Salt Lake City: University of Utah Press, 2002.

Barth, Gunther Paul. *Instant Cities: Urbanization and the Rise of San Francisco and Denver*. New York: Oxford University Press, 1975.

Bartiz, Loren. *The Good Life: The Meaning of Success for the American Middle Class*. New York: Harper and Row, 1990.

Booth, Douglas. "Gifts of Corruption? Ambiguities of Obligation in the Olympic Movement." *Olympika* 8 (1999): 43–68.

Bourdieu, Pierre. "The Forms of Capital." In *Handbook of Theory and Research for the Sociology of Education*, edited by J. Richardson, 241–258. New York: Greenwood, 1986.

Boykoff, Jules. *Activism and the Olympics: Dissent at the Games in Vancouver and London*. New Brunswick, NJ: Rutgers University Press, 2014.

———. *NOlympians: Inside the Fight against Capitalist Mega-Sports in Los Angeles, Tokyo, and Beyond*. Halifax, NS: Fernwood Publishing, 2020.

———. *Power Games: A Political History of the Olympics*. New York: Verso, 2016.

"The Broadmoor Colorado Springs: The Broadmoor's Past Is Legacy of Fame and Countless Memories." *Rangelands* 15, no. 5 (October 1993): 211–212.

Brown, Jen Corinne. *Trout Culture: How Fly Fishing Forever Changed the Rocky Mountain West*. Seattle: University of Washington Press, 2015.

Brown, Sam W. *Storefront Organizing: A Mornin' Glories' Manual*. New York: Pyramid Books, 1972.

Burbank, Matthew J., Gregory D. Andranovich, and Charles H. Heying. *Olympic Dreams: The Impact of Mega-Events on Local Politics*. Boulder: Lynne Rienner, 2001.

Burbank, Matthew, Charles Heying, and Greg Andranovich. "Anti-Growth Politics or Piecemeal Resistance? Citizen Opposition to Olympic-Related Economic Growth." *Urban Affairs Review* 35, no. 3 (2000): 334–357.

Carson, Clayborne. *In Struggle: SNCC and the Black Awakening of the 1960s*. Cambridge, MA: Harvard University Press, 1981.

Chafe, William. *Civilities and Civil Rights: Greensboro, North Carolina, and the Black Struggle for Freedom*. New York: Oxford University Press, 1980.

Childers, M. W. *Colorado Powder Keg: Ski Resorts and the Environmental Movement*. Lawrence: University Press of Kansas, 2012.

Clarke, Susan E., and Martin Saiz. "From Waterhole to World City." In *The Infrastructure of Play: Building the Tourist City*, edited by Dennis R. Judd, 186–201. New York: Routledge, 2003.

Coats, Denis, and Brad R. Humphreys. "Do Economists Reach a Conclusion on Subsidies for Sports Franchises, Stadiums, and Mega-Events?" *Economic Journal Watch* 5, no. 3 (2008): 294–315.

———. "The Growth Effects of Sport Franchises, Stadia, and Arenas." *Journal of Policy Analysis and Management* 18, no. 4 (1999): 601–624.

Cohen, Lizabeth. *A Consumer's Republic: The Politics of Mass Consumption in Postwar America*. New York: Knopf, 2003.

Coleman, Annie Gilbert. *Ski Style: Sport and Culture in the Rockies*. Lawrence: University Press of Kansas, 2004.

Collins, Robert. *More: The Politics of Economic Growth in Postwar America*. New York: Oxford University Press, 2000.

Cowie, Jefferson. *The Great Exception: The New Deal and the Limits of American Politics*. Princeton, NJ: Princeton University Press, 2017.

———. *Stayin' Alive: The 1970s and the Last Days of the Working Class*. New York: New Press, 2010.

Delaney, Kevin, and Eckstein, Rick. *Public Dollars, Private Stadiums: The Battle over Building Sports Stadiums*. New Brunswick, NJ: Rutgers University Press, 2003.

Dempsey, Chris, and Andrew Zimbalist. *No Boston Olympics: How and Why Smart Cities Are Passing on the Torch*. Hanover: University Press of New England, 2017.

Deutsch, Sarah. *No Separate Refuge: Culture, Class, and Gender on the Anglo-Hispanic Frontier in the American Southwest*. New York: Oxford University Press, 1987.

Diamond, Andrew J. *Mean Streets: Chicago Youths and the Everyday Struggle for Empowerment in the Multiracial City, 1908–1969*. Berkley: University of California Press, 2009.

Dichter, Heather L. "Corruption in the 1960s? Rethinking the Origins of Unethical Olympic Bidding Tactics." *International Journal of the History of Sport* 33, nos. 6–7 (2016): 666–682.

Dinces, Sean. *Bulls Markets: Chicago Basketball Business and the New Inequality*. Chicago: University of Chicago Press, 2018.

———. "Padres on Mount Olympus: Los Angeles and the Production of the 1932 Olympic Mega Event." *Journal of Sport History* 32, no. 2 (Summer 2005): 137–166.

Dittmer, John. *Local People: The Struggle for Civil Rights in Mississippi*. Urbana: University of Illinois Press, 1994.

Dorsett, Lyle W., and Michael McCarthy. *The Queen City: A History of Denver*. Boulder: Pruett Publishing, 1986.

Dyreson, Mark. "The Endless Olympic Bid: Los Angeles and the Advertisement of the American West." *Journal of the West* 47, no. 4 (Fall 2008): 26–39.

———. *Making the American Team: Sport, Culture, and the Olympic Experience*. Urbana: University of Illinois Press, 1998.

Dyreson, Mark, and Matthew Llewellyn. "Los Angeles Is the Olympic City: Legacies of the 1932 and 1984 Olympic Games." *International Journal of the History of Sport* 25, no. 14 (2008): 1991–2018.

Edwards, Harry. *The Revolt of the Black Athletes*. 50th anniverary ed. Urbana: University of Illinois Press, 2017.

Eisinger, Peter. "The Politics of Bread and Circuses: Building the City for the Visitor Class." *Urban Affairs Review* 35, no. 3 (2000): 316–333.

Ellis, Cliff. "New Urbanism: Critiques and Rebuttals." *Journal of Urban Design* 7, no. 3 (2002): 261–291.

Entman, Robert W. "Framing: Toward Clarification of a Fractured Paradigm." *Journal of Communication* 43, no. 4 (1993): 51–58.

Fainstien, Susan, and Robert Stokes. "Spaces of Play: The Impacts of Entertainment Development on New York City." *Economic Development Quarterly* 12, no. 2 (2000): 150–151.

Fea, John. "Lake Placid 1932." In *Encyclopedia of the Modern Olympic Movement*, edited by John E. Findling and Kimberly D. Pelle, 95–103. Westport, CT: Greenwood, 2004.

Fernández, Lilia. *Brown in the Windy City: Mexicans and Puerto Ricans in Postwar Chicago*. Chicago: University of Chicago Press, 2012.

Fogelson, Robert M. *Downtown: Its Rise and Fall, 1880–1950*. New Haven, CT: Yale University Press, 2001.

Foster, Mark S. "Denver 76." *Colorado Magazine* 53, no. 2 (Spring 1976): 163–186.

Fox, Kenneth. *Metropolitan America: Urban Life and Urban Policy in the United States*. Jackson: University Press of Mississippi, 1986.

Gallegos, Magdalena. "The Forgotten Community: Hispanic Auraria in the Twentieth Century." *Colorado Heritage*, no. 2 (1985): 5–20.

Gamson, William. "Bystanders, Public Opinion, and the Media." In *The Blackwell Companion to Social Movements*, edited by David A. Snow, Sarah A. Soule, and Hanspeter Kriesi, 242–261. London: Blackwell, 2004.

Garcia, Mario T., and Sal Castro. *Blowout! Sal Castro and the Chicano Struggle for Educational Justice*. Chapel Hill: University of North Carolina Press, 2011.

Garrow, David. *Protest at Selma: Martin Luther King, Jr., and the Voting Rights Act of 1965*. New Haven, CT: Yale University Press, 1978.

Goetz, Andrew. "Suburban Sprawl or Urban Centres: Tensions and Contradictions of Smart Growth Approaches in Denver, Colorado." *Urban Studies* 50, no. 11 (2013): 2178–2195.

Goldberg, Robert A. *Hooded Empire: The Ku Klux Klan in Colorado*. Urbana: University of Illinois Press, 1981.

Goodstein, Phil. *Denver in Our Time: A People's History of the Modern Mile High City*. Denver: New Social Publications, 1999.

———. *How the West Side Won: The History of West Denver/Auraria*. Denver: New Social Publications, 2015.

Gould, Richard. *The Life and Times of Richard Castro: Bridging the Cultural Divide*. Denver: Colorado Historical Society, 2007.

Gutiérrez, David G. *Walls and Mirrors: Mexican Americans, Mexican Immigrants, and the Politics of Identity*. Berkeley: University of California Press, 1995.

Guttmann, Allen. *The Games Must Go On: Avery Brundage and the Olympic Movement*. New York: Columbia University Press, 1984.

———. *The Olympics: A History of the Modern Game*. Urbana: University of Illinois Press, 2002 [1992].

Hall, Simon. *American Patriotism, American Protest: Social Movements since the Sixties*. Philadelphia: University of Pennsylvania Press, 2011.

Haney-Lopez, Ian. *Racism on Trial: The Chicano Fight for Justice*. Cambridge, MA: Harvard University Press, 2003.

Harris, Fred. *Now Is the Time: A New Populist Call to Action*. New York: McGraw Hill, 1971.

Hartmann, Douglas, "Rethinking the Relationship between Sport and Race in American Culture: Golden Ghettos and Contested Terrain." *Sociology of Sport* 17, no. 3 (2000): 229–253.

Harvey, David. *A Brief History of Neoliberalism*. New York: Oxford University Press, 2007.

Hauk, Paul. *Beaver Creek Ski Area Chronology*. Glenwood Springs, CO: US Department of Agriculture, US Forest Service, 1979.

Hays, Samuel. *Beauty, Health, and Permanence: Environmental Politics in the United States, 1955–1985*. New York: Cambridge University Press, 1987.

Hirsch, Arnold R. *Making the Second Ghetto: Race and Housing in Chicago, 1940–1960*. New York: Cambridge University Press, 1983.

Hjelm, Victor S., and Joseph P. Pisciotte. "Profiles and Careers of Colorado State Legislators." *Western Political Quarterly* 21, no. 4 (1968): 698–722.

Hoig, Stan. *The Sand Creek Massacre*. Norman: University of Oklahoma Press, 1961.

Horne, Gerald. *Fire This Time: The Watts Uprising and the 1960s*. Charlottesville: University Press of Virginia, 1995.

Hurley, Andrew. *Environmental Inequalities: Race, Class, and Industrial Pollution in Gary, Indiana, 1945–1980*. Chapel Hill: University of North Carolina Press, 1995.

Isserman, Maurice, and Michael Kazin. *America Divided: The Civil War of the 1960s*. 4th ed. New York: Oxford University Press, 2012.

Jackson, Kenneth T. *Crabgrass Frontier: The Suburbanization of the United States*. New York: Oxford University Press, 1985.

Joseph, Peniel E. *Waiting 'til the Midnight Hour: A Narrative History of Black Power in America*. New York: Henry Holt, 2006.

Judd, Dennis R. "Constructing the Tourist Bubble." In *The Tourist City*, edited by Dennis R. Judd and Susan Fainstein, 35–53. New Haven, CT: Yale University Press, 1999.

———. "From Cowtown to Sunbelt City: Boosterism and Economic Growth in Denver." In *Restructuring the City: The Political Economy of Urban Redevelopment*, 167–201. New York: Longman, 1983.

Kanellos, Nicolas. *Chronology of Hispanic-American History: From Pre-Columbian Times to the Present*. Detroit: Gale Research Group, 1995.

Kelman, Ari. *A Misplaced Massacre: Struggling Over the Memory of Sand Creek*. Cambridge, MA: Harvard University Press, 2013.

Keys, Barbara. "Spreading Peace, Democracy, and Coca-Cola: Sport and American Cultural Expression in the 1930s." *Diplomatic History* 28, no. 2 (2004): 165–196.

Killanin, Michael Morris, Lord. *My Olympic Years*. New York: William Morrow, 1983.

Lamm, Richard. "The Ultimate Problem." *Trail and Timberline*, no. 534 (June 1963): 111–112.

Lee, Chungmie. *Denver Public Schools: Resegregation, Latino Style*. Cambridge, MA: Harvard University Civil Rights Project, 2006.

Lenskyj, Helen. *Inside the Olympic Industry: Power, Politics, and Activism*. Albany: State University of New York Press, 2000.

Leonard, Stephen J., and Thomas J. Noel. *Denver: Mining Camp to Metropolis*. Niwot: University Press of Colorado, 1990.

Limerick, Patricia. *The Legacy of Conquest: The Unbroken Past of the American West*. New York: W. W. Norton, 1987.

Lipsitz, George. "Sports Stadia and Urban Development: A Tale of Three Cities." *Journal of Sport and Social Issues* 8 (1984): 1–18.

Llewellyn, Matthew P., and John Gleaves. *The Rise and Fall of Olympic Amateurism.* Urbana: University of Illinois Press, 2016.

Llewellyn, Matthew, John Gleaves, and Wayne Wilson. "The Historical Legacy of the 1984 Los Angeles Games." *International Journal of the History of Sport* 32, no. 1 (2015): 1–8.

Lo, Clarence Y. H. *Small Property versus Big Government: Social Origins of the Property Tax Revolt.* Berkeley: University of California Press, 1990.

Logan, John, and Harvey L. Molotch. *Urban Fortunes: The Political Economy of Place.* 20th anniversary ed. Berkley: University of California Press, 2007.

Long, Judith Grant. *Public/Private Partnerships for Major League Sports Facilities.* New York: Routledge, 2013.

Longhurst, James. *Citizen Environmentalists.* Medford, MA: Tufts University Press, 2010.

Lowitt, Richard. *Fred Harris: His Journey from Liberalism to Populism.* Lanham, MD: Rowman and Littlefield, 2002.

Mandell, Richard D. *The Nazi Olympics.* New York: Macmillan, 1971.

Manning, Christopher. *William Dawson and the Limits of Black Leadership.* Dekalb: Northern Illinois University Press, 2009.

Mantler, Gordon K. *Power to the Poor: Black-Brown Coalition and the Fight for Economic Justice, 1960–1974.* Chapel Hill: University of North Carolina Press, 2013.

Marin, Christine. *A Spokesman of the Mexican American Movement: Rodolfo "Corky" Gonzales and the Fight for Chicano Liberation, 1966–1972.* San Francisco: R and E Research Associates, 1977.

Mariscal, George. *Brown-Eyed Children of the Sun: Lessons from the Chicano Movement, 1965–1975.* Albuquerque: University of New Mexico Press, 2005.

Marsh, Thomas G. "Vance R. Dittman Jr.—Lawyer's Law Professor." *Denver Law School* 46, no. 2 (Spring 1969): 179–180.

Martelle, Scott. *Blood Passion: The Ludlow Massacre and Class War in the American West.* New Brunswick, NJ: Rutgers University Press, 2007.

Martin, Isaac William. *The Permanent Tax Revolt: How the Property Tax Transformed American Politics.* Stanford, CA: Stanford University Press, 2008.

McEncroe, Donna. *Denver Renewed: A History of the Denver Urban Renewal Authority.* Denver: The Denver Foundation, 1992.

Miguel, Guadalupe San. *Brown, Not White: School Integration and the Chicano Movement in Houston.* College Station: Texas A&M Press, 2001.

Miller, James. *"Democracy Is in the Streets": From Port Huron to the Siege of Chicago.* New York: Simon and Schuster 1987.

Mills, C. Wright. *The Power Elite.* New York: Oxford University Press, 1959.

Mollenkopf, John H. *The Contested City.* Princeton, NJ: Princeton University Press, 1983.

Molotch, Harvey. "The City as a Growth Machine: Toward a Political Economy of Place." *American Journal of Sociology* 82, no. 2 (1976): 309–322.

Montejano, David. *Quixote's Soldiers: A Local History of the Chicano Movement, 1966–1981.* Austin: University of Texas Press, 2010.

Moore, Louis. *We Will Win the Day: The Civil Rights Movement, the Black Athlete, and the Quest for Equality.* Santa Barbara, CA: Praeger, 2017.

Muñoz, Carlos Jr. *Youth, Identity, Power: The Chicano Movement.* New York: Verso, 2007.

Muñoz, Carlos Jr., and Charles Henry. "Rainbow Coalitions in Four Big Cities: San

Antonio, Chicago, Philadelphia, and Denver." *American Political Science Association* 19, no. 3 (1986): 598–609.

Murray, Michael "Denver: City Profile." *Cities* 19, no. 4 (2002): 283–294.

Nash, Gerald N. *The American West Transformed: The Impact of the Second World War.* Bloomington: Indiana University Press, 1985.

Navarro, Armondo. *La Raza Unida Party: A Chicano Challenge to the U.S. Two-Party Dictatorship.* Philadelphia: Temple University Press, 2000.

O'Connor, Thomas H. *Building a New Boston: Politics and Urban Renewal.* Boston: Northeastern University, 1993.

Olson, Laura Lee Katz. "Power, Public Policy and the Environment: The Defeat of the 1976 Winter Olympics." PhD diss., University of Colorado, 1974.

Oropeza, Lorena. ¡*Raza Si!* ¡*Guerra No! Chicano Protest and Patriotism during the Viet Nam War Era.* Berkley: University of California Press, 2005.

Pagán, Eduardo Obregón. *Murder at the Sleepy Lagoon: Zoot Suits, Race, and Riot in Wartime L.A.* Chapel Hill: University of North Carolina Press, 2003.

Page, Brian, and Eric Ross. "Legacies of a Contested Campus: Urban Renewal, Community Resistance, and the Origins of Gentrification in Denver." *Urban Geography* 38, no. 9 (2017): 1293–1328.

Philpott, William. *Vacationland: Tourism and Environment in the Colorado High Country.* Seattle: University of Washington Press, 2013.

Pieroth, Doris. "Los Angeles 1932." In *Encyclopedia of the Modern Olympic Movement,* edited by John E. Findling and Kimberly D. Pelle, 33–40. Westport, CT: Greenwood, 2004.

Piketty, Thomas. *Capital in the Twenty-First Century.* Cambridge, MA: Harvard University Press, 2014.

Podnair, Jerald. *City of Dreams: Dodgers Stadium and the Birth of Modern Los Angeles.* Princeton, NJ: Princeton University Press, 2017.

Price, Monroe E. "On Seizing the Olympic Platform." In *Owning the Olympics: Narratives of the New China,* edited by Monroe E. Price and Daniel Dayan, 86–114. Ann Arbor: University of Michigan Press, 2000.

Ralph, James. *Northern Protest, Martin Luther King, Jr., Chicago, and the Civil Rights Movement.* Cambridge, MA: Harvard University Press, 1993.

Reich, Kenneth. *Making It Happen: Peter Ueberroth and the 1984 Olympics.* Santa Barbara, CA: Carpal, 1986.

Riess, Steven. *City Games: The Evolution of American Urban Society and the Rise of Sports.* Urbana: University of Illinois Press, 1989.

———. "Historical Perspectives on Sport and Public Policy." *Policy Studies Review* 15, no. 1 (1998): 3–15.

———. "Power without Authority: Los Angeles Elites and the Construction of the Coliseum." *Journal of Sport History* 8, no. 1 (1989): 60–65.

Rome, Adam. *The Bulldozer in the Countryside: Suburban Sprawl and the Rise of Environmentalism.* Cambridge: Cambridge University Press, 2001.

———. *The Genius of Earth Day: How a 1970 Teach-in Unexpectedly Made the First Green Generation.* New York: Hill and Wang, 2013.

Rosentraub, Mark S. *Major League Losers: The Real Cost of Sports and Who's Paying for Them.* New York: Basic Books, 1997.

Rorabaugh, W. J. *Berkeley at War: The 1960s.* New York: Oxford University Press, 1989.

Rosentraub, Mark, and Mijin Joo. "Tourism and Economic Development: Which Investments Produce Gains for Regions?" *Tourism Management* 30, no. 5 (2009): 759–770.

Rothman, Hal K. *Devil's Bargains: Tourism in the Twentieth-Century American West.* Lawrence: University Press of Kansas, 1998.

Rothstein, Richard. *The Color of Law: A Forgotten History of How Our Government Segregated America.* New York: W. W. Norton, 2017.

Sage, George. "Stealing Home: Political, Economic, and Media Power and a Publicly-Funded Baseball Stadium in Denver." *Journal of Sport and Social Issues* 17, no. 2 (1993): 110–124.

Sarantakes, Nicholas Evan. "Moscow versus Los Angeles: The Nixon White House Wages Cold War in the Olympic Selection Process." *Cold War History* 9, no. 1 (2009): 137–157.

Schiller, Kay, and Christopher Young. *The 1972 Munich Olympics and the Making of Modern Germany.* Berkeley: University of California Press, 2010.

Schimmel, Kimberly S. "The Political Economy of Place: Urban and Sport Studies Perspectives." In *Theory, Sport and Society*, edited by Joseph MaGuire and Kevin Young, 235–251. Oxford, UK: Elsevier Science, 2002.

Schulte, Steven C. *Wayne Aspinall and the Shaping of the American West.* Boulder: University Press of Colorado, 2002.

Schwartz, Joel. *The New York Approach: Robert Moses, Urban Liberals, and the Redevelopment of the Inner City.* Columbus: Ohio State University Press, 1993.

Sellers, Christopher. *Crabgrass Crucible: Suburban Nature and the Rise of Environmentalism in the Twentieth Century.* Chapel Hill: University of North Carolina Press, 2012.

Senn, Alfred E. *Power, Politics, and the Olympic Games: A History of the Power Brokers, Events, and Controversies That Shaped the Games.* Champaign, IL: Human Kinetics, 1999.

Shaw, Randy. *Generation Priced Out: Who Gets to Live in the New Urban America.* Oakland: University of California Press, 2018.

Sheldon, Peter. *Conquer to Climb: The Untold Story of WWII's 10th Mountain Division Ski Troops.* New York: Scribner's, 2003.

Siegel, Barry. *Dreamers and Schemers: How an Improbable Bid for the 1932 Olympics Transformed Los Angeles from Dusty Outpost to Global Metropolis.* Oakland: University of California Press, 2019.

Stone, Clarence N. "Paradigms, Power, and Urban Leadership." In *Leadership and Politics*, edited by Bryan D. Jones, 135–159. Lawrence: University Press of Kansas, 1989.

———. *Regime Politics: Governing Atlanta, 1946–1988.* Lawrence: University Press of Kansas, 1988.

Sugrue, Thomas J. *Origins of the Urban Crisis: Race and Inequality in Postwar Detroit.* Princeton, NJ: Princeton University Press, 2005.

Tarrow, Sidney. *The New Transnational Activism.* New York: Cambridge University Press, 2005.

———. *Power in Movement: Social Movements and Contentious Politics.* New York: Cambridge University Press, 2011.

Trachtenberg, Allen. *The Incorporation of America: Culture and Society in the Gilded Age.* 25th anniversary ed. New York: Hill and Wang, 2007.

US Civil Rights Commission. *Mexican Americans and the Administration of Justice in the Southwest.* Washington, DC: General Accounting Office, 1970.

US General Accounting Office. *Olympic Games: Preliminary Information on Federal Funding and Support*. Washington, DC: GAO, 2000.

Vigil, Ernesto B. *The Crusade for Justice: Chicano Militancy and the Government's War on Dissent*. Madison: University of Wisconsin Press, 1999.

Walker, Donald L. "John A. Love: The Story of Colorado's Thirty-Sixth Governor." *Historical Studies Journal* 17 (Spring 2000): 1–59.

Walsh, James Patrick. "Young and Latino in a Cold War Barrio: Survival, the Search for Identity, and the Formation of Street Gangs in Denver, 1945–1955." Master's thesis, University of Colorado Denver, 1996.

Wamsley, Kevin. "Laying Olympism to Rest." In *Post-Olympism? Questioning Sport in the Twenty-first Century*, edited by J. Bale and M. Christensen, 231–242. New York: Berg, 2004.

Weiler, Stephen. "Pioneers and Settlers in Lo-Do Denver: Private Risk and Public Benefits in Urban Redevelopment." *Urban Studies* 37, no. 1 (2000): 167–179.

Wells, Tom. *The War Within: America's Battle Over Vietnam*. Berkeley: University of California Press, 1994.

Wenn, Stephen, Robert Barney, and Scott Martyn. *Tarnished Rings: The International Olympic Committee and the Salt Lake City Bid Scandal*. Syracuse, NY: Syracuse University Press, 2011.

White, Jeremy. "The Los Angeles Way of Doing Things: The Olympic Village and the Practice of Boosterism." *Olympika: The International Journal of Olympic Studies* 11 (2002): 79–116.

White, Richard. *"It's Your Misfortune and None of My Own": A History of the American West*. Norman: University of Oklahoma Press, 1991.

Whiteside, J. *Colorado: A Sports History*. Niwot: University Press of Colorado, 1999.

Whitson, David, and John Horne. "Underestimated Costs and Overestimated Benefits? Comparing the Outcomes of Sports Mega-Events in Canada and Japan." *Sociological Review* 54, no. 2 (2006): 73–89.

Whitson, David, and Donald Macintosh. "The Global Circus: International Sport, Tourism, and the Marketing of Cities." *Journal of Sport and Social Issues* 20, no. 3 (1996): 278–295.

William, Cheryl. "The Banff Winter Olympics: Sport, Tourism, and Banff National Park." Master's thesis, University of Alberta, 2011.

Wilson, Harold E. "Lake Placid 1980." In *Encyclopedia of the Modern Olympic Movement*, edited by John E. Findling and Kimberly D. Pelle, 373–379. Westport, CT: Greenwood, 2004.

Wilson, Wayne. "Los Angeles 1980." In *Encyclopedia of the Modern Olympic Movement*, edited by John E. Findling and Kimberly D. Pelle, 381–387. Westport, CT: Greenwood, 2004.

Witherspoon, Kevin. *Before the Eyes of the World: Mexico and the 1968 Olympic Games*. DeKalb: Northern Illinois University Press, 2008.

Zimbalist, Andrew. *Circus Maximus: The Economic Gamble Behind Hosting the Olympics and the World Cup*. Washington, DC: Brookings Institution Press, 2015.

———, ed. *Sports, Jobs, and Taxes: The Economic Impact of Sports Teams and Stadiums*. Washington, DC: Brookings Institution Press, 1997.

Index

Page numbers followed by f indicate illustrations.